In a Different Place

PRINCETON MODERN GREEK STUDIES

This series is sponsored by the Princeton University Program in Hellenic Studies under the auspices of the Stanley J. Seeger Hellenic Fund.

Firewalking and Religious Healing: The Anastenaria of Greece and the American Firewalking Movement *by Loring M. Danforth*

Kazantzakis: Politics of the Spirit *by Peter Bien*

Dance and the Body Politic in Northern Greece *by Jane K. Cowan*

Yannis Ritsos: Repetitions, Testimonies, Parentheses *edited and translated by Edmund Keeley*

Contested Identities: Gender and Kinship in Modern Greece *edited by Peter Loizos and Evthymios Papataxiarchis*

A Place in History: Social and Monumental Time in a Cretan Town *by Michael Herzfeld*

Demons and the Devil: Moral Imagination in Modern Greek Culture *by Charles Stewart*

The Enlightenment as Social Criticism: Iosipos Moisiodax and Greek Culture in the Eighteenth Century *by Paschalis M. Kitromilides*

C. P. Cavafy: Collected Poems *translated by Edmund Keeley and Philip Sherrard; edited by George Savidis*

The Fourth Dimension *by Yannis Ritsos. Peter Green and Beverly Bardsley, translators*

George Seferis: Collected Poems, Revised Edition *translated, edited, and introduced by Edmund Keeley and Philip Sherrard*

In a Different Place: Pilgrimage, Gender, and Politics at a Greek Island Shrine *by Jill Dubisch*

In a Different Place

PILGRIMAGE, GENDER, AND POLITICS AT A GREEK ISLAND SHRINE

Jill Dubisch

PRINCETON UNIVERSITY PRESS

PRINCETON, NEW JERSEY

Published by Princeton University Press, 41 William Street,
Princeton, New Jersey 08540
In the United Kingdom: Princeton University Press, Chichester, West Sussex

Library of Congress Cataloging-in-Publication Data

Dubisch, Jill, 1943–
In a different place : pilgrimage, gender, and politics at a Greek
island shrine / Jill Dubisch.
p.   cm. — (Princeton modern Greek studies)
Includes bibliographical references (p.   ) and index.
ISBN 0-691-02968-7 — ISBN 0-691-02967-9 (pbk.)
1. Mary, Blessed Virgin, Saint—Cult—Greece—Tinos Island.
2. Christian pilgrims and pilgrimages—Greece—Tinos Island.
3. Hieros Naos Euangelistrias (Tinos Island, Greece).   4. Tinos
Island (Greece)—Social life and customs.   I. Title.   II. Series.
BT660.T48D83   1995
306.6'6304249585—dc20   94-39673
                                                            CIP

Publication of this book has been aided by a grant from the
Princeton Committee on Hellenic Studies

This book has been composed in Sabon

Printed in the United States of America

10 9 8 7 6 5 4 3 2 1
10 9 8 7 6 5 4 3 2 1
(Pbk.)

In Loving Memory of Vasiliki Tze
She took two strangers into her life and made
them "διϰοί της"

We see the world not as it is but as we are.

—Talmud

Contents

Plates

Acknowledgments

THIS BOOK has been many years in the making, and during its long evolution I have had invaluable assistance from numerous friends and colleagues.

I would first like to thank Ray Michalowski for his constant encouragement and for his intellectual and psychological support in all phases of my research and writing. It is not always easy living with someone who is working on a book—or living apart from someone who is doing fieldwork—but his support has been constant and unflagging.

I would also like to thank my friends from Tinos: "Marina," "Marcos" and "Eleni," "Nikos," and all the others who gave me their time and their friendship and let me intrude into their lives. I am also grateful to the many pilgrims whom I observed, and to whom I spoke, for making this book possible.

A number of friends in Athens also played a part in developing my ideas and giving me insights through conversations, observations, and critiques, among them Akis Papataxiarchis, Deanna Trakas, Rom Gudas, Manos Anglias, and Marina Iossafides. I also wish to thank Mari Clark for letting me visit "her" village to speak to people there who had been to Tinos. Others whose insights and company proved valuable include Peter Allen, Ken and Ellen Robertson, and Tom Weisner. I am also grateful to George Moutafis and Vasiliki Galani-Moutafi, whom I visited on Mitilini, for their hospitality and for their help with my research there, as well as to various faculty and students at the University of the Aegean for a number of stimulating conversations that helped to spark my own thinking.

I also owe a great deal to the Women's Studies Program and the Southwest Institute for Research on Women (SIROW) at the University of Arizona for awarding me a Rockefeller Humanities Fellowship, which allowed me to spend the academic year 1988–89 at the university and to begin work on my book. It is difficult to imagine that I could have completed this work without the "jump-start" that this stimulating year provided.

In addition to the Rockefeller Fellowship, I have also received support from the Fulbright Foundation, the University of North Carolina at Charlotte, and Northern Arizona University for the various trips to Greece upon which much of this research has been based.

I would also like to thank the anonymous reviewers of my manuscript for their many helpful comments and corrections, as well as those who read various drafts of chapters in progress, including Peter Loizos, Michael Herzfeld, Mari Clark, Susan Phillips, and Liz Kennedy.

And finally, I would like to thank Julia Clebsch, graduate assistant and friend, for her tireless pursuit of articles and interlibrary loans, as well as her proofreading, photocopying, and bibliography work. Without her efforts, this book would undoubtedly still be in manuscript.

A Note on Transliteration

THERE IS no single system of transliteration that is accepted by all scholars of modern Greek, and the system I have employed here will certainly not please everyone. My aim, however, has been to present Greek terms in such a way that they may be pronounced reasonably correctly by non-Greek speakers while at the same time be recognizable to those familiar with the Greek language. To that end, I have employed forms with which not everyone would agree, and which, moreover, are not always entirely consistent (in those cases in which consistency would not lead to the best pronunciation by English speakers).

Several notes about specific transliterations: I have used *dh* for the Greek δ (pronounced like the *th* in *the*). I have also used *kh* in certain situations for the Greek χ, but only when this seemed to provide the best rendering into English phonology. In cases in which the Greek word already has a common transliteration into English, I have generally kept that form to avoid confusion. Hence, while I have rendered the name of the island on which I did research as Tinos (rather than Tenos, a form found mostly in older writings about the island), I have used the more common English forms for places with which English speakers may be more familiar: hence Mykonos (rather than Mikonos), Delos (rather than Dhilos), Aegina (rather than Ayina). In addition, when the name of a specific person has been transliterated from the Greek (as in the case of a Greek author whose work has been written in, or translated into, English), I have used the form employed instead of following my own system (e.g., Kharitonidou rather than Haritonidhou). In cases in which I have done the transliteration myself, however, I have been consistent with my own system. And finally, any transliterations found in direct quotes have been left in the form in which the author has rendered them.

In a Different Place

CHAPTER ONE

Introduction

THIS BOOK IS, first of all, a book about a pilgrimage site, the Church of the Madonna of the Annunciation (*Evangelístria*) on the Aegean island of Tinos, Greece, where I have been conducting research since 1986.[1] My account, however, is more than a simple ethnographic description. Indeed, in the context of contemporary anthropology, one would be hard put to maintain that any ethnographic description is ever really simple— or that any ethnography can be simply description. Acknowledging this, I seek here to experiment with several types of what might be termed "ethnographic exploration" in order to pursue the aims I have in writing this book.

First among these aims is the presentation and interpretation of the material on pilgrimage I have collected in the course of my research. This task—at first a seemingly straightforward one—has become, in the course of my writing, increasingly complex. This complexity is in part inherent in the subject matter I have chosen, that is, the topic of pilgrimage itself. But it is also the result of current intellectual challenges within anthropology and of developments in my own thinking, both of which in turn have influenced my relationship to the material with which I have been working.

This leads to my second goal, which is to explore certain facets of my own experience as a "participant observer." This exploration includes not only an examination of my experiences "in the field" but also a consideration of certain elements of my biography that are relevant both to my choice of study and to my theoretical perspective and that have affected my responses to the fieldwork "encounter." Gender is one such important biographical element that has shaped my work, but there are others as well, including my previous fieldwork experience and my personal experience with chronic pain. In exploring the impact of these elements on my work, I draw on current anthropological debates about reflexivity and about the necessity for understanding the anthropologist's place in relation to those whom she studies, especially in a postcolonial (and postmodern) world. As Myerhoff and Ruby put it, "to be reflexive is to be self-conscious and also aware of the aspects of self necessary to reveal to an audience so that it can understand both the process employed and the resultant product" (1982:6). I will consider the dimension of gender relevant in two domains of anthropological experience, to being "in the field" in the sense of research among people of another culture and to being "in the field" in the sense of working within the field of anthropology itself.

Gender, "the field," and considerations of self and other, are in turn related to a third area I seek to explore: the forms and process of ethnographic writing, and, beyond that, the act of writing itself. This is a topic that has received a good deal of critical attention recently in anthropology. Rather than being viewed as a "transparent" medium that simply "describes" another culture, ethnographic writing has come to be recognized as a literary genre with its own techniques for establishing authenticity and authority.[2] The deconstruction of anthropological writing has led some anthropologists to experiment with new forms of ethnography that seek to break with former conventions and assumptions. In my writing I have attempted to move away from the sort of "realist" account of "objective" facts recorded by an omniscient and invisible observer that was the characteristic mode of much of "traditional" ethnography (a mode still dominant when I began my career in anthropology). Instead I punctuate my account with analyses of my own writing as I experiment with different modes of presentation for different ethnographic purposes.[3] In addition, I seek to analyze the significance of writing in the relationship between the anthropologist and the people she encounters, and to use different forms of writing to subvert the normal anthropological presentation of that relationship.[4]

SELF-CONSCIOUS EXPERIMENTATION AND NECESSARY UNCERTAINTY

My experiments with ethnographic forms introduce an element of uncertainty, or at least indeterminacy, at various points in my account as I move through different modes of writing and through a range of different perspectives. Such indeterminacy is not unique, of course, to my account but is common to many "experimental" ethnographies. Nor should such a mode of writing be seen as a completely radical break with past ethnography. Debates over whether anthropology is humanistic or scientific, and over whether or not anthropology can be truly objective, have a long history in the discipline and prefigure the current postmodern critiques (Caplan 1988:8). And the technique of combining "objective" description with personal narrative is also not an entirely new one but rather may be inevitable in anthropology "because it mediates a contradiction within the discipline between personal and scientific authority," a contradiction that may be inherent in fieldwork (Pratt 1986:32). In addition, the blurring of boundaries that is taken as emblematic of postmodernism (see Pool 1991:313) may also be seen to some extent as inherent in anthropology insofar as "participant observation or fieldwork blurs the boundaries of the personal and professional, between subject and object" (Hondganeu-Sotelo 1988:611). Or as Hastrup puts it, "Fieldwork is situated between autobiography and anthropology. It connects an important personal experience with a general field of knowledge" (Hastrup 1992a: 117; see also Okely 1992).

What distinguishes the current experiments in ethnographic writing, however, is the deliberate questioning of the necessity to maintain boundaries between different modes of writing, and between the perspectives they represent, within the ethnographic account itself. No longer is the personal inevitably isolated within an introduction describing the "conditions of fieldwork," but rather the "I" of the anthropologist tends to wander freely throughout the ethnographic narrative, blurring the boundary between "personal" and "objective" and reflecting a greater self-consciousness about the anthropologist's own position vis-à-vis those of the culture being studied."[5]

Boundaries also may be blurred in other ways within these "experimental" ethnographies. One such blurring occurs in the freer movement between different realms of experience and different times and events within the ethnographic narrative structure. Such a method challenges the "traditional" form of the ethnography, a form that has generally been determined by a conventional set of assumptions regarding the ordering of material.[6] Some argue that such a break with conventional narrative structure is a better method of doing anthropology generally. Renato Rosaldo, for example, suggests that "social analysts should explore their subjects from a number of positions, rather than being locked into any particular one" (1989:169).

Part of the stimulus for employing such multiple positions in my own narrative was the subject of pilgrimage itself, a subject that continually challenged conventional ethnographic narrative structure and the ways in which fieldwork is carried out. I found that I required a variety of strategies in order to arrive at any sort of understanding of, or feeling for, that which I was studying, whether it was the experiences of pilgrims, the politics of pilgrimage, my own reactions to pilgrimage, or the notion of history as embodied in a pilgrimage shrine.

In addition to seeking to break with conventional narrative forms, many contemporary ethnographies reflect a certain self-consciousness about the act of writing. Among the ways in which this may be manifested is in the deliberate use (and self-conscious acknowledgment) of literary tropes, as well as in the manipulation of a variety of writing styles. Again reflecting the postmodern breaking down of disciplinary (and other) boundaries, inspiration for these new forms of writing is often drawn from other disciplines, especially literature (Fernandez 1986), and sometimes from the cultures being studied (e.g., Herzfeld 1985). Thus in addition to seeing pilgrimage itself as metaphoric, I have used, among other metaphors, those of text (chapter 9) and performance (chapter 10). These are part of my own "persuasions and performances" (Fernandez 1986), part of my mode of argumentation to the reader of my narrative. Indeed this introduction serves to prepare the reader for what follows by using some of the devices (such as movement back and forth from the personal and experimental to the theoretical) that will be used in the chapters that follow. Thus this chapter serves as a "frame" (in Bateson and Goffman's sense), telling the reader how to think about what follows (Birth 1990; Turner 1988).

Although the account that results from these efforts has at times a highly personal dimension, the result is not intended as autobiography[7] or confessional but rather as an elucidation of the relationship between the anthropologist and the field situation on the one hand, and the anthropologist's relationship to the theory and practice of anthropology on the other. Both of these relationships affect our understanding and portrayal of other peoples. In this respect my approach can be deemed "interpretive," insofar as interpretive anthropology, according to Marcus and Fischer, "operates on two levels simultaneously: it provides accounts of other worlds from the inside, and reflects about the epistemological groundings of such accounts" (1986:26).[8] At the same time, I am aware of some of the problems inherent in all forms of generalizing, including interpretive generalizing about meaning, and of the ways in which generalizations constitute "part of a professional discourse of 'objectivity' and expertise" and are "inevitably a language of power" (Abu-Lughod 1990:150).

As part of the blurring of boundaries, and because I believe that emotions can be a valuable source of insight in the practice of anthropology (see R. Rosaldo 1989:172), and that "the personal is theoretical" (Okely 1992:9), I have sought to use emotion—both my own and others'—in my narrative. Thus I have not isolated my own responses and experiences from other kinds of "data," but rather have sought to integrate them in a way that I hope will allow them to serve as a "window" for the reader as well as a pathway to theoretical insights. Such an approach gives fieldwork itself a central place in the development of anthropological theory. As Okely has pointed out, "The fieldwork experience is totalising and draws on the whole being. [But] it has not been theorised because it has been trivialized as the 'collection of data' by a dehumanised machine" (1992:3). In addition, because one of the aims of the experimental ethnography is to break down, at least to some extent, the distance between the observer and observed, my own placement at the scene—to use another metaphor—may help the reader vicariously to play a role in the drama as well.

"UNBOUNDING" THE PILGRIMAGE SITE

All of my experiments, however, are ultimately directed toward the goal of presenting to the reader a place and a way of life as experienced in the particular set of activities that cluster around a pilgrimage site.[9] This site is, in turn, a vehicle that I use for seeking to understand larger social, cultural, and political processes within contemporary Greek life, for no study of pilgrimage can ever be just about a particular pilgrimage "site." The site can be understood only as a setting for a wide range of behaviors, embodying multiple meanings and goals, and as both a part and a manifestation of many other aspects of a society—historical, social, political, economic, and religious. To some extent, of course, this is true of any anthropological field site. Indeed, as Clifford notes, in the contemporary world, with its complex political and historical relations, " 'the field' becomes more and more evidently an ideal construct" (1990:64). But the difficulties of delineating "the field" are particularly evident in the study of a pilgrimage shrine such as the Church of the Annunciation of Tinos. Both the pilgrims and, to some extent, those who serve them are a shifting population of diverse origins, participating in a repeated yet at the same time highly varied series of events. These events take place within a particular local context, but also within the context of a national—and international—religious tradition, and in a political environment that is both reflected in and shaped by events that occur at the place of pilgrimage.

Because all of this makes it exceedingly difficult to draw boundaries around "the field," I have used a variety of sources in addition to my own firsthand observations at the Church of the Annunciation. These sources include my earlier fieldwork in a more "traditional" village setting on the same island (see chapter 2), visits I have made to churches and pilgrimage sites in other areas of Greece, conversations with Greeks about Tinos and religion that occurred in a variety of settings (including a bar in Athens)[10] and not just in "the field," and the writings of numerous other anthropologists who have worked in Greece and elsewhere. In addition, I have drawn—perhaps somewhat eclectically—on a variety of other materials, particularly materials in Greek, including "local" writings on history and religion. Thus this book, although stemming from fieldwork done at a particular place, is more broadly "about" Greece and Greeks—or at least about certain facets of Greek society, history, religion, and world view. And perhaps more important, it is also about "Greekness," the frequently contested process of its definition, and its significance for particular individuals and groups within present-day national religious and political discourse.

This book is hardly unique in drawing on such a range of material, nor do I claim it to be. We are past the days when anthropologists could describe small communities as if they formed self-contained units for analysis. Indeed the best ethnographies today are no longer ethnographies in the local, narrow sense often exhibited by conventional ethnographies of the past. Several recent anthropological works on Greece illustrate this quite clearly. Loring Danforth's *Firewalking and Religious Healing* (1989), Jane Cowan's *Dance and the Body Politic in Northern Greece* (1990), C. Nadia Seremetakis's *The Last Word: Women, Death, and Divination in Inner Mani* (1991), and Michael Herzfeld's *A Place in History* (1991) all describe the complex interactions between the local, national, and even international dimensions of social life and ideology in Greece, while at the same time offering vivid and dynamic portraits of particular communities.

The pilgrimage site that is the focus of my study thus serves as a means for exploring a number of topics—including religion, gender, performance, and the nature of Greekness—as well as a means of examining issues of anthropological fieldwork, reflexivity, the nature of anthropological writing, and intimately connected to all of these, issues of being both a woman and an anthropologist. The topics I have chosen and my approach to them reflect the influence of two major intellectual currents of our time: postmodernism and feminism.

FEMINIST ANTHROPOLOGISTS AND POSTMODERN FEMINISTS

The term *postmodern* has a number of different meanings, perhaps almost as many as there are postmodernists.[11] Micaela di Leonardo suggests that "postmodernism" can have at least three different referents. One can speak simply of a "postmodern era" as a descriptive term for the current period in which postmodernism's challenge to the assumptions of modernity has been an important intellectual force. Or postmodern can refer to a "research stance, a set of tools for ground-breaking, perspective altering work." Or it can refer to an intellectual approach that seeks "to destabilize received conceptions of science, order, society, and the self" (di Leonardo 1991:24). In the first sense contemporary anthropology is of necessity postmodern insofar as it is practiced in a postmodern world. An anthropology that is postmodern in the second two senses, however, reflects at least a degree of commitment to a self-conscious and critical perspective, which, among other things, questions the neutrality and objectivity of science (indeed of all forms of knowledge), the universality of reason and "truth," the transparency of language, and the existence of a coherent stable self (Flax 1987:624–25), as well as the rejection of "metanarratives." Postmodernism also seeks to dissolve disciplinary and other boundaries, which may account in part for postmodern anthropologists' renewed interest in fieldwork and the fieldwork experience, an area in which boundaries are inherently blurred.

Although a number of anthropologists have critiqued postmodernism, especially for its antiscience stance and its presumed abdication from political struggle,[12] postmodernism has had a significant impact on both the theory and practice of the discipline. At the very least, it has become increasingly difficult for anthropologists to write in a manner that unselfconsciously assumes that all that is necessary in an ethnography is an exposition of anthropological "facts" objectively gathered and presented by a self-effacing observer. Even if one still believes this to be possible, it is a stance to be defended rather than assumed. Postmodernism, then, has demanded that a more critical eye be cast by anthropologists upon what we do and how we do it, and even postmodernism's opponents feel compelled to speak to at least some of its arguments.

Feminism is the other intellectual current affecting anthropology that has been influential in my work in a variety of ways, including both my choice of issues for study and my critique of anthropology. Yet the relationships between feminism and anthropology on the one hand, and feminism and postmodernism on the other, have not been entirely comfortable ones. There are those who maintain that feminism is inherently postmodernist in its challenge to Enlightenment assumptions regarding self, knowledge, and truth (see, e.g., Flax 1987:624) and in its dissolving of boundaries (such as those between the personal and the political). They would agree with Caplan that "feminism had already raised many of the major issues now preoccupying postmodernist anthropologists" (1988:10). Even those who take issue with the notion that feminism should adopt the postmodernist stance may acknowledge that both feminist and postmodernist philosophies "pursue a critique of the deep structures of society and of certain constricting forms of thought" (Tress 1988:196).

Yet there are feminists, anthropologists among them, who have criticized postmodernism for, among other things, its presumed political disengagement,[13] its failure to consider the dimension of power in social analysis (but see Pool 1991), its rejection of notions of truth and the integrity of the self, and the failure of mainstream postmodernist theory to take questions of gender seriously in its rereading of history and culture (see, e.g., Tress 1988; di Leonardo 1991:25–26; di Stefano 1990:75–76; Mascia-Lees, Sharpe, and Cohen 1989). Others argue that feminism (and even postmodernist feminism) must necessarily retain at least some ties to Enlightenment assumptions and so cannot be purely postmodern (see, e.g., Harding 1990:99–100). In addition, the charge has been leveled at postmodernism that it is a last-ditch attempt to maintain dominance by those whom feminism and other counterideologies have challenged. As

Hartsock puts it, "Why is it that just at the moment when so many of us who have been silenced begin to demand the right to name ourselves, to act as subjects rather than objects of history, that just then the concept of subjecthood becomes problematic?" (1990:163). Mascia-Lees, Sharpe, and Cohen make a similar observation: "Postmodern theorizing can be understood as socially constructed itself, as a metaphor for the sense of the dominant that the ground has begun to shift under their feet. And this social construction . . . is one that potentially may work to preserve the privileged position of Western white males," especially within the academic world (1989:17).[14] Thus while some would claim that the feminist critique has been a force in the development of a postmodern perspective, or at least would see postmodernism as a useful tool for feminists (see, e.g., Bordo 1990:154), others argue that postmodernism is a way of avoiding taking feminist (and other) critiques seriously, or at least a means of relegating feminism to one voice among many, with no superior claims to truth.

THE ISSUE OF A FEMINIST ANTHROPOLOGY

From the point of view of anthropology, feminism, while undeniably influential, has also been problematic. Although the last two decades have seen an explosion of anthropological studies on women and gender, these do not necessarily constitute a feminist anthropology, as Strathern (1988) and others have pointed out.[15] As Moore argues, "The real problem about incorporating women into anthropology lies not at the level of empirical research but at the theoretical and analytical level. Feminist anthropology is, therefore, faced with the much larger task of reworking and redefining anthropological theory" (1988:2; see also Dubisch 1991a; Benahib and Cornell 1987:1). Feminism and gender studies have often been ghettoized within anthropology, and not seen as relevant to "mainstream" thought (Caplan 1988:15; Dubisch 1991a:29–30; Moore 1988). "Women" continues to be the marked category. "Even when they present themselves as studying gender, feminist anthropologists are dismissed as presenting only a partial picture of the societies they study because they are assumed to be studying only women. Anthropologists study society, the unmarked category" (Abu-Lughod 1990:141). Men, even when they write only about men, are not writing *only* about men. In addition, as Strathern (who speaks of anthropology's "awkward" relationship with feminism) suggests, anthropology's very tendency to be open to multiple perspectives and approaches contributes to the ghettoization of feminist perspectives: "A milieu of tolerance has . . . reduced feminist scholarship to just another approach, one way among many into the data" (1987:280).

Some have questioned whether there can even be a feminist anthropology. Just as feminism provides a critique of anthropology, anthropology critiques the cultural bias and "the aims and political cohesiveness of feminism" (Moore 1988:10). Particularly insofar as feminism (or some forms of feminism) postulates a unitary and universal "womanhood" and a common history of shared oppression, it may find itself at odds with the anthropological emphasis on difference and on the cultural and historical contingencies that shape and divide women's worlds.[16] The relationship of the female anthropologist to the women she studies also comes into question here (see, e.g., Flax 1987:642). The female anthropologist's identification with women of other societies, despite differences of culture and power, is often taken for granted (by women as well as men) in a way that a male anthropologist's identification with men is not.[17] Hence the phenomenon of women studying women may be accepted as "natural." Some feminists have used the notion of a universal womanhood to see women of other times and cultures as representing both "ourselves" and, at the same time, the "other" of an imagined past state, either possessing what we have lost (for example, the primitive matriarchy, worship of the Goddess) or demonstrating the universality of patriarchy and female oppression (on this critique, see M. Rosaldo 1987; di Leonardo 1991:26–27). Feminist researchers, Stacey suggests, "are apt to suffer the delusion of alliance more than the delusion of separateness" (1988:25). Such ideas, critics have pointed out, are grounded in forms of social and economic relations, especially gender relations, characteristic of Western society (see Flax 1987:633; see also Sacks 1976). When one begins to question such ideas, some suggest, the analytic category "woman"—and hence an important pillar of a feminist anthropology—begins to dissolve (Moore 1988:7; see also M. Rosaldo 1987).[18] Nor are such critiques of feminism confined to anthropology. Pointing out that feminist analyses have turned from "phallo-centric narratives of our male-dominated disciplines" to critiques of feminist narratives themselves, Bordo notes that "it seems possible to discern what may be a new drift within feminism, a new scepticism about the use of gender as an analytical category" (1990:135).

In addition, while acutely aware of the issue of "otherness" (women so often having been the "other" themselves), feminists may also be guilty of the very practice for which they critique men, that is, of asserting the authority to speak for the other: "When feminists look overseas, they frequently seek to establish *their* authority on the backs of non-Western women, determining for them the meanings and goals of their lives" (Ong 1988:80). In this sense a feminist perspective can both represent and perpetuate the colonialism from which a contemporary anthropology claims to seek to liberate itself.

What, then—if anything—can anthropology draw from feminism?

What *should* it draw from feminism? Although I do not think that feminism has yet had the radical impact on anthropological theory that it deserves to have (some of the reasons for this are discussed below; see also Dubisch 1991a), it has shaped anthropology—and my own writing within anthropology—in several important ways, all of which are reflected in this book.

First, insofar as "the fundamental purpose of feminist theory is to analyze how we think, or do not think, or avoid thinking about gender" (Flax 1987:626), feminism has made it increasingly difficult (though unfortunately still not entirely impossible) to ignore gender as a significant category of social analysis, whatever one is studying.[19] Second, feminism has brought about increased self-consciousness about women's experience and its relationship to theory. Keohane and Gelpi argue that because "the construction of women's experience has never been adequate" and has been described and explained mainly by men, "feminist theory is fundamentally experiential" (1981:vii).[20] Flax goes further and suggests that all forms of theory, including but not limited to feminist theory, are dependent on and reflect "a certain set of social experiences" (1987:628; see also Harding 1990:95).[21] Such a stance further contributes to the breaking down of boundaries—between theory and practice, between the "subjective" and the "objective," between public and private experience, between the abstract and the concrete (see, e.g., Harding 1990). Within anthropology, women have begun to examine their own experiences, not simply as anthropologists and women in the field of fieldwork,[22] but also as female professionals in the "field" of anthropology, and to use these experiences as a basis for critiquing both theory and practice in their discipline. This second "field"—one's own academic one—and the ways in which one's work and the impact of one's work in this field are shaped by gender, have only recently begun to receive serious attention within anthropology. For me, as such analysis unfolds, it resonates with my own biography.

WRITING OTHERS, WRITING ONESELF

Although I have been writing about Greece, and about gender, for some time, and certainly recognized the role my own gender played in my choice of dissertation topic (and in male professorial indifference to it; see Dubisch 1986a), I thought that I could keep the study of women and the experience of myself as a woman separate, at least to some extent. In retrospect this seems naive. But I began my career as an anthropologist in the late 1960s, at a time when feminist consciousness was only beginning to penetrate the intellectual and political scene. Of course I realized even then that gender played a role in fieldwork—in the roles one was assigned or assumed, for example, and in the nature of the interactions one had with the "natives." And I also knew, without really analyzing it, that my interest in studying gender, or more specifically women ("gender," at the time, not yet being the widely used term it is now), was related to being female myself. But I felt no sense of universal sisterhood as the basis of my interest, only a concern that women and certain features of their lives were being overlooked or misrepresented by male anthropologists. In this sense, my interests in gender issues were typical of the time.[22] These interests persisted and evolved as anthropology—and anthropological interests in gender—changed. They persisted sometimes in spite of myself. Wanting to move beyond being a woman studying women (and by implication studying them only *because* I was a woman; see Moore 1988:7), I did not make gender a focus of my original research proposal on pilgrimage, the proposal with which I began the work I describe here. Yet gender became an unavoidable topic if I wished to do justice to what I observed and experienced (as this book demonstrates). In fact, my research on pilgrimage broadened my understanding of gender issues, and vice versa (see, e.g., Dubisch 1991a:41–44).

In addition, I certainly did not see in my earlier work that gender played a role in "writing up" my research (the phrase itself revealing the assumption of a straightforward objectivist relationship between field-note data and a final descriptive narrative). Yet, as Caplan has pointed out, "feminist anthropologists, in order to describe their object of study, have a double burden, since they have to use a language which is not entirely their own, but one dominated by male discourse" (1988:16). Recent attention to the relationship between writing and gender in anthropology has highlighted the ways in which both feminism and women's voices have been marginalized within the discipline. A number of female anthropologists have pointed out that when one surveys the recent discussions of anthropological writing and "experimental ethnographies," the examples cited of such ethnographies are almost always works written by men.[23] Neglected are a number of earlier works by female anthropologists that were "experimental" before the term came into vogue.[24] In many instances, the style in which these works were written—more personal, autobiographical, dramatic, and even emotional than the writing in "objective," impersonal standard ethnographies—doomed them to relative oblivion within the field, or at the very least to not being taken seriously as "real" anthropology. More successful were the women who learned to write in a more masculine, "objective" style. Since men have begun to analyze writing itself and to write experimentally, their writing has become cutting edge. One cannot help conclude, as Lutz does, that "certain types of discourse or approach are valorized *because* they are associated with the male" (1990:621; see also Caplan 1988:16). Thus one of my interests in writing this book is to explore not only issues of writing but the relationship between gender and anthropological writing as well.

In most of the writing from my first fieldwork I was conventional. Among other things, I dutifully sought, in good Weberian fashion (see R. Rosaldo 1989:170–73), to separate the "objective" world of my field data (written up in "fieldnotes") from the "subjective" world of the self (recorded in good Malinowskian fashion in my personal diary). The first was what I had "learned" (that is, "facts"), the second was what I experienced and felt, including daily events and problems that I encountered. A personal diary served, so I was taught, as an outlet for emotions and frustrations that (implicitly) had no place amid the "objective" data of my "fieldnotes." Although I did not entirely abandon this separation in notes taken during the fieldwork upon which this book is based, I found myself frequently blurring the lines between them. In this process, another conventional division—between "fact" and "theory"—also became difficult to maintain. As Kondo has put it in describing the strategy she employed in writing her ethnography *Crafting Selves,* "Experience and evocation can *become theory,* where the binary between 'empirical' and 'theoretical' is displaced and loses its force" (1990:8; cf. Okely 1992). Much (though not all) of my writing here bears the imprint of that breakdown of boundaries. To the extent that it does so, it constitutes what Abu-Lughod (1991) has called "writing against culture."

Abu-Lughod argues that the concept of culture, which emphasizes timelessness, coherence, and "otherness," and the generalizing that the concept of culture requires and upon which it bestows an aura of inevitability, are modes of creating difference and of preserving the authority of the observer. Generalization itself "is inevitably the language of power" (Abu-Lughod 1991:150). Abu-Lughod advocates shifting away from the concept of culture—"writing against culture"—and toward what she terms "ethnographies of the particular," which would present more of the complexities of the fieldwork experience. Her critique may reflect a common dilemma of the anthropologist, especially one newly returned from the field: the dilemma of trying to turn the particular into the general, the concrete into the abstract. I know it reflects my own experience in trying to "write up" my first fieldwork for my dissertation. Every time I wrote down a general statement about life in "the village," I felt dissatisfied, for such a statement inevitably violated my own experience of the complexities of village life. This life was full of particulars, not generalizations; it was peopled with individuals, not social categories. Yet I felt I was not being a good anthropologist if I could not "see" general patterns in what I had experienced, and I felt I *was* being a good anthropologist when I learned to write in the generalizations required by my field. While I think that a certain amount of generalization is necessary (and certainly it is practiced even by peoples of the cultures in which we work), Abu-Lughod's critique displaces generalization from its privileged position as the "right" way to do anthropology and opens up the possibility of other modes of anthropological presentation.

"OTHERNESS" IN THE EUROPEAN CONTEXT

I have discussed the issue of writing in relationship to a female self, and particularly the self of a female anthropologist. But there is another issue of writing, and of selfness and otherness, which I confronted in doing this work, and that is the issue raised by being an anthropologist working in a European society. Abu-Lughod has suggested similarities in the situations of feminist and what she calls "halfie" anthropologists—that is, those whose national or cultural identity is mixed, and who may even be studying, as anthropologists, those cultures that form part of their own heritage. In such situations, the "other" is at least partly the "self" (Abu-Lughod 1991). Most discussions of the self/other dichotomy, however, are based on the practices of a Western anthropology confronting and defining a non-Western other. Most American anthropologists studying Europe, on the other hand, are like the "halfie" anthropologist, studying the other who is also the self.[25] How does one construct the other when the other is European? How can one deny a history to those who invented it and who are part of one's own history? How can one write about those who are literate and can speak/write for themselves?[26] How does one deal with the writings of people of that culture in doing one's own work? How can one be an anthropologist among those who may themselves practice anthropology?

In the past, anthropologists (both American and European) who studied Europe sought to sidestep this dilemma by focusing on the more "exotic" areas of Europe (or perhaps *by* exoticizing such areas; see Herzfeld 1987a:91–92). One such area is the Mediterranean, a region that has often been viewed as "primal" compared to northern and western Europe (Sant Cassia 1992). Certainly Greece, on the "margins" of Europe (see Herzfeld 1987a), could be considered as falling into that category.[27] But even Greece has its own written history and its own scholars, including, in recent years, its own anthropologists. How do I deal with those who can debate with me in my own terms about the culture I have to come to "study," a culture of which they themselves are members? How do they receive my writings in relationship to their own work?[28] When I went to Greece in the summer of 1990, I visited a Greek woman with a recent Ph.D. in anthropology, for whose dissertation I had been an outside reader, and whose students are now doing anthropology in Greece. Who am I in this situation? And who is she? The other has now become the self, and this woman and I stand in a complex set of relationships to each other—as women, as anthropologists, as junior and senior, as Greek and non-Greek.

WRITING AS A WOMAN

Insofar, then, as a reflexive anthropology has come to critique the self/other dichotomy implicit in so much anthropological writing (a critique also intrinsic to much feminist theory), possibilities for a more "feminine" writing are opened up.[29] It can be difficult, however, for women in anthropology to write in this "feminized" fashion, especially since those women who have done so in the past have received little recognition, and their writing has often been devalued or ignored. Emotion, "irrationality," engagement, the struggle we undergo in "the field" to be both merged and separate (a struggle that we label "participant observation")[30]—these are intrinsic parts of the anthropological enterprise and underlie both anthropological understanding and anthropological writing. They are also, in our society's gender stereotyping, "feminine."[31]

Ironically, as ethnography becomes "experimental," male anthropologists may feel freer to experiment than female. Emotion is a sign, a mark of "otherness," of the primitive, of women, and women may seek to suppress this otherness in order to be accepted in a male-dominated or male-defined profession. By acknowledging their own emotions, however, anthropologists may cross the bridge to the other (Danforth 1989)—or at least meet the other halfway. For women, such a crossing over can constitute a double otherness that they may not believe they can afford.[32] In addition, the political project that feminist anthropology seeks to advance may seem to require writing in a more conventional anthropological mode in order to demonstrate that writing that addresses issues of gender can be acceptable as "good anthropology" (Abu-Lughod 1990:16–17). Thus while female anthropologists are now beginning to feel freer to experiment with textual innovation (and are producing excellent and interesting works as a result),[33] the self-conscious turn toward experimentation, and toward reflexivity and greater concern with emotion, although opening up more possibilities for both male and female anthropologists, has not automatically freed anthropology from the hegemony of male writing and male language.

CREATING ANTHROPOLOGY

Paul Rabinow, drawing on Geertz, speaks of anthropology as "fiction." By this he means not that it is false or that we "make it up," but rather that our accounts of other cultures are constructed; they are *made* (Rabinow 1986). This construction is the consequence of our interaction with the "other," our own background, training and orientation, and our own creativity. At first creativity seems antithetical to an "objective," scientific anthropology, which should report but not "create." And yet a "well-written" ethnography, one that holds our interest and conveys a vivid sense of another culture, is a creative endeavor, as is any ethnography. For fieldwork never presents us with a coherent account but rather with information and images that we must select and arrange and present and write about whether poorly or well, whether vividly or dully, using our own creative skills. It is furthermore a retrospective creation. From a present position of understanding we must recreate the always changing past experience of fieldwork (see Kondo 1990; Ottenberg 1990). As our sense of what ethnography should convey changes, these skills are especially challenged and anthropologists face "the creative possibilities released by loosening the strict codes that governed the production of ethnographies during the classic period" (R. Rosaldo 1989:38). Here again, as with self/other, emotional/objective, experience/theory, I saw boundaries if not dissolve, at least begin to blur as I wrote.

I have spoken of writing as if it involved only the present narrative. Yet the very process of anthropology begins in writing. Not only do we usually begin our research with a text—a proposal of some sort, presented to the appropriate persons or agency—we also create our experience in the field through writing, whether in fieldnotes or personal diary (Clifford 1986). By such means we "make sense" of what happens to us in the field, whether by categorizing events in certain ways or putting them in temporal sequence or relating them to other experiences.[34] There follow a variety of drafts in which material is written up for different purposes (a dissertation, a report to a granting agency, a symposium presentation, an article, a class lecture), drafts that intersect, interact, and build on each other. Each has its own appropriate form as mandated by the culture of anthropology. Thus any individual piece of writing is always the outcome of a series of writings, of the movement through a variety of texts (including, metaphorically, the field itself as text; see chapter 9).

Creation is not confined to the construction of one's object; it constructs the subject as well. In writing, one does not simply "express" oneself, as popular idiom would have it; one "creates" oneself. This is one reason why writing is so powerful. I have always enjoyed writing, beginning as a child when I wrote short stories and even novels for my own amusement. But for a long time I felt this creative power of my own writing to be realized only in writing fiction or poetry, or in a private journal. My "real" writing, my professional anthropological writing, I thought, was too constrained to be creative in this sense, constrained by a shared set of professional standards and by the conventionally agreed upon modes of presenting "facts" in appropriate language. Gradually I began to perceive that I had overlooked the ways in which anthropological writing, including my own writing, was creative as well—creative even within these constraints and even before the term "experimental ethnography" became a common phrase in anthropological discourse. Out of the multiplicity of ways in which even a single discipline allows its subject matter to be portrayed and transmitted, and out of the many possibilities for the subject matter itself, I had chosen certain ones. In doing so, I had not only created unique pieces of writing (as we all do) but also (as we all do) a professional identity, another act of "creation." (This is perhaps one of the reasons why writing is intimidating to many academics.)

To say, however, that anthropological writing is creative, that we "construct" the cultures we write about, that we should experiment with new modes of writing that break down boundaries we have constructed within ourselves and between ourselves and others—none of this means that anthropological accounts are or should be novels. I may "create" the people and situations I am writing about here, but I have not made them up. My accounts mesh with, overlap, confirm, and occasionally refute the accounts of others who have worked in Greece and elsewhere. This may be one means (and perhaps the only means) we have of arriving at a "truth" whereby this work, as well as others, may be judged (cf. Geertz 1973).

ETHNOGRAPHIES, POSTMODERN AND OTHERWISE

I have said that ethnographies are created, but the question of how they are created and even who creates them (the anthropologist, the "informants," the reader?) is currently the focus of considerable debate. Ethnography is inherently about writing, it is the means by which we make ourselves anthropologists as well as the means by which we create the object of anthropological study.[35] "Ethnography lies at the boundary of two systems of meaning and raises the question, how do we translate another culture through the vehicle of our own language?" (Caplan 1988:8). Writing always positions—it positions the writer, the reader, and those written about. One cannot write without a position: "Every view is a view from somewhere and every act of speaking a speaking from somewhere" (Abu-Lughod 1991:141). Yet it is well to keep in mind that everyone occupies a variety of positions. When I am in Greece, my positionality is complex. I may be an American grilled about Reagan's policies toward the Greek Socialist government (PASOK) and questioned as to why Americans elected Reagan as their president. I may be an established American anthropologist conversing with a younger Greek anthropologist about her own fieldwork. I may be an old friend to villagers I have known for over twenty years. I may be a source of revenue for an island shopkeeper. I may be just another foreign female in a tourist town to the Greek man on the prowl. So I am alternately and sometimes simultaneously positioned as female, American, anthropologist, tourist, friend, customer, lover, scholar, and even pilgrim. In addition, I am positioned by my own biography, my own experience (Hastrup 1992a:119; also Okely 1992). Thus I have sought to write from a number of these stances, and to make as clear as possible my multiple positions vis-à-vis those I am writing about.

This leads to a final question—can we as anthropologists ever escape writing itself? Are we trapped, and do we trap those we write about, in the net of our written words? Some anthropologists feel that we do and seek at least a partial escape from this dilemma in "polyphonic" ethnographies in which others are allowed to speak, and even to disagree with the anthropologist. Yet those voices still speak in words, and we as anthropologists have chosen which of those words to translate and we have written them down. The issue of voice is especially important with respect to women, whose views have been described as "muted" (Ardener 1975) and as subject to "verbocentric" male analysis (Herzfeld 1991a). How do we (male and female anthropologists alike) write about women when they may be unable, or unwilling, to "speak for themselves" (at least in words)?[36] There are no easy answers to this, and obviously I do not find a way out of words and writing in this book. Indeed, how can I?[37] I can only try to be conscious of what and how I write, and strive to make the reader conscious of the hidden agendas of my writing, as well as of its inevitable inadequacies. Ultimately, the author-ity is mine, and I must take responsibility for it.[38]

I have spoken throughout this chapter of the blurring and even dissolving of boundaries as characteristic of both feminism and postmodernism and as a feature of certain kinds of experimental anthropological writing.[39] It is this feature that perhaps most pervasively characterizes this work, and the one with which I struggled the most. The dissolving of boundaries is not complete—indeed I would not want it to be, for these boundaries still provide some of the structure of the work, and an important means of organizing and expressing what I wish to present. But at the very least I seek to question a variety of the separations anthropologists have made in our work: between self and other, between "fact" and theory, between emotion and reason, between the personal and the anthropological, between the field and the nonfield, between "history" and "story," between local and national, and as we shall see, even between the sacred and the profane.

CHAPTER TWO

The Pilgrim and the Anthropologist

TINOS: THE PILGRIM'S ARRIVAL

The summer traveler to Tinos will be struck first by two things about the island—the arid barrenness of the landscape, and the wind.

Tinos is a rugged island, one of a group of the Aegean Islands of Greece known as the Cyclades, a name derived from the fact that they form a circle (*kíklos*) around the ancient sacred island of Delos. For contemporary pilgrims, however, it is not Delos but Tinos that forms the sacred center of the Cyclades. These pilgrims come in droves during the summer months, in ships buffeted by the *meltémi,* the relentless north wind of summer. As the ships approach the island, steep rugged hills loom into view, their slopes dotted with tiny whitewashed villages. Dominating the landscape are the rocky escarpments of Exobourgos, the mountain that held the island's main town and fortress during the centuries of Venetian rule. Now, however, the island's main town is by the sea, sprawled along a waterfront lined with restaurants, hotels, shops, and boat ticket offices and encircling a man-made harbor cluttered with fishing boats, caïques, excursion boats, and yachts.

But the pilgrim approaching Tinos sees another sight as well, one that dominates the bustle of the harbor and town and draws the eye and the emotions. On board the ship, the devout cross themselves as this sight comes into view. It is the Church of the Madonna of the Annunciation (*Evangelístria*), the sacred home of the Panayía (All Holy One)[1] and the object of the pilgrim's journey. The church's whitewashed bell tower and ornate facade rise from a hill just above the town, visible from the sea even at night when the church's lighted outline shimmers like a beacon in the dark. As the ship draws closer to the harbor, another sacred place now comes into view. It is the whitewashed monastery of Kehkrovouno, perched high on the barren slopes above the town. This monastery was the home of Saint Pelayia, the nun whose vision led to the finding of the miraculous icon of the Annunciation, now housed in Tinos's famous church. The monastery is also a site of pilgrimage. Thus the two sacred places upon which the approaching pilgrim first lays eyes both gain their sacredness from female holy figures—the Madonna (Panayía) and a now-sainted nun.

The large passenger ships on which the pilgrims arrive make the run to Tinos daily either from Piraeus (the port of Athens) or from the fishing and resort town of Rafina (on the eastern side of Attica). In the busy months of the summer, there are usually four or five boats a day. Since most of these boats also go on to the tourist/jet-set resort island of Mykonos, they carry a mix of passengers—groups of young people dressed in the styles of the international youth culture; well-to-do Athenians on their way to vacations in Mykonos; families from Athens going to Tinos for pilgrimage or for their holidays; shabbily dressed pilgrims from mainland rural villages; groups of Gypsies in bright costumes; young couples carrying babies and laden with the paraphernalia of baptism; villagers and townspeople of Tinos returning from business trips to Athens; and groups of French, English, and Germans on tour who have discovered the "unspoiled" charms of Tinos and prefer it to "touristy" Mykonos.

Since most of the ships going to Tinos today are ferryboats and unload from the auto deck, disembarking passengers must crowd in the dark and cavernous hold with the cars and trucks as the ship is winched up to the dock.[2] The large doorway to the hold is lowered, and the passengers stream across the gangplank into the blinding sunshine—and the wind. Though many of the passengers are staying for several days, and a number will remain for weeks or even a month, everyone is in a hurry to disembark, and there is much jostling, shouting, and confusion as the passengers surge onto the concrete dock. Before all the passengers have straggled out of the hold, the cars and trucks have started up and begin to edge their way across the gangplank, adding to the confusion and the noise. A strong smell of diesel fuel hangs over the quay.

On the dock itself, behind a restraining metal fence, a large crowd awaits the passengers—women and men hawking rooms in hotels and private homes, islanders waiting to greet arriving relatives and friends, leaders of tour groups holding cardboard signs, and an occasional anthropologist, camera in hand. Beyond the crowds are lines of taxis and private cars as well as vans and buses emblazoned with the names of hotels, all waiting to convey the emerging passengers to their desired destinations. As the pilgrim tries to struggle through the confusion, white-jacketed men carrying baskets of *loukoúmia* (a locally made sweet) elbow their way toward the gangplank, hoping to sell their wares to the remaining passengers before the ship departs.

Many of the pilgrims disembarking will first seek lodgings for themselves. The stream of passengers gradually begins to disperse into little knots as some groups of pilgrims negotiate with potential landladies over the price of rooms, and others, suitcases and bundles in hand, head for lodgings that have been secured in advance. Many pilgrims, however—those who have come only for the day, or who feel the urgency of their sacred duties—will head directly for the church, trudging up the hill with their luggage. The pilgrim can thus join the crowd of devotees who, following the arrival of every boat on a busy summer day, stream up the main street to the church.

This street is a wide avenue about a kilometer in length, lined with shops at its lower end, and leading directly from the harbor to the church. As the pilgrims begin their ascent, they are assailed with the cries of the shopkeepers who stand outside their stores, hawking the items necessary for a successful pilgrimage: large candles (*lambádhes*) to be lighted in the church, metal plaques (*támata*) depicting the pilgrim's vow or request, and small bottles (*boukalákia*) for holy water (*ayíasma*). The merchants' cries ring in the pilgrims' ears as they begin to make their way up the hill: "*Lambádhes! Támata! Boukalákia yia ayíasma! Edhó lambádhes!*"[3] As the pilgrim ascends, the whine of a beggar woman may be added to the din, as she calls pitifully to those passing by to give her just a drachma or two to buy her bread. Thus the pilgrim's progress may be momentarily interrupted to purchase a candle, *táma*, or holy water bottle, or to give a few drachmas to the beggars by the wayside.

But for some of the pilgrims, their progress may be slower still, for they have made vows that they will ascend to the church not by foot but on their knees, or more difficult and painful still, on their stomachs, inching their way up the hill. It is women far more often than men who undertake such a difficult journey. On a busy day there may be a steady stream of such women on their knees, sometimes alone, but more often accompanied by another woman, husband, or children, crawling painfully up the hill. Sometimes they bear a burden on their backs that makes their passage still more difficult: a child (or a replica of one), a *lambádha*, an icon, a can of oil, or some other object, according to the nature of their request or vow. Other pilgrims may stop and watch these burdened ones for a moment. Some wish them success in their holy journey (*voithiá sas*). Others just stare with expressions of pity or curiosity. Shopkeepers along the way give encouragement or advice: "Go this way, around the cars." "It's not far, just take your time" (*sigá, sigá*). "You should put something on your knees." They may also bring water for the kneeling pilgrim to drink or splash upon her face.

At the height of the summer pilgrimage, and especially around the heavily attended festival of the Assumption or Dormition (*Kímisis*) on the fifteenth of August, large numbers of Gypsies add their colorful presence to the crowds. They, too, stream up the hill to the church, the women in bright dresses and scarves, shouldering bundles and blankets, bringing candles, oil, and sometimes sheep to offer at the church. Some come with a child who is "vowed" (*taméno*) and dressed in black, wearing a little black cap with a cross stitched on the front in red thread. Unlike the other pilgrims, however, the Gypsies do not seek rooms, for most of them camp in the churchyard, in the municipal park, or on the street.

Despite the incessant buffeting of the *meltémi,* it is hot in the midday summer sun, and the street seems to become increasingly steep as one ascends. At the top of the hill, where the shops end, is the municipal park, and some pilgrims pause here, taking advantage of the benches and the cool shade of trees to rest for a moment. Looking back down the street, one can see other pilgrims still struggling up the hill, and far below, the harbor and white-capped expanse of sea beyond, and the passenger ship now steaming toward Mykonos.

Only a little remains now of the pilgrim's journey. At the top of the hill, beyond the park, the street ends in a wide, paved expanse in front of the church. Short flights of steps lead up to a semicircular exterior courtyard laid with colored stones and edged by a low wall. People are sitting here and there, resting or perhaps guarding luggage and waiting for other members of their group who have gone inside the church. Suitcases and bundles of blankets are stacked along the wall, Gypsy children chase each other across the courtyard, and in the shade of the trees near the steps several local women sit, inquiring of the passing pilgrims if anyone wants a room.

This courtyard marks the first visible perimeter of sacred space since disembarkation on the island itself, and those who have not yet performed any ritual activity may pause to do so here—crossing themselves, removing their shoes (going barefoot is another common form of vow), or even falling on their knees to crawl the rest of the way to the church. Or they may wait to perform such devotions until they have crossed this courtyard and arrived at the arched doorways that open into the inner courtyard and the first full view of the church itself.

At the doorway stands a church employee, the first representative of the church and its regulations that the pilgrim has thus far encountered. This employee helps the pilgrims to remove the red paper wrappers from their *lambádhes,* gives information to those needing help, and refuses further entry to those who are improperly dressed. Visitors wearing shorts (men or women), miniskirts, bathing suits, or other "indecent" attire must either turn back or don appropriate clothes (which are provided by the church for those who neglect to bring their own). This attempt to guard the purity of the sacred space is not always successful, however. Even when the "guard" is there, it is possible for the scantily attired visitor to enter through another, unguarded doorway to the interior courtyard, and from there to ascend the steps to the sanctuary.

A set of marble steps leads up to the courtyard from each of the two entry gates, and groups of pilgrims may be posed on these steps having souvenir photographs made, either by a member of their own party or by the professional photographer who waits just inside the gate. The upper courtyard is an open area paved with square marble blocks, encircled by the church and the buildings housing the church offices, museums, meeting rooms, and so on. Pilgrims may be camped in the courtyard on blankets in the shade of trees or balustrades, or along the balconies of the second floor of the encircling buildings or even just outside the doors of the main sanctuary. (Those who have not brought their own blankets may borrow them for no charge from the church.) Bundles of bedding and clothes are stacked everywhere and families rest in the shade, eating their lunch.

To the right as the pilgrim ascends the courtyard steps is a fountain donated by a Turkish official who was cured of syphilis by the holy icon, and directly ahead is the second set of marble steps that ascends to the sanctuary. If it is a very busy day, a line may have already formed outside the church door, and even down the steps. Women on their knees may be working their way up the steps on this final stretch of their journey, and the other pilgrims stand aside to let them by. If the day is not so busy, however, pilgrims ascend the steps directly and turn left along the balcony to the main doorway of the church.

It is dim inside the church, the interior lit only by the sunlight streaming from the high windows and by the candles burning in the candelabra in front of the icon. Just inside the door to the pilgrim's left is a carved wooden counter with a slot where the pilgrim can drop money and pick up candles of various sizes as offerings. A church employee stands behind the counter, stuffing paper bills into the slot with a stick, since on a busy summer day the offering box fills rapidly. Pilgrims who have brought oil to offer may first turn right upon entering the church, toward another counter where offerings of oil are accepted and small bottles of consecrated oil given out. On this counter also stands one of the church's most famous offerings—a silver orange tree bearing votive lights on its outstretched branches.

The pilgrim lights the candles or *lambádhes* and places them in one of the candelabra before passing behind the row of candelabra and in front of the icon itself. On a very busy day, the attendants may instruct people to do their devotions (*proskínima*) first and then light a candle afterward, in an attempt to keep a more orderly line. It is an attempt that is not usually successful, and when there is a constant stream of pilgrims, a small traffic jam may form in the area around the icon. (On especially busy days, a church policeman, or *ikonofílakas*, stands at the church door, blocking further entry with his outspread arms until the congestion has cleared, anxious pilgrims pressed behind him.) Eventually, one by one, each pilgrim passes in front of the icon, bending to kiss it and making the sign of the cross three times. The icon itself, resting in an elaborate icon stand, is not visible for it is covered with some of the many jewels that have been given as offerings. All around it other offerings are arranged as well: small replicas of ships hanging from the icon stand, bouquets of fresh flowers, embroidered cloths, pots of basil.

Some pilgrims simply perform the minimal devotions in front of the icon, but others have a more elaborate ritual to carry out. This may consist of making the sign of the cross over the icon three times with one of the metal plaques (*támata*) representing the pilgrim's request and then dropping the *táma* in the box by the icon provided for the purpose. Or it may involve tucking flowers or some other offering next to the icon. Or a pilgrim may perform a more elaborate devotion by kneeling in front of the icon stand and kissing various parts of the stand as well as the icon itself. Those who have crawled to the icon on their knees usually perform such devotions first and then rise to kiss the icon, their arrival at the sacred spot signaling the end of their painful pilgrimage. Children are lifted up to kiss the icon, parents grasping tiny hands to demonstrate how to make the sign of the cross. Some of the devotions carried out at the icon are intensely emotional as women weep and cry out to the Panayía to grant their prayers and onlookers sigh and wipe away their own tears, murmuring *Panayía mou* (my Panayía). Retarded children may fuss or shout as their parents attempt to lead them to the icon's healing power. Although those waiting may grumble if someone takes too long in front of the icon, no one is rushed or pulled away. A church employee sits patiently, even stoically, to one side of the icon stand, reaching out periodically to wipe the much-kissed glass with a cloth or cotton pad, but otherwise there is little interference with the constant flow of pilgrims filing by.

Once past the icon, the main objective of the pilgrim's journey has usually been accomplished. Some pilgrims may leave at this point, exiting by one of the side doors of the church. But many stay, perhaps moving around to pay their devotions to the other icons in the church, particularly the silver- and gold-covered icon showing the Dormition (*Kímisis*).

They may also admire the many offerings hanging from the ceiling of the church—lamps, replicas of ships, and a variety of other *támata*. They may also write names of friends and family members and requests for their health on little slips of paper that they put in a wooden box or give directly to the priest, who will read the names during services. They may kneel at the altar rail or to one side of the church to pray. They may stay for prayer services (performed each afternoon in the summer and timed for the arrival of the boats). Or they simply sit quietly for a while on a chair or bench, watching the other pilgrims, absorbing the atmosphere of the church.

On a busy day, the church buzzes with activity that seems at first chaotic. Even during services people continue to move around, engaging in their own rituals, talking, coming and going as they please. There is a hum of voices, a child crying, a woman praying. The church is pungent with the smell of melting wax, crowded bodies, and the lingering scent of incense from the service. Church employees work constantly beside the flaming candelabra, snuffing and removing the lighted candles to make room for new ones, their dark work jackets splattered with wax. A female employee scrapes up melted wax from the marble floor and then polishes the brass railing around the icon with a cloth. Outside, people rest on the stone benches in the shade of the arcade that runs along the second level of the church, chatting with fellow pilgrims, waiting for other members of their group to emerge. "Where do we go for holy water?" pilgrims ask each other, and other more knowledgeable pilgrims direct them downstairs, to the chapel beneath the main church where they will find the holy water font. Perhaps on the way they will stop to look through the doorway of the mausoleum to the *Elli,* the Greek battleship that was torpedoed in 1940 by an Italian submarine while it was anchored at Tinos to celebrate the fifteenth of August. If a family has brought a baby to baptize, they will also go to this lower part of the church, for here the baptismal fonts are found, and on a busy summer weekend a constant stream of baptisms is performed.

On important festival days such as August 15 (the day of the Dormition), March 25 (the day of the Annunciation and also Greek Independence Day), and July 23 (the feast day of St. Pelayia), these activities are intensified. Thousands of people pour off the boats in the days preceding the festival, bearing their luggage, their children, their ailments, hopes, and fears. They stream up the hill to the church, filling the courtyards and the steps, crowding into the stuffy, candlelit interior. It is usually at such times that the most desperate supplicants come, and in hundreds of individual rituals extremes of human suffering are dramatized—a woman struggling up the church steps on her stomach, bearing her paralyzed child on her back; a Gypsy man crowned with thorns, a large wooden cross weighing on his shoulders, trudging up the hill; a woman in black crawling with agonizing slowness toward the church, crying out that she cannot make it for the devil has possessed her and is holding her back; a woman on her knees bearing on her back a frail, sickly child who she believes has been bewitched.

At such times there is an all-night service (*olaniktía*), and pilgrims spend the night inside the church, or sleep on blankets in the inner courtyard or even just outside the main doors. In the morning, the icon is carried in a procession down the main street to the podium by the waterfront. During the procession, many pilgrims kneel in the center of the street to have the icon passed over them, and often those bearing the icon must slow in order to accommodate all of those seeking to squeeze beneath. (On the day of Saint Pelayia, the icon is transported up to the

1. Pilgrims lining up on the steps at the Church of the Annunciation, waiting their turn to enter the chapel

monastery where Pelayia lived.) At the waterfront (where there is a small town square, or *platía*, with a podium), speeches and sermons are given by the various dignitaries who have come for the event. The icon is then carried back to the church while the pilgrims gather up their belongings and make their way to the docks to crowd aboard the ships that will carry them home. And the anthropologist, emotionally and physically exhausted from days of observing, talking, photographing, and toiling up and down the hill to the church, trudges wearily back to her apartment to write up her notes.

TINOS: THE ARRIVAL OF THE ANTHROPOLOGIST

When I arrived on Tinos in the summer of 1986 to do research at the Church of the Evangelístria I was returning after an absence from Greece of seven years. Much had happened during those seven years; indeed, much had happened to me since my original fieldwork on Tinos in 1969–70. I was returning now on my own pilgrimage, hoping not only to explore the theoretical and ethnographic interests I had developed since my first fieldwork, but seeking both professional and personal revitalization as well. Unlike many of the other pilgrims who come to Tinos, however, I was not seeking healing—or so I thought. But perhaps I was, for in the years preceding my return, I had suffered considerable psychic and physical pain. Among other things, a very serious back problem had altered my life in a number of profound ways. Not only was the pain itself sometimes difficult to endure, but the experience of and continuing concern with this pain had led to depression, self-absorption, difficulties in personal relationships, and challenges to my own identity, an identity that had been based, in part, on *doing* certain kinds of things. It did not help that when my back problems began, I had just turned forty. I felt old and feared the inactivity and the restrictions on my life—including restrictions on doing fieldwork—that chronic pain would impose. Moreover, I feared the pain itself, for at its worst, before I found therapy that would at least make it manageable, it was at times so severe I could think of nothing else.

I had also reached an impasse professionally. Like most cultural anthropologists, I had done my original fieldwork while in graduate school, spending thirteen months on Tinos in the small village of Falatados from 1969 to 1970, gathering material for my doctoral dissertation. Although I visited Greece periodically afterward, returning briefly to the village each time,[4] I had not done another major research project. There comes a point in time, however, when one must face the issue of "returning to the field," whether because of institutional expectations, the threat of personal burnout, or simply because one is an anthropologist and that is what one does. I had reached the stage where I had begun to ask myself, "What next?" I had explored several possibilities, postponing the idea of returning to Greece. There were various reasons for this postponement: the desire to explore a new area rather than returning to the old, the fear of physically not being able to travel and do fieldwork because of disability and pain, and the fear of loneliness. In the end, perhaps like any pilgrim, I felt the need of renewal from another visit to the sacred site, in my case, a return to "the field." It was with some trepidation, however, that I finally did make plans to return, not certain that I would be able to carry out these plans because of the problems with my back.

I was also anxious about going back into the field alone. In my original village fieldwork I had been accompanied by my husband, who had provided both companionship and help with my work. While a brief return trip by myself to the village in the summer of 1975 after my husband and I had separated had shown me some of the advantages of being in such a situation alone (deeper immersion in the language, less distance between myself and the villagers), this did not allay my anxiety. I was not going back to the village, after all, but moving into a new research situation. My partner at the time was not able to accompany me, as he had other professional commitments and interests (though he did visit for a while).[5] I was anxious about being a woman alone in Greece, and anxious about the ways I might find myself restricted because of my gender. Since problems with my back had deeply undermined my sense of self-confidence, all of these issues loomed even larger than they might have at an earlier point in my life.

I had chosen the research project that I did for several reasons. Studying the Church of the Annunciation seemed to me one way of moving beyond the limitations of a village study, as well as advancing my own growing interests in religion and in interpretive anthropology. The healing dimension of the shrine also appealed to my interest in medical anthropology. In addition, I felt that the project would help to correct what I had come to perceive as an oversight or blindness on my part where the church was concerned, which had led me to overlook some of its local and national significance (Dubisch 1988). I also thought that the project I had conceived—to examine the political and nationalistic dimensions of pilgrimage as manifested in this particular shrine—would be a relatively straightforward one, an important consideration given certain constraints of funding and time. I was already familiar with the site and knew a good deal about the background of the project and I had personal ties in Greece. In addition, I knew the language (though my Greek was rusty after seven years away). Once I began my work, however, the project proved to be much more complex and difficult than I had imagined it would be, and led me well beyond the pilgrimage site itself.

I arrived on Tinos on June 17, 1986, with the *meltémi* blowing fiercely. After nearly a month spent in Athens, brushing up on my Greek, renewing old friendships and forming new ones, and recovering from a somewhat unexpected case of culture shock, it was a relief to be away from the city and back on the island. I knew that an apartment was waiting for me, since this had been arranged in advance and my landlady was to meet me at the dock. When I emerged from the dark bowels of the ship, I anxiously scanned the unfamiliar faces of those waiting at the waterfront, hoping that someone would approach. As I stood uncertainly, buffeted by the wind, an attractive woman of about my own age with curly blond hair and fashionable glasses approached me tentatively. Was I an American professor, she asked me in Greek, and did I speak Greek? Our relief was mutual as I said yes. She told me that her name was Marina[6] and laughed as she recounted how she had already approached several foreigners with that question, not knowing exactly how to recognize me. She took my bags and we headed across the dock toward the apartment that was to be my home for the next four months.

It was a relief to settle in and unpack in quarters that were much more spacious than the hotel room where I had spent my month in Athens. After I put away my belongings, Marina took me grocery shopping, pointing out the shops where (according to her) the best produce and groceries were to be found. These chores completed, I left my new apartment to renew my acquaintance with the town.

Tinos had changed in the years since I had last visited. The building I would be living in was new, as were many of the other buildings on the edge of town. There seemed to be even more shops, especially more tourist shops, and more hotels. There were also more foreign tourists than I had seen before (foreign tourism had been virtually nonexistent when I first did fieldwork in 1969–70), and there were signs in languages other than Greek. There was a video store, and places to rent cars and motorcycles, and there was even a disco. (Later I would find that there was also topless bathing at the beaches.)

Yet at the same time there was a welcome familiarity to it all. As I walked around the town, I savored this familiarity—the broad *paralía* (waterfront) lined with restaurants, cafes, hotels, and shops (many of them the same ones I remembered from fifteen years earlier), the boats docked at the wharf—brightly painted fishing boats, excursion boats to Delos and other islands, private and chartered yachts—the traffic (worse now), and the crowds of pedestrians out for an evening stroll (*vólta*). All of this evoked poignant memories of my earlier years on the island. I had returned to a familiar place.

The next day, after spending the morning organizing my quarters and writing up some notes, I went down to watch the boat from Athens arrive, observing the crowds of passengers as they spilled onto the dock and headed toward town and the church. I began to walk with the crowd of pilgrims, intending at first simply to stop someplace along the way for lunch. But then I found myself walking up the hill toward the church with the pilgrims instead, caught up in the purpose, the object, of their pilgrimage. I had for the first time a glimpse of what it means to the people who come to Tinos to arrive at the island, to climb up that hill to the church. While recognizing that there was a certain illusion in this experience, I did nonetheless feel, if only briefly, some of the excitement and power of the pilgrimage, of the sacredness of the destination ahead of me, and of myself, however fleetingly, joining with the others in that purposeful journey up the hill. At that point it was more than I was ready for, to be caught up so immediately in the emotional power of the pilgrimage, and although later I made this journey countless times, that day at least, I did not complete the climb.

The ambivalences that surfaced that afternoon continued to haunt me during the course of my fieldwork. They were in part ambivalences of a personal nature, having to do with my own relationship to and feelings about what I was studying. These ambivalences were heightened by the fact that I was also uncertain what role my own feelings should be allowed to play in my professional understanding of what I observed. This was particularly important, I found, because much of what I observed was of a highly emotional nature, both for myself and for those making their pilgrimage. Yet, as in the above account of my experience that first day, I distrusted my emotions, seeing them (at least at first) as impediments to my own observation and understanding.

In addition, as time went by I discovered that doing fieldwork in the town of Tinos was a radically different experience from my earlier fieldwork. In my first research trip to Greece I had lived in a village of 370 people that was located about a half hour by bus from Tinos's main town. In this tiny community it was difficult to be anonymous. My husband and I lived in the house of a family, nearly everyone in the village knew who we were, relationships were personal, and we were often and relatively easily drawn into people's lives. There were many contexts for engaging in conversations, and a variety of ways to observe and participate. Just *being* there yielded rich material for the anthropologist.

Working in the town was both easier and more difficult. It was certainly materially easier. Instead of a house with no running water and a pit toilet, I had an apartment with a fully equipped bathroom (and even a hot-water heater) and a kitchen with a refrigerator. All the amenities I needed were available in the town's many shops. (I did not have to "go to town" to shop as I had when I lived in the village.) In addition, because I was more anonymous, the town afforded me a privacy I had not enjoyed in the village. The other side of privacy, however, was invisibility and loneliness. The townspeople, unlike the villagers, were used to dealing with strangers, both foreign and Greek, and it was easy to place me in that stranger category, which was a distancing one. Even when I broke through that distance, however, and established a somewhat more personal relationship, I found that people were extremely busy in the summer (the time when I was usually there since that is the time of most intense pilgrimage) and unable to offer me the sort of hospitality that would have been the village norm (a fact that my landlady, busy at the family store until midnight seven days a week, would sometimes lament to me). The casual "hanging out" that had occurred easily in the village, and that had always yielded information and insights as well as social bonds, was thus much more difficult in the town. I found myself buying a variety of trinkets from shopkeepers as a means of starting conversations and asking questions, and I spent many an evening hour sitting in my landlady's store. In addition, the pilgrims, who were the main focus of my research, were a shifting population whom I could never get to know well individually. Though I could constantly observe their passage and the variety of their individual and collective acts, conversations with them were often brief and our interactions transitory.

There was an additional psychological difficulty working on the island. When I first went to Tinos in 1969, it was relatively undeveloped as a tourist site, and few foreigners came there. Today, while the villages remain mostly (though by no means completely) unaffected by foreign tourism,[7] and while the main business of the town is still pilgrimage, increasing numbers of foreigners are now visiting (chiefly Germans, French, and English). In addition, more Greeks are now coming to Tinos, not as pilgrims, but for summer vacations. This creates difficulties for the anthropologist who finds herself sharing the space where she has come for work with those who have come for pleasure. I admit that there were certain advantages to being in a tourist site—an abundance of restaurants and services, the availability of several beaches. But I found it extremely difficult to work, and to live by myself, in a place where others came to enjoy themselves, and came in the company of lovers, family, and friends. Moreover, when one works in such a place it is hard to be taken seriously, either by those who live there or by others (such as academic colleagues) to whom one laments about the difficulties of fieldwork. Local people couldn't always understand what I was doing. Why did I spend so much time at the church? Why didn't I go swimming? Why was I there alone? Since the exact nature of my work was somewhat obscure to most local people (and sometimes also to me), even those who knew that I was a professor doing research on the church could not refrain from putting me in the same category with other kinds of summer visitors (a category that, for them at least, made a good deal more sense). Hence not only did I not receive reinforcement from my surroundings for the idea that I was doing "fieldwork," but also my own experience of the contrast between what I was doing and what those who were in Tinos for vacation were doing added to the difficulty of my situation.

Pain and illness are always harder to manage when one is living in a strange place, and far from home. In the end, however, I suffered less from the physical pain of my back than from the loneliness of fieldwork in a place where local people are exhaustingly busy and the subjects of my research transitory, and from the inherent methodological problems of studying a pilgrimage site, problems that sometimes seemed overwhelming. Yet at the same time I think that my own physical problems underlay much of my response to what I experienced on Tinos. Most important, perhaps, these problems led me to understand, much more than I would have at an earlier time in my life, the pain and suffering that would lead people to seek healing at the shrine, and they produced in me emotional responses to many of the things I saw, responses that came to play a significant part in my fieldwork and, later, in my theoretical understanding of what I encountered.

ANTHROPOLOGY AS PILGRIMAGE

Anthropologists have sought to apprehend the nature of fieldwork with a variety of analogies—the analogy of childhood socialization, of the anthropologist as stranger, of the anthropologist as the participant in a game trying to learn the rules, of the fieldworker as second-language learner.[8] All of these are ways of trying to grapple with fieldwork as an experience that is at the core of the discipline yet lacks a disciplinary consensus as to its nature and methods. To this I add my own analogy, perhaps an obvious one but meaningful in the context of my own research—the analogy of anthropology as a pilgrimage.[9] There are several ways in which we can draw such an analogy.

First, anthropology, like pilgrimage, obviously involves a journey. Like the pilgrim, the anthropologist must leave home and travel to a special place, a place with transformative powers, a place that can provide the pilgrim/anthropologist with answers to prayers/questions. In the "field" the anthropologist is in a liminal state, just as the pilgrim is.

Both the anthropologist and the pilgrim may experience things during the journey that do not occur at home—which is, of course, very much the point of the trip. In the field, requests are made and may even be granted. "Miracles" may occur in which the veil between self and other, the profane and the sacred, is rent, and the anthropologist, like the pilgrim, will return home to bear witness with tales of these miracles, recounted to either confirm or shake the faith of those who have remained at home, and perhaps to inspire others to make the sacred journey as well. And like the pilgrim, the anthropologist may suffer in this journey, but through this suffering experience a transformation so that the person who left is not the person who returns. Behind both the pilgrim's journey and the anthropologist's lies the same basic premise: certain places are different, and miracles can happen there.

CHAPTER THREE

The Anthropological Study of Pilgrimage

WHEN I FIRST began my research on pilgrimage at the Church of the Annunciation on Tinos in 1986, the phenomenon was not one that had been well studied by anthropologists. Aside from Victor Turner's works on pilgrimage as ritual and on the place of pilgrimage in the Christian tradition (1974, 1979; Turner and Turner 1978), works that provided much of the initial inspiration for my own research, there existed only a handful of anthropological studies of pilgrimage. Recently, however, anthropological interest in the topic has burgeoned. While there are still no general theoretical works of a scope to rival Turner's, there have emerged a number of monographs and articles, many of which critique Turner's theories.[1]

Just as anthropological attention to pilgrimage has grown, so has pilgrimage itself flourished. Far from dying out in a purportedly secularizing world, pilgrimage has adapted to, and even benefited from, contemporary modes of transportation and communication. Planes now carry Muslim pilgrims to Mecca, and Greek pilgrims travel in groups to Tinos and other Greek shrines by bus and boat. Pilgrimage is often more organized, easier, and safer than in past times. It is also more widely advertised. Television and newspapers carry stories of pilgrimage events. The miracle-working site of Medjugorje, in the former Yugoslavia, has been featured in *Life* magazine and on the television program "Unsolved Mysteries." New pilgrimage sites such as the Church of St. Rafaíl on the Greek island of Mitilini (Lesvos) are popularized by the media as well as by word of mouth. Nationalism and pan-national religious movements and ideologies provide a further impetus to pilgrimage.[2]

What accounts for the current popularity of pilgrimage? What accounts for increasing anthropological interest in pilgrimage? And, conversely, what accounts for earlier anthropological neglect of such a widespread phenomenon? Are the increase in popularity of pilgrimage and the increase in anthropological interest in the phenomenon related, and if so, in what way? And perhaps equally important, in all of these different kinds of journeys, can we find anything in common? Is there anything that allows us to speak of "pilgrimage" in a general sense (including both contemporary and historical pilgrimage in our designation), or can we only speak of "pilgrimages"? And given the nature of pilgrimage, which involves journeys, sometimes long ones, over different kinds of space, and pilgrimage sites that engage a constantly shifting set of personnel, how can pilgrimage be studied by the anthropologist?

PILGRIMAGE IN TIME AND SPACE

At the heart of pilgrimage lies the notion of a journey (see, e.g., Morinis 1984). A journey involves two important dimensions—time and space. What distinguishes pilgrimage from other journeys is that its time and space are not ordinary time and space. Moreover, pilgrimage is both a "real" journey and a symbolic or metaphoric one in which spiritual and/or social transformation takes place.

Pilgrimage is based on the belief that certain places are different from other places, specifically, that they are in some sense more powerful and extraordinary—what Preston (1992) calls "spiritual magnetism." This power can not only be experienced by the pilgrim who visits such places; it can also be taken home in one form or another—whether as a feeling of spiritual renewal, as a healed illness, as a physical object imbued with the sacred power of the pilgrimage site, or as a transformation in one's social status. Often there is some *thing* at the site of pilgrimage that provides a center for the pilgrimage space. This "thing" may be a church or other sacred structure that has additional functions as well as being a locus for pilgrimage.[3] In such places, other ritual activities not directly connected to pilgrimage may also occur. (For example, the church at Tinos provides regular services for the local population as well as daily prayer services that coincide with the arrival of the boatloads of pilgrims.) Other sites, such as Medjugorje, have become the focus of pilgrimage only because of miraculous events that have drawn crowds of the faithful and hopeful to that particular spot.

Eade and Sallnow emphasize that the role played by the physical locale varies from one pilgrimage situation to another. A pilgrimage site may be a place where the divine has manifested itself (as at Lourdes or Medjugorje). Or the terrain itself may give birth to a pilgrimage site that is part of an animate landscape. Pilgrimage may also center around a sacred person, such as a living saint. Or the pilgrimage site may derive its holiness from the fact that it corresponds to a holy text, as in Christian pilgrimage to Jerusalem in which various sacred points provide movement through the textual accounts of Christ's life and death (Eade and Sallnow 1991a:6–8). Yet in all these cases, whatever the nature of the sacredness that provides the rationale for the journey, this sacredness is nonetheless geographically located, requiring the pilgrim to venture away from home to a different place to experience it.

In fact, any place may become a locus of pilgrimage. All that is required is that people go there with a sacred purpose and that the site become known for its powers, drawing still more people there. Sometimes pilgrimage sites are established with official sanction, but there are also many cases of pilgrimage sites (such as Lourdes and Medjugorje) that owe their existence to popular belief and only later became officially sanctioned. By going in large numbers to a place believed to be sacred, devotees in effect *create* a pilgrimage site. In contrast, other sites may become pilgrimage sites through official promotion, and the miracles that occur there are promulgated by church and lay officials, whether for political reasons, as a means of renewing faith, or in order to create renown for a particular site or region. Some believe this is what happened at Tinos, where the establishment of the Church of the Annunciation coincided with the establishment of the first independent Greek state (see chapter 9). Turner suggests that pilgrimage sites are usually spatially peripheral (part of what he terms the "anti-structural" nature of pilgrimage). They are "out there," tending to be located outside the main administrative centers of church and state (Turner 1974:192–96), though especially famous pilgrimage sites may, in time, become highly developed centers of ritual and ecclesiastical activity. Such peripherality may vary, however, according to the nature of the political and religious system within which pilgrimage takes place. Cohen, for example, postulates that the location of pilgrimage sites "out there" is particularly characteristic of the Christian tradition. In other religious traditions, such as Islam and the religions of India, where there is a close relationship between the political and religious domains, the separation between pilgrimage sites and secular centers may be absent (E. Cohen 1992:35).

Pilgrimage is part of more general patterns of visiting sacred places, patterns that have a long history in many religious traditions, past and present. In many of the religions in which pilgrimage is found, individual worshipers may make a variety of visits to nearby sacred places, visits that are not necessarily viewed as pilgrimage, nor as in any way "extraordinary." In this respect pilgrimage forms a continuum with other sorts of religious activity involving special places, from a brief visit made by an individual to a local church or tomb or other sacred spot, to more difficult journeys to distant places drawing thousands of worshipers every year. The idea of the journey, however, remains basic to pilgrimage and sets it apart from other visits to sacred places. Thus a woman from one of the villages of Tinos who simply takes the bus to town to visit the Church of the Annunciation and a woman who journeys there from Thessaloniki in northern Greece may have the same purpose in mind for their visit, but the experience is different for the one who must journey from afar. Nor is this simply a matter of the distance involved. For the village woman, the church at Tinos is familiar, part of her local geography and a source of local identity and pride (see Dubisch 1988). For the woman from

Thessaloniki, however, the church at Tinos is "exotic." When I asked people who had traveled to Tinos from other areas of Greece what their impressions were, they not only spoke about the church itself and the events they witnessed there, but also frequently made comments about the island landscape—its barrenness, the wind, the lack of trees—and about the town and its inhabitants. For these individuals their journey to Tinos was definitely a journey to a different place. At the same time, we must not lose sight of the common feature that the church at Tinos exhibits for anyone, whether from nearby or far away. That common feature is its sacredness as a place where the everyday world comes close to, even touches, the spiritual world, and where the everyday world is altered by such an encounter.[4]

In addition to centering around a different sort of place, pilgrimage generally involves a different sort of time, time that is removed (to some extent at least) from ordinary life and that may reenact events associated with gods, saints, martyrs, and other sacred beings (see Turner 1974:207; see also Bowman 1991).

Thus time figures in pilgrimage sites in other ways than just the ritual journey of the pilgrimage. Time is also involved in the sense of time as history; that is, there is a past event or set of events associated with most pilgrimage sites that gives them their special character and serves to justify the pilgrimage journey. These events are ones involving a bridge between worlds. During such events, the power of the spiritual world crosses over in one way or another into the mundane world, whether it is through an apparition, the occurrence of miracles, or simply the spiritual renewal experienced by the pilgrim. Over the course of time, events that continue to occur at the pilgrimage site become part of this history and add to its range of meaning for devotees, inspiring further pilgrimage. At the same time, the history of a pilgrimage site differs from secular history for it both is and is not linear. Although its power usually derives from specific past events, a pilgrimage site also gains power from the belief that what happened in the past may occur again (Turner and Turner 1978:6).[5] As Ross, speaking of Christian women's religious geography in the Holy Land, puts it, such sites are "legitimated by God's interactions with human persons" so that "historical places are no longer mere historical places; they are now sacred spaces, bearers of a divine presence which has the power to recall the past to the present and to awaken in believers the religious response of the scriptural figures who prefigured and accompanied Christ" (1991:101).

Another temporal element of a pilgrimage shrine is the staging of calendrical rituals that draw large numbers of people. These rituals usually commemorate and celebrate parts of the shrine's history, or reflect other sacred associations of the pilgrimage site. For example, at Tinos, though

pilgrimage may take place at any time of year, it is the holy days associated with the Panayía (particularly the days of Annunciation and the Dormition) that draw the greatest crowds. Smaller shrines may experience
pilgrimage only during such events. On these special occasions, the sacred
power of both time and space is magnified. When calendrical rituals provide the major impetus for pilgrimage, pilgrimage may become highly
seasonal in nature, as was the case, for example, in much historical European pilgrimage (Nolan and Nolan 1989:53).

A pilgrimage site is not an isolated place or event. Not only does it fit in
complex ways into a larger religious tradition (within which it may be
either marginal or central) but it may also be part of a network or field of
pilgrimage sites. Within this field, sites may be hierarchically ordered,
with shrines being of greater or lesser importance, as measured by their
"catchment" area (some of the most famous sites, such as Lourdes, cut
across national boundaries) and by the number or type of visitors (Bhardwaj 1973). Or sites may be officially ranked within a particular religion,
such as Mecca in Islam and Jerusalem in Christianity (see Turner 1974;
Turner and Turner 1978). Pilgrimage may rotate from one site to another,
depending on the particular event in the liturgical calendar associated
with the site, or sites may even compete with one another. (For example,
in Greece, there are at least three places that have major celebrations
drawing pilgrims on August 15, the Day of the Dormition—Tinos, the
nearby island of Paros, and the site of Panayía Soumela in northern
Greece, which draws many Pontic Greeks.)[6]

In summary, then, pilgrimage depends on (1) the association created
within a particular religious tradition of certain events and/or sacred figures with a particular field of space, and (2) the notion that the material
world can make manifest the invisible spiritual world at such places.[7]

To anthropologists whose training and tradition have emphasized the
notion of a field "site"—a physically and socially bounded space that can
be studied by the methods of participant observation in a specified cycle
of time (Clifford 1990)—the study of pilgrimage offers special challenges.
By its very nature pilgrimage, although centered around a specific place,
violates notions of boundedness. Pilgrims leave their own space and join
with strangers to whom they have not been connected previously in order
to take part in events that are outside the normal flow of daily life. The
boundaries of the pilgrimage site itself, which at first seem clearly to de-
lineate a sacred space with a devotional focus, become blurred, and then
dissolve, as pilgrims scatter and return to their homes, taking something
of the pilgrimage site with them, spiritually and materially. The pilgrimage site is a web—at its center the object of devotion, but with
strands spun outward both by the pilgrims and by other forces (such as
the media, the church, and national politics), all of which advertise and

promote the site, and create mutable and sometimes conflicting meanings. Thus the site is permanent through the presence of its physical center, which provides a magnet to pilgrims, but impermanent and constantly fluctuating in its personnel, as well as mutable in the accumulations of its history and in the meanings assigned to it over time.

In addition, a pilgrimage site is connected in complex ways to the nonsacred world around it. It has economic, social, and political ramifications for the local community, the region, and even the nation. Thus "as anthropologists, we must regard the pilgrimage system . . . as comprising all the interactions and transactions, formal or informal, institutionalized or improvised, sacred or profane, orthodox or eccentric, which owe their existence to the pilgrimage itself" (Turner and Turner 1978:22; cf. Crumrine and Morinis 1991:9).

It is perhaps these peculiar features of pilgrimage that were, on the one hand, responsible for earlier anthropological neglect of the topic, and that, conversely, have now become a stimulus for contemporary anthropological interest in the phenomenon. The earlier neglect certainly inspired Turner's interest in pilgrimage. Observing pilgrimage in Mexico, he notes that the phenomenon there, and in other parts of the world,

> was a great popular process, demographically comparable to labor migration, involving millions of people the world over in many days and even months of traveling, rich in symbolism and undoubtedly complex in organization, and yet very often ignored by the competing orthodoxies of social science and religion. . . . In the case of the anthropologists, there may have been a combination of causes: the concentration . . . on the elicitation and analysis of highly localized, fixed, and focused "structures" and "patterns" . . . coupled with an almost obsessive emphasis on kinship, law, politics, and economics rather than on religion, ritual, metaphor, and myth. . . . Religious leaders, on the other hand, have been silenced by their ambivalent feelings about pilgrimages. (1974:187)

The factors Turner elucidates also suggest the reasons for the contemporary popularity of the study of pilgrimage. Not only have many anthropologists become more interested in studying ritual, symbol, and meaning, but also the "traditional" limited study of a small community as an isolated unit has become both increasingly unsatisfactory within a changing discipline and increasingly unfeasible within a changing world. This is both a challenge and a problem for contemporary ethnography: "If ethnography once imagined it could describe discrete cultures, it now contends with boundaries that criss-cross over a field at once fluid and saturated with power" (R. Rosaldo 1989:45; cf. Appadural 1991). The study of pilgrimage thus offers one means for anthropologists to transcend localism and to tie into regionalism, nationalism, economics, politics, and larger religious traditions without at the same time abandoning the microfocus and "thick description" that for many are the hallmark of good ethnography (Geertz 1973).

There are, however, multiple ways to study pilgrimage. To begin, one can study pilgrimage as experienced by a specific group of people who journey from their home community to a pilgrimage site, or one can study a pilgrimage *site* with all its shifting population and complexity. Each yields different, if complementary, results. The first tells us much about pilgrims, the relationship of pilgrimage to their daily lives, and the meaning pilgrimage holds for them. The second tells us much about a pilgrimage place and its relationship to larger cultural systems, as well as something of the varying groups of people who journey there. An example of the first approach is Ann Grodzins Gold's study of the various forms of pilgrimage undertaken by members of a Rajasthani village, "a village whose residents are much else before they are pilgrims" (1988:2). She distinguishes three kinds of pilgrimages villagers may undertake: to the shrines of regional gods, to the Ganges to submerge the bones of the recently deceased, and journeys made "to wander."[8]

The study of pilgrimage sites, on the other hand, can not only tell us what pilgrimage shrines mean in the context of the local community, but can also yield information about pilgrimage in a broader context, including the ways in which pilgrimage centers connect within regions and articulate with larger religious traditions. Mary Crain's work on the pilgrimage shrine of El Rocio in Andalusia exemplifies this approach. She describes the manner in which pilgrimage there has been transformed from a local religious ritual to a national festival and the conflicts and problems this has created for the local population (Crain 1989; see also Murphy 1989, 1994).[9]

There is a third approach to pilgrimage, and that is a macrolevel view that examines systems of pilgrimage within particular religious traditions. Much of Turner's work on pilgrimage in Mexico and western Europe falls into this category (Turner 1974; Turner and Turner 1978), as do several studies of pilgrimage in India.[10]

My own study is in some ways a mix of approaches. Although I have focused on a particular pilgrimage site, and on the ways in which this site and the events that occur there have taken on meaning in a national context, my long association with the island of Tinos and my fieldwork in a small village there have given me a somewhat different perspective than I would have had if I had arrived "cold" at this particular site. And because I was interested in the multiple contexts of both the church and pilgrimage to it, I chose to use multiple approaches. I observed pilgrims and their rituals extensively, both inside and outside the church; I talked to pilgrims to learn where they were from and the purposes of their journey; I conversed with townspeople to discover their opinions about pilgrimage and pilgrims and the significance of the Church of the Annunciation in local identity as well as in the local economy; I talked to employees of the church to learn their views about what they observed there, to obtain information about the church itself, and to gather stories about pilgrimage; I observed tourism in order to analyze the differences between tourism and pilgrimage; I read a variety of materials about the church written by local authors; I gathered information from the files of the local newspapers to learn about past pilgrimage events and other local matters; I talked to villagers I knew and attended a baptism of a former villager at the church; I visited the monastery where an elderly nun had the vision that led to the finding of Tinos's famous miracle-working icon and I spoke with some of the nuns; and I studied and asked questions about the variety of religious objects offered for sale by merchants in the town (and even bought some myself).

Nor was my research bounded by the island. Although my focus on the pilgrimage site itself meant I was unable to observe pilgrims in their daily lives, I did visit a village on the mainland that was being studied by another anthropologist and had the opportunity to talk to a number of villagers who had gone to Tinos on pilgrimage. In addition, in the summers of 1990 and 1993, I visited several other pilgrimage sites in Greece to provide myself with comparisons to pilgrimage on Tinos. I also examined icons in museums, especially icons of the Madonna, and read of their histories and miracles. And since the Church of the Annunciation is a national shrine, everywhere I traveled in Greece (or anywhere I encountered Greeks outside of Greece), I would ask people I met whether they had been to Tinos, and if so, why they went and what their impressions had been of the island and the church.

PILGRIMAGE AS RITUAL

I have suggested that one of the reasons that pilgrimage has recently been drawing anthropological attention may lie in the fact that it is a local phenomenon with nonlocalized connections, amenable to anthropological participant observation and microanalysis, yet offering the opportunity to examine larger-scale social forces as well. An additional reason for the appeal of pilgrimage for contemporary anthropology may lie in the complex and dynamic character of the ritual of pilgrimage, a ritual that reflects and responds to a variety of both constant and changing beliefs, values, and needs. Thus pilgrimage lends itself to an approach that regards ritual as process rather than as fixed structure, and that sees meaning not as fixed but as multiple and mutable and often contested (e.g., Eade and Sallnow 1991). In this sense, pilgrimage may constitute a perfect postmodern subject for the anthropologist.

Victor Turner provided the first major theoretical model for the study of pilgrimage, comparing pilgrimage to a rite of passage in its ritual structure, a structure that includes separation of the pilgrim from ordinary life, the liminal period of the pilgrimage journey, and the return to ordinary life (1974, 1979; Turner and Turner 1978). Turner suggests that pilgrimage "succeeds the major initiation rites of puberty in tribal societies as the dominant historical form" (1974:182). In contrast to a rite of passage, however, pilgrimage was viewed by Turner as a form of "anti-structure," characterized by liminality and communitas. It is the desire to experience such communitas, according to Turner and Turner (1978), that constitutes the major motivation for pilgrimage.[11] Communitas such as that experienced in pilgrimage carries an inherent social critique, "for its very existence puts all social structural rules in question and suggests new possibilities" (Turner 1974:202). In addition, pilgrimage becomes a metaphor for other kinds of journeys, whether actual physical quests or inward searchings, whenever the sojourner "goes on a long journey to find out who he or she really is outside 'structure'" (1974:182). Pilgrimage, as opposed to rituals of tribal societies, is a voluntary activity, undertaken at the option of the individual.[12] For this reason, Turner and Turner suggest, "pilgrimage is perhaps best thought of as 'liminoid' or 'quasi-liminal,' rather than 'liminal' in Van Gennep's full sense" (1978:35).

For Turner, the liminality of pilgrimage helps to explain its resurgence in the contemporary world: "During the present transitional period of history, when many institutionalized social forms and modes of thought are in question, a reactivation of many cultural forms associated traditionally with normative communitas is occurring" (1974:172). Turner suggests that this is connected with a growing contemporary interest in the occult, visions, and other kinds of liminal religious phenomena.

In addition, both improved means of transportation and the mass media have facilitated this renewed interest by making shrines more known and access to them easier. But there is more to mass communications than the simple facilitating of pilgrimage, for the media themselves, in their appeal to a diverse mass audience, may serve as facilitators of communitas in large-scale, industrialized societies (Turner 1974:217). Another feature of pilgrimage that makes it adaptable to the contemporary world is its ability to address multiple and changing concerns. Thus although pilgrimage is an old practice, pilgrims can use their journey to address such current problems as drug addiction and safe airplane travel, and to have their automobile blessed. Pilgrimage rituals can be constantly reinscribed with meaning, in part, perhaps, because they are often created by and depend on individual desire and popular practice, and hence are always in process.

Several features of Turner's general schema have been criticized by anthropologists doing studies of pilgrimage in specific cultural settings. Turner's work focused on elucidating commonalities, not differences, among various pilgrimage sites. As anthropologists study pilgrimage sites in different religious, social, and political contexts, Turner's schema has been modified, and elements other than the ones he stressed have begun to emerge as more significant in defining the nature and parameters of pilgrimage.[13]

Particularly criticized has been Turner's idea of "anti-structure," specifically the concepts of liminality and communitas as applied to pilgrimage. A common element in most of these criticisms is the observation that pilgrimage, rather than being a journey away from the structures of everyday life and into a world of liminality and "anti-structure," often reflects the obligations and concerns of everyday social life such as those of family, patronage, and obligations to the dead. Moreover, such critiques suggest, social distinctions and hierarchies, such as those of class, caste, status, gender, occupation, and local identity, are not necessarily dissolved during pilgrimage but continue to structure relationships and generate conflicts, even within the pilgrimage journey. As Sallnow puts it, describing pilgrimage in the Andes, such pilgrimage is "a complex mosaic of egalitarianism, nepotism, and factionalism, of brotherhood, competition and conflict" (1981:176). Pilgrimage may reflect and reinforce, as well as mask, social hierarchy and social difference. Dale Eickelman, in his study of Moroccan Islam, notes that in pilgrimage to the tomb of a saint (*marabout*) "the inequalities implicit in everyday social relationships are preserved" (1976:173) and "the pilgrimage to Boujad largely constitutes a continuation of the ordinary social order" (1976:175). Similarly, Messerschmidt and Sharma (1981) found that in Hindu pilgrimage in Nepal caste relations were scrupulously observed.

Even when the ordinary social relationships are suspended or muted, this does not necessarily lead to communitas. Sallnow (1981), for example, argues that in Andean pilgrimage a new supralocal arena of competition is created in which new social alignments may arise (see also Murphy 1994). At a wider level, pilgrimage may also have integrative and legitimizing functions for larger political units or groups. For example, Hindu places of pilgrimage, according to Bhardwaj, "have knitted the linguistically diverse Hindu population socially, culturally, and spatially at different integrative levels" (1973:228).[14] Moreover, different kinds of pilgrimage may exhibit different kinds of features, including different degrees or forms of liminality and communitas. Betteridge suggests that local pilgrimage in Iran, for example, is liminal in that it is "on the fringes of orthodox religious practice; it is theologically interstitial" (1985:31). The same could not be said, however, for pilgrimage to Mecca, which is a core ritual practice of Islam.

Turner has also been subject to criticism for adapting the terminology of a rite of passage to create his model of pilgrimage, and for focusing on the ritual and experiential aspects of pilgrimage and neglecting its other dimensions, such as the social and the political. In addition, critics suggest, Turner has overlooked the wide range of individual motivations (in addition to the desire for communitas) that may inspire the pilgrim to her or his journey (see, e.g., Morinis 1984). Pilgrims may go on a pilgrimage as a remedy for very concrete problems of everyday life, and not necessarily for some "higher" spiritual purpose. In addition, a pilgrimage site may have very different meanings for different groups of pilgrims, depending on social class, ethnicity, and religious background (see, e.g., Bowman 1991). Beyond this, as Sallnow suggests, Turner's schema can be criticized for its deterministic approach to a highly variable phenomenon: "The study of pilgrimage, by the very nature of the phenomenon, demands that *a priori* assumptions concerning the relationship between religion and society be abandoned. . . . The link between ritual and secular processes should be regarded as analytically determinable in each case, rather than simply assumed" (1981:179).

These more recent studies have provided a better understanding of pilgrims, and of their different kinds of personal involvement in pilgrimage ritual, and a better sense of the great variety in pilgrimage journeys and sites. Critiques of "liminality" and "communitas" as defining features of pilgrimage have led to a better understanding of how pilgrims participate in a wide range of sacred activities and for a wide range of purposes: from the Moroccan women who journey to the sanctuaries of saints seeking a space and power of their own in a patriarchal society (Mernissi 1977), to the "yupeez" who come to the Andalusian pilgrimage shrine of El Rocio to be seen and to participate in a media-constructed nostalgia for "tradition" (Crain 1992); from the Indian villagers who journey to the Ganges to submerge the bones of dead kin (Gold 1988), to the woman who ascends on her knees to the church at Tinos because she made a vow to the Panayía when her child was ill.

These critiques thus point out the difficulty of trying to develop general models of pilgrimage. The diversity of pilgrimage activities and the diversity of the cultures, past and present, within which pilgrimage occurs show pilgrimage to be a highly complex and multifaceted phenomenon. Moreover, at any one pilgrimage site there may exist a variety of views of pilgrimage, depending on the identity of the participants and the activities taking place, views that may even come into conflict on particular ritual occasions (see Dubisch 1990a; see also Crumrine and Morinis 1991; Eade and Sallnow 1991b; Murphy 1994). For example, members of the religious hierarchy may stress the sort of communitas emphasized by Turner, postulating a common identity and equality among the worshipers as proclaimed by the religious tradition. Such was the message of several sermons to pilgrims I heard on holy days at Tinos. An individual pilgrim, on the other hand, may be intent upon her child's illness or upon some other painful problem for which she seeks relief and pay very little attention to sermons or pronouncements by priests or other officials. The degree to which pilgrims are "liminal" may also vary. Women in Greece, for example, may experience some of Turner's "anti-structure" by their participation in a group tour to a famous shrine, a trip that provides a release from everyday obligations, even if they also carry offerings and requests on behalf of family members at home. And pilgrims who visit sacred sites at the time of major events attended by thousands of other pilgrims, events where a high degree of emotional intensity is generated, may experience a greater degree of both liminality and communitas than those who come alone on quieter days. Thus "anti-structure" might best be viewed as a dimension of pilgrimage, more or less present depending upon the participants and the occasion (or upon the particular religious tradition; see Messerschmidt and Sharma 1981:572), rather than an element with an absolute presence or absence.

Although his ritual schema has been criticized for being too rigidly deterministic, Turner has called attention to the emphasis in his work on "performance, move, staging, plot, redressive action, crisis, schism, reintegration, *etc*. To my mind, this stress is the 'postmodern turn' in anthropology" (1979:65). In this turn, he suggests, performance would move to the center stage of anthropological observation, and "postmodern theory would see in the very flaws, hesitations, personal factors, incomplete, elliptical, context-dependent, situational components of performance, clues to the very nature of human process itself" (1979:66–67). For Turner one of the important features of rituals (including pilgrimage) is that they seek to deny this mutability and flux of social life: "By dint of repetition they deny the passage of time, the nature of change, and the implicit extent of potential indeterminacy in social relations" (1979:68). At the same time, ritual is part of that indeterminacy. This makes an analysis of ritual necessarily dynamic, contextual, and open-ended.

Yet perhaps a postmodern understanding would reject the very notion of "pilgrimage" as a category of ritual activity. To speak of pilgrimage in a broad comparative sense is to assert the authority of generalization and to create the sort of timeless and coherent other (in this case, the pilgrim) that Abu-Lughod (1991) critiques when she urges us to "write against culture." Certainly, as those studies that criticize Turner's model argue, once pilgrimage is examined in specific contexts, it reveals itself as a polymorphic phenomenon, different not only in form and meaning from one cultural setting to another, but also in its forms, motivations, and meanings within a single context.[15] In light of this, perhaps the term *pilgrimage,* like other anthropological categories such as kinship, gender, and religion, ought be subject to critical rethinking, and perhaps even dropped from our vocabulary.[16]

There is some merit to such a suggestion. In Islam, for example, there is distinction between the *hajj,* the pilgrimage to Mecca, which is obligatory for those who are able to make it and which is timed to the Muslim lunar calendar, and *ziyara,* a journey to another kind of religious shrine such as that of a saint (Eickelman 1976:173).[17] The term *yatra,* which Gold translates as pilgrimage in her study of a Rajasthani community, refers to "wanderings" or movement from place to place. Such journeys "are united by a common involvement with death" (Gold 1988:59). Sered reports that in Israel the term *aliya* has multiple meanings: return from the Diaspora to live in the homeland, the passage to heaven of a saint, pilgrimage to a shrine, and (for men) being called to bless the Torah in the synagogue (1992:19–20). And as I will show in the next chapter, Greek also does not have a word exactly equivalent to the English term *pilgrimage;* the Greek *proskínima* has a different field of reference, for it refers more generally to devotions at a church, and not just to those involving a journey.[18] Thus to label certain ritual activities as "pilgrimage" and distinguish them from other religious activities may obscure the continuities between ritual (and other) behaviors on the one hand, and on the other hand may blur significant differences among the various activities we broadly characterize as pilgrimage. A Greek village woman tending the grave of a dead child, for example, may have more in common with a woman traveling to Tinos to fulfill a vow she made to the Panayía when her child was ill than either has with a politician who visits Tinos as a highly publicized political act. But it is the activities of the last two that are lumped together and labeled "pilgrimage."

Yet at the same time I am reluctant to abandon the term *pilgrimage* entirely. While the differences among pilgrims are sometimes considerable, I am also struck by the similarities in the practice of journeys to sacred places even among quite different religious traditions. While accepting that generalization can do violence to the complexity of life and tends to assert the authority of the anthropologist over the "other," I find that generalization such as that embodied in the term *pilgrimage* can also moderate "otherness" by showing us similarities in the midst of difference (as in my own metaphoric application of the concept of pilgrimage to anthropology). Such generalization obviously calls for caution. (I certainly do not wish to postulate a *Homo pellegrinus*.) But it also opens up possibilities for understanding, some of which I seek to explore in this book.

"Oriental" Pilgrimage

Chapter 2 placed me "in the field" at my research site and sought to place the reader there as well. Chapters 1 and 3 have placed me "in the field" of anthropology itself, each in a somewhat different way. Chapter 1 placed me in terms of larger intellectual orientations and personal biography. This chapter places me in terms of the ways in which anthropologists have dealt with a particular category of human activity, a category we have labeled "pilgrimage," and thus serves to situate my writing in relation to a body of writing by others on the subject. The concept of pilgrimage as a category of ritual activity is itself a creation of the anthropologist's culture, though not purely an anthropological creation (that is, the concept enjoys an existence outside anthropology). Anthropologists have further defined and refined the concept, however, and examined its applicability to ritual journeys in other cultural settings. Such examinations problematize the category, raising the question of whether or not there is any such thing as "pilgrimage." The answer, I have suggested, is both yes and no. I have chosen, for the moment at least, to place myself in a position of accepting the category, if only for utilitarian purposes, and as a means of illuminating my own research, which drew at least part of its initial impetus from that category, that is, from the desire to study a "pilgrimage site."

But there is an additional reason for my wishing to continue to speak of pilgrimage, and that is to draw Greek pilgrimage out of the "margins" (cf. Herzfeld 1987a) and into the mainstream of anthropological discussion. Turner and Turner's 1978 book is titled *Image and Pilgrimage in Christian Culture*. Yet "Christian" turns out to refer only to *western* European Christianity (including Catholicism in Latin America). Completely omitted is any mention of the Eastern church. The Turners are hardly alone in this oversight. Like "woman," the Orthodox forms of Christianity are the marked category (see chapter 11).[19] Similarly, other aspects of Orthodoxy are little dealt with in comparative studies of religion. The Orthodox Madonna, for example, is rarely considered in general works on the Virgin Mary in Christianity. Likewise, Orthodox pilgrimage has generally been ignored or overlooked in the literature (anthropological and otherwise).[20]

One can certainly find pragmatic reasons for such neglect. Post–World War I and II political arrangements have, until recently at least, inhibited Western scholarly access to many of the Eastern Orthodox countries, and religious activity in these countries has often been discouraged or actively suppressed by their governments. In addition, the relative autonomy of each national Orthodox church may make less likely the sort of cross-national pilgrimage found in Catholicism (such as that exhibited at Lourdes or Medjugorje), which draws both popular and scholarly attention to the phenomenon.[21] And historically, Ottoman rule may have inhibited the development of pilgrimage within those Orthodox populations under its sway. Pilgrimage such as that which I observed in Greece may thus be a relatively late, and a highly nationalistic, phenomenon. Certainly pilgrimage to Tinos's famous church begins with the struggle for, and establishment of, an independent Greek state (though there is some evidence of earlier pilgrimage there as well; see chapter 7).

All of these are certainly factors in the relative neglect of Orthodoxy in the anthropological (and other) literature. I would suggest, however, that there is another (nonpragmatic) reason for such neglect, and this is Orthodoxy's "orientalism," an orientalism whose ambiguous (and ambivalent) nature is particularly exemplified by Greece.

Michael Herzfeld has spoken of the "marginal" position of Greece, both within anthropology and for the West generally. The purported progenitor of Western civilization, Greece is at the same time "orientally polluted" (Herzfeld 1987a:177) by its long association with, and domination by, the East (especially the Ottoman Empire), a split, Herzfeld suggests, that is felt by Greeks themselves.[22] Greek Orthodoxy is similarly liminal and "polluted," Christian in its profession and certainly in its origins and yet at the same time oriental in its ritual and its material trappings, at least in the eyes of the "West." Like the East, Orthodoxy remains an oriental mystery.

In some of the following chapters I will seek to show the ways in which I believe this "marginality" of Orthodoxy can illuminate anthropological understanding of religion, and conversely how an examination of Greek religion (as manifested in pilgrimage activities) can illuminate anthropology. In order to do this, I examine not only the activities connected with pilgrimage but also my own responses to Orthodox religion and its rituals, the role of gender in religion, and notions of history and time.

CHAPTER FOUR

Observing Pilgrimage: Churches, Icons, and the Devil

> All sites of pilgrimage have this in common: they are believed
> to be places where miracles once happened, still happen, and
> may happen again.
>
> —Turner and Turner 1978:6

ON THE EVENING of August 12, 1986, at around eight o'clock, I left my apartment on Tinos accompanied by a visitor, my partner and companion Ray, who had come to visit me for six weeks.[1] It was Ray's last evening on the island and we had planned a nice dinner at our favorite restaurant. Since it was still a little early to eat (by Greek standards), we thought we would first take a stroll along the waterfront and perhaps sit at a sidewalk cafe and watch the passing crowds.

It was only a few days before Tinos's main religious holiday, the celebration of the Dormition on August 15. Thousands of pilgrims had already descended on the island in anticipation of the holiday, and the streets were crowded. As Ray and I drew close to the main street, I suggested that we walk up to the church for a few minutes just to see if anything interesting was happening. As it turned out, we did not have far to go to discover what I was hoping for. Not quite halfway up the hill, just past some of the shops selling candles, *támata,* and little bottles for holy water, we noticed a woman in black lying face down in the street. Around her clustered perhaps a half dozen onlookers. An elderly woman—that was my first thought—collapsed while trying to fulfill her vow to reach the church on her hands and knees.

Drawn by the crowd, we moved closer. Women on their hands and knees were so common this time of year as to attract little attention. The fact that this woman was causing passersby to stop and stare was not only interesting in itself, it offered the anthropologist an opportunity as well. Since a small crowd of Greeks had already stopped to watch the woman lying in the street, I knew that I could join them without disturbing the woman (at least any more than she was already disturbed) or engaging in "foreign" behavior. (There was a Greek-American photographer there, taking photographs in the woman's face, and even that she hardly seemed to notice.)[2]

As we drew closer, I realized that the woman was not old, as I had originally thought. She was young (about twenty-five, I soon learned) and in great distress, such distress that my next thought was that she must be very ill. She would rise from her prone position to her knees, crawl a few steps, and then collapse, crying out to the woman accompanying her, "Maria, I can't! I can't!" (*Dhen boró! Dhen boró!*). Maria, for her part, walked stolidly alongside, pacing herself to the woman on her knees, staring straight ahead and praying. When her companion collapsed, she paused to make the sign of the cross over her head with the crucifix she bore in her hand.

We had now joined the crowd on the sidewalk. I was interested in observing such a vow "in action" and hoped that, because of the onlookers and the woman's particular difficulties, I would learn a little more about the nature of the vow than was usually possible when I observed women in the act of crawling on their knees to the church.

The crowd of onlookers was a shifting one, as some observers moved on and others passing by stopped to watch. It was not a passive audience, however.[3] Some of the passersby and some of those watching from the doorways of shops along the street stepped up to the woman and encouraged her not to give up, to complete her *táma* (vow). "*Káne kouráyio!*" they told her. "Have courage! Keep going!" (The phrase can be translated both ways.) As we watched, a Gypsy woman with scabbed knees stopped to tell the young woman that she herself had done it (gone up on her knees) and surely the other woman could too.

The outside lights of the church had been illuminated just after we arrived on the scene, and they shone invitingly, outlining the building at the top of the hill. A man who had just joined the onlookers bent over the young woman, telling her that the lights had been turned on for her. "The Panayía is waiting for you" (*I Panayía se periméni*), several other onlookers added.

It was my sense at this point that those watching viewed the woman's verbal and physical expressions of her difficulty as overdone, perhaps even a little self-indulgent. After all, she was engaging in an endeavor that is fairly commonplace at the shrine, and one that at this time of year is accomplished daily by women older and more feeble than she. Maria, the woman's companion (who, I learned later, was her sister), kept encouraging her to go on, at one point pausing to look around in embarrassment at the crowd that had gathered. "Look," she said to the other woman (who had once again collapsed), "people [*o kósmos,* the world] are watching you."

I was fascinated by this unfolding drama, wondering if the woman was going to make it, wondering what was wrong with her. Was she paralyzed, Ray and I speculated, or did she have some other debilitating illness? I was reluctant to leave until I had learned more. Ray, a social scientist though not an anthropologist, was also fascinated by the drama, and even though he did not speak Greek, he was willing to linger if that was what I wished to do. Little did I know at that point, however, that it would be almost two and a half hours before we would finally be able to have dinner together.

The woman on her knees continued to have difficulty. She would get up and crawl rapidly for a few yards on her hands and knees and then collapse again, crying out. At one point she shouted, "My head! My head!" and her sister bent to make the sign of the cross over her head. At another point she cried, "He'll kill me!" As she collapsed once more face down on the ground, a middle-aged woman in black pushed her way through the crowd, and kneeling down by the young woman's side, she slipped a protective amulet of colored string around her wrist. She then took the crucifix from the sister and made the sign of the cross over the fallen woman and applied holy water to her face. By now people were beginning to wonder what was wrong with the young woman, as it became evident that her difficulty was no ordinary one. "She has her cross" (*éhi to stavró tis*), the sister replied, and "she has a sin" (*amartía*).

By this point, the crowd around the young woman had grown quite large and the spirit of the onlookers had turned into one of active participation. People shouted encouragement: "You're getting closer!" (*kondévis*), or even "You've arrived!" (*éftases*).[4] Ray had wandered off at this point, stationing himself along the wall of the park to watch from a distance. From this vantage point he was later able to estimate the crowd at about seventy-five people. Perhaps thirty-five of them were actively helping the woman, verbally or otherwise. As the crowd increased, I found myself pushed back, so that eventually it became difficult to hear everything said directly to and by the woman and her sister and I began to rely, as others in the crowd did, on the exchange of information among those watching. Newcomers came up to ask what was happening and were given the latest information by those already there. I participated in this information exchange as I was occasionally asked by someone what the woman "had" (*ti éhi*), that is, what was wrong with her. Wanting to remain as inconspicuous as possible, I kept my answers brief. I wished neither to interfere in any way with the drama being enacted nor to be distracted from it by questions about myself as a foreigner.[5]

In a period of about an hour and a half, the young woman had covered perhaps a quarter to a third of a kilometer and reached a point approximately three-quarters of the way to the church. (A healthy woman is normally able to cover this distance on her knees in thirty to forty-five minutes.)

At this point the woman's problem began to be revealed more clearly as word spread through the crowd that she was possessed by the devil (*dhemonisméni*), who had got inside her head (*bíke mésa sto kefáli tis*). He had entered her, it was said, when, at the age of eighteen, finding herself not yet engaged, she had resorted to magic to remedy her state. This had afforded the devil his opportunity. "The magic did it to her" (*i mayía tin ékane*).[6] As the story unfolded, I moved excitedly back and forth between Ray, still at the margins of the crowd, and the people gathered around the possessed woman, relaying the latest news to him and then hurrying back to learn more.

While all of this was going on, there was no sign of activity at the church. Vespers had ended, the exterior church lights were on, and the priests had gone home. The only encounter the possessed woman had with anyone "official" on her painful journey up the hill occurred when several members of the crowd accosted a young nun walking down the street, her briefcase in her hand. They urged her to speak to the possessed woman, to give her the aid of her own holiness, and somewhat reluctantly the nun let herself be led to the young woman's side. I was too far away to hear the exchange between them as the nun knelt down, but she stayed only a few moments and then rose silently and left.

People in the crowd seemed to have much more definite ideas of what to do than the nun did, for they continued their efforts to help the young woman. Some made the sign of the cross over her, children were sent running up the hill to fetch holy water from the church, others chanted the Lord's Prayer. A woman in the crowd was explaining to several young girls that when the devil got inside someone, that person could do whatever she/he wanted (*óti théli;* no gender is indicated in the verb form) except go to church. That's why the harder the young woman on her knees tried to get to the church, the more the devil held her back. A woman standing near me commented several times to another woman, "And to think our children don't believe . . . " If only they could see this, she went on, they would know that the devil was real and active in this world. Another woman remarked that here in Greece there were some people, that is, Greeks, who were not even Christians. At this point I sought to make myself even more inconspicuous, a little uneasy as a non-believer in the midst of this drama of faith and dangerous powers.

As the woman neared the church, the crowd continued to grow, augmented by Gypsies camped at the top of the hill. She was now surrounded on all sides by onlookers and there were constant cries of "Open up! Open up!" (*Aníkste to!*) to try to part the crowd so that the woman could see her destination—the church ahead of her crowned by its lighted cross.

By the time the woman began to make her way up the first set of steps and across the outer courtyard of the church, the crowd had grown to perhaps 150 or more, many of them Gypsies. Two Gypsy men had now taken charge. (Until now the participants in the drama had been almost all women.) They yelled at the crowd to step back and make way so that the woman could ascend the stairway to the outer plaza of the church. At this point there was some discussion among people near me about whether or not the church would be open when the woman arrived. Several people agreed that even if the doors were closed, it wouldn't matter. The young woman could at least view the icon through the window and then could come back the next day for her *proskínima* (devotions). Some people were indignant that the church should be closed at all. What were those people who came on the late evening boat to do if they could not go to the church when they arrived?

From the time that she had drawn near the church, the possessed woman had begun to move more rapidly. Since the large crowd prevented us from getting close to her as she passed through the entryway into the inner courtyard of the church, Ray and I hurried through the other entrance and up the steps to the church balcony and stood at the top of the stairs, where we could watch her arrival at the door. It did not take her long to crawl up the two flights of marble steps to the balcony. A little girl shrank back in fear against her mother as the woman crawled past, and her mother bent over to reassure her. Even when the devil passed so close to her, he could not harm her, the mother said, as long as she believed strongly in God.

The church was indeed closed at this point; the church doors locked. (It was now 10:30. The woman had taken two and a half hours to crawl from the place where I had first seen her to the doors of the church.) A number of pilgrims had spread out their bedding on the balcony and were already asleep when the crowd arrived. Those sleeping by the main door of the church were rather rudely awakened by the Gypsy men who had taken charge and were told to make way for the woman approaching on her knees. When the woman reached the church doors, she stood up and kissed the doors and then briefly prayed. (The interior of the church would have been dimly visible through the glass, and she could have seen the icon stand, but the icon itself is always locked away at night, just before the church closes.)[7] Shortly afterward, I had a glimpse of her being led away down a hallway behind the sanctuary by one of the women in the crowd. They were chatting normally together as they walked. Obviously the devil no longer held the woman in his thrall.

Ray and I finally made it to dinner. Whatever we had planned for our last evening together, it certainly had not been this. I found myself in a very mixed emotional state. On the one hand I was probably as stimulated and excited as I have ever been during fieldwork. At the same time I was distressed by the thought that after the ship left for Piraeus the following day, I would be alone and would not see Ray again for several months. The evening was thus simultaneously a high and a low point of my time in the field.

Part of the excitement I felt was due to all that I had learned. There were many days in which I felt (whether accurately or not) that I had learned little or nothing. Yet here, in a short and dramatic space of time, I had observed so many things directly relevant to my research that I hardly had time to absorb them. The whole event was what Fernandez (1986) has called a "revelatory moment" (in this case a revelatory two and a half hours). This does not mean, of course, that the revelations all occurred to me on the spot. Many came as I later thought and wrote about the event.

But there was another source of the excitement that infected me that evening, and this was the "exotic" nature of what I had seen. This sense of the exotic is often missing in fieldwork in Greece. Or, perhaps more accurately, the exotic often lies buried, requiring a certain amount of digging to recover—the surface familiarity frequently obscures the underlying difference. Just as the young woman's demon possession was not immediately apparent, the exotic may hide beneath the surface of seemingly routine activities and events. And it is, after all, the search for the different that sends anthropologists on their own pilgrimage. The belief that in the different the "ordinary" will be more clearly revealed to some extent justifies the whole anthropological enterprise.

There was, however, another side to my fascination with the exotic nature of what I had just observed. In the anthropological preoccupation with the interconnections between the moral and religious systems of community life in Greece, the "irrational" and "exotic" are often overlooked or relegated to a marginal position ethnographically.[8] This is related to some of the ways in which anthropologists generally write about religion on the one hand, and on the other hand to the peculiar position of Greece as both within and outside the cultural domain of the West, an issue raised at the end of chapter 3. The particular event I have just narrated, in conjunction with other activities I had observed at the church, provided a challenge to "rational" accounts of Greek religion, accounts that tend to focus on belief and its verbalization and neglect ritual and "action." As I seek to show in the following chapters, the drama of the possessed woman not only illustrates some of the important features of pilgrimage to the Church of the Annunciation and of religion generally in Greece, it also illuminates some significant points about fieldwork. In addition, in my recounting of it, I have sought to illuminate some features of anthropological writing.

A third reason for the fascination and excitement that the possessed woman's journey generated for me lay in its dramatic structure and its cathartic conclusion. It is true that the woman did not actually reach the icon (which would have made the conclusion of her journey even more dramatic), but she did obviously defeat the demon possessing her, and

I witnessed her return to (seeming) normalcy.[9] Her drama obviously gripped the other onlookers as well, many of whom, if they did not actually believe they saw the devil in action (and most of those around me did seem to believe), were at least caught up in the evident reality of the woman's difficulty and suffering. But what was it about the drama that enthralled *me?* Was it simply the anthropological data it provided and the chance to see in dramatic and extended form the pilgrimage activities I had come to observe? I think that there was something more, something that made me more than just an "objective" observer collecting data. I was caught up in the drama in an emotional way as well. What I did not experience, however, was the sense of danger that others in the crowd (such as the child on the stairs) experienced. The same was not true of Ray, who had been raised in the Catholic faith. "I've never been so close to the devil before," he remarked afterward, his comment in no way a joke. Although he was now a nonbeliever, he elaborated later, the social context in which he found himself, surrounded by believers in the grip of the drama of possession, in combination with his own Catholic background, created for him an atmosphere in which the devil was a reality. (As we will see in the next chapter, something similar happened to me later with a dangerous situation and a vow.)

The next day, after Ray had left, I hurried back to my apartment, tidied up, and then spent the rest of the day writing an account of the events of the night before. This task helped to occupy my during an otherwise painfully lonely day. In the days that followed, up to and through the hectic activities surrounding the fifteenth of August, I was prey to all the mixed emotions generated that evening when we watched the possessed woman crawl up to the church. Though stemming from my own personal circumstances, these emotions—or so I felt—tied me in some way to the thousands of pilgrims I observed during this time.

Observing Pilgrimage: The Impressionist Tale

I have opened this chapter with what Van Maanen (1988) calls an "impressionist tale." I have done so in order to show how a particular body of anthropological "knowledge" is arrived at and written about and how anthropological questions are asked and answered. Impressionist tales, according to Van Maanen, are designed "to startle their audience." They are woven from vivid "metaphors, phrasings, imagery, and most critically, the expansive recall of fieldwork experience," all "put together and told in the first person as a tightly focused, vibrant, exact, but necessarily imaginative rendering of fieldwork" (Van Maanen 1988:101–2). Although such tales are told to illuminate certain general features of the culture the anthropologist is studying, the events narrated are not ordinary ones. On the contrary, "what makes the story worth telling is its presumably out of the ordinary or unique character. Impressionist tales are not about what usually happens but about what rarely happens. They are the tales that presumably mark and make memorable the fieldwork experience" (Van Maanen 1988:102).

Why then, if it recounts something so unusual, would one choose to tell an impressionist tale? Why would I choose to recount an instance of possession (not a common reason for pilgrimage, especially today)[10] and to use it to open my chapter on pilgrimage? The reason is this: "Impressionist tales present the *doing* of fieldwork rather than simply the doer or the done. . . . The story itself, the impressionist's tale, is a representational means of cracking open the culture *and* the fieldworker's way of knowing it so that both can be jointly examined. Impressionist writing tries to keep both the subject and the object in constant view. The epistemological aim is then to braid the knower with the known" (Van Maanen 1988:103; italics mine). To put it another way, the object of the tale is to "exploit the intrusive self as an ethnographic resource rather than suffer it as a methodological hindrance" (A. Cohen 1992:226). Impressionist tales are about the action involved in doing anthropology, about experience, about practice. They are part of what Okely terms "the autobiography of fieldwork," which seeks to rescue fieldwork from its position as "the mechanical collection of data" and challenges "the new emphasis on fieldwork as writing [that] sees the encounter and experience as unproblematic" (Okley 1992:3).

Although the impressionist tale seeks to bring the reader into a more immediate, sensual contact with the field, it cannot in itself put the reader completely in the place of the anthropologist (just as the anthropologist, though on the scene, cannot be in the place of the observed). My own presence in, and reaction to, the drama of the possessed woman was conditioned by both my own previous understanding of the situation (my knowledge of "normal" pilgrimage activities, my knowledge of Orthodox belief and practice) as well as by personal factors, some of which I have included in my tale.

I first wrote this story for a meeting presentation,[11] making it the beginning and core of a paper on popular religion in Greece. This paper has since been rewritten and published as part of a volume on popular faith and religious orthodoxy in Europe (Dubisch 1990a). However, there are some differences between the tale as I originally wrote it and the tale as it is written here. Some of the differences are stylistic. Other differences are due to my including in the tale some of the information that had formerly been presented as analysis. But the most significant difference has to do with the placement of myself within the narrative. My earlier version, while told in the first person, sought to efface that person fairly early in the narrative. Once I had come upon the scene in which I found the possessed woman, the "I" in effect soon disappeared. No longer was there an observer, only the observed. As I have told the tale here, however, "I" have stayed with it until the end. I have also made visible the person who accompanied me, and included his role in the tale, as well as some discussion of the emotional state created by the imminence of his departure. And I have told, as best as I could remember, something of my own reactions as the tale unfolded and after it had ended, and attempted to tie these into some general concerns I had about my fieldwork.

This rewriting is not a critique of my earlier version. That earlier version, however, does not suffice for what I am trying to do now, which is to account for not only what I learned during my work, but how and why I learned it—and how I am writing about it—as well.

I said above that I wrote of my own reactions "as best I could remember them." This brings me to another reason for the impressionist tale. As Van Maanen points out, "There is . . . a great disparity between the way fieldwork is written about and the way it is talked about" (1988:108). In informal conversation, fieldworkers have many stories to tell about particularly interesting or amusing events. And yet fieldwork is not generally presented in this manner when it is "written up." The impressionist tale, because it takes more the form of these informal, oral narratives, has, as Van Maanen suggests, an air of intimacy about it. Such details as our own reactions to what we observe, who we were with when we observed it (spouses, friends, lovers), how we may have been included in or frightened or embarrassed or angered by what was unfolding around us are usually suppressed in the final written narrative that we present professionally. But they are also separated by our writing during fieldwork as well, in the way we record what we experience and observe.

An ethnography cannot be all impressionist tales, however, if only because such tales cannot really "speak for themselves" (though they may sometimes seem to do so). They are, after all, a convention, just like any other convention of ethnographic writing. In that sense they are deceptive, for behind their vividly depicted scenes lies a not-immediately-apparent backstage, and a host of props, including the knowledge, assumptions, and emotions of the anthropologist who has selected the particular events for her narrative.

It is time now to move to that "backstage."

I begin by drawing upon anthropological studies of religion in Greece —my own and others'—as the necessary context in which my understanding of pilgrimage has been forged.

RELIGION AND EVERYDAY LIFE IN GREECE

Anthropological studies of Greek Orthodoxy have generally focused on religion in the context of community life: the manner in which religious beliefs are articulated with other social values such as family, "honor," and neighborliness; the ways in which official religion meshes with local practice; the attitudes that the laity hold toward the church establishment and its practitioners; and the interrelationship between religion, gender ideology, and gender roles.[12]

In much of Greece, and certainly in the areas of rural Greece most studied by anthropologists, religion is inextricably entwined with daily life; indeed, through its yearly cycle of holy days and its life-cycle rites, religion has served, and still serves, to structure daily life in numerous ways (see Hart 1992; du Boulay 1974). Religion is lived, acted, and made materially manifest through the many churches scattered around the countryside, in the numerous icons found in churches and homes, and by dozens of commonly performed rituals, ranging from those as modest as making the sign of the cross to the rich and emotional celebrations of Holy Week.

At the same time, in part precisely because it is so inextricably interwoven in the fabric of daily life, religion is, in some sense, taken for granted by many of its practitioners. It is less an object or means of contemplation than a set of acts one performs, not only inevitably, but almost naturally (part of what Bourdieu has termed *habitus;* Bourdieu 1977). As Roger Just puts it, "Religion [in Greece] is not something to be pondered; it is part of a given identity. One is a Christian because one believes; one is a Christian because one is Greek; what one believes is that one is a Christian Greek" (1988:9). The simple statement "I believe" (*pistévo*) can suffice as an expression of the basic principle upon which the individual's relationship to Greek Orthodoxy is founded. While one might proclaim belief "in" (God, Christ, the Panayía), beyond that most of the villagers I knew, and Greeks elsewhere as well (see, e.g., Just 1988), are little given to discussion of points of doctrine or to articulating specific "beliefs" (and may indeed show considerable skepticism regarding some of the dogmas promulgated by the church).

Either in spite of or because of the deep-rootedness of religion in Greek identity, identification with one's religion does not necessarily involve attending formal church services, and church attendance varies widely by individual, as well as by gender (women on the whole attend more than men) and by class. In the village where I lived, it was only on certain major occasions, and particularly at Easter, the major Orthodox holy day, that everyone in the village was likely to be found in church. For some individuals (particularly men) the only event other than Easter likely to draw them to services was a life passage rite—a baptism, wedding, or funeral.

In my own earlier village fieldwork, I found that most discussions of religion (and most points of comparison about religion) centered around what one did rather than what one believed. "What do you do at funerals in America?" I was asked. "Do you have saints' days? Do you have icons? Do you fast?" Villagers were anthropologists, too, in their interest in cultural similarity and difference (cf. Gold 1988), and they were aware (though sometimes in a vague way) of other religions. They were most knowledgeable about Catholicism, because the island has a large Catholic population (see chapter 7), and Catholicism is similar enough to Orthodoxy to be considered a Christian religion (cf. Just 1988) while also exhibiting points of contrast. (For example, one contrast that both Orthodox and Catholic islanders emphasized was that Catholics have statues instead of icons, and they cross themselves differently from the Orthodox.)[13]

In such discussions the anthropologist's own religion inevitably became an object of inquiry. I was accompanied during this earlier fieldwork by my husband, who was Jewish. I myself had converted to Judaism after my marriage. Despite the large theological differences, we found it surprisingly easy to make comparisons between Jewish and Orthodox ritual practices, comparisons that seemed to make an otherwise obscure religion more understandable to the villagers (for example, Jews fast, have a ceremony comparable to baptism, and have mourning and memorial rituals).[14] Protestantism, on the other hand, though known to the islanders and occasionally mentioned when they asked about the religion of foreigners, is somewhat mysterious, hardly to be considered a religion at all because it has little of what many Greeks consider essential to religious practice (such as saints' days, icons, ritual). It is sometimes difficult for Greeks to believe that Protestants are really Christians. This attitude was typified by a seller of religious trinkets to whom I spoke just outside the Church of St. Nektarios on the island of Aegina in the summer of 1990. After we had chatted for a while about the church and the pilgrims who came there and he had recounted to me some of the miracles that had occurred at St. Nektarios, he asked where I was from. When I told him, he said, "In America, they are Catholics, aren't they?" I said yes, and also Protestant. "Protestants aren't Christians," he said. "*They* believe they are," I replied. "Excuse me," he retorted, "they may *believe* that they are, but they aren't" (Cf. Just 1988).[15]

Of course it is difficult and somewhat misleading to speak uniformly of "Greeks" when discussing religion, for a variety of reasons. Even though approximately 98 percent of Greeks adhere to the Orthodox faith, there is a small minority of Greeks who are non-Orthodox (Catholics, Muslims, Jews, and some Protestants).[16] In addition, while most anthropological studies of religion in Greece have been conducted in small rural communities, the handful of anthropological studies conducted in other settings suggest that attitudes toward religion and religious practice vary not only by region but also by class (see, e.g., Faubion 1994; Bennett

1988). For example, a number of educated, urban Greeks I have known have indifferent or skeptical attitudes toward religion and/or hostile feelings toward the Greek Orthodox church and its politics, and seldom, if ever, set foot inside a church. (One such urbanite to whom I spoke about my research called priests "witch doctors," comparing them to the *brujos* [witches] of Latin America.) And yet for such individuals religion is often viewed as part of their national cultural heritage. Even those most hostile to religion and the church, and the most likely to scoff at those who are religious, may admire a particular vernacular church or a fine icon or speak of the beauty of the Orthodox liturgy and the rituals of Holy Week. Such individuals may even seek out religious practices deemed "traditional" as part of an interest in their national heritage, just as urbanites return to the countryside to seek national roots in "the village."[17]

Even those who consider themselves devout Orthodox Christians, however, do not necessarily demonstrate reverence for the church and its functionaries. As I discovered in my own work, and as has been noted elsewhere in Greece (see Just 1988), villagers' version of religion, and what they consider important in the practice of their faith, may differ from that which the church professes or condones. The clergy themselves seldom receive great respect in village life, and may even be the object of ridicule or fear (see, e.g., Blum and Blum 1970; Herzfeld 1985; Just 1988). On Tinos, for example, there were people who believed devoutly in the Panayía and the miracle-working powers of her icon, but at the same time were very critical of the Church of the Annunciation as an organization and of those who ran it, feeling that the church had too much money and wielded too much power (even though it also supported charitable works and such projects as road building and restoration of village churches).

In addition, there is a variety of religious activities in which individuals participate that take place outside the church and outside official jurisdiction, including many of those that occur at pilgrimage sites such as Tinos. The events surrounding the pilgrimage of the possessed woman described at the beginning of this chapter are just one example. Less dramatic rituals also take place daily in ordinary life, such as those carried out by women who tend family gravesites, light candles and offer prayers in front of the household icons, and care for the small, privately owned churches found in many areas of Greece (see Dubisch 1983). Insofar as Greek Orthodoxy is very much about *practice*, about doing rather than simply about believing, ritual activities, whether within or outside the boundaries (physical and jurisdictional) of the church, actually *constitute* religion for many Greeks (rather than "expressing" or symbolizing it).[18]

This brings me to another important feature of religion in Greece—its material manifestations. Greek Orthodoxy does not make a dualistic division between the material and the spiritual world; rather, the material world can make manifest the holy (see Ware 1963). Hence Orthodoxy is a tactile and sensual religion. Rituals are often long and elaborate. Churches are rich with ornamentation and filled with icons, lighted candles, and offerings. They are also places of activity—worshipers light candles, kiss the icons, hang *támata* from the iconostasis. The Greek landscape itself is a visible manifestation of the holy, dotted with tiny churches and roadside shrines. Often these rural churches (and sometimes urban ones as well) define local geography, lending their name to the location in which they are found (for example, St. Barbara, Holy Cross). In addition, a wide variety of religious objects such as medallions, crosses, blue beads, and philacta can be encountered throughout Greece—in cars and buses, in shops, on babies, and on personal possessions—protecting them against the evil eye and invoking holy powers against other threats to property, family, and health.

CHURCHES, SAINTS, AND HOLY DAYS

After many years of working in Greece, I had come to take many of these material aspects of Orthodoxy for granted. In addition, since Orthodoxy was the only Christian religion with which I had any prolonged or intense contact, it had come—to some extent at least—to form my model for religious practice. Hence it took an "outsider's" comment to make me reflect on the nature of a "church" in Greece.

This comment came from a British friend, raised Protestant and unfamiliar with Greece, who came to visit with his wife in the summer of 1986. We toured the island, and he was puzzled by all the churches he saw. "Why doesn't every village just have one church?" he wanted to know. "Why are there so many?" (I sensed some accusation of extravagance in his question.) Since I had come to take the existence of the many churches for granted, my friend's "naive" question forced me to reflect on the nature of Greek Orthodoxy and its differences from Western Protestantism, differences that underlay his puzzlement. Part of the answer to his question, I think, lies in the fact that the various sorts of buildings that non-Greeks might label as "churches" (and even as "Christian churches") may differ significantly in function and meaning from "churches" in British and American society.

In Greece churches are intimately connected with the Greek pantheon of saints and with the Orthodox liturgical cycle. Every Greek village and town has at least one main church (in which regular weekly services as well as life-cycle rituals are generally held) and often several lesser ones, and in many parts of Greece there are small churches scattered throughout the countryside. These rural churches are particularly noticeable in the Cyclades. Tinos alone has over seven hundred (Dhorizas n.d.). Every church is associated with a particular Orthodox saint or with a specific day in the holy calendar. Each village celebrates its own saint's day (*paniyíri*), usually the day of the saint associated with the village's main church. Members of neighboring villages come to participate in the church services, to partake of local hospitality and visit friends and relatives, and to enjoy the dancing and drinking, which continue in the village tavernas late into the night. Depending on the saint's day and the time of year, people may come a long distance to attend such celebrations. Although rural depopulation has greatly reduced these events in many areas, they used to be an important source of socializing and entertainment, and provided an opportunity for the display of hospitality so important to village and family reputation.[19]

Each individual church usually has its own saint's day or holy day celebration, consisting of (at a minimum) a liturgy and the serving of some refreshments. If the church is located in the countryside, an excursion may be made of the event, with refreshments carried along to be served after the services. On Tinos, many of these small country churches are privately owned, and in addition to paying for the once-a-year services, the owners have the responsibility for maintaining the church, keeping it clean, and lighting the oil lamp on the eve of holy days. Thus at dusk before any holy day one sees dotted over the hillsides of Tinos the lights of oil lamps burning in the windows of these little whitewashed churches.

In addition, individual saints may be seen as serving different needs within a locale or community. Some saints are known for responding to particular kinds of troubles. (St. Nikolaos, for example, is particularly helpful to sailors; St. Paraskevi helps those with eye troubles.) Other saints, while enjoying a national reputation, nonetheless may have special local significance, and may not even have churches dedicated to them outside the local community. St. Pelayia (the nun whose vision led to the finding of the icon of the Annunciation on Tinos) and St. Nektarios of Aegina are two examples of such local saints (though Nektarios now enjoys a much wider reputation).

Since every Orthodox church, large and small, is dedicated to a particular saint or holy day, Greek Orthodox churches make manifest the liturgical cycle and the Orthodox pantheon. Some holy personages such as the Panayía may be celebrated on a number of different holy days. (Her churches are named for these different days, for example, the Day of the Annunciation, the Day of the Dormition.) Churches also tie particular communities and localities to these figures, and hence to Orthodox cosmology. In addition, saints connect individuals to the Orthodox ritual

2. A small roadside shrine dedicated to the Panayía

cycle. Most Greeks are named after saints, and it is customary to celebrate one's name day rather than one's birthday.[20] On name days, the
family as a whole receives visits and congratulations.[21] Name days are
collective also in the sense that one celebrates at the same time as all
others with that name, united with these others by a common connection
to the divine in the form of the holy personage from whom one's name is
derived.

Individuals and families may be connected to saints in another way.
Many of the small churches in Greece are privately built and maintained.
Their construction may have been the result of a vow, or even a vision, or
an expression of thanksgiving to a particular saint. Many churches thus

have stories connected with them. For example, a church just outside the village in which I lived was jointly owned and maintained by my land-lady's family and another family in the village. The church was called "God covered" (*Theoskepastí*). It was built into the rocky hills in a place where, according to my landlady, a dense cloud is said to have concealed a group of islanders when they were fleeing from invading Turks. The church was built in thanksgiving for, and commemoration of, this mira-cle.[22] Hence churches may embody important past events (in this case a protective manifestation of divine power at a point of ethnic crisis), and mark earthly places where the power of the divine was, in one way or another, made manifest. In this manner the sacred is localized and individualized.

For these reasons churches vary in their reputation (cf. Betteridge 1992). Throughout Greece, there are particular churches that draw large numbers of pilgrims on their saint's day or festival. These shrines and the saints they commemorate may serve as the focus of local identity (Kenna 1977). For example, when I interviewed people in a village in the Pel-oponnesus about their pilgrimages to the Church of the Annunciation at Tinos, a number of those interviewed mentioned to me the Church of St. Nektarios on the nearby island of Aegina, where they had also frequently gone on pilgrimage. These local churches may have unique features that distinguish them from other churches. The Church of St. Spiridhonos on the island of Kefalonia, for example, contains the preserved body of the saint. And the Church of Taksiarhis (the archangel Michael) on the island of Lesvos boasts a rare three-dimensional icon made of earth soaked with the blood of martyred monks.

Foremost among all the Greek saints is the Madonna or Panayía. In fact she is the central figure in religious devotion generally, and her aid is less "specialized" than that of some of the other saints—she can be ap-pealed to for a wide variety of problems and needs. Churches dedicated to her and her holy days outnumber those of any other single saint. On Tinos, 83 of the 514 Orthodox churches on the island are dedicated to her (more than twice as many as any other single saint or holy day) and 43 of the 208 Catholic churches (Dhorizas n.d.). The Panayía has many local manifestations. For example, on Tinos there are churches dedicated to the Panayía Faneromeni (the Madonna who has appeared or mani-fested herself), Panayía Mirtidhiotissa (Madonna of the myrtles), Panayía Eleousa (the compassionate Madonna), Panayía Spiliotissa (Madonna of the Cave), as well as the main church dedicated to the Madonna of the Annunciation (Evangelístria) (cf. Kenna 1977). The Panayía can also serve, as she does at Tinos, as a representation of Greece itself (see chap-ter 11).

All of these interconnections—among churches, saints, holy days, local communities, and individuals—reflect and assert an intimate relationship between the material and the divine worlds. The churches themselves connect the sacred to the earth, and particular manifestations of the sacred to particular locations on the earth. In addition, every church, whether national cathedral or tiny country chapel, is constructed according to a plan that both creates and manifests this connection. Because of this plan, no Greek church is completely unfamiliar to the Orthodox. The worshiper enters the church expecting to find, at a minimum, an icon on a stand by the doorway, usually an icon representing the saint or holy event to which the church is dedicated (though this may be at the front, near the altar, in a large church). In front of the stand will be a candelabrum, and there will be a table or stand with candles and a box in which to leave monetary offerings. There will often be other icons as well, on stands or hung upon the walls. At the back of the church, opposite the main doorway, is the altar screen (témblas or iconostásis) painted with scenes from the life of Christ, along with individual icons. In larger churches the altar table will be behind the screen (an area forbidden to women). Larger churches will be laid out in a "cross in square" pattern, with large pillars dividing the main area of the church (Hussey 1986:362), and Christ the Pantokrator gazes down from the ceiling, while the heavenly host and various saints and scenes from Christ's life are depicted on the vaults and walls (Hussey 1986:359). In addition, every church, whether large or small, will have offerings presented by the faithful, either as permanent parts of the church (for example, an icon hung on the wall or an icon stand), or as temporary ones (such as flowers or támata). And whether the church is large or small, worshipers will know what to expect when they enter, and what to do while they are there.[23]

It should be clearer now what the meaning of a "church" is in the Greek Orthodox setting. Above all, a church is a means of connection between the material world and the spiritual world, and between the human and the divine. Each church represents a particular manifestation of such a link. Thus every church, as a physical object, has a meaning, connecting people and the space and time in which they move to a spiritual world represented by specific holy personages and by the liturgical cycle. But these churches are themselves linked to this spiritual world in a particular way—through icons.

ICONS IN ORTHODOX TRADITION AND PRACTICE

Icons are central to any understanding of the Orthodox church. Every church has its main icon, usually located on a stand to the left as one enters the church. This icon represents the saint or event to which the church is dedicated. (For example, the main icon of the Church of the

Annunciation shows Gabriel appearing to Mary with the announcement of Christ's birth.) Icons also cover the screen separating the altar from the main part of the church. These icons are arranged in a prescribed traditional and symbolic order, with icons of Christ, the Panayía, and the saint of the church's dedication occupying the center panels (see Kenna 1985: 359–62; see also Cavarnos 1977:22–23). Most churches have other icons as well. In the Church of the Annunciation, for example, an elaborate icon depicting the Dormition and decorated with silver and gold[24] is prominently displayed in its own stand on the right-hand side of the church, and there are many other icons placed elsewhere throughout the sanctuary, most of them gifts.

Icons are not simply to be looked at. Rather, they are the center of a set of behaviors referred to in Greek as *proskínima*—the devotions one performs upon entering any church. At the minimum, these devotions include lighting a candle, kissing the central figure(s) of the main icon, and making the sign of the cross. (I have never seen a Greek pilgrim fail to perform this basic devotion.) *Proskínima* may also include additional acts—kissing of the other icons, genuflecting, and so on. (*Proskínima* also carries the idea of submission, as reflected both in kissing the icon and genuflection.) *Proskínima* may be carried out in the absence of other religious rituals (as when one simply visits a church), or if one enters during services (at the minimum, one kisses the icon near the doorway, even if further devotions are not possible at that time). On a holy day, one might speak of going to the church *na proskiníso*, to "make my devotions," this being a self-explanatory act; both the act itself and the reasons for it are contained within the phrase. Another commonly used phrase, *n'anápso éna kerí* (to light a candle), refers to this act metanymically; the lighting of the candle stands for the devotions as a whole.

The Greek word for icon—*ikóna*—means "picture" or "image" or "representation" and is applied to mundane pictures as well. An icon may be referred to as a holy picture—*ayía ikóna*—or simply as an *ikóna*. Unlike the statues found in Catholic churches, icons are not dressed or otherwise covered in different ways during the cycle of the holy year, although offerings may be hung upon them by the devout. (The icon of the Annunciation at Tinos is completely obscured by jewelry given as offerings.) Icons also may be taken out of the church in procession at certain times of year. And they may be appealed to for various favors. Icons are given gifts (in the form of offerings) and given as gifts, both by ordinary people and (in the past) by the Byzantine emperor to state officials, provincial governors, and foreign allies (Başğmez 1989:12). And they also give gifts (in the form of answered prayers).

Although icons of saints may purportedly be based on the features of the living person, they are not meant to be naturalistic. Rather, they represent the saint's holiness. Icons have a calm, static character, no matter what the event being depicted. Heads are generally placed in full or three-quarter face, and the eyes gaze outward, engaging the viewer while at the same time maintaining a certain inward quality (Kenna 1985). The background of the icon is often gold, as are halos and highlights. Gold symbolizes "the presence and power of God, the uncreated and uncorruptible light, spaceless and timeless" (Kenna 1985:352). The name of the saint or the event being depicted is painted on the icon as well. Icons may be instructive or didactic, seeking to teach or to remind people of the major events of Christianity (such as the events of the life of Christ), or they may be devotional, depicting particular saints who act as intercessors (Başğmez 1989).

The veneration of icons is a significant feature of Orthodox Christianity, and one that has at times been a point of contention within the church. The use of icons goes back to the first century A.D. and has its origins in the rudimentary symbolic forms used by early Christians (Cavarnos 1977). Early icons were also pictures to make eminent priests and monks known to future generations and to preserve their memory (Başğmez 1989:9). The first important iconographic decorations of churches were mosaics, an art form borrowed from the ancient Greeks and Romans. Other decorations were done on panels, a form that Cavarnos suggests goes back to Egyptian tomb paintings of the Roman-Greco period (Carvarnos 1977; see also Başğmez 1989). The use of pictorial representations increased with each century until the outbreak of Iconoclasm in 726. During the Iconoclast period (726–843) a large number of icons were destroyed. The end of the Iconoclast controversy, however, firmly established the place of icons within Orthodox devotion: "The close association, even synonymity, of the Orthodox faith and icons is stressed in the annual festival, marking the end of the Iconoclast dispute in A.D. 843, which takes place on the first Sunday in Lent and is known as both 'the triumph of Orthodoxy' and as 'the restoration of the Ikons'" (Kenna 1985:367–68; see also Ware 1963:39).

Orthodox theologians are careful to emphasize, however, that the veneration of icons is not to be considered idolatry. "The icon is not an idol but a symbol; the veneration shown to images is directed, not towards stone, wood, and paint, but towards the person depicted. . . . Because icons are only symbols, Orthodox do not *worship* them, but *reverence* or *venerate* them" (Ware 1963:40). In Greek the distinction is between *latría* (worship) and *proskínisis* (devotion or respect). Icons, according to Ware, are "one of the means which the church employs in order to teach the faith" (1963:41). Cavarnos, quoting St. Photios, Patriarch of Constantinople, states that "icons not only teach, as do written accounts, but in some instances they are *more vivid* than written accounts, and hence *su-*

perior to the latter as a means of instruction" (Cavarnos 1977:31; see also Başğmez 1989).

Icons are emblematic of the Orthodox view of the relationship between the material and spiritual worlds. Orthodox theologians reject forms of religious dualism that repudiate material images of the divine. For the Orthodox the doctrine of the Incarnation shows that the human and the divine are not mutually exclusive, and that the divine is, moreover, accessible to the senses. Ware argues that because God took human form, such material representations as icons are not only appropriate but also essentially bound up with the Orthodox belief that "the whole of God's creation, material as well as spiritual, is to be redeemed and glorified" (1963:42). The icon, in effect, bridges the tension between this world and the next. Icons are not meant, however, to be representational in the sense of imitating nature. "True iconography is intended to take us beyond anatomy and the three-dimensional world of matter to a realm that is immaterial, spaceless, timeless—the realm of the spirit, of eternity. And hence the forms and colors are not those one customarily observes around him, but have something unworldly about them" (Cavarnos 1977:38). As Başğmez puts it, "The objects and figures depicted are shown as objects and figures of a world that resembles our world yet at the same time is different from it" (1989:16). In a further extension of the idea of the icon, each person can also be viewed as an icon, or image, of God (Ware 1963:224–25).

In actual practice, and in popular experience, the distinction between the icon as material object and what it is meant to represent is not always clearly maintained, nor is the distinction between *latría* and *proskínisis* always behaviorally evident.[25] In fact, icons are often viewed by devotees as containing, rather than simply representing or channeling, the divine power they depict (cf. Kenna 1985:346). Stories told by pilgrims and the remarks of those visiting the shrine at Tinos, for example, suggest that many of them see the Panayía as residing in her icon. In one instance, an elderly man I interviewed told me that during World War I the Panayía left her icon in Tinos and went "up" (*epáno*, that is, the front in northern Greece) to help the troops who were fighting there. She returned to the church in the form of a white dove on the night of her holy day (March 25). A woman, when I asked her why people go to Tinos, replied, "For the Panayía" (*yia tin Panayía*), as if she resided in her icon. In one account of the nun Pelayia's vision (which led to the finding of the miraculous icon), the Panayía speaks to the nun of her "house" (that is, icon) in the field just outside the town, and of how she is weary of being buried there (see chapter 8). Both pilgrims and local people on their way to the church speak of going to the Panayía (*stin Panayía*). The Church of the Annunciation, both as a physical place and as an institution, may also be referred to simply as "the Panayía." Similarly, people often speak directly to icons, addressing them with their concerns and prayers.[26]

Consistent with this view of the holy figure as contained in the icon, icons may be seen as having personalities and wills of their own, making demands on human devotees. Loring Danforth (1989), in his study of the Anastenaria (ritual firewalkers) of northern Greece, has described the ways in which icons that have been neglected or confined make known their desire to "come out" and be properly cared for by afflicting individuals with illness or other problems. On Tinos a number of the icons found in the island churches have stories attached to them that show the icons as active participants in their own discovery and in the building of the churches to house them. In one such story, a fisherman went to investigate a light that had been seen at sea. When he arrived at the spot, he discovered an icon of the Panayía. As soon as he picked it up, he found himself on dry land and on the road to the village. After he had walked with it for a while, the icon suddenly became too heavy to lift. As it was growing dark, the fisherman did not know what to do and he prayed to the Panayía to give him strength to carry the icon to some nearby ruins. The icon then became light enough for him to carry it to that spot, and the next day the fisherman returned with some fellow villagers and they decided to build a church where the icon had been left.[27]

As such stories show, it is not simply *through* an icon (as a representation), but *to* an icon that many supplicants appear to speak. Icons are not only part of the devotee's relationship to the divine, but are themselves active participants in this relationship. This becomes particularly manifest at the Church of the Annunciation, both in the devotional acts carried out in front of the icon and in the verbal expressions of the pilgrims who congregate there, who may address the Panayía in very personal terms, asking for her favor or grace (*hári*) or thanking her for her help. On the saint's day of Pelayia, as I was following the icon as it was carried in procession from the church, many of the boats in the harbor sounded their horns in a cacophony of greeting as the icon approached the waterfront. "Why are they doing that, Mama?" a little boy near me asked his mother. "We are thanking the Panayía for her grace" (*Efharistoúme tin Panayía yia tin hári tis*), the mother replied. And as the possessed woman crawled painfully toward the church, onlookers encouraged her by saying, "The Panayía is waiting for you."

A view of icons that sees them only as symbolic and representational does not account for the differential power of icons. Some icons are known for their special powers and draw devotees from beyond the icon's local radius. Central to the understanding of the Church of the Annunciation of Tinos is the miracle-working (*thavmatourgós*) nature of its icon. It is this miracle-working power (*káni thávmata*) that is cited by many pil-

3. The miraculous icon of the Annunciation, housed in an
elaborate icon stand and covered with offerings

grims as their reason for coming to the church, whether they come specifically to invoke the Panayía's aid in their particular problems or simply as
religious tourists to see the church that the icon's/Panayía's power has
wrought and to view the many offerings displayed in the church that attest to the miracles that have occurred.

The term miracle (*thávma*) is officially reserved for those acts that alter
seemingly hopeless and generally medically untreatable conditions. A
nineteenth-century work on the Church of the Annunciation, for example, defines a miracle as something that does not get better through a
doctor's skill but only through God (Pirgos 1865:9n). Common examples
of miracles cited to me by pilgrims, church officials, and islanders were
such occurrences as a mute person speaking, a crippled person walking, a
sick child cured, a mad person made well, instances where the change in
the supplicant's condition was dramatic and immediately apparent. In

4. Pilgrims line up in the main street on the Day of the Annunciation, waiting for the icon to pass over them

another sense, however, any answered prayer that changes existing conditions (for example, effects a rescue or cure) could be termed a miracle insofar as it is interpreted as the working of divine power in everyday life. In this sense, events are not chance, but have meaning. As a booklet describing the various miracles that have occurred at Tinos puts it, miracles are "the powerful presence of God in our life" (S. Lagouros n.d.:7).

The meaning associated with miracles is enhanced in the liminal context of pilgrimage, where the ordinary may become extraordinarily significant (see, e.g., Betteridge 1985). Expectation and the receptive state of mind engendered by pilgrimage, especially during major pilgrimage events, do indeed create an atmosphere in which pilgrims expect to see—and do see—visions and miracles. For example, on the evening of August 15, 1986, when I went up to the church for the *olaniktía*, I found a knot of people gathered in the plaza in front of the church, staring up at the bell tower. I joined them and asked someone why people were staring. I was told that there was a figure of a man discernible in the tower, and the same answer was given to others who came up to join the shifting population of observers. It was never clear to me or to anyone else I queried what the significance of this figure was, but the readiness to see the unusual is typical of the heightened liminality of major pilgrimage events and is one of the factors that leads pilgrims to make their journey on such occasions.

Although I was told by church officials that today a doctor attests to the validity of miracles before they are officially recorded at the church, many "miracles" of the more ordinary sort are described in church pamphlets, in local newspapers, and in other writings about the church, and appear to be based simply on the testimony of those to whom they occurred. In addition, when a miracle takes place at the church, it is publicly broadcast by the ringing of the church bells, and the townspeople immediately know what has happened.

Stories of miracles are also circulated by word of mouth, and there is an oral tradition of miraculous happenings, consisting of pilgrims' own experiences and of events they have heard recounted by other pilgrims (cf. Slater 1986). The telling of such stories is a common type of exchange among pilgrims, especially at major festivals, when crowds are large and pilgrims more likely to fall into conversation with one another. Such tales, individually and collectively, reinforce faith and bolster hope.[28] In the summer of 1988, for example, while standing with a group of pilgrims just outside the church, I heard a story of a child who had been vowed (*taméno*) to the Panayía and who had fallen overboard while his family was traveling by boat to Tinos. Unaware of the accident, the captain had sailed on. But the Panayía was watching over the child, the storyteller said, and it was picked up by another ship that was passing by. Since no one knew the identity of the child, it was brought to the church when the boat arrived at Tinos. When the grieving parents came to the church, they found the child waiting for them beside the icon. The other pilgrims listening to this story nodded knowingly, impressed with this confirmation of their faith.

Icons—and the saints they represent/embody—thus tie the material world to the spiritual, material objects to abstract ideas, acting through the medium of "miracles" (broadly defined). In one sense, of course, any religious symbol makes such a connection—that is what religious symbols are all about. But what is significant about icons for many of the devout is not the abstract meaning icons supposedly convey; rather it is the *experience* of the spiritual world that they make possible. This experience occurs both through the tangible presence of the icon and through the granting of requests to supplicants. In addition, the numerous votive offerings that particularly powerful icons acquire are another tangible manifestation of divine power. Icons offer an experiential grasp of their religion to the Orthodox, rather than (or in addition to) an intellectual one.[29]

This brings me back to an earlier point—that Greek Orthodoxy is a sensual religion, but particularly a visual and tactile religion. For this reason, a purely intellectual approach—that is, a description of beliefs and moral values—cannot encompass the "meaning" in the largest sense (meaning as total experience) that Greek Orthodoxy holds for many of its adherents. In addition, icons cannot be understood outside the context of that experience. Icons in an art gallery or museum, for example, are removed from the setting, both physical and behavioral, that gives them meaning, and in such a context often seem lifeless and flat. Just as the icons represent the possibilities of human connection to and participation in the divine, so human devotees are required to give the icons life in the material world. It is in the context of the church and in the presence of the faithful that icons come alive.

Although there is no church without icons, icons may be found outside churches, in household shrines. While churches may be considered "houses" for icons, houses in turn take on a spiritual dimension through the presence of their icons. The tending of these icons, including lighting the oil lamp at the shrine (*iconostási*), is generally the duty of the woman of the household (see Dubisch 1983; see also Kenna 1976; Pavlides and Hesser 1986). Icons are also connected with other social units, and may take on particular importance as the focus of community identity in situations of upheaval and migration. In such circumstances, displaced groups may carry their icons with them, making them the spiritual center of a new community. Renee Hirschon (1989) describes such a process in the Asia Minor refugee community she studied in Piraeus, and Loring Danforth (1989) describes a "genealogy" of icons among the Anastenaria (refugees from what is now Bulgaria and Turkish Thrace), a genealogy that replicates the system of social descent.

INTERIOR BELIEF AND EXTERIOR ACT

I have emphasized the importance of ritual acts and the material objects around which acts may center in Orthodox Christianity as it is practiced by many Greeks at Tinos and elsewhere. This should not, however, be taken to mean that the internal state of devotees and their beliefs are not important as well. As onlookers commented while the possessed woman crawled up to the church, one must have faith to hold the devil at bay. On several occasions I heard negative comments from islanders about the faith of today's pilgrims. Those who come nowadays no longer believe, they said, and come to Tinos only for a vacation, not for a real pilgrimage. One island woman told me it is because people no longer believe that so many bad things are happening in the world today. Several pilgrims, describing to me the miraculous visions of the Panayía that have appeared in the church, stated that not all of those present saw these visions, and stressed that one must have faith to see. A (male) friend of mine from the village of Falatados, a great skeptic in religious matters and a frequent critic of the church, said that he believed that miracles really could occur, but only to those who truly had faith.

Nonetheless, it is in general accurate to say that popular religion in Greece, like popular religion in many Catholic countries (see, e.g., Brettell 1990), is more outward than inward looking, more concerned with external images, with the public and communal than with the interior or the mystic. Pilgrimage may thus be a particularly appropriate expression of religiosity in such societies. In Greece this may in turn be related to a more general social concern with outward appearance as opposed to inner state, to what Herzfeld (1986) has termed a "fundamental concern with display and concealment."[30] This does not mean that Greeks feel that inner states do not exist, only that one cannot know the inner state of another with any accuracy or confidence (see, e.g., du Boulay 1974; Herzfeld 1985). Hence the importance of the public act or performance through which inner states are made visible. Thus while a vow may be made "inside oneself" (see chapter 5), it finds expression in a public, ritual act, whether one as simple as lighting a candle in a nearby church or as dramatic as crawling up to the church at Tinos on one's knees. For the woman possessed by the devil, her interior "sin" was made visible by her public suffering. Those who come to be cured of illness or other physical problems display their suffering as well, either through visible signs of their affliction, or through the act of pilgrimage itself and the acts and objects associated with it. The votive offering placed in the church is also a visible, public manifestation of faith. In this sense, icons, too, find their social place, for they are visible, material, and public manifestations of what is otherwise invisible and privately experienced.

I began my discussion with a section titled "Religion and Everyday Life." While pilgrimage is not an everyday event (at least not for the pilgrim), it is rooted in other features of religious life that are more closely entwined with daily life. The closeness of the material world and the divine, as represented by icons, churches, and miracles (in the broadest sense of the term), means that the spiritual world, while sometimes awe-inspiring, is also close and familiar. Many of the townspeople and villagers I know, and certainly most of the pilgrims, have a sense of this closeness and familiarity. It is a sense expressed in many of the ritual activities connected with pilgrimage. Timothy Ware has noted the "informality" of worship found in the Eastern Orthodox religion. Churches do not have pews, and worshipers often move around freely during services, coming and going as they please, sometimes even talking quietly to one another. As Ware says, "They are at home in their church . . . children in their father's house. Orthodox worship . . . could . . . be described as 'homely': it is a *family* affair" (1963:276).

I suggested earlier that there is a wide range of ways in which Greeks may choose to be attached to their religion, and even those who feel most alienated from the Orthodox church and its rituals may nonetheless view the Orthodox religion as part of their cultural heritage as Greeks and find some facet of it to admire or some activity to make their own. The wide range of possible religious activities, the number of religious objects (including icons and churches) connecting the mundane to the spiritual world, and the "informality" of religious observance allow for great flexibility in the ways in which people experience their religion. It may also account, in part at least, for the Greek Orthodox religion's suitability as a unifying national force. I will save this topic for a later chapter, however. I now turn to another major element of Greek Orthodox religious practice integral to pilgrimage—the vow.

CHAPTER FIVE

Pilgrimage Observed: The Journey and the Vow

PILGRIMAGE INVOLVES by definition a journey of some sort, usually one of enough distance to constitute a hardship, or at least an inconvenience, to the pilgrim.[1] With today's rapid and comfortable transportation, however, pilgrimage to Tinos cannot be considered too great an ordeal (though on major holidays the crowded passenger ships can make the journey an uncomfortable one, and winter storms or the *meltémi,* the summer wind, can create rough seas). Pilgrims arrive on large passenger boats, a journey of three to four hours from Piraeus. On Tinos they can stay in private rooms and hotels and eat in restaurants. However, the difficulties of the journey, both financial and physical, vary by social class. For the poorer pilgrims the trip is more difficult, especially if they must come from distant areas of Greece. If they cannot afford rooms, they may have to sleep in rooms provided by the church, or if these are full, in the churchyard or the streets, and they eat the food they have thriftily brought along.[2]

Although improved transportation has relieved some of the hardships of the journey for today's pilgrim, in the past the trip could be a difficult and even dangerous one.[3] This was particularly so in March, at the time of the celebration of the Annunciation (March 25), which used to be the major holy day celebrated at the church.[4] Old people described how the storms that were common at this time of year could make the journey extremely unpleasant, especially in the smaller, slower boats of the time. Not everyone was intimidated by these hazards, however. One elderly woman from the Peloponnesus told me about a trip she had made to Tinos during a storm. Everyone else had been afraid, she said, but not she. After all, they were all going to the Panayía, who surely would protect them on their journey. Another old woman from the same village recounted, with a certain self-satisfaction, how she ate and drank during the journey, despite the fact that everyone around her was seasick. Once they arrived at Tinos, these elderly pilgrims told me, passengers were ferried to shore in caïques, since no dock existed there at the time. Once on the island, pilgrims had to travel by donkey if they wished to visit the monastery or other inland places, for in those earlier days the island had no roads.

In addition to externally imposed hardships, pilgrims can turn the journey into a difficult one by the nature of their vows. For those going on their knees, or bearing some burden as they toil up the hill to the church,

5. Pilgrims on their knees ascending the steps to the church

pilgrimage can indeed become an ordeal, and sometimes a very painful one, both physically and emotionally, as they express and seek help for their ailments and difficulties.[5]

In chapter 2, I gave an impressionistic sense of what pilgrims "typically" do when they come to the Church of the Annunciation. Let us now look more closely at what actually constitutes a pilgrimage.

As explained earlier, there is no exact equivalent in Greek to the English term *pilgrimage*. A person coming to visit the Church of the Annunciation is called by a term—*proskinitís*—that can be translated as "pilgrim." But to translate the noun form of what such an individual does—the *proskínima*—as "pilgrimage" is to impose a meaning on it that is too narrow and that isolates it from its religious context, since in Greek the term *proskínima* refers more broadly to the set of devotions performed upon entering a church. One may have traveled a great distance to perform these acts, or one may have simply gone around the corner to a village church. Use of the term *pilgrimage,* then, marks off the activities of the sort I observed at Tinos in ways they are not necessarily marked off by the pilgrims themselves, at least not verbally. However, while a journey to Tinos exhibits continuities with other forms of Greek religious behavior (some of which were presented in chapter 4), it exhibits differences as well, differences that may be qualitative and part of a continuum of religious practice but are nonetheless significant.

Pilgrimage, as the term is generally used in English, refers to an act that is usually centered around a physical goal: that is, the pilgrim seeks to reach a physical place that is, or that contains, the object of the journey. In the case of pilgrimage to Tinos this goal is the Church of the Annunciation, or more specifically the miraculous icon or the Panayía herself (as she is embodied, for many pilgrims, in the icon). Pilgrimage also has another, less materially apparent, goal: the satisfaction of the need or desire that draws the pilgrim, whether that need is for some specific request to be answered, the thanking of the divine power that has granted the request, the wish for the general spiritual benefit of contact with the icon's holiness, or simply to see a famous holy place (in which case the visit may be less a pilgrimage and more a sort of "religious tourism").

At the church, the devotions in front of the icon constitute the essential core of *proskínima*. It is the minimum that any pilgrim must perform, and except for the large crowds that may be present and the acts carried out in conjunction with special requests, it does not differ from the devotions one would carry out upon entering any church. Once this minimum is completed, some pilgrims simply leave the church by one of the side doors. Others, however, may engage in various activities connected with pilgrimage. Some may even linger in front of the icon, kneeling before it, kissing the stand as well as the icon itself, making extended appeals to the Panayía. Normally little effort is made by church functionaries to enforce any sort of order on the pilgrims, who carry out their *proskínima* in their own order, and at their own pace. An exception occurs during the events surrounding the fifteenth of August, when church police—*ikonofílakes*—may guard the doorways, controlling the number of pilgrims who enter at any one time, moving people out immediately following their devotions at the icon, and blocking entrance to the church at the side doors so that pilgrims can enter only through the main door.

Once their devotions in front of the icon have been completed, pilgrims may make the rounds of the church, performing devotions in front of the other icons, admiring the many offerings, and even taking photographs. They may obtain consecrated oil or bread from church employees, or bring oil or bread as offerings. Pilgrims bring a variety of other offerings as well—flowers, *támata*, wine, embroidery—sometimes placing their offerings directly beside one or another of the church icons. The large candles—*lambádhes*—are also offerings.[6] Larger donations of money, jewelry, and the like are made through the church office, where they are recorded. Pilgrims may stay for prayer services, or they may leave before or during such services. Many pilgrims also visit the chapel below the main church, where they can obtain holy water, and they may wander around the church grounds to view the museum of Tinian artists, the displays of old icons, the chapel of St. Pelayia, the bookstore, the art gallery (its holdings of paintings and other objects given as gifts to the church), the mausoleum of the *Elli,* and the statues and other marble works that decorate the courtyard. Most pilgrims, however, confine their attentions to the main sanctuary and to the chapel of holy water (*zoodhóhos piyí,* the Life-giving Well) below the church. Pilgrims who have come to baptize a child must make arrangements for this at the church office. (Baptisms are held only during certain hours.) Either before or after the baptism, members of the baptismal party will perform their *proskínima* in the main sanctuary of the church.

Though not all churches that are pilgrimage sites offer the possibility for baptisms (and probably none baptize on the scale achieved at Tinos during the busy summer months), many of the features of pilgrimage described thus far for Tinos are to be found at other pilgrimage sites in Greece as well. Each has its unique features (which is, after all, what draws pilgrims to the site), but they have common features as well: a holy icon or other sacred object, stories of miracles, special days of celebration, offerings, holy water, and so on. Thus every pilgrimage site is both special and at the same time familiar to the pilgrim who journeys there.

THE SACRED JOURNEY

Turner has spoken of the "increasing sacralization" of the pilgrim's route as the site of pilgrimage is approached (1974:182). This sacralization is defined by religious tradition, by the official structure of the church, and by the behavior of the pilgrims. The entire island of Tinos is considered by many inhabitants to have a sacred quality by virtue of the presence of the church, and a local writer refers to it as "the island of the Megalohari" (S. Lagouros n.d.:7). At one point during the late 1960s (under the junta and before I arrived to do my original fieldwork) church officials reportedly forbade miniskirts on passengers who disembarked on the island.

Today there are no such restrictions on dress, and topless bathing and discos have invaded the island. But there is still a zone around the church where discos and bars are forbidden.[7]

The church is, of course, a sacred precinct. As mentioned earlier, a church employee stands guard at the entrance to the inner courtyard, to make certain no one enters who is inappropriately attired. It is not uncommon for pilgrims to bring their own more modest clothing to pull over shorts and short skirts, but if the pilgrim has not been so thoughtful, the church will loan such items so that the pilgrim can enter the sacred grounds properly dressed.[8]

In other respects, however, it is the pilgrims, both collectively and individually, who determine, through their own behavior, the degrees of sacredness of their route. Many cross themselves when the Church of the Annuciation is first sighted from the boat; others do so as they disembark. Those who have vowed to ascend to the church on their knees usually begin their arduous journey at the quay. Others may wait until they arrive at the steps of the church.

The possessed woman described earlier viscerally displayed the increasing influence of the sacred. At the beginning of her long struggle up the hill to the church, she could barely move, so strongly did the devil hold her back and seek to prevent her movement into sacred space. Then, as she drew closer, the holy power of the Panayía gradually began to exert itself, the devil was forced to lose his hold, and the woman started to move more freely.[9] The loosening and eventual removal of her headscarf as she struggled up the hill, a gesture often preceding release of emotion among Greek women (Caraveli 1986), indicated the evolution of the young woman's own emotional state. Even though the church doors were locked when she arrived, it was sufficient for her merely to peer into the space where the holy icon was housed for her exorcism to be complete.

Sacredness is a matter not only of space but of time. As mentioned earlier, certain holy days are thought to be particularly propitious ones to make a pilgrimage to the church. On occasions such as August 15, the atmosphere is highly charged, emotionally and spiritually. Many will attend the all-night vigil olaniktía which is held the night before the holy day,[10] and I have had several people tell me of seeing the Panayía appear in the church during this vigil.

This does not mean, however, that pilgrimage is entirely a sacred event, or to put in another way, it does not mean that there is an absolute separation between the sacred and the profane, or between religious and everyday life. Not only are religious holidays occasions for socializing and entertainment, but during pilgrimage to Tinos everyday life may invade "sacred" space.[11] One of the remarkable sights on the days preceding the feast of the Dormition, for example, is the hundreds of pilgrims camped in the churchyard. One must step over or around prone bodies to get around the yard or across the balconies. (The church even distributes blankets for the pilgrims who camp outside.) People eat, talk, or sleep. Women wash dishes and pans and even clothing in the faucets of the churchyard. Children run everywhere (see Dubisch 1994).

In addition, pilgrims may combine pilgrimage with a vacation.[12] One morning, in the summer of 1986, I came down the stairs from my apartment to find two rather portly middle-aged women seated at a small table in the garden. They were sisters, my landlady informed me, and they came to Tinos every summer, renting one of the lower (cheaper) rooms in the apartment building. Later, when I talked to them, I learned that they had vowed to spend a month in Tinos every summer in gratitude to the Panayía, who had cured one of the sisters, as well as various family members who had been ill. The two women visited the church frequently during their stay and also made excursions to the monastery where St. Pelayia had lived. But they also spend a considerable amount of time relaxing and eating (they always seemed to have pastries, cheese, or some other treat on the little table).

It is common for those pilgrims who stay longer than a day or so to visit other sites on the island (not just religious sites such as the monastery, but also villages, windmills, and other island attractions), to take excursions by boat to the nearby islands of Delos and Mykonos, and to go swimming and shopping. These activities might be seen to have a certain commonality, however, for as Turner and Turner point out, there is a similarity between pilgrimage and more playful travel away from home: "A tourist is half a pilgrim, . . . a pilgrim is half a tourist" (1978:20; see also Smith 1992).

Once the *proskínima* is completed at the church, we might speak of the "desacralization" of the pilgrim's route back into the town, which usually proceeds down the street of shops paralleling the main street to the church. (Merchants speak of this descent of the pilgrims from the church as "the return," *i epistrofí*.) The shops offer a wide variety of religious and secular souvenirs. Icons and incense may be displayed side by side with suntan lotion, snorkling gear, Smurf T-shirts, *loukoúmia* (a local sweet), and cups that say (in Greek) "from Tinos with love."[13] It is a rare pilgrim who leaves Tinos without some material remembrance of the visit, and sometimes as much time is devoted to the choosing of gifts and souvenirs as to devotions at the church.

At the same time, although a number of itinerant merchants set up stands selling religious objects and other souvenirs just before the major holy days, one does not find at Tinos the fairs or carnival atmosphere characteristic of pilgrimage in some other areas of Europe or in Latin America,[14] nor is there any selling in the precincts of the church itself. Even

Gypsies, who elsewhere engage in itinerant merchant activities, come to Tinos largely for the religious event and do relatively little trade. Nor does one find in the town the dancing and music characteristic of the village *paniyíria*. Such activities are not carried out in or around the church; one must go to the villages themselves for such celebrations.

This does not mean, of course, that there is not an important economic dimension to pilgrimage. In addition to the vast amount of wealth collected by the church—part of which is redistributed to the islanders in the form of good works—many of the townspeople depend, directly or indirectly, upon pilgrimage for their living. Pilgrims rent rooms, eat in restaurants, buy food and souvenirs, purchase bus and boat tickets, and contribute to the island economy by providing a market for local farmers and jobs for both townspeople and villagers.

So far I have spoken of the sacralization of the pilgrimage journey in terms of space, centered on the Church of the Annunciation. Sacredness is not, however, a simple matter of geography. It is not only on Tinos that the power of the Madonna of the Annunciation is felt. She can extend her help anywhere, no matter how distant the supplicant from her church, and the influence of the divine may linger with the pilgrim even after departure. For example, I heard a story of a woman who had a vision in her hotel room while visiting the island, and another story of a miraculous cure that occurred after the pilgrim disembarked upon her return home. In the latter case, the pilgrim was a child who was mentally ill; as she stepped off the boat from Tinos, a vision of the Panayía appeared to her and after that she was well. A woman in a village in the Peloponnesus spoke to me of a general sense of spiritual fulfillment she felt after her pilgrimage to Tinos. That sense was fading, however, and she hoped she could sometime return to the church so that it could be renewed. Pilgrims also carry the sacred influence of the pilgrimage site home with them in the form of objects: holy water, consecrated oil, and other items acquired on their pilgrimage. And they may create their own holy objects, for example, by rubbing a piece of cloth or cotton over the icons.

In addition to afternoon prayer services in the summer, vespers are held at the church every day of the year, along with regular Sunday and other holy day services. There are also ceremonies accompanying the putting away and taking out of the icon when the church closes and opens, and some pilgrims attend these as well. For those who cannot afford the price of rooms, there are rooms available at the church where pilgrims may stay for free.[15] Such long-term stays bring the afflicted into prolonged contact with the holy atmosphere of the icon. Pilgrims may also take other excursions around the island, the most common being to the monastery of Kekhrovouno, where the nun Pelayia had the dream that led to the finding of the miraculous icon.

The manner in which pilgrimage is conducted varies to some extent by social class. More extreme sorts of behavior (such as crawling on one's knees) appear to occur mostly among pilgrims of lower socioeconomic status. Gypsies are especially likely to engage in more dramatic forms of behavior at the shrine. Poorer pilgrims (including Gypsies) are usually the ones who stay in the rooms provided by the church or sleep in the court-yards or the streets, and they usually keep their stay brief. More affluent pilgrims generally stay in better accommodations and are more likely to combine their pilgrimage with vacation (though they may also come for a brief pilgrimage, as, for example, for a baptism).[16]

Townspeople recognize a definite distinction among different types of pilgrims. They view the events of the fifteenth of August with some am-bivalence, for the occasion draws what they consider to be a poorer class of people, people who do not spend much money on rooms, food, and souvenirs. (Included in this class are Gypsies, who are commonly believed to steal.) Merchants breathe a collective sigh of relief when the holiday is over, for after that a more affluent class of visitors (*kalós kósmos*) begins to arrive for pilgrimage and holiday.[17]

It should be emphasized, however, that pilgrimage to the Church of the Annunciation and belief in the miracles of the icon are by no means only characteristic of the poor. People of all classes, and all ages, come to the church. The many spectacular offerings of jewelry, silver, and gold attest to the Panayía's help to the affluent. And the patriotic importance of the church in Greece (see chapter 9) means that major ritual events such as the fifteenth of August are always attended by a high-ranking representa-tive of the current government.

So far I have been describing something of the "shape" of pilgrimage as I observed it at Tinos. This "shape" has certain general features that one would find at other Greek pilgrimage sites as well. But each site also has its unique features, and while the pilgrim would find much that is familiar from one pilgrimage site to another, she or he would also encounter dif-ferences. An example of such differences can be seen at the monastery of St. Rafaíl on the island of Lesvos, which I visited in the summers of 1990 and 1993. This is an increasingly popular pilgrimage site, where the "newly appeared" martyred saints Rafaíl, Nikolaos, and Irini are com-memorated.[18] There are several small chapels at the monastery in addi-tion to the main sanctuary, one of which contains the tomb (*táfos*) of St. Rafaíl. This tomb is an important focus of pilgrimage activities, some of which were unfamiliar to me from my own work at Tinos. For example, I observed people taking a piece of string and making the sign of the cross along the length and width of the tomb. Some pilgrims took a wad of string and performed a similar act. One woman took such a wad and rubbed it on one eye, crossed it on the tomb, rubbed the other eye, crossed it again, and then rubbed it on her heart. Clothing and towels are also left at the foot of the tomb to absorb the power of the saint.

Pilgrims were also bending over to put their ears to the *táfos*. I asked a woman next to me what it was they heard. "A sort of 'thump-thump,'" she said. "A knocking," another bystander replied. A third woman commented that she had put her ear to the tomb and heard nothing and then removed her earrings and heard the sound twice. She went on to suggest that the saint is moved to such manifestations by emotion, by a tear. (She herself became emotional as she talked about it.) "If one truly believes" (*pistévi pragmatiká*)," another bystander commented, "one can hear the saint." As I stood watching, five or six people stood with their ears bent to the *táfos,* listening in silent concentration. I was struck by the quietness of the scene, a stark contrast to the constant activity to which I had become accustomed in the church at Tinos, and I found myself moved much as the woman to whom I spoke had been.

As the example of St. Rafaíl shows, each pilgrimage site might be said to have its own "traditions," formed not only by the site's unique history but also by the particular pilgrimage practices that have developed there. Although church personnel are present to direct pilgrims and answer their questions, much of the information regarding these practices seems to be passed on by the pilgrims themselves, whether at the pilgrimage site or after the pilgrimage, in conversations with those back home.

Within the parameters of both the general "shape" of pilgrimage and the particular practices of individual shrines lies a wide scope for individual variation. Indeed this variation is one of the striking features of a pilgrimage site, and it highlights the degree to which pilgrimage is an individual act, initiated, orchestrated, and carried out by the pilgrims themselves, with little or no oversight or control by officials of the church.[19] The possessed woman, for example, carried out her pilgrimage and achieved resolution of her problem with help from her sister and her fellow pilgrims. It is the pilgrims who decide the nature and the form of their vow and the kind of offering they will make. They may record the offering in the official records of the church, or they may make it quietly on their own. They may ask a priest to read the names of loved ones in the prayer services, or they may complete their entire pilgrimage without even having seen a priest. They may choose to engage in conventional activities such as going on their knees or listening at a saint's tomb, or they may invent entirely new acts of pilgrimage. It is this voluntary and "creative" dimension of pilgrimage that gives it its particular form and power and that helps to create the "traditions" characteristic of each pilgrimage site.

It may also lead pilgrimage to be viewed with a certain ambivalence by the official church. Although pilgrimage sites may be promoted by the church, in the final analysis it is the pilgrims themselves who determine

6. Women fulfilling vows by ascending to the church on their knees. The standing woman carries *lambádhes*

what becomes a place of pilgrimage, and who, despite official attempts to control the pilgrimage process itself, give pilgrimage its final "shape" (Dubisch 1990a; see also Turner 1974).

PILGRIMAGE AND THE CHURCH

The Church of the Annunciation at Tinos thus exhibits both similarities to and differences from a "typical" village church. It serves an entire nation, rather than a local community or even a region, and it draws its largest crowds not for the "routine" celebrations of the liturgical cycle, but for the special events that give shape to pilgrimage. Church services, that is, officially organized and controlled activities, thus determine attendance at the church to a much lesser extent than they would at a community church. Much happens—indeed in many ways more happens—outside the structure of these events. While even in a village church one will find a considerable amount of coming and going during services (there are no pews in Greek Orthodox churches), on busy days at the Church of the Annunciation such coming and going is constant.[20]

While the church is an important part of island identity, it does not serve the community in the same way as a village or neighborhood church (although local people may also attend Sunday or other holy day services at the Church of the Annunciation, just as they would at a village church). This difference is clearly illustrated by baptisms. Though islanders as well as pilgrims may have their children baptized at the church, the ritual as performed at the church is not a singular communal event but one of a series of baptisms (in the busy summer months, almost a production line), which may be observed by complete strangers (since many people wander through and stop to watch) instead of only members of one's family and community. Baptisms are also not performed in the church itself (as they would be in a village) but in the baptistry, which is located off the chapel of the Life-giving Well. For pilgrims, the baptism is usually attended by only a small party of relatives. Often people pose in the church courtyard with the baby afterward for a round of photographs, and if there is a meal eaten together, it is generally done in a public place, in a restaurant, rather than in someone's home.

The Church of the Annunciation is a complex institution of national and even international dimensions, a political and economic power (both locally and nationally), and a philanthropic institution that controls a vast amount of wealth. The church also operates a school for priests, and visiting priests frequently conduct services. In addition, the church is a significant local employer (as well as a generator of business through pilgrimage). All of this gives the Church of the Annunciation a character and an influence that goes beyond that of any more localized church.[21]

There is another sense in which pilgrimage makes the Church of the Annunciation different. Although the activities there both reflect and reveal significant features of Greek Orthodox religion, in certain ways they are also atypical. Part of this atypicality is a result simply of the sheer numbers of people who come, most of them strangers to one another, and of the emotional intensity that such numbers generate. Because so much of pilgrimage is focused on problems to which people seek or have sought help, pilgrimage rituals tend to center on individuals or discrete groups.

This is only partly offset by the common involvement in others' difficulties that may be created by pilgrimage. It is this dimension of pilgrimage— that is, the reasons for and process of its undertaking—to which I will turn next.

THE VOW

On July 23, 1986, the saint's day of Pelayia,[22] Ray and I ascended to the monastery of Kekhrovouno. It was here that the elderly nun Pelayia had the dream that led to the finding of the icon of the Annunciation, and every year on this day the icon is carried in procession from the main church up the winding mountain roads to the monastery.[23] The monastery was crowded when we arrived. Services were being conducted in the church, pilgrims were wandering through the monastery's maze of narrow whitewashed streets, visiting the gift shop and the small cell where Pelayia had lived, and nuns in black robes scurried back and forth. After touring the monastery, we escaped the crowds for a moment to wander down a path that led away from the main buildings and toward the cemetery so that I could show Ray the chapel where the bones of deceased nuns were stored. On the way back, we encountered a man alone on the path, Greek, perhaps in his thirties. I asked him (in Greek) if he knew when the procession with the icon would be starting its descent back to the town. When he realized we were Americans, he switched the conversation to English and proceeded to tell us his story.

He had come to Tinos by "pullman," with a group from Thessaloniki, he told us. But he had lived eleven years in the United States. While he was living there he had been struck by a car in a hit-and-run accident and was left by the roadside, where he bled considerably. He was finally found and spent three months in the hospital, undergoing surgery, which repaired most of the damage of the accident but left him with one improperly set knee, which he was unable to bend. He returned to Greece to live with his parents and found a Greek doctor who fixed the knee so that it could bend, though it was still not completely well and he had some pain. It was for that reason he had come to the shrine, to see if a pilgrimage could help complete his cure. It was a miracle he had been found after the accident, he said, and a miracle that he had encountered the doctor in Greece who had improved his knee so much. He had heard of the miracles that occurred at Tinos through the television coverage of pilgrimage. If one has faith, one never knows what could happen, he told us. He could very well get better, he reasoned, so why not come and try.

Pilgrims come to Tinos for a wide variety of reasons. For many, such as the man at the monastery, the shrine offers relief for specific problems, usually problems of illness, disability, and pain, either one's own or that

7. A stand displaying *támata, lambádhes,* and bottles for holy water

of close family members. One may come directly, as this man had done, to make a request for healing and to experience the power of the icon. Or one may come because one's prayers to the Panayía have already been answered, and the pilgrimage is the promised return for this answered prayer. In the latter case, pilgrimage is motivated by a vow (*táma*).

As mentioned earlier, the word *táma* (plural: *támata*) can mean either a vow itself or the metal plaques depicting a vow or request. These plaques are brought to the church and left as offerings. Although they are especially evident at pilgrimage sites, *támata* may be left at any church. It is rare to enter even the smallest Greek church and not find several hanging on one or more of the church's icons indicating favors requested of or granted by the icon's saint. (Other objects besides plaques may be left at churches—indeed almost anything can be given as a gift, from flowers to sheep to icons to furnishings for the church.[24] These are not called *támata*, however, but are referred to as "offerings" (*afyerómata*).[25]

The fact that *táma* is used both for a vow and the object that represents it further illustrates the close relationship between the material and the spiritual. But *táma* as "vow" has an important range of meanings only partly encompassed by *táma* as physical object. To say, as many pilgrims do, "I have a vow" (*ého táma*) is widely enough understood so as to be self-explanatory. No further statement is necessary to explain a pilgrim's presence at the church, or the activity (whatever it might be) that one engages in while there. A pilgrim may also use the verb form, *tázo* (I vow), usually in the past tense: *ého táksi* or *étaksa* (I have vowed or I made a vow).

Vows involve a very personal relationship between the person making them and the spiritual being to whom they are addressed. Vows are made "inside oneself," and the nature of the vow may or may not be verbally revealed, even though the fact that one has made a vow is displayed—publicly and sometimes dramatically—in the act of pilgrimage. Some pilgrims readily revealed to me the nature of and reason for their vow, while others kept these reasons completely secret, even from those closest to them. Even among those who were willing to say why their vow had been made, few cared to elaborate on its nature. A vow, then, is a very personal act, however public its actual fulfillment may be.

Vows represent an unmediated relationship between the person making the vow or request and the divine personage to whom the appeal is directed. Vows, I was told, are not required or supervised by a priest or other religious authority. Hence they are a very direct connection between the individual worshiper and particular spiritual beings. Moreover, I would argue, they should not be seen as an extension of worldly patronage relations (as in the idea of a "patron saint"), as has been argued for parts of the Catholic world.[26] The vocabulary pertaining to vows and pilgrimage is applied to a religious context only and is not used in the realm of mundane social relations.[27]

How and why do vows come to be made? In order to answer this question, we must once again consider the relationship of the divine to everyday life in Greece. Just as the material and spiritual cannot be separated, the divine and the mundane cannot be seen as separate in the context of daily life. The divine is believed by many to be revealed in daily events, and secular happenings often are given a spiritual significance by their association with the holy. For example, the association of the raising of the flag of Greek independence with March 25, the Day of the Annunciation (see chapter 9) is seen by the faithful as not coincidental but as laden with divine significance. In this sense, things do not happen "by chance"; there are spiritual forces at work in people's lives. This belief leads individuals to search for the spiritual significance of events. For example, the son of my landlady, Marina, had been in a serious accident the year before I arrived to do fieldwork at the church. The young man spent a long time in the hospital, and his mother was frantic with concern. Eventually, however, he recovered. Marina told me that she intended to build a small church to St. George in her backyard in thanksgiving. The accident had not occurred exactly on St. George's day, but that had been the nearest holy day, so she attributed her son's escape from death to this particular saint.[28]

Given this intervention of the divine, it is reasonable to expect that one can call on spiritual beings to help with the concerns of everyday life. Some idea of the range of such concerns can be gathered by a perusal of the *támata* for sale at the stands lining the main street to the church. Most are inexpensive pressed-tin plaques that depict various parts of the body (heart, eyes, limbs), as well as whole figures of women, men, and children. They may also depict houses, automobiles, ships, wedding crowns, airplanes, cows, cribs, and babies—a varied array of persons and things that may be the object of desire or concern. Some *támata* are of soldiers, for the anxious mother whose son is going into the army. When I inquired about a *táma* for a friend who was worried about not getting tenure at his university, and hence not being able to marry his fiancée, the shopkeeper from whom I was making my purchase first suggested that I buy a *táma* with wedding crowns,[29] and then when I explained more fully the nature of the problem, suggested one of a man in a business suit.

In addition to these inexpensive ready-made plaques, one can purchase *támata* of silver and gold in jewelry stores, or have them made to order in any form one wants. Many such made-to-order *támata* hang permanently in the church, including ones in the form of elaborate ships (from sailing ships to modern vessels), a map of Cyprus, babies, a fork, and a silver orange tree (see chapter 9).

While vows or requests can involve anything that is of value in life, they frequently center on concerns of health, both one's own and that of one's family. A wide range of physical and mental problems are brought to the Madonna of the Annunciation at Tinos (and to other shrines elsewhere in Greece) for help. Women's special concern with the health of children is clearly reflected at the shrine, as mothers crawl on hands and knees with small children on their backs, or lead a child dressed in black who is "vowed" (*taméno*). Women also may appeal to the Panayía to conceive a child.

A second important category of vows and requests made to the Madonna at Tinos concerns sailing and the sea. The Panayía's protection over seafarers is attested to by the many votive offerings at the church that depict ships. These range from sailing vessels to steamers to small caïques. Offerings may be made for a safe journey by those who are about to sail, and ships may also be brought to Tinos to be blessed, especially when they are first launched. An old man from the mainland told me of traveling to Tinos during World War I on a navy ship that went to donate a large bell to the church. A friend who does history lectures on a small cruise boat told me that the boat had been taken to Tinos to be blessed before it began its voyages. On such occasions, the icon is carried down to the harbor from the church.

Vows may be made by sailors in the throes of terror and despair, as they appeal to the Panayía to save them. Such vows account for the large number of marine offerings (Florakis calls these *karavákia támata*) that decorate the church. For Florakis, such offerings are sailors' spontaneous responses to the fear and emotion evoked by situations of danger (1982: 69). In this aspect of her aid the Panayía at Tinos represents the island's— and Greeks'—intimate and often hazardous relationship with the sea. In acknowledgment of this, the boats in the harbor are decorated on the major holy days honoring the Panayía and the icon, and it is a navy guard that escorts the icon in procession on August 15.

A vow can be anything one chooses. Although there are conventional things one can do to fulfill a vow—walk barefoot up to the church or on one's knees, light a candle, bring oil or wine or flowers—and although the majority of vows are of such a nature, the vow and its fulfillment are individual matters and can, in theory at least, take any form. Thus there are always individual variations. The more arduous physical vows generally seem to be those of poorer pilgrims, who have only their bodies and suffering to bring as offerings; richer gifts are donated by the more affluent.[30]

One symbolically powerful *táma* is the wearing of black, a color normally reserved for mourning.[31] A child who is *taméno,* for example, may be dressed in black for its pilgrimage, the black clothing removed after the child has been brought before the icon. Women may also wear black for their pilgrimage, changing into everyday clothes and leaving their more somber garb as an offering once the pilgrimage is finished. (I have seen women changing their clothing right behind the icon after the festival of the Dormition on August 15.) Since black is the color of death and mourning (and is usually worn only by adult women, never by children),

8. Gypsy pilgrims with sheep and *lambádhes*

the wearing and shedding of black clothing in this context is a symbolic resurrection and provides a powerful representation of the new life that the Panayía provides. Black places the wearer in a clearly liminal state, which is then shed at the end of the pilgrimage.[32]

Although pilgrimage has been important at the Church of the Annunciation since the finding of its miraculous icon (see chapter 9), the nature of the problems for which pilgrims seek relief has changed somewhat over time. For example, it used to be common for women to loosen their hair as they walked up to the church, an act that has now lost its significance in an age of shorter haircuts (though I have seen this done occasionally by Gypsy women, who still wear their hair long). *Támata* depicting automobiles represent the concern over a relatively recent danger, as do those that depict airplanes. New problems also afflict parents these days. For example, my landlady Marina told me of a recent case of a boy with a drug problem whose mother brought him to the church, hoping the Panayía could help. (The trip was unsuccessful, apparently, as the boy overdosed while he was there.)

One concern that seems to be a constant, however, is illness. The contemporary medical system has not erased this concern, as the man I met at the monastery shows. Not only can medicine not solve all problems, but many Greeks seem to take a pragmatic attitude toward seeking a cure for problems of health—one consults a doctor, but one also prays to the Panayía or a saint (cf. Blum and Blum 1970). The two approaches are by no means incompatible. As the man to whom we spoke at the monastery suggested, all cures are in some sense miracles.

One can see, then, that the shrine is adaptable, or rather, that people adapt the shrine to their changing needs. The contemporary world has not eliminated the need for miracles, though it has changed to some extent the kind of miracles that are required. Part of this adaptability comes from the open-ended nature of requests and vows, and from the fact that requests are by no means automatically granted. One must have faith for miracles to occur. Sometimes a supplicant must spend a long period at the church, or come on a number of consecutive occasions before any improvement takes place. But even if there is no guarantee of help, as the man at the monastery put it, it is nonetheless worth a try.

FULFILLING THE VOW

Once a request has been granted, the vow may not be immediately fulfilled. When I asked people what happens when someone makes a vow but does not carry it out, there seemed to be no definite answer. Nothing happens, one local woman told me. It's just that one *should* do it. She then went on to quote a saying: "To the saint" (*ston áyio*)—that is, she explained, "To the icon [*stin ikóna*] is like to a child" (*íne san sto moró*). In other words, a saint is like a child to whom one has promised something and who will remember and demand it.

My friend Eleni from the village of Falatados commented that it is hard to know when a vow has *not* been carried out. The individual making the vow may not have the money to make a pilgrimage immediately, for example, but may make it later when finances and time allow. One example of this was a girl whose family had moved to Australia. When she was a baby she fell sick, and her parents vowed to bring her to Tinos to be baptized at the church if she got well. The girl recovered, but her parents were not able to carry out their vow for sixteen years. The girl was a young woman when they finally brought her to the church for her baptism.[33] At what point, Eleni asked, could one say that the parents had not fulfilled their vow? In fact, in the end, they *had* carried it out. Similarly, my landlady, Marina, took several years to fulfill her vow to build a little chapel to St. George in her yard. But she continued to speak of it as something she planned to do, and therefore it could not be considered at any point as a vow unfulfilled. (When I visited in the summer of 1990, she had actually finished the building, though it did not yet have an altar and had not had a service performed.)

There are stories, however, of attempts to get out of one's vow through deceit, and these are a different matter. I did not come across any such stories when I was in Tinos, but a man on Lesvos told me the story of his aunt's child who disappeared for two days because the aunt had not kept a vow she had made to Taksiarhis. Thus just as vows may be made on behalf of others, so a saint's wrath at a vow unfulfilled can fall upon those close to the maker of the vow.[34]

What seems to be important is not necessarily whether one fulfills a vow immediately, but rather the nature of one's *intent*. As long as the intent is there, and the vow is made in good faith, the vow cannot be considered unfulfilled. It is only when the person making a vow has the intent to avoid it that retribution follows. And that intent to deceive is difficult to conceal from a saint.

Not everyone who comes to the Church of the Annunciation does so bearing a particular request or seeking to fulfill a vow. Some come either because the church is famous and visiting churches is a pleasurable kind of sightseeing, or they come for the general benefit of visiting a holy place, for "the good of it" (*yia to kaló*). One may also take away some object associated with the shrine, in effect, taking home some of the power of the shrine itself. Such objects might include one of the charms called *philactá* into which are sewn such materials as incense from the church or dried bits of flowers left as offerings; or perhaps some of the dirt by the holy water font in the lower chapel, which represents the dirt of the field in which the icon was found.[35] Pilgrims may also buy literature at a shrine, either works about the shrine and its miracles or general works on religious matters. At the monastery, items made by the nuns are also for sale.[36]

A vow is generally made in the context of daily life, though frequently in a situation of crisis or difficulty within that daily life (the illness of oneself or a family member, failure to conceive a child, or a possible danger in the future). Vows must therefore be understood within their social context (cf. Christian 1981:31–32). Since so many vows concern health, it is not surprising that one sees many women on pilgrimage to Tinos, for it is women who are responsible for both the family's physical and spiritual well-being. For the most part, pilgrims do not go on pilgrimage alone. They go with family members—a husband, sister, children, a child with its grandmother—or with neighbors or friends. Even those who do not accompany the pilgrim physically may nonetheless be brought on the pilgrimage in spirit. A pilgrim's vow or request may be on behalf of another person, especially a family member, or pilgrims may include family or neighbors in their general prayers. And the pilgrims who write names on the slips of paper to be read by the priest during prayer services will frequently include on the slips a number of names of those left back home. A pilgrim can also make a vow on another's behalf, or light a candle, if the person in question cannot come—for example, if she or he is too ill to make the trip. And pilgrims also bring back items for those left behind—holy water or consecrated oil, icons or *philactá,* or perhaps a more secular souvenir. I myself have lighted candles at the church for friends and brought back oil and holy water to people in Athens.

The *táma,* then, is a central feature of pilgrimage, representing the request and the promise of the devotee to a holy personage, as well the response of the divine to this request. A vow in turn centers around a particular material manifestation of the divine—the icon—present in a specific sacred geographical place. In this sense the vow is self-explanatory when given as a reason for pilgrimage. It is expressive both of one's connection to the divine and of one's earthly connections and obligations. A painting in the church's gallery of Tinian artists illustrates this well. The painting shows a woman in black, with an obviously sick child, also in black, reclining across her lap. The woman is looking down at the child with tender concern. The picture is titled simply *To Táma* (The Vow).

PILGRIMAGE, LIMINAL AND OTHERWISE

It is clear that pilgrims to Tinos (and to other shrines in Greece) do not sever, even temporarily, their social bonds, or leave behind the social networks that enmesh them in everyday life. While to some extent pilgrims do experience a "release from mundane structure" (Turner and Turner 1978:34), at the same time they by no means leave this structure behind. Pilgrims are not atoms, stripped of identifying social features and free to connect with other like atoms in the pilgrimage journey. Not only is much of pilgrimage motivated by and carried out in the context of significant social relationships, but also many pilgrims come engrossed in their own acts of devotion, having little involvement with the hundreds of others who may be carrying out their own devotions concurrently, but separately.

This does not mean, however, that pilgrimage to Tinos is devoid of any sense of communitas, as postulated by Turner. If we see such communitas as relative rather than as an absolute condition, and as a potential inherent in the pilgrimage rather than as a defining feature, the concept does offer insight into some of what the observer sees, and the pilgrim experiences, during pilgrimage. In the case of the possessed woman, for example, I observed a number of pilgrims joined together in a common purpose, helping a fellow pilgrim to complete her vow, and collectively defeating the forces of evil as well. On other occasions, however, I witnessed hundreds of pilgrims simultaneously engaged in individual rituals (such as crawling on their hands and knees to the church) with little or no contact among them and little interest exhibited by the pilgrims in what others were doing.

Communitas, then, varies both by occasion and by social group. Particularly dramatic dramas of pain (such as that of the possessed woman) may draw onlookers together as fellow pilgrims identifying with the sufferer. Women especially may stop to watch other women on their knees, sighing "*Panayía mou*" and even wiping away a tear before they move on. On the occasions of major festivals, such dramas increase in number as thousands of pilgrims descend upon the church. The sheer numbers of pilgrims who come at such times, resulting in a large number of pilgrimage "dramas," creates an emotional atmosphere generally absent in "everyday" pilgrimage. Social class may also influence the sense of communitas. Those pilgrims who must sleep in the rooms or courtyard of the church are brought together in a context that erases normal physical structures and places pilgrims in a common situation where communitas may be fostered. Despite this, it is obvious that social difference is not dissolved in pilgrimage. And for the most part, only the poorer pilgrims camp in the churchyard and streets, and thus are separated from the more affluent, who can afford hotels and private rooms. In addition to spatial separation, there is some temporal separation as well. More affluent middle- and upper-class pilgrims may avoid Tinos on such occasions as August 15, preferring instead to come at other, quieter times.

Turner speaks of marginality and liminality as characteristic of the pilgrimage state. Certainly we can see pilgrims performing their vows as being in a liminal ritual state, whether they are crawling on their knees, wearing black, carrying a child, or bringing an offering to the church. And even the observer can see the release from that state experienced by many pilgrims who have completed their devotions in front of the miraculous icon. The women who shed their black clothing behind the icon stand and leave it as an offering shed their burden as well. Nor need one's liminality and release be expressed in any dramatic way. Simply having made a vow places one in a liminal situation, which is relieved only when the vowed pilgrimage is carried out.[37] One day I watched a Greek family from Florida who had come to the church do their *proskínima*, the ordinary *proskínima* that any pilgrim makes. "I feel relieved," the man said in English to his son as they started back down through the street of shops. ("Unfortunately they have made it into a marketplace," he added disapprovingly in Greek, gesturing toward the shops and stands.) A Greek woman from Australia to whom I spoke at the church of St. Rafaíl on Lesvos described to me the psychological release provided by her pilgrimage. The anxiety was lifted from her, she said.

Although liminality is an important dimension of pilgrimage, one might ask to what extent pilgrimage creates liminality and to what extent it tends to draw people who are already liminal in some way. Gypsies, for example, are socially liminal to begin with. Women are another category of pilgrims whose normal social liminality may find a particular expression in the context of pilgrimage (see chapter 10). At the same time, pilgrimage may be a way of trying to overcome liminality, to connect, to identify oneself with the core symbolic structures of one's society. Liminality, like communitas, is not necessarily an inherent feature of pilgrimage to Tinos but is variable, situational, and fluctuating.

A pilgrimage site, then, is formed in complex ways. While the physical locale to which sojourning pilgrims direct their footsteps is the most obvious focus of pilgrimage, and the means by which pilgrimage is most immediately and clearly apprehended, pilgrimage is a concept and a force that exists outside that immediate locale as well. It exists in the power of a shrine's holiness, which may be far-reaching (in this case extending to all Greeks, even when they are on the other side of the world) and long-lasting (whether the long-term effects come from being healed, from having a request granted, or simply from the spiritual well-being that the pilgrimage may generate). The Church of the Annunciation at Tinos has come to form part of many Greeks' religious experience and part of the religious geography of their world (even if they have not actually visited the church). It is a spiritual resource to which believers can turn when the problems and worries of everyday life threaten to overwhelm them, and where they can find relief and answers to their prayers.

THE ANTHROPOLOGIST'S VOW

On August 6, 1988, while back in Tinos for further fieldwork, I attended a baptism at the Church of the Annunciation. The baptism was of the sixteen-year-old girl from Australia (mentioned earlier) whose parents had made a vow when she had fallen ill as a baby that they would baptize her at the Church of the Annunciation if she were made well. Due to the expense and difficulty of the journey, they had not been able to make the trip until the girl was grown. The family was originally from the village of Falatados, and I had met the girl, Vasiliki, a few days earlier at the house of a couple who were related to her family. It was this same couple, Marcos and Eleni, who invited me to the baptism at the church and then suggested that I come up to the village afterward for the baptismal dinner. "How will I get back to town?" I asked, knowing that the last bus from the village left at 5:30 in the afternoon. "Don't worry," Marcos replied confidently, "I'll take care of getting you back." Although I was somewhat concerned by the vagueness of this promise,[38] I was eager to attend the dinner, particularly since such social events were rare during my fieldwork on pilgrimage. Thus the invitation offered not only the opportunity to have closer contact with the baptismal party, but a chance for some company and relaxation as well. So, putting aside my doubts, I rode up to the village with Marcos and Eleni in their truck after the baptism.

It was a lovely evening, cooler up in the village than in the town, and the baptismal party had spread a big table under the trees in the outdoor restaurant on the edge of the village. Although I felt a little awkward as an outsider (I didn't know most of the other members of the party), I reminded myself that I was an invited guest of relatives of the baptismal family and set out to enjoy the evening.

I was a little disappointed, however, in the seating arrangements. I was placed at the end of the table, in a position in which the only people I could talk to easily were Marcos and Eleni. Moreover, Marcos, who had been drinking quite a bit (having begun earlier at a restaurant in town), did much of the talking, making it difficult to hear the conversation at the other end of the table. Thus I was able to catch only scraps of some very interesting discussions elsewhere at the table, including an argument about whether or not the baptism (which differed in several significant ways from a child's baptism) had been done properly.

At about 1:00 A.M. the party broke up and Marcos and Eleni and I went to another village restaurant, which had a band. Eleni and I had already agreed that I would take a taxi to town since Marcos had had so much to drink. I was rather tired by this time and did not wish to drink anymore. Nor did I know the men at whose table we now sat. Marcos, however, was in his element and showed every sign of being able to keep going till dawn. I began to feel a little panicked. My days on the island were limited, the following day was a Sunday (a major pilgrimage day, especially for one-day visitors), and I could see the day being lost to any fieldwork if I did not get back to my apartment soon and get a reasonable night's sleep. Marcos's only response to my concern was further reassurance that he would take care of me.

Had the occasion been a real *paniyíri* of the sort I remembered from my days of fieldwork in the village, there would have been a steady stream of taxis ferrying people from the town and other villages (since at 1:00 A.M. things would just have been getting into full swing). But this was just a Saturday night with a hired band, and besides, as I soon realized, many of those who had come were summer visitors with their own cars or motorbikes.[39] Finally, at around 2:00, I went inside the restaurant to call a taxi from the taxi stand in the main town. There was no answer, and I realized that no one was on duty at that late hour. Marcos kept offering to drive me back (at some unspecified time), but I decided that perhaps I should just give in and agree to an earlier suggestion he had made that I stay at his house for the night. This proved a problem also, however, for it was obvious that Eleni was not at all happy with the idea. Several of their nieces were visiting and there were no extra beds. Marcos's suggestion that I share a bed with Eleni while he went somewhere else was no more eagerly received by her than by me.

I was feeling extremely tired at this point, after eight hours of talking, eating, and drinking. I was also experiencing considerable back pain after sitting for so long in straight-backed village chairs. Finally, it was decided that all three of us—myself, Marcos, and Eleni—would drive to the town and that Marcos would return to the festivities later. I felt bad pulling Marcos away from his fun, and I knew that the other men at the table thought I was being silly (just like a woman, they were probably saying to themselves, dragging a man away from a good time), but I was so worn out at that point that I didn't care. Walking to the truck, I began to cry, telling Eleni that it was the pain in my back that was bothering me, which was true, though not the whole truth.

Marcos is a man who holds his liquor well; his drinking simply intensifies his normal exuberance, the state Greeks call *kéfi,* the high spirits induced on such occasions by alcohol, music, and sociability (see Cowan 1990).[40] In addition, he knows the winding island roads from the village to the town well, having driven them regularly much of his adult life. Therefore I did not really feel apprehensive until we began our descent down the mountainside. At this point I realized he was much more drunk than I had thought. He had obvious difficulty controlling the truck on the narrow roads, even though he proceeded quite slowly, and on several occasions he came sickeningly close to the steep drop-offs on the edge, turning only at the last moment to take the next curve. It did not help my own terror that Eleni surreptitiously crossed herself each time Marcos began his negotiation of a new bend in the road. I did not want to die here, I told myself. Yet I truly feared that I might if we went over the edge and down one of the steep slopes. Without even pausing to think about it, I spontaneously made a mental vow that if I arrived safely in the town, I would light a candle the next day in the church.

Once in the town, Eleni and I both got out of the truck, refusing to drive along the waterfront with Marcos, and we made our way on foot together to my apartment. I offered to put both Marcos and Eleni up for the night, but Eleni had decided to either stay with her daughter (who lived in town) or take a taxi back to the village. Marcos later showed up at my apartment, asking if I knew where Eleni had gone. I could tell him no more than she had told me. He hadn't seen her in the street, he said. Then he left.

It was not until the following Monday that I learned the finale to this little drama. Marcos had returned to the village without Eleni—who had, as I suspected, stayed with her daughter—and had rejoined the party at the restaurant, staying until around 5:00 in the morning. Needless to say, I felt terrible about the whole incident. I had caused trouble for my friends, spoiling Marcos's *gléndi*,[41] placing both of them in jeopardy from Marcos's drunken driving, and in general acting like a silly *kséni* (foreigner). I had also been terribly concerned about Marcos's driving back up to the village alone, which he had been determined to do. While I knew that much of the problem had been caused by Marcos's excessive drinking (which, in retrospect, I realized had grown worse over the years that I have known him), I also blamed myself for having created the situation in the first place.

The next morning (Sunday) I went up to the church before the boats arrived with their crowds of pilgrims and lighted the candle I had vowed.

CHAPTER SIX

The Observer Observed

MY OWN "VOW" reflects a particularly complex, long-term, and even intimate relationship with a certain set of religious practices. As I look back on my earlier fieldwork, I realize that religion was part of my experience of Greek life almost from my first days in the village. This is illustrated by an entry in my journal on August 4, 1969, about two weeks after my husband and I had settled in Falatados. I spent part of this day with some village women, accompanying them to their garden in the countryside. It was a frustrating experience for me as I struggled to carry on a conversation in my fledgling Greek and worried about whether or not I was behaving appropriately. Sitting on the ground with the women and their children, sharing a freshly split watermelon, I sought to grasp something of the "feel" of the lives of these people I had come to "study." Later, in the early evening, as we headed back to the village, I heard the church bells ringing and I was told by one of the women that they were ringing for the dead (*ta nekra*). I had a sudden strange feeling at that moment of the very real existence of these dead.

This moment from my early fieldwork is perhaps the first one in which I *experienced* religion in Greece. But what does such "experience" mean for the anthropologist in the context of fieldwork? In what ways can I use my own experience as someone outside this particular cultural context in order to convey the experience of those within it? Is such a translation even possible? Or should the observer herself simply be effaced without being observed?

EMOTION, OBSERVATION, AND FIELDWORK

In his book *Culture and Truth: The Remaking of Social Analysis,* Renato Rosaldo describes how he came to understand the statement of the Ilongot headhunter that "rage, born of grief, impels him to kill his fellow human beings" (1989:1). After years of seeking to discover a "deeper" explanation of headhunting than that offered by his informants, Rosaldo finally came to understand the force of the headhunter's statement when his own wife, Michelle Rosaldo, died from a fall while they were doing fieldwork together in the Philippines. Shaken by rage as well as grief, Rosaldo was brought to recognize a dimension of emotion that he had failed to discern before—the dimension of anger that can exist within grief. At the same time, he did not equate his anger with that experienced by the Ilongots: "Ilongots' anger and my own overlap, rather like two circles, partially overlaid and partially separate" (1989:10). Separating the angers, Rosaldo points out, are differences in the cultural form that emotion takes and the consequences that result from such differences. (He did not, for example, go headhunting after his wife died.)

On August 17, 1986, I made the following entry in my journal:

> Things that I feel can help me understand the shrine and the people who come to it, to some degree, at least: the pain in my back, the search for & despair of a cure, trying to cope with the idea of a permanent disability, the pain of separation from Ray and wanting to safeguard him and assure his safe travel and our own eventual reunion.
>
> From watching people coming to the shrine—the idea of sacrifice is a very profound one, a transcendence of the self, offering something intimately connected to one's life.

Then on September 15, 1986, after returning to Tinos from a conference:

> Arrived yesterday—finally—left my luggage at the store and went up to the church like a true pilgrim to light three candles: for Margaret, Ray and myself. A strange feeling walking up to the church—a centered-ness, a purpose, a goal once I got off the boat—different from just walking up there with the pilgrims.

And finally, another notation, this one on July 23, 1988, St. Pelayia's day, when the icon is taken up to the monastery and then brought down in procession:

> I stayed [in town at the waterfront] for the return procession of the icon, falling in behind the crowd as the icon proceeded up the main street to the church. How well can one compare one's own feelings in such an event, I wonder, with those of the other participants? Of course there is a whole set of meanings attached to these rituals, not just religious, but social—chatting leisurely with companions as the procession moves up the hill—which I do not share in. At the same time I felt an odd and pleasant sense of community, and even a sense of well-being and catharsis after the event.

REVEALING THE OBSERVER

I opened chapter 4 with a long description of an event, the exorcism of a possessed woman, in which I was an observer, and I described the manner in which I created from this event an "impressionist tale" and the way the event itself served for me as a "revelatory moment." Chapter 5 closed with another story, one in which I was much less an observer, and which also constituted—in its own way–a "revelatory moment." But what, in the end, was "revealed" by these events, and what did my own emotional responses tell me in each case? And do these responses constitute the sort of "overlapping circles" of which Rosaldo speaks?

To begin with, I have used both events to reveal certain patterns and problems of fieldwork: the methods of observation I employed; the opportunism that was a necessary part of observing pilgrimage; my concerns about being intrusive or disruptive in what I felt to be a sensitive situation; the frustration I felt in not having opportunities for deeper relations with pilgrims; my loneliness and my desire for social contact; and the emotional strain generated by fieldwork, which was exacerbated by frequent exhaustion and by chronic pain.

My own patterns of observation are illustrated by the incident of the possessed woman. To some extent these patterns followed the patterns of pilgrimage itself. I did most of my study during the summer months, when pilgrimage is at its peak.[1] The rhythm of pilgrimage was dictated by the arrival of the daily passenger ships (as many as four a day, and sometimes more, during the height of the summer).[2] Disembarkation marked the starting point of this final leg of the pilgrimage, and the beginning point for my own observations as well. I would walk with those pilgrims who went directly to the church.[3] I would note what these pilgrims did along their route, what sort of groups they traveled with (singly, with children, as couples, groups of women), what they stopped to purchase, and what they did as they approached and entered the church. I would talk to individual pilgrims as the opportunity arose. I often stayed at the church for one of the prayer services, which were timed to coincide with the arrival of the boats. Sometimes I would "hang out" just outside the church, on the balcony or in the courtyard, watching the various activities, listening to conversations, and speaking to people who were waiting there.

I also visited the church at quieter periods (for example, in the morning before the boats arrived), to talk to church employees, to observe the generally more leisurely activities of the pilgrims who came at such times, and to study the interior of the church. On major holidays, the church would be busy throughout the day (not just when the boats arrived) and so my interactions with and observations of the pilgrims were more continuous. I also talked with local residents about pilgrimage. Since many of the townspeople with whom I interacted were merchants, and our interactions took place in their shops, I often found myself initiating a conversation through questions about religious objects, and then, in the end, buying something as well. And on Pelayia's saint's day as well as nonholy days I visited the monastery where the nun Pelayia had lived.

As I worked I developed a series of questions about pilgrimage, vows, attitudes, and beliefs, to which I sought answers through observations and questions. But I often found myself in the course of my fieldwork unable to obtain clear answers to certain of the questions I had formulated. Sometimes pilgrims were simply unwilling to talk to me. This unwillingness, in most cases, was probably due less to my not being Greek than it was my being perceived as an educated non-pilgrim. For example, one day early in my fieldwork I approached a group of women camped in the churchyard and asked if I might take their picture. I asked as a matter of courtesy, not thinking they would mind. But the women were very suspicious and uncooperative. Was I a journalist, they wanted to know. Why did I want their pictures? I tried to explain that I was an American professor doing a book on pilgrimage to Tinos, but they refused me permission to photograph. Later I realized that in recent years pilgrimage to Tinos has become something of a media event, and that some pilgrims feel defensive about their pilgrimage, sensing that it is regarded as quaint or backward by educated urbanites (a type exemplified by journalists).[4]

Some pilgrims were quite willing to strike up a conversation with me and to exchange information. But even here I often had difficulty getting answers to my questions about pilgrimage and vows (though pilgrims were happy to provide such personal information as where they were from, who their families were, and who were the people with whom they were traveling). Sometimes I felt quite frustrated at the thought that people around me knew everything I wanted to know, but I couldn't tap that knowledge.

Part of my difficulty can be attributed to the fact that I was working for the most part with a transitory population, with whom it was difficult to develop rapport or engage in extended conversations.[5] My own personality also played a role—I find it difficult to begin conversations with complete strangers and so every day of working with pilgrims was a struggle.[6] But I came to realize that the difficulty I was experiencing went beyond the obvious factors of my foreignness and the pilgrims' transitoriness. The major problem with my questions was that the pilgrims to whom I spoke did not necessarily "know" in the sense in which I wanted to know. "Why did you come here?" I would ask. "I have a vow" would be the reply. "Why is she on her knees?" I would ask the companion of a woman crawling up to the church. "She has a vow," the companion would say. Much of the time I could get no further than that, and additional questions were often met with a shrug.

I was looking for the essence of what I was observing in words, for it was through words that I would explain my observations not only to myself but also to others. Yet I came to realize that this "verbocentric" emphasis was leading me astray and contributing to my frustration. It was leading me to intellectualize and rationalize something that was neither intellectual nor rational. I was looking for the essence of what I wanted to learn in words, in what people would *tell* me, and giving lesser attention to what I saw and felt. Beyond this, like Rosaldo's refusing to accept the simple force of the headhunter's statement that he hunted because of rage born of grief, I refused to accept the simple and self-sufficient force of the statement "I have a vow."

Here I think is where my own experience of making a vow, unpremeditated, spontaneous, born in a very Malinowskian fashion from my own intense fear and my own desire to survive, helped lead me to greater understanding of this dimension of pilgrimage. A vow is, in this respect at least, a very simple and straightforward thing. Even I—with only an outsider's experience of the church and no belief in the power of saints and icons—even I might make one. Moreover, once I had made it, and reached my destination safely, I would not have dreamed of not fulfilling it. Had anyone asked me why I was going to the church that Sunday morning, and had I replied, "I have a vow," the understanding would have been perfect between us—or so at least we might have assumed. More accurately, our understanding would have been like Rosaldo's "overlapping circles," sharing an emotional core that is the center of a vow but surrounding that core with a quite different set of cultural understandings. For the Greek pilgrim, the vow is embedded in a set of cultural beliefs and practices that precipitate the vow and give it meaning, whereas my own vow was generated by proximity to these beliefs and practices resulting from my work as an anthropologist, by a kind of fieldworker's *habitus*.

Despite these differences, my making of the vow was a "revelatory moment" for me. Since many of the religious activities I sought to understand had a taken-for-granted nature for those involved, and since "understanding" of these activities was experienced, and "meaning" frequently was emotional, my own experiences as I observed (and even to some extent participated in) pilgrimage activities and my own emotional responses became crucial to me in my work. Eventually I even learned (though not with a complete cessation of my frustration) to take my lack of success in obtaining satisfactory verbal responses as itself a part of my "data."

I have spoken of "emotion" as if the term referred to only the dramatic and painful, the serious or the sad. But there is another element to pilgrimage, indeed to religion generally, that should not be overlooked in Greece—religious activities are often enjoyable, even fun. I have described how pilgrims, especially those who come with an organized group, may visit such nonreligious sites as Delos and Mykonos, and go swimming and shopping in addition to visiting the church. Although as an observer with stricter notions of the separation between the sacred and the profane I made a distinction between what were for me two types of activities, I do not know that such a distinction would necessarily be made by most of the pilgrims. The religious, the social, and the recreational are closely bound in Greek life. A saint's day celebration, for example, may involve church services; visiting from house to house to share food and drink; and music, socializing, and dancing at tavernas in the evening. While some individuals may emphasize one part over the other, all are inter-twined in the notion of a saint's day or *paniyíri*.[7]

Similarly, a trip to Tinos may be in the nature of an excursion for many who come. Religious at its base, it is nonetheless recreational as well. In fact, the religious dimension, though serious, is also recreational (cf. Nolan and Nolan 1989). Pilgrims enjoy the spectacle of a procession, the impressive display of religious artifacts in the church, the services, and the general atmosphere of the occasion. And although local people may criticize those who come to Tinos only for an excursion, islanders may also be caught up in the enjoyment of events. For example, on the day of St. Pelayia, a holy day with significant local dimensions, I followed the procession of the icon through the town after it was brought back from the monastery. It was accompanied by flaming torches as it was carried along the waterfront in the dusk, and then up the hill toward the church. "Pretty, isn't it," commented my landlady, Marina, as she came out of her store to watch the procession, while I sought to capture the beauty of the moment on film in the rapidly fading light.

Other shopkeepers emerged from their stores as the procession made its way up the hill. One young woman from a produce stand told the woman next to her to watch her child and she ran, laughing, into the street to duck under the icon. Later I asked her why she had done it. She shrugged, smiling, and said it had just seemed like a good thing to do.

I have spoken of the dramatic atmosphere of pilgrimage, and of the emotions out of which a vow may be born. But the other side of the coin is pilgrimage's sometimes startling taken-for-granted quality. Shopkeepers along the main road to the church, for example, will offer matter-of-fact advice to the pilgrim on her knees as to the best way to get around parked cars, suggest that the pilgrim use some sort of knee pad, and even offer water, as if the activity they are witnessing is a perfectly normal one— which in a sense it is, at least for them. I was struck by this assumption of normalcy when I was looking at some *támata* outside a store one day. The owner came out and asked if I wanted a *táma*. I asked if it were possible to offer a *táma* for a friend who was ill (a question I had been asking people that day, with a particular Athenian friend in mind), and he said yes. I then asked if she herself would have to come later, and he said no, I could offer the *táma* for her. He then went on to say that I needed a *táma* with a picture of a woman, and that I should make the sign of the cross with it over the icon three times and then put it in the box next to the icon. He then informed me that he also had *lambádhes* in case I needed some later. The conversation could not have been more matter-of-fact had we been discussing vegetables for my supper instead of my religious needs. Though I was obviously a foreigner, the shopkeeper took my needs and purpose for granted as completely normal, requiring neither explanation nor justification.

RELIGION AND THE CHANGING OBSERVER

In order to understand my particular responses to pilgrimage and the activities surrounding it, I needed to sort out my own feelings about religion, and particularly my feelings about the religion I was observing. As I noted earlier, all observers are positioned, but in multiple and sometimes contradictory and inconsistent ways. My own positioning includes being an anthropologist in a postmodern world, being a Westerner studying Europe, and being a woman. In addition, my age, personal suffering, and certain aspects of biography have also placed me in my relationship to my subject and created a certain kind of observer. Positioning is not static, of course. Among other things that my work at the Church of the Annunciation led me to confront was why and how my own views of Greek Orthodox religion had changed over the years and why my attitude toward the Church of the Annunciation had moved from one of relative indifference to making this same church the focus of my later research (see Dubisch 1988). These changes were the consequence of changes in my own life, my experiences with religion in Greece and elsewhere, and changes in my own thinking as an anthropologist (in turn related to changes in the discipline itself).

In order to grasp the dimensions of such change consider the following excerpt from my diary, from December 1, 1969, during my first period of fieldwork:

> Memorial service today for the husband of the woman in Vlasados [a nearby village], held in the little church by the cemetery. Had the feeling I have every now and then that I don't really like this religion, despite its beautiful trappings. The music seemed grating today, the priest's voice pompous and droning, the humble attitudes of the people there irritating.

Contrast this with the following from my more recent fieldwork at the Church of the Annunciation, written on July 23, 1988, after I had attended some of the celebrations of the holy day of St. Pelayia. (On this day, the icon is carried at an early hour from the Church of the Annunciation up to the monastery. I had arisen before dawn to arrive at the church.)

Impressions: a chilly dawn with a sharp wind, the warm breath of the church wafting from the doorways, a compound of incense, candle flames, and body heat.

I have come to like the complexity and liveliness of the service. There is always something happening—people coming & going, filing in front of the icon, going to the other icons, etc.—in addition to the service itself. People cross themselves, kneel, hum or sing along with parts of the service. I think most other religious services would seem dull to me.

(As I will show, it is significant that the above observation was recorded not in a personal diary but in my general fieldnotes.)

Despite a strong interest in religion, I had little in my personal experience that equipped me to understand religion when I first did fieldwork in Greece. I had been raised with minimal religious instruction, in a vague sort of Protestantism that involved no regular churchgoing. The only holy days celebrated in my family were Christmas and Easter, and only the former had any religious overtones. Either in spite of or because of this lack of religious exposure, I was (at least as I remember) interested in religion (particularly its mystical aspects) from a fairly early age. I was especially interested in religious ritual (probably one of the reasons why I found Protestantism relatively unappealing). When I went to graduate school, one of the main interests I listed in my application was religion (even though this was not the topic of my first fieldwork). Ironically, my most prolonged exposure to religion, which came in early adulthood, was to two faiths quite alien to my earliest religious instruction—Judaism (to which I converted shortly after my marriage in 1968) and Greek Orthodoxy (to which I was exposed during fieldwork). I liked Judaism for its ethics and its rituals. I eventually came to like Orthodoxy for the richness of its churches and the emotional appeal of its liturgy.

Age had been another factor in my changing relationship to religion. Renée Hirschon has suggested that in Greece an individual's relationship to religion varies with the life cycle. Older people, seen as already closer to the hereafter, are, and are expected to be, more involved with religion than the young (Hirschon 1983). A similar phenomenon may be observed in the United States as well, and may explain why many "baby boomers" who, once they had families to raise, began to return to church. Certainly my own understanding of the reasons people turn to religion has been enhanced by the experiences I have had over the twenty years since I first did fieldwork.

When I first did fieldwork in 1969–70, however, I was a different person, positioned differently with respect to my subject matter (and working in a different world as well). As the excerpt from my journal of this

period indicates, I was not entirely comfortable with the Orthodox religion. Part of my discomfort probably stemmed from my own lack of
religious background. Agar speaks of the "traditions" involved in the ethnographic encounter: "Ethnographies emerge out of a relationship among
the traditions of ethnographer, group, and intended audience" (1986:19).
For the ethnographer in particular, traditions provide "resources available to make sense out of experience" (1986:18). In my case, the only
religious tradition that could serve as such a resource was Judaism, and
particularly Jewish rituals, but this religion was so new to me that it could
hardly be said to be a personal tradition. I had little experience of how to
be religious. Hence my discomfort with (despite my interest in) the rituals
of the Greek Orthodox church.

It was this discomfort, perhaps, that partially explains my general neglect of the Church of the Annunciation during that first period of fieldwork. I was not "listening" to what islanders said about the shrine and its
importance.[8] In part my failure here was a consequence of my own cultural positioning. At Tinos I observed very public and very emotional
manifestations of religiosity antithetical to my own (vaguely Protestant)
middle-class American background. In addition, pilgrimage frequently
involves supplication, again often of an emotional and public sort, which
is antithetical to my society's notions of self and dignity (as reflected in
my journal comment on "humble attitudes"). And finally, Orthodox religion involves many material objects, suggesting superstition and even
idolatry to an observer raised with Protestant values. All of these elements
are particularly "embarrassing" in a religion that is supposedly Christian
and in a society that is viewed by many Westerners as the progenitor of
Western culture. Hence Orthodoxy has often engendered negative feelings
in foreigners.

Such attitudes were well expressed by an American woman who owned
a shop in Tinos. In a conversation I had with her one day she stated her
disapproval of all the women who ascended to the church on their knees.
She didn't see the point of it, she told me. It was all too emotional. While
acknowledging that religion shouldn't be all intellectual, she felt that it
shouldn't be all emotional either. She went on to say that she thought that
Greeks were not really deeply religious. They performed lots of religious
acts such as making the sign of the cross, but then would turn around and
cheat their neighbors. Although I certainly did not share this woman's
opinion, her comments reflect a set of attitudes about religion typical of at
least certain segments of my own society, a set of attitudes that in both
subtle and not-so-subtle ways had affected my own reactions to religion
during my fieldwork in Greece.

One might say that I brought enough of a religious tradition to my

work to make me uncomfortable with certain features of Greek Orthodoxy, but not enough to give me guidelines on how to behave in a religious context or to provide a field of contrasts to sharpen my vision. I
often took things for granted in Greek Orthodoxy that those with a more
explicit religious upbringing might have found unusual or problematic.
The puzzlement of my British friend about the number of churches on
Tinos, for example, a puzzlement I had never experienced myself, led to
my thinking more deeply about what a church meant in the Orthodox
tradition. My friend Ray, who was raised Catholic, was startled, and even
shocked, to see Greek worshipers splashing themselves with holy water
and eating consecrated bread (as well as carrying it from the church and
passing it to their friends). His reactions made me reflect on the "homey"
nature of Greek religion and on the familiarity and ease exhibited by its
devotees in many Orthodox rituals and practices. Thus it was often more
through the eyes of friends rather than through my own that I became
aware of religious difference.

THE OBSERVER "DOING"

When I came back to Tinos in 1986 to study pilgrimage, I was obviously
placing religion at the forefront of my attention. I had come to terms with
some of the problems discussed above and had done considerably more
thinking about religion generally (aided in part by years of teaching an
undergraduate course in the anthropology of religion).[9] However, when I
began my research I was confronted with a very practical problem—what
should I actually *do* at a church? This was something I had never worked
out satisfactorily in previous fieldwork, but it became especially important in my work on pilgrimage since I would be spending considerable
time in church. I did not feel comfortable entering a church as a tourist,
that is, as someone who had simply come to view an interesting sight (as I
saw other foreigners do). But what was I, not only non-Orthodox but a
professed non-Christian, to do? Should I kiss the icons? Should I make
the sign of the cross? The first was difficult because, like genuflection, it
was antithetical to my Western, and particularly American, notions of self
and dignity. The second seemed inappropriate given my postmarital conversion to Judaism. At the same time, I wished to both blend in and show
respect.[10]

I eventually arrived at a compromise I have seen other non-Orthodox
foreigners familiar with Greece arrive at as well: upon entering a church I
put money in the offering box and light a candle.[11] The lighting of the
candle is an almost generic symbolic act (and found in Judaism as well as
Christianity) and it satisfied my desire to perform an appropriate ritual
without forcing a meaning on such a ritual that violated my own faith (or

lack of faith). In addition, from a practical anthropological point of view, my simple ritual act moved me more "inside," for a Greek always *does* something in a church; to not do anything marks one off as a foreigner who is not connecting appropriately with the surroundings. Once I had performed this act, I could move freely about the church as I wished, and as I saw Greeks doing, examining the other icons and the offerings, standing and listening to services, or taking photographs. Lighting a candle thus provided "passage" into the church and allowed me to blend with the worshipers and neither stand out nor give offense.[12]

But my relationship to the church and the religion it represents was not so simply resolved by adopting a satisfactory ritual behavior. Fieldwork at the church was an emotional experience. It is difficult, for example, to watch a woman crawl up the stairs to the church on her stomach, bearing her totally paralyzed daughter on her back, making her agonizing way to the icon and crying to the Panayía for her aid and not be profoundly moved. The tearful prayers of pilgrims at the icon, the shouts of retarded children, the sight of badly crippled supplicants making their way up the stairs to the church all add to the emotional atmosphere. Indeed being moved by the pain of others is one of the experiences of pilgrimage. But the emotionality in my work was due not only to the experience of watching people in need and in pain, but also to the rituals I attended at the church. There were times when I was caught up in the beauty of the service and even had to remind myself to watch what the people around me were doing. It was not simply the liturgy itself that created this effect, but also the involvement of those around me, which drew me into the community of ritual and faith. At one point, for example, during prayer services, when the priest emerged from behind the altar to cense the congregation and the icons, he swung the censer directly toward me as I stood watching. This act seemed symbolically to include me in the community of those joined together by the fragrant clouds of incense floating through the church.[13]

These rituals, over time and through fieldwork, became part of my own history, my own memories, so that they are—as experiences—now part of my own identity. I would not argue, however, that the familiarity that such occasions acquired for me was the same as it would be for a Greek Orthodox pilgrim. Rather, I see it once again as part of Rosaldo's "overlapping circles."

Another area in which I had to work out an accommodation between my own role as an observer and the nature of what I was observing was photography. Taking photographs was an important part of my fieldwork, especially since the material and visual not only were striking elements of pilgrimage but also came to represent a significant part of my understanding of religious ritual. At the same time, the camera is not a neutral device. Not only are there pilgrims who resent having their picture taken (as my earlier example of the women in the church courtyard illustrates), but the possession of the camera marks one as an observer and an outsider in the context of pilgrimage. This does not mean that the Greeks who come to the church never bring cameras. Many do, and take pictures both inside and outside the church. But the kind of camera I usually carried (a Nikon with a zoom lens) was not the sort used by most pilgrims (and was probably part of the reason I was sometimes taken for a journalist), and I often photographed objects and events that would not be photographed by the pilgrims themselves.

The camera creates a peculiar relationship to one's surroundings.[14] It is a distancing device, not only placing a physical object between the observer and observed but also clearly turning what is observed into an object. Hence I was sensitive about taking obvious pictures of individual pilgrims, even when they were intent on their vows and clearly oblivious to anything else. (The Gypsies were the only pilgrims who chose to be actors—rather than passive objects—in the photographer/photographed relationship, insisting on posing for me when they saw I had a camera in my hand.) The camera also shapes what one chooses to see, for it seeks out what is "photogenic," that is, the striking and different, and often passes over what is more mundane. I frequently had to work to get my camera to follow my own experience, that is, to focus on what I saw without the camera, and I sometimes made lists of what I wished to photograph so that I would have a more complete visual "record" of my experience.

While ironically the camera has allowed me, through my extensive selection of slides, to portray much more vividly the phenomenon of pilgrimage to members of my own society, there is no question that, to some extent, the camera came between me and what I was studying. Thus I was torn between my participation in two different worlds—the world "back home," in which I would be making presentations about my research, and the world of pilgrimage, which absorbed me while I was in Greece. The following excerpts from my journal illustrate this ambivalence about the camera. The first is from July 23, 1988, the day of St. Pelayia:

> . . . set my alarm for 5:30 so I could be up for the early service and procession. I slept restlessly, and of course awoke well before the alarm. I went up to the church and stood just outside the doorway behind the icon for the service. When I saw them pick up the icon, I hurried down the steps, and had just begun to take pictures, when the battery on the camera gave out. I was upset not only because I had some good shots lined up, but also because with the new lens [a zoom], they were shots of a sort I hadn't been able to get before. On the other hand, I wasn't as upset as I might have been since I had just been thinking

that sometimes the camera gets in the way of both participating and observing. So I simply became a participant, falling in with the crowds trailing behind the icon, following it down the hill and along the waterfront.

And from August 16, 1986, following the Day of the Dormition:

> . . . taking photographs was also a problem—on the one hand, there were so many things I wanted to document photographically (in addition to photographs it was just too hard to pass up) but I felt later that my photography perhaps got in the way of my observations.

WHO IS THE OBSERVER?

On August 10, 1988, I made a "pilgrimage" of my own to the village of Falatados, site of my first fieldwork. The object of my journey was twofold: to visit the village cemetery in order to take pictures there for a paper I was working on about the changing material markers of death, and to locate the bones of my former landlady, Vasiliki, who had died prior to my return to the island in 1986. Thus in this small journey the "personal" and the "professional" were intertwined.

Burial customs in Greece vary by region, but they often involve rites of "secondary burial," that is, the disinterment and redisposal of the bones of the deceased after a specified period (on Tinos, after three years).[15] I knew that in the village the bones were placed in boxes in an ossuary in the church next to the cemetery, and it was this church that was my destination.

It was midafternoon, and the whitewashed lanes were deserted as I made my way to the edge of the village where the cemetery stood. Once there, I found myself faced with a wealth of visual information. Not only was I able to take more systematic and complete photographs of the cemetery than I had during my original fieldwork, but I also found interesting changes had occurred since that fieldwork, both outside, in the cemetery, and inside, in the ossuary. Inside, for example, I noted that not only were many of the boxes for the bones of the recently deceased much more elaborate than the simple wooden boxes that had held the bones in the past, but also marble markers had been built inside the ossuary to honor the memory of certain individuals (replacing the temporary markers erected at the gravesite), and there were flowers, candles, and other offerings.[16] I photographed a number of these markers and offerings, pausing every now and then when, sadly, I recognized the name of someone I had known on one of the boxes. I could not find the box with Vasiliki's bones, however, and I scanned the floor-to-ceiling stacks of boxes, looking for it. I knew that she had died in Athens (after a sudden, brief bout with cancer), but I had been told that her bones had been brought to the village after the mourning period.

Finally I found her box—a simple, almost shabby, tin affair, with a tiny, barely recognizable photograph attached and her name written in faded ink. I felt a little indignant that her bones had been shelved in such a mean container. I also felt very strange standing there staring at that little box, knowing that the bones that lay inside belonged to someone to whom I had been very attached, and who had played an important role in my life in the village. I realized that this was an experience I would never duplicate in my own society. One might visit a gravesite, but one would not visit the bones of a departed one. What was stranger still, however, was to realize that, although I had lost several relatives who were quite dear to me (including all of my grandparents), I had never visited the gravesite of any one of them. It was odd to experience in another cultural setting something I had never had the opportunity to experience in my own. As I lit a candle to place in the candelabrum in honor of my dear friend's memory, I wondered, Who am I?[17]

I seemed to be a ghost, I think, to the woman rounding the corner to the back of the church as I left the ossuary. She stopped, startled, her hand to her heart as I emerged into the cemetery. I apologized and left the churchyard, heading back into the village. As I made my way back through the narrow village streets I had the oddly mingled sense of both belonging and not belonging. To the woman at the cemetery, I was a stranger who startled her. Yet I had not been at the cemetery simply as a tourist or anthropologist, a mere observer. I had been there "doing" something as well.

Later that afternoon, I dropped by Vasiliki's old house, having been told that her husband, Mihalis, would be there. I was greeted by Vasiliki's son and daughter-in-law, who had come for a summer visit. We sat around a table with the widower, catching up on news. As we talked, Mihalis started to become agitated, and finally tears began streaming down his face. Our reminiscences had reminded him of better days, his daughter-in-law explained, when my husband and I had lived in the village, his wife had been alive, and we had good times together. It was with a good deal of emotion that I embraced Mihalis as I left, both of us crying. I wondered if I would ever see him again.

Later, as I headed back to town on the bus, I thought of the village I was leaving behind, of the people I had known there who were now dead, of the way the village had become depopulated in the years since I had lived there and how its older way of life was dying as it became more and more a place of summer homes for now-urban villagers. I thought particularly of Vasiliki's house, once so well kept, with a flourishing garden, now shabby and neglected, and of the son's plans to restore it in "authentic" village style (not like the villagers themselves were doing, he informed me, a trace of disdain in his voice). And I wondered about my own life, and how, in ways that in retrospect seemed as much chance as design, it had somehow been intertwined with these people and this place for so many of my adult years.

Fieldwork poses a variety of challenges to identity, and numerous other anthropologists have reported moments such as I have just described, moments of wondering "Who am I?" At such times the line between observer and observed grows thin, blurs, and occasionally disappears (see Wengle 1988). For me, the long period of my life occupied by my association with Greece and especially with Tinos (virtually all of my adult life, beginning with my first fieldwork in 1969–70) has added to the confusion. And familiarity with the place where I am "conducting research" eventually makes observation not easier, but more difficult, not only because of emotional attachments of the sort I have just described, but also because what was once unfamiliar, exotic, and interesting can easily become routine.

Thus I was taken off guard when I returned to Tinos in the summer of 1988 and ascended to the church for services on the eve of St. Pelayia's day. Although the crowds were there, and although I had timed my arrival for this event, I found myself unable to take an interest in what was going on. I was not only unable to really "see" things, but I found myself, quite simply, bored. Though fortunately this boredom abated during my stay, I realized that if I were to carry out further research on pilgrimage, I would have to find a means of creating a sense of "difference" to make myself aware of and interested in what I was doing. (For example, I sought to overcome this "overfamiliarity" on my next trip to Greece by visiting some other pilgrimage sites.)[18]

In situations such as making a vow, lighting a candle for friends, going to pay my respects to my landlady's bones, getting caught up in the rhythm of pilgrimage, and even becoming bored, I have blurred the line between observer and observed. This is worrisome, and even perhaps guilt inducing. Have I ceased to be an anthropologist? Or, worse perhaps, am I simply playing games, playing at the culture I have come to observe, clumsily donning a kind of behavioral "native dress"? Yet fitting in is not mere "play" but a response to our surroundings and to the pressures, whether overt or subtle, placed on our behavior by those with whom we are interacting. This response has a "practical" dimension for the anthropologist —we want to fit into our surroundings so that our work of observing will be easier. It also has a psychological dimension in that the approval of those around us is satisfying and makes us feel competent in the culture (cf. Kondo 1990). Through such "secondary identification" we respond to the challenge to identity posed by fieldwork (Wengle 1988:32–33). Under such circumstances not only does the question "Who am I?" become particularly acute, but the very notion of a "self" as a consistent, "inner" being is called into doubt (Kondo 1990). If the inner person is a cultural person rather than an essence separate from the outside "objective" world, then that inner person, that "self," must be to some extent affected by whatever outer world we find ourselves in and by the way we behave in order to fit into that world. In that sense, we are not one self but many overlapping and sometimes inconsistent ones. Although I do not become a Greek when I am in Greece, perhaps I have a "Greek self," manifesting itself more strongly when I am in a context in which that self has been shaped and where it is reinforced, leading me to such acts as making a spontaneous vow and crossing myself without thinking during a service in the church.[19]

Part of the reason such problems loom large for us may stem from our anthropological dichotomies. The very phrase "participant observation" implies a balancing act. Use of the two terms suggests that while both activities are part of fieldwork, they are nonetheless separate. Observing, implicitly, requires (or perhaps *is*) separation, and implies a self that is and can be kept separate from what is observed. It is in part because of this that the issue of emotion becomes so complex and problematic. Emotion is involvement, hence not separation, hence not observing. These anthropological dichotomies have been the source of some of my own struggles and doubts during fieldwork and in the analysis of my fieldwork. Once I began to include my own emotions as part of my observing, and as a vehicle toward understanding (and not simply as separate, private, to be acknowledged only in a secret journal), then I could begin to place the kinds of experiences I have been describing in perspective and make use of them. At the same time I can avoid the objectification of self that occurs through divorcing these emotions from myself and from the personal meaning they might have for me. This has required, among other things, rethinking anthropological writing.

This brings us back to the "impressionist tale."

Telling Tales

The personal reactions of the anthropologist to the fieldwork situation— emotions, frustrations, idiosyncratic daily experiences—are conventionally supposed to be recorded in a daily journal or diary. Such reactions, we are advised as graduate students, are to be kept separate from our recording of "objective" data—from that part of our writing we call "fieldnotes." The diary is personal. We may never expose its contents to others' gaze. (Or perhaps, as with Malinowski's diary, our diaries will be revealed only upon our death.) In the diary we can find an outlet for the emotions (anger, fear, disgust, despair—as well as joy and exhilaration) that presumably should not color our final, objective report of our work.

Fieldnotes, on the other hand, are ideally something one should be able to pass on to other anthropologists. Fieldnotes are presumably a check on one's analysis of the material collected during fieldwork, as well as a potential source of data for others. I used to feel guilty about my fieldnotes, large portions of which other anthropologists would find it difficult if not impossible to use. For example, many of my earlier fieldnotes from the village contain initials for names,[20] and make reference to incidents that would be hard to piece together into a larger picture without my own background knowledge of the people involved and my own memory as "glue."

Eventually I realized, however, that this ideal of "fieldnotes" may be something of a myth in anthropology.[21] I began to realize this when I started going back to my earlier fieldnotes and found myself feeling frustrated at what I found—or rather, at what I didn't find. Instead of providing me with a wonderful storehouse of data that I could later reexamine in the light of new ideas, my fieldnotes represented (naturally enough) the interests and understandings I had at the time I lived in the village—that is, my interests and understandings as a graduate student in the late sixties—and my view at the time of what constituted the proper sort of "data" that an anthropologist should collect (cf. Ottenberg 1990:153). I do not mean to say my notes are now totally useless; indeed they are not. But neither do they provide me with a rich store of material crying out for reanalysis. More frustrating than this, however, was the dryness of these notes. I wished—too late—that I had put more of myself into them, that I had described my feelings and activities as part of the recording process. As a consequence, I have found myself turning more and more often to my diary as a source of information from that past fieldwork period.

In my more recent fieldwork, I continued to keep a journal, separate from fieldnotes. Among other things, this journal provides me with a temporal record of my activities. But the nature of my fieldnotes has changed considerably. Some of these notes are still structured as pieces of "information," but I have also broken down the boundaries that separate one kind of recording from another. Thus on the one hand I have taken to writing more of my observations in a narrative style, linking events, using descriptive language to evoke the sensual aspects of what I have observed, and recording my own feelings. On the other hand, I have also taken to writing analytic pieces as part of my fieldnotes, breaking down the other significant separation that is supposed to characterize such work—that between "data" and "analysis" or "theory." In writing this book, I came to wish I had carried this breakdown further. Even when working with this more recent material it is sometimes difficult to put together my observations and my reactions to what I was observing.

In the end, my aim (as I see it now, though only partially realized) was

to overcome the schizophrenia often induced by anthropological fieldwork and by the ways in which, implicitly or explicitly, many of us have
been taught about how it should be done.[22] This schizophrenia results
from the threefold separation I have just mentioned: on the one hand the
separation of "objective" gathering of data from the emotions that inform
and are generated by such collection, and on the other hand the separation of "objective" data collecting from the theories that in fact not only
determine what is perceived as data but perpetuate the very idea of "objectivity." These separations have only recently come to be challenged in
some of the new, "experimental" ethnographic writing in which personal
narrative, more or less "conventional" anthropological description, and
theoretical analysis form a rich and mutually nurturing mix. At the same
time, we still do not know how the fieldnotes are written upon which
such ethnographies presumably are based.[23]

Even my new (and still evolving) manner of writing during the process
of fieldwork does not provide me with all that I need in order to write an
account such as I am undertaking here. My impressionist tale is a case in
point. Earlier, I stated that in the version of the possessed woman's drama
written for this book I had included some of my own reactions and
concerns "as best I can remember." The day after the events occurred I
wrote as complete an account as I could of all that I had observed, putting
it in narrative form, adding details at the end (and later) as I remembered
them. (I also had jotted down a few things immediately after the event as
aids to memory; cf. Ottenberg 1990.) In addition, I recorded some of my
feelings about the excitement of the event in my diary. When I wrote the
first paper drawing on the event (about two and a half months later),
some further details came to mind as I began to tie my tale into my
paper's theme (in turn tied to the theme of the session in which it was
being presented). But other parts of the narrative had not been written
before I set them down on these pages, and they came to mind only in the
entirely new context created by the writing of this book.[24] It is in the
doing, and the thinking about doing, of this tale that I have come to
realize the truth of Van Maanen's description of fieldwork: "Fieldwork, at
its core, is a long and social process of coming to terms with a culture. It
is a process that begins before one enters the field and continues long after
one leaves it. The working out of understandings may be symbolized by
fieldnotes, but the intellectual activities that support such understandings
are unlikely to be found in daily records. The great dependency commonly claimed to exist between fieldnotes and fieldworkers is not and
cannot be so very great after all" (Van Maanen 1988:118; cf. Kondo
1990).[25]

My impressionist tale of the possessed woman is a particular kind of
ethnographic genre, contrasting on the one hand with realist tales, and on

the other hand with what Van Maanen calls confessional tales. If ethnography "rests on the peculiar practice of representing the social reality of others through the analysis of one's own experience in the world of these others" (1988:ix), and its method on the "bedrock assumption that 'experience' underlies all understanding of social life" (1988:3), then the impressionist tale, which focuses not just on what has been "objectively" observed (the realist tale) or upon the observer (the confessional tale), is particularly suitable for the ethnographic task. It places the ethnographer in the scene she is observing and shows the mutual dependency of observer and observed, constituting what Tedlock (1991) has called a "narrative ethnography." Since one of the aims of my own ethnography is never to let the observed and the observing drift too far apart, it seemed appropriate to open my discussion of pilgrimage with an impressionist tale.

As recent critiques of anthropological writing have made clear, what an ethnography seeks to convey cannot be understood separately from the conventions of narrative used to convey it. The language in which we write fieldwork is not a transparent one, revealing ethnographic "truth" through a simple and straightforward clarity of words. An awareness of modes of writing, including the ones I myself am using, is a necessary part of ethnographic analysis. Moreover, "cultural description . . . can not erase the presence of and role played by emotion, presupposition, and artistry in ethnography" (Van Maanen 1988:12). One of the points I have sought to make about religion in Greece generally, and pilgrimage to the Church of the Annunciation on Tinos in particular, is that religion must be seen, at least in large part, as experiential and emotional, its essence apprehended sensually, and not always susceptible to being conveyed in words. In order to overcome the paradox that I must, however, communicate this essence in words, an impressionist tale and other modes of writing that link my own experiences and emotions to the rituals and other activities I observed have been interwoven with more conventional ethnographic description and analysis.

But a single tale, no matter how dramatic or revealing, cannot tell all. And a pilgrimage site contains many tales—indeed such tales in important ways create the pilgrimage site. As Turner and Turner suggest, "Every pilgrimage has a local and a regional history; responds more or less sensitively to a national history; and especially in the case of the most important pilgrimages, is shaped and colored by international, even world history" (1978:23). But what exactly is history in the context of a holy shrine? And does history mean the same thing for the pilgrims at the shrine as it does for me, the outsider, the Western academic? These are some of the issues I wish to explore in the following chapters as I examine the stories of an island, an icon, and a nun.

CHAPTER SEVEN

An Island in Space, An Island in Time

SO FAR I have brought both the pilgrim and the anthropologist to Tinos and have described something of the activities of each at the pilgrimage site. These activities are located within two larger fields: the practices and beliefs of the Greek Orthodox religion on the one hand, and the practices and beliefs of anthropology on the other. Up to this point Tinos, the island, has remained in the background, noted merely as the location of the Church of the Annunciation, as the site of my earlier village field-work, and as a place to which both pilgrim and anthropologist must travel by boat.

But the island is more than a physical setting. It derives meaning from, and imparts meaning to, the church and its miraculous icon, and it has its own story to tell, a story that both ties it to and makes it different from the other islands of the region. In part, the very fact that it is an island helps to give it a unique identity. Therefore some background on Tinos is essential for our understanding of pilgrimage.

TINOS TODAY

Tinos is one of a group of Aegean islands known as the Cyclades (*Kik-ládhes*). Like many rural areas of Greece, most of the Cyclades are se-verely depopulated, as large numbers of their inhabitants have migrated to Athens or abroad.[1] Many of the Cycladic islands have experienced internal population movements as well, with islanders moving from vil-lages into the islands' main towns. On Tinos, for example, while the is-land as a whole has been steadily losing population, the population of the main town has actually increased, from approximately 3,000 in 1969–70 to a little over 4,000 as of the 1981 census (declining to 3,569 according to the 1991 census).[2]

When I first did fieldwork on Tinos, the village where I lived had al-ready experienced considerable out-migration (see Dubisch 1972, 1977), mainly to Athens. More recently, although out-migration continues, many of the village young people seem to be establishing themselves in the main town through jobs, businesses, or marriage, as opportunities in the town are enhanced through the growth of tourism, summer visiting, and pil-grimage. For some, at least, this has provided an alternative to migration to Athens.[3]

The rugged beauty of the Cyclades, the individuality and variety of the islands, and the relatively unspoiled nature of many of the lesser-known islands are now drawing both Greeks and foreigners in large numbers. Twenty years ago passenger ships to many of the islands were small, slow, and often old. Now many islands are served by large, relatively new and relatively fast ferryboats, and some are served by air as well. Recently hydrofoils ("Flying Dolphins") and catamarans have been put into service among a number of the Cycladic islands, including Tinos, making them even more accessible. Increased tourism and summer visiting by Athenians have led to an expansion of businesses on many of the islands. Restaurants, hotels, rental rooms, tourist shops, and bars flourish in what were once quiet towns. Farmers, fishermen, and producers of local handicrafts find increased outlets for their goods. The construction industry has also grown on a number of islands as more shops, hotels, apartment buildings, and summer homes for affluent urbanites are built. On Tinos a variety of public works have been undertaken (building and repair of wharves, roads, and the like) and more public functionaries are now required: more tourist police, harbor police, and other civil servants.[4] I also found motorbike and car rental establishments, video stores, and bars when I returned to the island in 1986, businesses that had not been there in the 1970s, and that serve both tourists and the local populace.

On Tinos, the growth in the main town has had effects throughout the island, as villagers find expanded markets for their goods and services, or as they commute to town to work in restaurants, stores, construction, or other businesses. Visitors are also increasingly finding their way to the rural villages, for, ironically, as the island towns grow larger and more crowded, many vacationers now seek the peace and beauty of the countryside. In the village of Falatados, where I did fieldwork, for example, at least one woman now rents rooms in her house to summer visitors, both Greek and foreign; the owner of one of the tavernas has added a "hotel" to his taverna in the form of rooms for visitors; and a new taverna opened in the village in the late 1970s and now caters to outsiders as well as villagers. Although both village tavernas draw local people, they would find it difficult to survive in the depopulated village without the patronage of summer visitors who come to experience "traditional" village food and a rural atmosphere. A number of houses in the village (family houses or newly purchased ones) are being renovated, and I learned in the summer of 1993 that a village house has been purchased by an American and his wife who are resident in Greece. The building and renovation give the village an odd face—more prosperous looking now than it was when I first lived there over twenty years ago, yet in fact a depopulated shell of its former self.

Each Cycladic island has its own special character, customs, dialects, and history, which is part of their attraction for visitors. The island of

Syros, for example, was once the main port of the new nation of Greece. It still has an active shipyard, and is the seat of both a Catholic and an Orthodox archbishop, as well as of the head of the provincial administrative unit, the *nomós*. The island of Naxos is the largest of the Cycladic islands. Long under Venetian rule, Naxos was the seat of a dukedom, and the dukes of Naxos wielded considerable power in the region during the three-hundred-year period of their rule. Naxos boasts early Cycladic works of art (the large stone figures called *koúri*), an ancient temple of Apollo,[5] and a Venetian walled town nestled within the structures of the present-day settlement.

The Cycladic island that is probably best known to foreigners is Mykonos. It has long been a jet-set and tourist resort and now has a reputation as an international gay meeting place, with discos, bars, and nude beaches.[6] Although the island has maintained the picturesque maze of narrow streets and the brilliantly whitewashed houses that first made it attractive to tourists, tourism itself has completely transformed the island, leading many tourists to search for places that are "unspoiled" (such as some of the less well-known Cycladic islands).

For many Greeks, however, the sacred center of the Cyclades is Tinos. And unlike many of the other islands, Tinos, with its Church of the Annunciation and its miraculous icon, has had long experience with visitors, ever since the discovery of the icon and the building of the church in the early nineteenth century (see chapter 9). Although both foreign tourism and summer visiting by nonpilgrim Greeks have increased greatly in recent years, the overwhelming number of visitors to Tinos come because of the Church of the Annunciation and its miraculous icon, and it is pilgrimage that has created the particular character of the main town and given the island of Tinos its fame. For many of the islanders, the finding of the icon "begins" Tinos's history. But the roots of this history stretch further into time than that.

TINOS: THE PAST

Tinos has been occupied since the Bronze Age, its first known settlements dating from about 3000–4000 B.C., and archaeological sites have been uncovered in several locations on the island. A temple to Poseidon (who, according to tradition, had rid the island of its serpents) has been found at Koinia, several kilometers outside the present-day town, and a temple of Dionysios apparently stood where the Church of the Annunciation stands today. The ancient capital was located near the present town, possibly at Kionia.[7] Tinos was independent for many centuries but came under the rule of the Athenians in 664 B.C. Tinos then passed to a variety of rulers —Persians, Thebans, Macedonians, Ptolemenians, and eventually, in 146

B.C., to the Romans. In the first century B.C., many pilgrims visited Tinos for its temple of Poseidon. According to Frazee, at that time Tinos's famous temple was a Sanctuary, and it was visited during Hellenistic and Roman times by pilgrims. An eating hall and a hotel were located nearby (Frazee 1988). Tinos seems to have been relatively prosperous at this time, perhaps benefiting from the status enjoyed by neighboring Delos as a free port (Frazee 1988), although another author suggests that it had been economically ruined by the preceding centuries of invasion and conquest (Koukas 1981).

Although the exact date of the arrival of Christianity in Tinos is uncertain, the conversion of the island may have occurred sometime in the early fifth century, or perhaps earlier (see A. Lagouros 1965:25–26). Frazee states that Christianity arrived sometime during the Roman period, and that "according to tradition," St. John, having spent his exile on Patmos (another sacred island), came to Naxos to preach, and Christianity spread to the rest of the Cyclades from there (1988:5). Lagouros states that the first church or cathedral (naós) on Tinos was built where the temple of Dionysios had stood. According to Lagouros, this church contained the icon of the Annunciation, which he attributes to the Apostle Luke (known as a painter of icons as well as a physician). The church was dedicated to John Prodhromos (John the Baptist) and to the Madonna (A. Lagouros 1965).[8]

The history of Tinos during the Byzantine period is obscure. Dhorizas suggests that this was a difficult time, since all of the islands, including Tinos, were subject to repeated depredations by pirates, Turks, Arabs, and other raiders, and beset by famine, plague, massacres, captivity by raiders, and even earthquakes (1976:9). At the beginning of the Iconoclast period in 727, Muslim raiders roamed the Cyclades, meeting with little resistance. During this period a man named Stephen joined forces with the theme (political-military unit) of Hellas to overthrow the Byzantine emperor Leo III. The seamen of the Cyclades joined him and the Cycladic fleet was destroyed by Leo. "The islands sank back into obscurity, used as a place of exile for iconodules. Possibly at this time the miraculous icon of Tinos . . . was buried by a displaced exile from Constantinople" (Frazee 1988:8).

In the eighth century a plague that began in Momnevasia to the north moved into the Aegean, killing perhaps a quarter of the population there (Frazee 1988:8). From the ninth century, the Arabs menaced the islands until the Muslims were expelled from the area by the Byzantine emperor Nikephoros Phokas when he conquered Crete and the Cyclades. In 1083 the emperor Alexios Komnenos established an independent metropolitan of the Cyclades. At this time the islands were a major source of sailors for the emperor's fleet.

Cycladic architecture supposedly derives its distinctive character from these perilous centuries. Villages were built within walls for protection, their streets a maze to confuse raiders, and their walls were left the natural color of the stone in order to blend with the hillsides and be invisible from the sea.[9] Churches from the Byzantine period are also found all over the Cyclades.

During the Middle Ages, Delos, Mykonos, and Tinos were included in the *theme* of the Aegean Sea, "but nothing specific is known of them for centuries. It is only when the Latin conquest takes place [1204] that they return to the light of history" (Frazee 1988:56). The Fourth Crusade, which led to the conquest of Constantinople and division of the Byzantine Empire between the Venetians and the Crusaders, ushered in the Venetian period of Cycladic history. Although only the island of Andros was given to the Venetians as part of the partition, bands of Venetian soldiers and adventurers soon seized a number of the other islands as well. Naxos was wrested from Genoese pirates by Marco Sanudo, a nephew of the Venetian doge Enrico Dandolo, who had accompanied the Fourth Crusade. Sanudo eventually visited most of the other Cyclades. In 1207 two of Sanudo's associates, the brothers Andrea and Geremia Ghisi, took Tinos, Mykonos, and the by then uninhabited island of Delos. (They also held the northern Sporades and part of Kea.)

Frazee suggests that the Venetians met little resistance in the Cyclades. Many islanders may have despaired of the Byzantine Empire's ability to defend them from pirates and felt that only Venice had a fleet strong enough to provide adequate protection. In addition, Sanudo avoided conflict with the local Greeks by respecting their customs and by making it clear to local leaders (*archontes*) that he did not intend to institute social revolution (Frazee 1988:14–15).

Tinos was probably rather sparsely inhabited at this time, mostly by farmers engaged in subsistence agriculture, a supposition supported by Dhorizas's observation that repeated catastrophes had served to keep the islands at a low and not very diversified state of development (1976:10). It is not certain how many Venetian families came to settle on Tinos— perhaps thirty to forty (Frazee 1988:56). Families from other Italian cities also came, since rulers of the islands wanted colonists. The Venetians would have married into local Greek families, provided the civil service and a military force, and been supported by lands received in a feudal arrangement (Frazee 1988:56). According to Lacroix, the Venetians did not maintain regular troops on the island but organized the inhabitants so that they could be quickly mustered at a single signal (1881).

Along with the settlers to Tinos came Latin Catholic clergy and a Catholic bishop, who took over the Orthodox cathedral of St. Nikolaos and the properties attached to the Orthodox see. Only a *protopappas*, a "head priest," chosen by the Orthodox but confirmed by the Latin bishop, would have been permitted to reside on the island. Greek clerics had to acknowledge the Latin bishop's authority, pay him part of their revenues, and commemorate both the pope and the Latin patriarch of Constantinople in the liturgy. Latin altars were put up in Greek churches and the Catholic bishop became the chief administrator of Byzantine monasteries and convents. The *protopappas*, along with the parish priests, would have had to go outside the island (again with the bishops' permission) to seek ordination, and was subject to the authority of the Latin Catholic authorities (Frazee 1988:56–57). Frazee suggests that such changes affected most of the Greek Christians minimally. The actual number of Latin clergy in the islands was few and their congregations small. Orthodox pastors were not troubled in their office or property as long as they cooperated with the Latin rulers. According to Frazee, the division between Latin and Orthodox was more cultural than doctrinal, since few were aware of the nature of the doctrinal differences dividing the churches (1988:22). Greeks, however, were regarded as second-class Christians and had to march behind Latins in any joint celebration (1988:57).

At the beginning of the Venetian period the Cyclades seem to have experienced a certain amount of prosperity. Even though there were continued problems with piracy, island commerce was enhanced by the greater security provided by the Venetian fleet, which allowed wheat, wine, oil, and other island products to be shipped. Tinos shared in this prosperity, producing mostly agricultural products (Frazee 1988:72–73). During the Venetian period, the island's capital was moved to the highest point of the island, the rocky peak of Exobourgos. This was obviously for defensive reasons, as the rugged 540-meter peak provided a formidable deterrent to attack. The fortress was built on the peak itself, with the walled Venetian town just below. Outside the walled town lived the Greeks, who served those dwelling within. When pirates attacked the island, the inhabitants fled for shelter behind the walls of Exobourgos. The contemporary visitor can still find the remains of the stone walls and steps of the town and fort clustered along the steep slopes. With exposure to the constant island winds, and the chill clouds that sometimes settle over the peak even when the rest of the island is sunny, the walled fortress must have been an uncomfortable location for the Venetian families and soldiers who lived there. On the other hand, it did provide an effective point of defense. In 1570, for example, at the time of the Cypriot war, Selim II landed three thousand Turks at Tinos. He pillaged the island but was unable to take the fortress (Lacroix 1881).

The Latins became the landowners of the island, with most of the native Greeks paying their lords a certain percentage of their crops.[11] Tinos passed through a succession of Ghisis (see Dhorizas 1976; Slot 1982) until the close of the fourteenth century, when Giorgio Ghisi had no children. He willed his possessions to Venice, which took over direct rule of Tinos, Mykonos, and Delos when he died in 1390. At this time, the islands were in poor condition. They were constantly being raided by pirates of various nationalities, against whom the Venetians were able to provide little protection, and islanders were frequently carried off into slavery. The populations of Tinos and Mykonos declined and many of the island fields lay empty (Frazee 1988:101). A series of arrangements for governing the islands was made during the following decades, but the islands continued to decline as successive governors milked them for their own profit (Frazee 1988:105).[12]

With the fall of Constantinople to the Ottoman Turks in 1453, the situation of the Cyclades became even more difficult. For the next two hundred years, Venice and Turkey engaged in a series of wars, and with every outbreak of war, Tinos and Mykonos became exposed to attacks both from the Turkish navy and from Ottoman privateers (Frazee 1988: 105). Perhaps the worst depredations were those of the Turkish admiral Khair el-Din, known as Barbarossa, who set out in 1537 to devastate the Aegean, killing and enslaving the populations of the islands. Tinos managed to hold out against him, with only three villages reportedly surrendering, but the Turks did capture and settle on Mykonos. In a treaty signed in 1540, after the Holy League (consisting of the papacy, Venice, and the Hapsburgs), which had been formed to oppose Barbarossa, abandoned its war with the Turks, Venice ceded Mykonos to the Ottomans. All of the remaining island princes of the Archipelago (as the region of the Cyclades is sometimes called) became Ottoman tributaries. Tinos's defenses were strengthened in anticipation of further attack, and in the years that followed, as the island became a place of refuge for those fleeing from the Turkish-held islands, its population increased from influxes of these Orthodox refugees. Opposition to Turkish rule was not necessarily universal among the Cycladic islanders, however, many of whom believed they would be better off under the Ottomans.

In the early seventeenth century, Tinos seems to have grown more prosperous, apparently gaining importance from its role as a Venetian (and Christian) stronghold in an increasingly Ottoman sea. Tinos had strategic importance for Venice in protecting Venetian ships sailing through the Dardanelles, and the Venetians sought to build the island's prosperity in order to encourage resistance to the Turks (Slot 1982:158). The island was extensively cultivated and many walled terraces were built during this time. By 1613 fields on Tinos had been converted to vines to increase the productivity of the soil, but this made the island more dependent on the import of wheat, not a good situation considering the island's precarious and isolated position. The vines were later ordered torn up, but the fields replanted in wheat did not have the yield they previously attained (Slot 1982:159). Frazee estimates the population during this period to have been around ten thousand and suggests that in order to provide for this population, the cultivation of silk was undertaken. Not only could it be used as a cash crop for export, but also the cultivation was intensive and did not require large amounts of land (Frazee 1991:137). Silk was exported to Italy and, after 1670, also to France (Slot 1982:28–29).[13] A visitor to Tinos in 1614 estimated that three-fourths of the island population were Catholic (Frazee 1991:137), while Slot estimates that about 50 percent of the island population were Catholic (1982:14). An increasing number of Orthodox villages were being built during this period in the northern and southern parts of the island. Although Orthodox, they were under the jurisdiction of the Latin bishops and were required to follow the liturgical calendar determined by the Latins. Some villages were mixed Catholic and Orthodox (as they are today), but others were separate.

It is unclear when Muslim inhabitants (aside from administrative functionaries) began to settle in the Cyclades. This probably occurred after 1590. But they did not have mosques or *kadis* and depended for their protection on Ottoman institutions outside the Cyclades (Slot 1982:107). The actual number of Turkish Muslims resident in the islands was probably only two to three hundred, and it was the presence of the Turkish fleet that made Ottoman control possible in the area (Slot 1982:117). The Greek church had little difficulty in adapting to the Ottoman regime since its position in the empire was more favorable than its position had been under the Latin rule. Greek churches were emancipated from Latin control and many Latins converted to the Greek (Orthodox) rite, preferring to be Orthodox under Ottoman rule since being followers of the Latin rite put them under suspicion as subjects of the pope (Slot 1982:109).

The situation in the Cyclades by the late seventeenth century is described by Slot: "The Cyclades had become a disputed region where no one could any longer exercise any decisive influence. A nearly total anarchy reigned" (Slot 1982:230). Although the islands at this point seemed to be returning to the Occidental sphere of influence as Turkey grew weaker and the Venetians and French became more active in the region, Slot suggests that the local population had grown further and further from the Francokratia and that the character of insular society had become increasingly Ottoman (1982:230).

Tinos resisted various Turkish onslaughts as the century progressed, and the harbor of Tinos became a rendezvous for Christian corsairs who preyed upon Ottoman ships. A 1665 visitor estimated the population of Tinos at twelve thousand: eight thousand Catholic, four thousand Orthodox. In 1670 the British traveler Randolph counted thirty villages on the island, with an estimated twenty thousand people, the large increase (if these figures are accurate) perhaps due to Cretans seeking refuge on Tinos after Crete was ceded to the Turks in the treaty of 1667 (Frazee 1991: 139). Venice was paying a tribute to the Ottomans at this time for its right to hold the island, though this did not stop the Turkish assaults. The island fortress at Exobourgos continued to prove impregnable, but in 1701 a French visitor to the island, Baron Pitton de Tournefort, was distressed to see how the fortress was being neglected by the rector (Frazee 1991:139). His distress turned out to be well founded. In 1714 Turkey declared war on Venice. On June 5, 1715, a Turkish fleet appeared off the coast of Tinos and landed a force of twelve thousand on the island. With apparently no effort at resistance, the Venetian rector agreed to hand over the island to the Turks. Islanders today say that he was bribed by the Turks with gold.[14] Negotiations allowed the garrison defender and all others who wished to go to Christian lands to depart and a large number of the island's inhabitants left (Slot 1982:253). The leading two hundred noble Catholic families were exiled by the Turks to North Africa. A Turkish garrison of one thousand was established in the fortified city and other Muslim colonies were placed around it (Slot 1982:253). Two years later, in 1717, a Venetian fleet appeared off the island. According to one version of what followed, the Turks fled in a panic, destroying the fortress. The Venetians did not retake the island, but without the fortress Tinos could not be securely colonized and was no longer of any strategic importance to either Venetians or Turks (Slot 1982:253–54). With the fortress of Exobourgos destroyed, the island's capital town was moved to its present location by the sea. Tinos was the last of the Cycladic islands to fall into Turkish hands.

Although the Turks are today viewed as both the traditional and the contemporary enemy of the Greeks, Ottoman rule rested very lightly (and relatively briefly) on Tinos, and the island seems to have prospered during this period (see Dhaskalaki-Dhoriza 1982:128). There was no Turkish settlement on the island, only an agent of the Porte, and the islanders were left to govern themselves through their own community council, though they paid taxes to Constantinople. Although protected by an agreement with France that extended over the Catholics of the Ottoman Empire, many Catholics chose to migrate, and their numbers were reduced to five thousand by 1746. Population estimates for the island during this period range from eleven thousand (Frazee 1969:173) to twenty-five thousand (Zallony 1809:xii) to twenty-eight thousand (A. Lagouros 1965).[15]

The Englishman Lord Charlemont, who traveled to Tinos in 1749, noted that Tinos, in common with Naxos, enjoyed the privilege of being free of the visits of the Captain Pasha, and that the deputy agent residing on the island was the only Turk living permanently there. Tribute to the

Porte was paid in silk. Lord Charlemont comments: "This freedom from oppression is easily to be observed in the state of the country, which is beautiful and well-cultivated, and in the appearance of the inhabitants, who are industrious, well-clothed, happy, and lively" (1984:61). He goes on to note that there were sixty-four villages on the island, some of them very small; that there was good pasture and excellent fruit; and that the island was well planted, especially in mulberry trees (the leaves of which were used to feed the silkworms). In addition, "the dress and manners of the inhabitants bespeak their affluence, and content is visible in every countenance" (1984:62).

Zallony distinguishes three classes of islanders during the Ottoman period: nobles, bourgeois, and peasants, with the first category disdaining the others and the second category distinguished by their "urbanité" (1809:80). He notes that "la plupart des Tiniens voyagent," but they love their "patrie" and hence always return (1809:78). From Zallony's description of local dress, especially of the upper and middle classes, it appears that the inhabitants were much influenced by European styles and, to a lesser extent, by Turkish as well. He noted that European dress was common among the nobility and among young Tinians who had traveled to Constantinople, Smyrna, or Europe.

Both Charlemont and Zallony commented on the position of women on Tinos. Charlemont's attention was captured by the beauty of the Tinian women, and he noted their skill in dancing, both in the Greek dances and in the minuet. He contrasted Tinos with Athens, where women were more reserved and young girls were seen only in church, a situation he attributes to the continuance of ancient traditions rather than to Turkish influence (1984:126). Zallony describes the women of Tinos as "plus spirituelles que les hommes, vives, enjouées, jolies, les femmes sont en même temps modestes et decentes" (1809:69). He adds that "elles n'en sont pas moins cependent maitresses absolues dans leur ménage" (1809:70).

Zallony also notes what he terms an "inveterate hatred" between the Latin Christians and the Orthodox. In the summer, he recounts, when drought occurred, the adherents of each rite would go to their respective churches to pray for rain. Later, when the drought was broken, arguments would break out over which prayers were the effective ones (1809: 56). According to Zallony, "ces idées superstitieuses" lose their force in the Adriatic and large cities, where they give way to theological discussions comparing the two rites (1809:57).

Despite the relative lightness of Ottoman rule upon the island, in 1821 Tinos joined the Greek uprising for an independent state of Greece. The inhabitants of Tinos sent letters of solidarity, money, ships, and men to aid in the struggle (see Dhaskalaki-Dhoriza 1982). The Greek cause was not supported by all Tinians, however. The Catholic population, prosperous under Ottoman rule and fearful of their own status under a new, Orthodox state of Greece, remained neutral. Or perhaps neutral is not quite the exact term, since they continued to send their representative to pay taxes at Constantinople and to declare their loyalty, and were furthermore suspected of providing information to the Turks (Frazee 1979).

When early in 1823 a miraculous icon was found on Tinos in a field just outside the main town, the event took on a particular significance. In the turbulent period of the struggle for an independent Greece, the finding of the icon seemed to signal divine approval of the Greek (Orthodox) cause (see chapter 9). Although no fighting took place on Tinos, the island did feel the effects of the war through the arrival of shiploads of refugees fleeing Chios and Psara, where thousands had been massacred by the Turks (Frazee n.d.:32).

After the War of Independence, Tinos and the other Cycladic islands became part of the kingdom of Greece, formed in 1832. This new nation was small, comprising only the Cyclades, Attica, and the Peloponnesus. The Greek irredentist struggle (the *Megáli Idhéa*) was to continue into the next century, enlarging the political boundaries of Greece, until 1922, when the Greek defeat in Asia Minor by the Turks put an end to Greek expansionism. The addition of the Dodecanese islands, ceded by the Italians after World War II, gave Greece its present-day boundaries.

Estimates of the population of Tinos at the time of independence, as might be expected, vary considerably. Lagouros gives the population from 1824 to 1830 as a little over twenty-one thousand (1976:63), though other estimates go as high as thirty thousand, and about the same for the middle of the century. The population gradually decreased during the next hundred years, and was down to under eight thousand by 1980. During the period following independence, Tinians migrated both temporarily and permanently to Constantinople, or "the City" (*i Pólis*), as it has continued to be called by Greeks, until halted by the Greek defeat in Asia Minor in 1922, an event still referred to by Greeks as "the Catastrophe" (see Hirschon 1989). At this time many Tinians already in the City were forced to flee. Since then, migration away from the island has been mainly to Athens (see Dubisch 1972, 1977).

Tinos as Sacred and Greek

This brief account has sought to locate Tinos in time. It reveals something of the "marginality" of both Tinos and the Cyclades both in the sense that the islands have existed for centuries on the margins of various empires and in the sense that they have existed on the margins of Western history, caught up in the West's politics and conflicts, but seldom if ever playing any decisive role. The account also shows the Cyclades on the margins between East and West, not just between the Christian West and Islam, but also between Western and Eastern Christianity. Indeed, from the point of view of religion, this latter conflict has played a more important role in the islands than the conflict with the Ottomans, for Islam itself never gained a stronghold there even under Turkish rule. On Tinos, however, because of the discovery of the icon of the Annunciation in 1823, religion came to play a significant role in the island's relationship to the Greek struggle for independence and in its position within the new Greek state. In turn, religion itself played a role in defining that state.

The Eastern Orthodox church has been officially separate from the Roman Catholic Church for over nine hundred years and differs from it in ecclesiastical organization and points of doctrine, as well as in the geographical distribution of its adherents. Those of the Orthodox faith often see themselves as the first Christians, representatives of the faith from which all other Christian faiths have been derived (Just 1988).

On Tinos, as the above account has shown, the Eastern Orthodox and the Latin rites came into an intimate and sometimes conflict-ridden relationship, as the declining Byzantine Empire was dealt its first fateful blow, not by the now traditional enemy—the Eastern and infidel Turk—but by the Christian powers of the West during the Fourth Crusade. The Eastern, that is, Oriental, as opposed to Western, nature of the Orthodox church is highlighted in this series of events, as it was besieged by those who professed a faith and adhered to the rites of a church to which the Orthodox church had once been joined.

When the Greek revolutionary leaders met on January 1, 1822, to adopt a constitution, its first article stated, "The established religion of the Greek State is the Eastern Orthodox Church of Christ" and added that "the government of Greece, however, tolerates every other religion, and its services and ceremonies may be practiced without interference" (Frazee 1979:321). Many high church officials were opposed to the move for independence (including the patriarch, Grigorios V), but local priests often participated actively in the struggle (Frazee 1977). While within Greece today there is a small percentage of Greeks of other faiths (including the Catholics on Tinos and some of the other Cycladic islands), to be Greek and to be Orthodox are very nearly synonymous. Greece today "is now the only country in the world that is officially an Orthodox Christian country" (Campbell and Sherrard 1968:189).

Nationalism and religion are thus closely intertwined in the history of modern Greece. This association is clearly demonstrated at Tinos, where the very beginning of the Greek nation was believed to have received divine validation through the discovery and subsequent miracles of the long-buried icon of the Annunciation. The major holy day for the church at Tinos, the Day of the Annunciation on March 25, is also Greek Inde-

pendence Day. On this occasion the religious and the patriotic are officially joined in a variety of rituals. Thus Tinos's history does not end with
the War of Independence. Indeed, for some it is at this time that the most
significant part of Tinos's history begins.

TINOS AND THE "LIGHT" OF HISTORY

Upon learning that I am an anthropologist and that I have done work in
Greece, many people, academics and nonacademics alike, assume that I
am an archaeologist and that I have done my research on ancient Greece
—so much is the present Greece overshadowed by Western images of the
classical past, an image filtered through the lens of the West's own historical agenda. Thus unlike cultural anthropologists working in most other
countries, I must designate my geographical specialization as "modern"
Greece. This viewing of modern Greece through the prism of ancient
Greece has played a crucial role in the development of Greek identity and
played a significant part in Greek history and politics (see Herzfeld 1987a).

As the brief and often sketchy account given here makes clear, the history of Tinos over the last two thousand years can also be seen (or
"read") as echoing many important themes of European history, including the movements of peoples, the confrontations of world religions, and
the clashes and conquests of states and empires. But it echoes these
themes from the point of view of a society that stands "on the margins"
(Herzfeld 1987a). Not only is Tinos (along with the other Cycladic islands) caught between East and West, but it also emerges as a largely
passive player in the dramas of conquest, moving to center stage only in
its stubborn resistance to the Turks, becoming the last of the Cyclades to
fall to Ottoman rule, and then a century later as the home of the miraculous icon of the Annunciation, discovered during the difficult years of the
struggle for an independent Greece.

In writing about Tinos, I have given it a character, a role as a distinctive
entity. It is easy to do so because Tinos is an island, with definite (perhaps
deceptively definite) physical boundaries. Separated from and yet in touch
with its neighbors, on the margins of and yet connected with the ebb and
flow of history, Tinos exercises a particular fascination. Overshadowed in
the ancient world by its neighbor Delos, annexed to or ruled by one or
another distant or near federation, ruler, state, or empire, a virtually independent principality flourishing, declining, flourishing again, a last Western outpost against the Turkish East, an early sign of hope in a time of
revolution, a beacon to the Orthodox within and outside the new state of
Greece—Tinos has gone through all of this to come into its own as a
sacred center of modern Greece, embodying all the glorious and not so
glorious past. Tinos thus stands revealed as more than just a barren and

picturesque island for tourists, and more even than a popular pilgrimage site. The present, seen in previous chapters as so vital, colorful, and overwhelming, is revealed now as simply a moment, and perhaps even a rather minor one, in a long span of the island's time.

And yet the island's time is in some significant sense not its own, for the island moves in and out of history, revealing "history" itself as something determined by others. Indeed, it raises the issue of what *is* history. In particular, Tinos's past emerges in relationship to the West, which in a sense determines what is history and what is the appropriate object of history. As Frazee says of the early centuries of the Christian era, "Nothing specific is known of the islands for hundreds of years," and it is only with the Venetian occupation, that is, with the penetration of the West, "that Tinos and Mikonos again come into the light of history" (1988:56). Without that light, Tinos is unknown, dark, not really of history. And although several accounts of Tinos's past have been produced by local authors in recent years,[16] they must rely mainly on the reports of foreign travelers, writers, and scholars, especially for the early periods of the island's history.

History is, moreover, male history, structured by men's time, a sequence of events, with men as the chief—indeed, for the most part, the only—actors (see Dubisch 1991d). This is true even though the brief version told here is by a woman (myself). Women are a separate category in such a history, an "other," an object. In travelers' accounts the appearance and character of the island women are often described as a distinct local feature, thus forming an "other among others," an object of commentary for the foreign visitor.[17] In this sense, we might see *all* Greeks in this history as "women," for they are the ruled and the written about. Thus the history I have recounted here is a Western history, and only in small part a story told by the Greek islanders themselves. Yet in the telling of what seems at first to be simply a conventional background sketch against which to set my account of the church and its icon, I seek also to subvert the very conventionality of this account and to bring to the center those who have been marginal in their own history.

Thus I proceed by recounting the story of a nun, an icon, and the building of a church.

CHAPTER EIGHT

Writing the Story/History of the Church:
The Panayía and the Nun

ON JULY 9, 1822, an elderly nun named Pelayia, who lived at the monastery of Kekhrovouno on the island of Tinos, had a vision. This vision appeared to her in the form of a woman surrounded by light who came to the nun as she slept. This lady approached Pelayia's humble bed, and speaking to her, told the nun to go to the *epítropos* of the monastery and tell him to excavate a field outside the town, a field belonging to one Andonis Dhoksaras, in order, in her words, to find "my house" and there to begin "the building of my temple" (*ktísimo tou naoú mou*).

Pelayia awoke from this dream filled with fear, uncertain whether the vision she had seen had been truly divine or simply her own fantasy. Deciding it had been the latter, she did not follow the instructions given her in the dream but simply went about her normal routine. The following Sunday the vision once more appeared, but was once again discounted by Pelayia, who was a humble person (*tapinós ánthropos*) and didn't believe that it was her place to see such an exalted personage as the Panayía.

On July 23, 1822, the same magnificent woman once more appeared. This time she was angry, telling the nun that if her instructions continued to be ignored, cholera would fall upon the island. At the woman's commanding (*prostaktikó*) tone of voice, Pelayia awoke. With her eyes open, she still saw the woman, whose appearance combined both magnificence (*megaloprépia*) and sweetness (*glikítita*). Pelayia found that her lips were unable to utter a word. Only for a brief moment was she able to collect herself and stutter, "And who are you, Lady, that you command that of me?" At this question, the divine woman gestured at the surroundings as if to indicate the entire world and said, "I come to announce a great joy." Pelayia fell to her knees and responded, "Let the heavens praise the glory of God."

The next day, after the divine liturgy, Pelayia went to the abbess of the monastery and told her of the vision, and the abbess, because she knew of Pelayia's virtue and her ascetic life, believed her story and sent her to the churchwarden, Stamatelos Kagkadhis, who lived in the village of Karyia. After listening to her story, the *epítropos* sent her to visit the bishop, Gavriíl, in the same village, who believed her account as well.

According both to historians of the time and to traditional accounts, Gavriíl was a most excellent (*áristos*) prelate. Upon hearing Pelayia's story, he sought without hesitation to turn the divine command into reality. He also recalled the narrative of an old man, called Giouzes, who had said that, according to the old inhabitants of the island, there had been a princedom in the field of Dhoksaras and that one day there would be a princedom again: "a principality to which people will come from the farthest reaches of the world in order to pay their respects" (*na to proskinoún*). Thus the vision strengthened the bishop's confidence that in the field was an ancient temple or church (*naós*) and an icon hidden in the earth.

At the beginning of September 1822, the work of digging up the field was begun, but nothing was discovered. Only the ruins of a building were found, along with a dried-up well. The diggers continued their work for two months, and then their enthusiasm cooled and they abandoned the project. At that point, cholera appeared on the island. Kagkadhis believed that the cause was indifference to the building of the church as directed by the dream. Thus, upon the order of Gavriíl, and at the request of Kagkadhis and of the inhabitants, the excavations were zealously begun again. A committee (*epitropí*) was formed that oversaw the excavations and the building of the church, a committee that included Kagadhis and several other islanders, with Gavriíl as president. From the villages of Tinos, villagers came down every day in shifts and thus the work progressed.

The laying of the foundations of the church began on January 1, 1823. Church officials, notables, and the people (*o laós*) all came, and it was necessary to have a blessing with holy water, which of course required water. At the moment that someone left to fetch water from the town, a child who was near the dried-up well shouted for them not to go because the well was full. Everyone thanked God for the water, and the sick who washed with it became well. Gavriíl sprinkled the water on the foundations and the church was dedicated as the Life-giving Well (*Zoodhóhos piyí*).[1] Within a short space of time the work was finished because, with the cessation of the cholera, the finding of the holy water, and all the other miracles that were happening every day, enthusiasm for the church grew and the difficulties lessened.

On January 30, it was the turn of the inhabitants of the village of Falatados to work on the building of the church of the *Zoodhóhos piyí*. At two in the afternoon, one of the workers struck a piece of wood while digging. Cleaning it off, he saw that it depicted an angel with a lily. Immediately the workers began to dig for the other half and very quickly it was found. On this half was the Mother of God (*Theotókos*, Godbearing) seated on a throne. The workers joined the two pieces of wood and there before them was the Annunciation (*Evangelismós*).

Crying, those present at the event sent the news to Falatados, to the other villages, and to the town, and the news created great joy (*hará*) throughout the island. Local people and strangers (*kséni*) came to kiss Her (the Panayía's) Holy Icon, bearing oil lamps, and with tears in their eyes lined up to pay their devotions (*na proskinísoun*). On February 2, the first procession of the icon took place through the narrow streets of Tinos.

The icon depicted the Annunciation, and although the worker's shovel had cut the icon in two, neither the angel Gabriel nor Mary had been damaged. The back of the icon was charred. It is believed that this is because the icon was originally housed in an early Byzantine Church of St. John, burned by raiding Saracen pirates in the twelfth century. Part of the foundation of this earlier church can be seen in the church of the *Zoodhóhos piyí*, which is now underneath the main church of the Annunciation. The icon itself is attributed to St. Luke.

After finding of the icon, it was decided to build a larger church in order to carry out the command of the Mother of God, and in the name of the Annunciation. Accordingly, an architect from Smyrna was invited to come to Tinos and to stay there while drawing up a plan for the church. The plan was developed quickly and the building was begun immediately. All the people (*laós*) helped: rich and poor, notables (*árhondes*) and artisans, local people and strangers (*kséni*),[2] women and children offered their services with enthusiasm. The rich donated money and jewelry. The poor worked without pay. Despite all these efforts, several times the money for building ran out, but always some miracle intervened and the work was able to continue. Marble from the quarries at Panormos, on Tinos, was used in the construction, as well as marble taken from the ancient site of Kionia, a short distance from the town, and from the ancient sacred island of Delos. The church was inaugurated within a year, though not completed for eight years, and from that time until the present the divine liturgy and vespers have been held every day of the year.

Several miracles occurred early in the history of the icon and the church. One was the rescue from the cholera epidemic. As soon as the icon was discovered, the epidemic stopped, and no further cases were reported. Another miracle was the filling of the dry well during the building of the first church, providing water for its sanctification. A third miracle was the saving of the English frigate (recounted in chapter 9), which led to a donation of money allowing work to continue on the church. At the same time, the church had begun to acquire a wider reputation, for there are accounts of numerous supplicants, both from the island and from elsewhere, who began at this time to come to the island with their requests.

READING AND WRITING AN *ISTORÍA*

The foregoing is a brief and seemingly straightforward account of the finding of the miraculous icon and the building of the Church of the Annunciation, which now houses it. It is taken mostly from an anonymously written pamphlet published and distributed gratis by the church, a pamphlet written in Greek and titled "Description of the Discovery of the Miraculous Icon of the Annunciation in Tinos in the year 1823." This pamphlet is also available in several other languages, including English. The account, as written in this pamphlet, is presented as history, that is, as a description of actual events as they occurred in the past. Obviously, however, for it to be read as such assumes a readership for whom such things as visions of the Madonna, divine intervention in everyday life, and the occurrence of miracles are historical—or historically possible—events. My own presentation is written as if both I and those who will be reading this chapter share such assumptions. My account is not set off by indentation or quotation marks as if presenting a narrative by "natives." I have not punctuated the account with such phrases as "it is believed," "it is said," "according to," and "I was told." In other words, I have written as if what I wrote had the same status as the history of Tinos presented in the preceding chapter—a "real" and "factual" account, at least as far as we can know it.

Yet at the same time, there are a number of concealed elements at work here—concealed in the very act of writing, as well as in the persona in which I wrote—elements that subvert and contradict the historicity of this writing. In order to reveal what these elements are, we must once again turn to the subject of writing, both writing in general and anthropological writing in particular.

Writing itself has come to be viewed, at least by some anthropologists, as a political act, an act that conveys a message about the difference between those doing the writing and the written about. Writing tells us much, it is argued, about relations of dominance both within and between cultures. Who has the authority and the power to write, and about whom? How is such authority announced and sustained in the writing of particular ethnographies? What is history—a necessarily written account and the product and possession of the dominant and colonizing—and how does it differ from legend and myth, which characterize the "other," the dominated and colonized? How does the emphasis we place on writing both result from and sustain this division between self and other, the literate and the nonliterate, those with and those without history?

Greece offers a fruitful context in which to examine some of these issues. The Greek word *istoría* can be translated as either "story" or "history." This ambiguity (from the English speaker's point of view) is one that I find useful in thinking about my own writing of the finding of the icon. Herzfeld contrasts the use of *istoría* with the definite article (*i istoría*), indicating "history" in its most general sense, with the use of the term with the indefinite article (*mia istoría, a* story) or in the plural (*istoríes,* "stories," accounts of specific events) (1987a:42–44). The former, one can argue, is what "we" write about "them," as well as "official" nationalistic history (Herzfeld 1987a:43–44). A "native" account that is labeled *the history* within its own cultural context may thus be reread and rewritten by the authority (anthropologist or other scholar in the Western European tradition) as *a story.* In my own analysis of how I write about the finding of the icon and the origins of the church, I chose to use the Greek word, taking advantage of its ambiguity (for English speakers) in order to discuss some of the problems in writing about what others tell us, whether the telling takes place in oral or written form.

The view of history as *istoría,* that is, as a cultural construct, is at odds with a positivist view of history that sees past events as having "really" happened and the task of the historian (or other scholar) as the empirical one of "discovering" them.

But the term *istoría* can be applied to what anthropologists write as well. Rabinow points out that fiction and science are now held by many to be complementary rather than opposed: "Advances have been made in our awareness of the fictional (in the sense of 'made,' 'fabricated') quality of anthropological writing and in the integration of characteristic modes of production" (1986:243). Clifford points out that the term *fiction,* as used in recent textual theory, "has lost its connotation of falsehood, of something merely opposed to truth. It suggests the partiality of cultural and historical truths, the ways they are systematic and exclusive. . . . Even the best ethnographic texts . . . are systems, or economies, of truth. Power and history work through them, in ways their authors cannot fully control" (1986:6–7). In this sense, my rendering of the *istoría* of the icon is part of the creation of my own anthropological *istoría,* an *istoría* that includes what I have chosen to exclude from my account as well as the rhetorical devices I have used in presenting it.

One of the kinds of "power" that "works though me" is the power of writing. The relationship between "author" and "authority" and between authority as "knowing" and authority as "power" is clear.[3] The one who writes "has the last word."[4] The one who writes transforms "story" into "history." There is an irony, of course, in this act, for while writing creates history, in anthropological writing it removes those written about from history by "freezing" them into an ethnographic present (Fabian 1983; see also Herzfeld 1987a). Control over the written word has historically been both the hallmark of authority and the means of its exercise, a dividing line between the powerful and the powerless, between "us" and "them." Moreover, to write is to bestow permanence on the transitory and thus to control time. "Real" history, with its events occurring in "real" time, is thus created by the writer and is opposed to the "false" history of myth and legend, which exists in the unreality of timeless time (and may be recounted in the present tense by the anthropologist, thus removing it from "real" time; see Davis 1992a:19).

My own historical situation places me in the category of those who write, rather than those who are written about. Yet my situation is at the same time ambiguous, for although as an anthropologist I am part of a Western European tradition that both dominates and studies the exotic other, as a woman I am also the dominated (and exotic) other—not the writer but the written about, not the reader but the read.[5]

How do I, as an anthropologist and therefore writer (for to be the first requires the second), escape the authority of the written in writing about others, an authority compounded by my place in history and by the very act of writing?

One way of escape lies in taking seriously the writings of those who usually are the written about, that is, "native accounts." Thus we examine history as it is written about by the "other" and anthropology as it is constructed by "halfie" anthropologists (to use Abu-Lughod's term). Indeed all anthropology by "natives" must to some extent be a "halfie" anthropology, given the perhaps inescapably Western nature of anthropology. Moreover, Western anthropological accounts of their own culture may provide the impetus for non-Western peoples to take up the discipline themselves. As Gefou-Madianou points out in her discussion of the writing of ethnographies of Greece by non-Greeks, "Despite the fact that many of their works were written in English and French and published abroad, they inspired young Greek students of other disciplines to turn their attention to the study of anthropology, especially as a means of discovering their own cultural identity" (1993).

At the same time, escape from domination may also occur through writing, as in the writings of women who seek to escape or resist masculine domination, and by the "other" to escape or resist the domination of the West, and particularly of Western history and anthropology. In this manner, identity and self are created out of the very tool of oppression—that is, writing. To not write, in a literate world, would be to leave this creation in the hands of others.

This brings me back to my account of the *istoría* of the icon.

I first began to think about the different ways of telling this *istoría* after a conversation with a friend in Athens, a non-Greek who has resided a long time in Greece and who speaks and reads Greek fluently. He had been writing an article about the history of the church on Tinos. In discussing the article with me, he speculated as to whether or not one might ever be able to learn what had *really* happened. Had the icon really been buried all those centuries in the ruins of a Byzantine church? Was the icon really as old as was claimed, and could it actually have been painted by Luke? His questions interested me, not so much because I was interested in the answers but because of my own reaction to his raising them. I myself did not doubt the *istoría* I had heard and read. That is not to say that I "believed" it either. What I did believe was that it was believed by those who told it to me. Hence, while I found my friend's questions interesting, I realized I had devoted very little thought to the issue of what "really" happened over a century and a half ago.

I had occasion to think more about this reaction when I returned to Tinos in the summer of 1988 for the festival of St. Pelayia on July 23 and the celebrations of the fifteenth of August. During the interval between these two events, I was visited by another anthropologist, one whose specialty was not Greece. He had read some of my writings, and during his stay we visited both the Church of the Annunciation and the monastery at Kekhrovouno. It was obvious, however, that these two places held none of the interest for him that they did for me. But I was a little taken aback when he remarked, with a certain amount of indignation, that he didn't believe that the Madonna had really appeared to a nun many years ago and revealed to her all that I had written and spoken about. Both the comment and the tone of voice surprised me. My first impulse was to respond with, "Of course not. It's only a story—*their* story." But I did not say that. Instead I refused to offer an opinion about the truth or falsity of the accounts; determining their truth or falsity was not my interest or my intent.

My friend's frustrations are echoed sometimes by students in my anthropology of religion classes when I refuse to translate what I have described into their own terms or to fit it into their own understanding of causality (what they call "explaining"). For example, when I show a film on the Anastenaria, the firewalkers of northern Greece who dance across a bed of hot coals while in a trance state, the students want to know how they do it. "What keeps them from getting their feet burned?" they ask. They turn to me to tell them what is "really" happening. It is an answer I refuse to give, at least in the terms they wish. "Perhaps they are protected by St. Constantine," I suggest, offering the explanation that the firewalkers themselves give. The students' own understanding of the world is confounded both by what they have seen and the reaction of their professor to their questions. I have refused to "translate" for them or to sanction their own attempts at such translation, and they are left frustrated and disturbed.[6]

What my friend (and my students) would like to have me say is that perhaps the nun simply had a dream, its visionary content exactly what one might expect from an aging ascetic nun who had spent virtually her entire life in the convent. Because those in authority believed her story (for whatever reasons—perhaps they saw it as a political opportunity), this dream led to a series of actions that resulted in the unearthing of an ancient icon. The discovery of the icon may simply have occurred by chance. Or perhaps both the nun and those she told about her dream knew that a church had once stood in the field. It was not so remarkable that an icon should be buried in the ruins of a church, nor that a dry well, once excavated, might be unblocked and begin to flow again. Nor is it odd that in those difficult early days of the Greek War of Independence both priests and populace would be looking for reassurance and hope. Given their own religious beliefs, and the propensity to see religious significance in events (see chapter 6), the islanders seized upon these occurrences as signs of divine favor. Such an interpretation is appealing because it fits with Western, scientific notions of causality while still taking account of the "facts" of the story. On the other hand, one can see such "explanations" of what "really" happened as simply additional *istoríes*, telling as much about the tellers as about "history."[7]

There is another possible interpretation that also accords with Western views of causality and of human nature. This interpretation views the entire event as a hoax concocted by the Orthodox religious establishment to further commitment to the cause of the Greek uprising and to provide a symbolic focus for the newly formed nation. Credence is lent to such an interpretation by the fact that the large Catholic population on the island had chosen to remain neutral in the struggle and also by the fact that there seems to have been no official resistance to Pelayía's account or to accepting the authenticity of the subsequently discovered miracle-working icon. Moreover, the finding of the icon and the building of the church were by all accounts undertaken under the supervision of church officials, further supporting the idea that the whole event was manufactured by the church.

This is a satisfying rendering of the *istoría*, for unlike one that depends on a belief in visions or miracles for its acceptability, this both dispenses with and gives an explanation for such *istoríes*—that is, they were fabrications designed to support a particular set of interests. In addition, this rendering postulates as motivating factors not faith and divine forces, but politics and secular power struggles, much more acceptable motivators than the divine. Thus while the divine authenticates history for those who wrote the church pamphlet, it undermines the account's status as "real" history for those outside that framework of belief (and such outsiders can be Greeks as well as non-Greeks).

But I think there is a further dimension to my friend's indignant comment. This has to do with Greece's particular and ambiguous position as both "us" and "them," a topic explored extensively by Herzfeld (1987a). Insofar as Greeks fall into the category of "us,"—that is, those of a Western European tradition—we expect them to exhibit true "history." If I were to recount, for example, some equivalent *istoría* from an African or Melanesian society, it could be much more readily categorized as "myth," no matter what the form in which I told it, and there would be no attempt to "explain" it, or at least to render it in "rational" historical terms. But Greeks—at least the modern ones—are not supposed to have myths. Rather, they have history, for they exist in real (that is, European historical) time and are part of our own past. A "history" that includes visions and miracles (treated as "real" events) confounds this notion, making Greeks ambiguous—are they "us" or "them," self or other? In addition, a subtext of a number of the writings on the *istoría* of the Church of the Annunciation is the implication of an always present and divinely ordained Greece. Such a teleological view, while certainly not absent in Western history, nonetheless tends to delegitimize this *istoría*. Insofar as the Greeks are "us," such *istoríes*, presented as history, threaten our notions of history, reality, and time, a threat not posed by the *istoríes* of more exotic societies. A further problem occurs when these *istoríes* are written by the "natives" themselves, for to write is to cross the line into history, or at least into the category of those who (like anthropologists) claim the authority to decide the status of others' *istoríes*. For all of these reasons, I suspect, my friend would have reacted quite differently had he visited me doing fieldwork on a Melanesian island and I had given him a similar account of the origin of a sacred site.

There is an irony in anthropology's treatment of writing, for while we speak of the power and dominance involved in writing and critique our own forms of writing, we have tended to privilege the verbal in our study of the "other." That is, anthropology has taken as its special subject matter those peoples who are nonliterate, or marginally literate within their own societies. Anthropologists concerned with these issues have suggested various ways to address the problem of writing and dominance. One way is to extend the idea of writing metaphorically: "All cultures write." Thus other forms of cultural expression are placed on a par with writing. Another attempt to find a way out of the dominance conferred by writing is through "polyphonic" ethnographies, in which the "natives" are allowed greater latitude to "speak for themselves." And yet the anthropologist is still in control of the final written product and still must select the situations in which the other voices will be recorded and choose which voices will be transmitted to the reader. In addition, much of the speaking of others makes no sense to the reader without some context, and this context must, of necessity, be conveyed/created by the anthropologist in order to render it in terms understandable to the audience.

Even when others write, they do not necessarily "speak for themselves." I said that I presented the *istoría* of the icon as I found it written, but this is not really true. The pamphlet from which the account was taken is in Greek and intended for a particular Greek audience, an audience that brings to the account a different understanding than is brought to it by my own audience. My reading of the pamphlet, as a non-Greek, is a kind of ethnographic eavesdropping, a conversation "overheard" instead of one in which I am a direct participant. Thus even though I am presenting an *istoría* based on a native text, a written text, I am not simply a conduit. First of all, I have preceded this account with a number of chapters that provide the context in which (I claim) the account must be understood. Without this background, the reader would have no means of apprehending the *istoría* or determining its significance. Of course I have not left that determination up to the reader, but have in the opening chapters, which present the setting and activities associated with the pilgrimage site, exercised my authorial power of selection. And since "context" for me includes the anthropological context, that has been discussed in several chapters as well.

Moreover, in recounting the *istoría* itself, I have not presented word for word everything included in the pamphlet but have made certain selections, selections that reflect interests and conclusions of my own formed prior to the writing (some derived from reading other texts on the subject), as well as the presumed interests of my intended audience. Certain things have been left out; others have been emphasized. And because the accounts I have used for this part of my narrative are in Greek, I have had to translate them, which requires a further selection process since many, if not most, words require choosing among possible English words and phrases for their most appropriate rendering. The words I select reflect not only my own understanding of the passage in Greek but also my own style in English, which guides my transformation of sentences and phrases into readable English. By including the Greek words in parentheses I have sought to lend authenticity to my rendering, but it is a device to be used sparingly since it can become confusing for the reader. At the same time I have tried to keep some of the "flavor" of the original Greek. But this is a tricky undertaking. Poorly done, it can seem to mock the original by an inferior or awkward form of English. For this reason, there are places in the narrative where I abandoned a strict rendering of the Greek altogether in favor of an English phrasing that conveyed the sense rather than the style of the Greek.

In part to address some of the issues I have raised regarding history, I have written the *istoría* in a "realist" ethnographic mode. That is, I have presented it as if it were "really" history. I have used my own "author-ity" as the writing ethnographer to confer a similar authority on the (anonymous) person who wrote the text on which I have drawn. Because I sought to present the material in this "realist" mode, I have left out certain things that, for my readers, might seem inappropriate to that mode.

What sort of things did I leave out? For one, I left out the prologue to the pamphlet, which is addressed to the Panayía and which praises, among other things, her countless miracles. I have also omitted or toned down overly strong expressions of faith. This is "translation" in the larger sense in that I am trying to translate from one reality to another, from an account that is realistic to those recounting it, to one that carries a similar sense of realism for those who will be reading my translation.

This assumes, as all ethnographic writing does, a certain kind of reader, and herein lies one of the difficulties of rendering my *istoría*. My account has assumed a nonbelieving reader, most likely an anthropologist or other social scientist, or possibly a student. The account on which I am drawing assumes a very different sort of reader, someone who is, if not a believer, at least someone who is ready or likely to believe. Insofar as I see my task as that of evoking another reality (see Tyler 1986), I wish to present a narrative that is believable, in some sense at least, to the nonbeliever, a challenge I have tried to meet through the use of a "realistic" form. By doing so, I hope (among other things) to provide some sense of how this *istoría* appears to those who narrate it.

A further problem would arise had I drawn on material already translated into English (such as the English version of the church pamphlet). Here choices have been made prior to my own reading. An additional dilemma arises because sometimes the English in such works as pamphlets includes misspellings, odd phrasings, and inappropriate use of words. Yet if I wish to discuss the ways in which the church and its *istoría* are presented to foreigners, these are the texts I must use. Is it appropriate to quote such texts verbatim, even when they contain errors? Or does such quotation simply serve to bolster the dominant position of the writing anthropologist by implying (to most English speakers who might read it) the inferiority of those who seek to write in my own language and signaling that we need to take their writing less seriously than we otherwise might? By showing the "natives'" semiliteracy in my own language, I undermine the authority that would normally inhere in writing.[8]

In Greek the language of such accounts is the language of belief and it is as such that I have attempted to render it, making it stylistically continuous with the history of the island as recounted in chapter 7. I might have begun my account differently. For example, I could have stated that "church pamphlets and books written about the church give the following account of the discovery of the icon and the building of the church." I might have made more use of such phrases as "it is claimed," "according to," "people believe that," and other markers that serve to distance myself and my readers and signal our possible doubts about the account. Instead I left out all such references and presented the *istoría* as straightforward "fact," even inserting endnotes as I would in any other section of the book.

But this rather "dispassionate" rendering conceals some important items in my own agenda that have guided my selection of what to include in the *istoría*. Moreover, if all history is partial (in both senses of the word), then one must expect, and indeed require, more than one *istoría*. My account was taken mostly from a pamphlet distributed by the church and hence represents its agenda. There are other accounts as well, some more detailed, some offering slightly different versions of events. It is not my task here to determine which version is "true." Nor do I wish to cast doubt on all of them ("because there are different *istoríes* this obviously cannot be history"). For those who recount these *istoríes* they tell of things that "truly" happened. Yet the accounts are also false, for they are told, as are all *istoríes*, from a particular perspective, whether that perspective is of church official, islander, Orthodox believer, scholar of Tinos—or anthropologist.

My own agenda will become apparent as I proceed with the following chapters, but I will anticipate several things here. I am interested in the Panayía's request (and hence have rendered it verbatim as it is recorded in the pamphlet). I also want to emphasize the complex gendered hierarchy of religious authority; the commanding divine figure is the Panayía, but the nun Pelayia must act within a constraining structure of male authority, which is responsible for carrying out the divine request. I am also interested in the descriptions of local participation in the uncovering of the icon and the building of the church. Thus I have planted seeds of the "plot" that will unfold in later chapters (cf. Becker 1986:105). By doing this I have perhaps invalidated earlier claims, for these elements of plot are not necessarily those that concern those who penned the original Greek narrative. Thus comes the confession: I am writing my own *istoría*, not theirs.

WRITING THE "REAL" *ISTORÍA*

Let me add one more *istoría* to that I have already constructed in order to illustrate how the authenticity of what I relate might be falsified from within, simply through the choice of words I use. This rendering is my own, drawing upon the "facts" of the other accounts.

Church pamphlets and works of local historians give the following account of the discovery of the holy icon of the Annunciation: In the summer of 1822, an aging nun named Pelayia, resident for most of her humble life in the holy monastery of Kekhrovouno on the island of Tinos, is visited by a mysterious but impatient vision in the form of a lady surrounded by light. From this vision, Pelayia receives somewhat mysterious but rather detailed instructions. "I can no longer stand being where I have been for so long," the vision states, "there in a dusty field, in my buried house. Go tell Stamatelos Kagkadhis to have my home uncovered, there in the field of Andonis Dhoksaras. If he does not obey my orders, a divine sword stroke will smite everyone!"

Despite this grim warning, Pelayia at first does nothing about what she has seen and heard, not believing that her humble person could be the recipient of so grand a vision. The mysterious lady appears a second time, and then a third. Exasperated now, she delivers a rather grim threat: "Listen for the last time, Pelayia; if you do not do what I have told you, I will erase your name from the book of life!"

These threatening words cause Pelayia to awaken from her sleep, whereupon she finds that the vision is still before her. She is struck into near dumbness but manages to gather her wits enough to question her vision about her identity. The vision replies indirectly, with words of the Evangelismos, to let Pelayia know that it is indeed the Panayía who is commanding her. Convinced at last of the reality of her vision—whether because it continued into her waking state, whether because of the direct revelation of the identity of her mysterious visitor, or whether as a consequence of the grim personal threat the Panayía held over her (more convincing apparently than the threat of cholera or "sword stroke" to smite the general populace)—Pelayia, finally certain that her vision is truly divine, informs the abbess about what she has seen.

None of the accounts tell us anything about Andonis Dhoksaras, whose field is so precisely indicated by the Panayía, nor do we learn if he was ever compensated for the loss of his land. Perhaps the glory of having the icon found there was compensation enough.[9]

It is tempting to write this way, with a disbelief that is revealed through style yet does not violate or directly challenge the "facts" of the *istoría*. Disbelief is indicated not only by my choice of adjectives and ironic tone and by such speculations as why Pelayia was finally convinced or how Andonis Dhoksaras felt about his land (speculations that would occur to neither the writers nor the intended readers of the accounts on which I draw), but also through the use of the present tense throughout the narrative. The present tense removes the account from "real" time, hence from history, and places it in the realm of legend or myth; it becomes a story, not a history. Since the use of the present tense is a common dramatic device in the recounting of "stories" in both Greek and English, the *istoría* of Pelayia's vision is, through this device, placed in such a category of popular or "folk" narrative (and hence made less true than "real" history).[10] And since this use of the present tense is associated with less educated people—rural "folk," peasants, the lower classes—employing it here places the *istoría* in an inferior relationship to literate traditions, despite the fact that it is taken from written sources. These sources are thus treated as "no more than" folk narratives, their "literacy" diluted or denied. On the other hand, use of the past tense, as in the first accounts I gave, associates the *istoría* with literacy and hence with history.

Through such stylistic means, I can distance both myself and the reader from the account, without pronouncing on its truth or plausibility. In addition, I can impress and entertain the reader by my cleverness with language. Both the reader and I can, if we wish, treat the *istoría* as an amusing or interesting tale by an observer more sophisticated than the original storyteller. Here I not only exercise my anthropological "authority," but through my writing I create my anthropological persona, playing with the "native" account to confirm and enhance my own superior— because more knowledgeable and literate—position.[11]

Ernestine Friedl, in the introduction to her ethnography *Vasilika,* points out that one of the advantages for anthropologists in working in what she terms "old national cultures" is that they can draw on the work of other specialists, in this case, both Greek and non-Greek (1962:4–5). But what I have been attempting to show is that the relationship of the anthropologist to the written work of the society being studied is not a simple or straightforward one.[12] By writing the *istoría* of the icon several ways, I have rendered the status of that *istoría* ambiguous. In doing so, I seek to address several dilemmas that face me in using so-called "local history" (the phrase itself implies that it is something less than "real" history), dilemmas that are a consequence of my own position as anthropologist and therefore writer and representative of the Western European tradition, with all its ideological, political, and economic weight. At the heart of the dilemma is my relationship to the material itself, a relationship expressed in my writing. Am I writing *about* it, or *from* it? Is it simply one level of "native" account and therefore "true" only as author-ized by the anthropologist? If so, then I treat it as simply *mia istoría.* Or are these accounts data in a positivist sense, that is, real "facts" on which I can base a "real" history? But if I treat the accounts as true "history" in the Western sense of the word (that is, as truth as distinguished from "stories"), am I not doing violence to them by imposing my own concept of what history is or ought to be? Should I critique them as I might critique the work of colleagues? To do so might be to misrepresent them. To not do so, on the other hand, might be viewed as condescending, again removing these materials from the category of "real" history, therefore placing them in an inferior position to other kinds of writing. (After all, one does not critique a myth, at least not now when we are no longer concerned with the one "true" version of a myth; that is, we do not treat myth in the same manner we treat history.)

In addition to the anthropologist's relationship to the "native" written accounts (which is part of the anthropologist's relationship to the "natives" themselves), there is an additional point to be considered. These accounts are, obviously, written by those who are themselves literate, that is, people in authority, whether officials of the church or local scholars. Through writing, they declare the historical truth of the *istoría*. This itself must be considered in relationship to those who are not doing the writing, a point explored more fully later. Moreover, we need to consider the extent to which the dominance of Western European ideas of history, writing, and "truth" shape the way local historians and other scholars write, leading them to seek to turn their *istoríes* into (Eurocentric) history (of the sort presented in chapter 7; cf. Herzfeld 1987a:133).

WRITING THE WOMAN: THE *ISTORÍA* OF ST. PELAYIA

One person who cannot speak in this account is Pelayia. A central character in the *istoría* of the church, she mediates between the human and the divine. It was through her that the lost past was uncovered and recovered and a future Greece given symbolic form. Yet for all of this she is the written about, and not the writer (though we are told that she had learned her letters). A woman of great holiness, chosen to receive the message of the holiest woman of all, she is nonetheless constrained by the structures of male authority through which the commands of the divine must be enacted, and is written about, both contemporarily and thereafter, by men. (Even the Panayía exercises authority over her by writing, threatening to erase her from the book of life.)

And yet I have puzzled over the question of to what extent I should (or must) view her as a woman. Should she be seen instead as simply a holy *person* (*ánthropos*), one who had, after all, renounced most, if not all, of the experiences and roles through which womanhood in her society supposedly was defined? Is my own agenda emerging here, and am I attributing a significance to Pelayia's gender that is inappropriate in this particular context? Am I projecting the categories of my own society in giving gender a wider context of significance than it may have in the society I am studying? Or is it some assumption of a universal "sisterhood" of women that makes me so interested in Pelayia's story (cf. M. Rosaldo 1987)?

And yet perhaps, paradoxically, one of the things that so intrigues me about Pelayia's life is my inability to imagine it despite our shared gender. Nor is it only the span of time that makes such imagining difficult. In my visits to the monastery of Kekhrovouno, I found it difficult to comprehend the nuns' way of life. Their very withdrawal from, and even in some senses challenge to, the way of life that supposedly unites women worldwide— that is, marriage, sexuality, childbirth, and motherhood—further removes them from my own ability to identify, or even empathize, with them, and their long black robes and severe black cowls both mark them off and conceal them, as women and as human beings.[13]

Yet the fact that Pelayia was a woman is not irrelevant to her *istoría*. I will tell this *istoría* now in my own words, drawing on the written texts available to me, as well as on oral statements from islanders and on my own observations.

Not very much is known, it seems, about Pelayia's life. According to one of her biographers (S. Lagouros 1979), she was born in 1752 in the village of Kambos, the daughter of a priest named Nikiforos Negrepondis[14] and of a mother whose name was unknown but who came from the village of Tripotamos. She was given the worldly name Loukia. She apparently had three sisters, but nothing is known about them. According to one biography, the priest's family led a life of simple and pure faith, "close to nature and to God" (S. Lagouros 1979:7). Loukia lived with her family in a rural environment, with three country churches nearby. In this period, when Tinos was under Turkish rule, there were no schools on the island,[15] and her biographer suggests that Loukia learned her first letters from her father and spent her time helping her mother with housework and assisting her father with his holy duties and with the care of the churches close to the house. From her earliest years, her biographer tells us, Loukia "had chosen her road" (S. Lagouros 1979:8) and knew she wished to dedicate herself to God. After her father's death, when Loukia was twelve, her mother sent her to live with her aunt in Tripotamos, and from there she paid frequent visits to the monastery of Kekhrovouno, where another aunt was a nun, with the name Pelayia. It was thus perhaps natural enough for the young Loukia to choose to follow the life of a nun, and at the age of fifteen she entered the monastery, where she lived until her death in 1834.

The monastery of Kekhrovouno, where Loukia/Pelayia spent most of her life, is dedicated to the Dormition of the Madonna (*Kímisis tis Theotókou*). The exact date of the founding of the monastery is unknown. One of the nuns at the monastery told me it was founded in the seventh century, but other sources give different dates. A story (shall we call it myth or history?) written by a philologist appeared in a local paper; it gives the following account of the monastery's beginnings:

> Opposite the monastery, below the mountain of Exobourgos, is the village of Tripotamos. Before the monastery was built, on its site there was a small church [*mikrí eklisoúla*] of St. John. Two orphan girls, good and God-fearing [*kalés ke theofovoúmenes*], who lived in Tripotamos would see a light on the side of the hill every night. This continued for many evenings and finally they decided to investigate. When they arrived they saw the little church of St. John. When they returned to the village, they told the villagers about it. The girls decided to go back and build a room [*kámara*] there and to remain because they believed the light to be something important and holy [*theikó*]. However, they had no money. But the villagers helped them out, and thus they built their room and lived there. Little by little, they built other rooms and other young women came to stay. Thus the monastery gradually came into existence and became the monastery of Kekhrovouno, many years ago. (Amirolis 1972)[16]

The monastery was in existence in 1207 when Tinos was captured by Ghisi, duke of Tinos and Mykonos. It thus appears to be of the Byzantine period.[17]

The monastery is built on the side of a mountain, visible from the sea and from the town, exposed to the winds that buffet the island. In the summer it is cooler than below in the town, and in the winter it is cold and damp. In construction it is like the island villages—clustered buildings along narrow winding streets, the whole enclosed in one outer wall pierced only by tiny windows, this a necessity for defense in the days when pirates frequently raided the island. Such walls can still be seen here and there in some of the island villages, but the monastery is the best-preserved example. Today all the buildings of the monastery are whitewashed, the gleaming walls in picturesque contrast to the bright flowers and green vines grown by the nuns. But in earlier, more perilous times, the stone walls would have been left bare to blend with the rocky landscape so that they would be less easily spotted by raiders from the sea (Kharitonidou 1984).

There is no information about how many nuns were resident in the monastery at Kekhrovouno when Pelayia first came to live there. In these earlier times monastic life flourished on Tinos, but today all the island's monasteries stand deserted except for Kekhrovouno and one Catholic monastery at Loutra (open only during the winter months, when it serves as a school for Catholic girls). At Kekhrovouno, however, the monastic life is still followed by some sixty nuns,[18] practicing a form of noncommunal monasticism, an old system whereby nuns live in their separate cells, cooking and eating in groups of two or three.

Kekhrovouno, like other sacred places, has a history of miraculous happenings, which are commemorated and embodied in its physical structure. One example is a painting on the wall of the chapel of the Life-giving Well. The chapel had once been a room used for storage. One night the nuns heard shouting. When they went to the room to investigate, they found the painting there, as well as a spring from which holy water is now drawn. This icon cannot be altered. If one goes to fix or polish it, I was told, nothing happens. Another miracle also involved a wall, one that sprang up miraculously to shield the nuns from view when the monastery was attacked by invaders.

The monastery undoubtedly owes its present-day prosperity, if not its continued existence, to Pelayia's vision over 150 years ago. The monastery itself is an object of pilgrimage, where devotees come to see the humble cell in which the Madonna appeared to the elderly nun, and to hear accounts of the monastery's other miracles. And once a year, on July 23, the date of the Panayía's final, decisive appearance to Pelayia and now the feast day of St. Pelayia, the Panayía returns to the monastery as her icon is carried up in procession from the town for a day of celebration at the place where the process of its rediscovery was begun.

What was life like for a woman on Tinos in the mid-eighteenth century, a woman born into a priest's household in a small village, under the relatively benign rule of the Ottoman Empire in its fading days? Pelayia was a rural child, tending the country churches with her father, not part of the bustling, more cosmopolitan prosperity of the town (which would have been a long walk or donkey ride away, down the steep mountainside along a narrow path bordered by stone walls). What was it like to enter the monastery at the age of fifteen, an age when other girls most likely would have been contemplating marriage, and to live there for the rest of one's life, a span of over sixty-five years? It is not just Pelayia herself that the answers to such questions would reveal, but an entire time and place.

The icons of Pelayia depict a woman with a lined, ascetic visage, her face framed by the severe black head covering of a nun, gazing straight ahead with the characteristic expressionless yet penetrating gaze of a Byzantine icon, revealing little of the person, everything of the saint.

By all accounts Pelayia continued her life of simplicity and piety from the time of her vision until her death. She did not live in obscurity during those years, however, for many visitors came to visit her in her humble cell and to receive her blessing. Moreover, her recent sanctification shows her to have a more general religious significance, according to a local newspaper, O Fáros tis Tínou (The Lighthouse of Tinos). A story in the June–July 1971 issue points out that the canonization of the Blessed Pelayia demonstrates that even in our time the church has saints to offer, in

9. St. Pelayia. Icon in her chapel at the Church of the Annunciation

the form of those who show themselves to be instruments of God and organs of the fulfillment of God's will (1971, nos. 131–32).

Pelayia died on April 28, 1834. She would have been eighty-two at the time. She had lived long enough after her vision to witness the establishment of the first state of Greece and the institutionalization of the Church of the Annunciation as a major pilgrimage site. She was buried in the cemetery of the monastery, and when, as was customary, her bones were later disinterred (presumably after three years, since this is the normal time period today on the island), the church foundation (*ídhrima*) sought to acquire them to be placed in the Church of the Annunciation. The nuns, however, wished to keep her in the monastery, and apparently they prevailed, for her bones were interred behind the altar in one of the monastery churches.[19] For some reason, however, the exact place of interment was forgotten, and there was considerable excitement when, during church renovations undertaken in 1950–51, some bones were found underneath the marble behind the altar. As the finding is recounted (both in written accounts and orally), the sweet smell that emanated from the site, and from the skull when it was disinterred, announced the resting place of a saint, and the bones were assumed to be those of Pelayia.[20] They were placed in her cell (now a pilgrimage site) until 1973, when after her canonization a church for her was built at the monastery. The bones now reside in an ornate stand near the main entrance of this church, and through the glass top of the stand the dome of the skull can be seen.

Pelayia's cell has been turned into a small chapel and museum. Here one can see her simple living arrangements (the rooms not so much different from what can still be found in some of the older village houses today), the small, hard bed on which she lay and her wooden pillow. A painting of Pelayia's vision hangs on one wall, and in the main part of the chapel a glass-fronted cupboard houses some old icons dating from the time period when Pelayia lived. Accounts of the miracles performed by Pelayia since the recovery of her bones are recorded at the monastery and have added to her *istoría*, which did not cease with her death, but lives on in these and other ways. In addition, her sanctification was an important event for the island, to judge by local newspaper stories at the time.[21]

Pelayia's life, as presented today, is an example of piety and faith, a *woman's* piety and faith. The divine will is revealed not to the wealthy and powerful, but to the humble and poor—in this case to a nun known for the purity and simplicity of her life. Pelayia serves as an example, not in her way of life—for certainly not all women are exhorted to be nuns— but in her faith. Pelayia has little or no voice of her own in this history. She is spoken to and spoken of, but does not speak for herself.[22] Yet she and her history are an essential part of the church and of pilgrimage, for it was through her that the icon was (re)discovered, and this is materially embodied in her representations in the monastery (her cell, chapel, church, bones) and in the Church of the Annunciation (where there is a chapel dedicated to Pelayia below the main church), as well as in the verbal and written stories of the church's history (including sermons on such occasions as her saint's day).

When I first approached the writing of this chapter, I saw it as a fairly simple task. I would use whatever written materials were available, in Greek or other languages, as well as oral accounts and my own observations in order to construct a chapter titled (tentatively) "The History of the Shrine." But I was not completely naive in approaching this task, for the word *interpretation* also lurked in my mind as part of what I both needed and wanted to do. What I did not foresee was that straddling a position between *istoría* as history ("background") and *istoría* as story (requiring "interpretation") would present such a radical challenge. As I worked, however, I came to realize, as Hastrup has put it, that "the range of 'otherness' also incorporated a vast number of separate histories" (1992b:1). The Western sense of history, a sense that assumes a linear progression of events (see Hastrup 1992b; Davis 1992b), dominated chapter 7's discussion of the history of Tinos. In that discussion, I pointed out that the island has generally been viewed by historians as having a history only insofar as it was implicated in Western history. This chapter, on the other hand, has suggested the possibility of "other histories," or as Davis (1992a) has put it, a "history of the people without Europe."

What makes the history of the icon as recounted in this chapter a confusing one is that the form in which this history is generally recounted resembles Western notions of history: a sequence of events arranged in chronological order, cause and effect, linear time. And yet what is acceptable as cause and effect to the narrators of this history turns out to be subversive of the notion of history in the Western sense. Divine intervention, visions, miracles—these are not the forms of cause and effect with which Western historians normally operate. Moreover, upon closer examination, time itself proves not to have the linearity the narrative at first seems to suggest. Rather, there are elements of inevitability in the account of the icon's finding, foreshadowed in the prophecies that preceded the discovery, and of cyclical time, echoed in the themes of the parallel resurrection of the icon and of Greece (both in turn associated with the Annunciation, the announcement of Christ's birth).[23] Time thus becomes more than a linear series of happenings linked by cause and effect; rather, as Herzfeld puts it, time "becomes a play of ideas about inevitability and the specificity of historical events" (1992a:63).

In seeking to come to terms not only with different versions of an *istoría* but also with different views of what is history, I have found myself shifting among many positions as I write, resulting in a stance that Clifford has termed "believer-skeptic" (1986:111). While wanting to write a "history" in my own terms, I find that to reconstruct the written accounts in these terms is in fact to dismiss them as history and to make them stories instead, and to claim for myself the sole authority to create an "authentic" past. Yet since I cannot remove my own voice, I have tried to make my account multivocal—or polyphonic, though in a somewhat different sense than Tyler (1986) means—as one way of creating a sense of another experience and another reality. I have done so by presenting the accounts, to some extent at least, in their own terms and by contrasting this presentation (through several forms of narrative) with ways I might present these *istoríes* in my own reality.

Obviously writing is not unconnected from reading—each assumes the other. My own choices about how to write about the material I have covered here depend on my reading of it. Mostly, however, I have been concerned with how to render the material to my own audience through my own writing. The next chapter examines the perspective of the "reader" and expands the idea of writing, reading, and texts beyond the written word. At the same time it carries forward some of the questions I have been exploring with respect to history, for as I shall show, "reading" the Church of the Annunciation carries us into issues of national and local identity, and as Davis suggests, "There is no identity . . . without a past" (1992a:21).

CHAPTER NINE

Of Nations and Foreigners, Miracles and Texts

IN THE EARLY 1880s an Englishman named James Theodore Bent made a tour of the islands of the Cyclades. He visited Tinos twice on his travels, once to attend the festival of the Annunciation on March 25, and the second time, not quite a year later, to tour the island. Unlike many such travelers to Greece, Bent did not confine his attentions to antiquities but was also interested in contemporary customs and was willing to learn modern Greek. Nonetheless, he saw many continuities between the modern Greeks and the ancients, and drew upon both past and present in describing what he saw at Tinos.

Here is Bent's introduction to his experiences at the festival of the Annunciation:

> Of the many existing points of connection between old and new Greece one of the greatest is the love of panegyris; these religious festivals are still numerous in Asia Minor and in the islands as of old, and are characterized now as then by a mixture of devout earnestness and general sociability.
>
> In every branch of the religious life the religious susceptibility of the Greek of today is as it was when St. Paul wrote of them as being too superstitious, too devoted to the countless gods of their country. In short, this country, the former hotbed of polytheism, has in no way changed its character yet. (1965:231)

Bent went on to describe how pilgrims came to the Church of the Annunciation from all parts of the Greek world, and noted that "those who contend for the Slavonic origin of the modern Hellenes would do well to spend the feast week at Tenos, where they would satisfy themselves, beyond a doubt, that the Greek who goes to the island of Tenos today is a lineal descendant of the Greek who went to the neighboring island of Delos to worship two thousand years ago" (1965:232).

Thus for Bent the festival he observed at Tinos represented both cultural and racial continuity with ancient Greece. However, he was not blind to the contemporary significance of the shrine, and to the fact that its founding coincided with the establishment of the new state of Greece. He commented on the large numbers of pilgrims coming to be healed, and then went on:

> This is only the general aspect of the pilgrimage; politically and socially the effect is wider. The birth of the panegyris at Tenos was coincident with the regeneration of Greece, and in the working of Greek politics for the last sixty

years the annual excursion to Tenos has formed an important factor. Dissatisfied Cretans, oppressed Greeks from Asia Minor here meet the free sons of new Hellas on free Hellenic soil, and in this island yearly are sown seeds of revolt against Turkish rule, which the pilgrims take home and spread broadcast on fertile ground. (1965:232)

Bent was only one of many travelers, Greek and foreign, to visit Tinos during the nineteenth century after the finding of the icon. Following the icon's discovery and the building of the Church of the Annunciation, Tinos became both an important pilgrimage site for the Orthodox and a curiosity to attract the adventurous foreign visitor. Although there were other pilgrimage sites in Greece, some relatively localized, others drawing devotees from a wider area, the Church of the Annunciation rapidly acquired importance as not only a national pilgrimage site but, as Bent notes, a panhellenic one as well. The reasons for this have to do with the timing of the finding of the icon, a timing that, as we shall see, can be "read" in a variety of ways. Thus for James Theodore Bent the Church of the Annunciation at Tinos and the ritual events that occurred there were a text that spoke to him of both the old Greece and the new, and of the cultural links joining the one to the other.

THE ANTHROPOLOGIST'S RETURN

My own initial "reading" of the shrine and its festivities was somewhat different from Bent's.[1] When I arrived in Tinos to do fieldwork for my doctoral dissertation in late July 1969, I intended to focus on the study of a village, not on a miraculous shrine. In fact, I did not even realize before I made my first visit that Tinos housed such a celebrated place of pilgrimage. And although I observed several of the celebrations associated with the Church of the Annunciation during the course of fieldwork, including the Day of the Dormition, my observation of these events was incidental to my research. My main concern when I first arrived was settling into my fieldwork site, the village of Falatados, about 15 kilometers from the main town. Stories of a miraculous shrine and its miracles of healing were not what I had come to study, and I was frankly uncomfortable with the crowds and the emotional fervor associated with events at the Church. Nor did I find the church itself aesthetically appealing. Crowded with the many offerings of the faithful, it appeared to me overly ornate and lacking in the more austere charm that characterized many of the village churches. I did not neglect the Church of the Annunciation completely when I wrote up my research—it was, after all, what made Tinos famous and an important part of the "background" material I needed to include when writing about other topics. But it remained just that—background—and not a focus of my interest or research.

It was the islanders themselves who would not let me completely over-look the church. When told that I had come to study the customs and the history of the island and village (the closest I could come at the time to explaining why I was there), several islanders told me that all I needed to know of the history of the island were two things: the story of how the island had fallen from Venetian into Turkish hands by the treachery of the Venetian commander and the later discovery and subsequent miracles of the the icon of the Annunciation. The islanders' insistence on telling me the story of the shrine and my own tendency to ignore their insistence in favor of what I regarded as more "anthropological" topics were, I feel now, related. It was not simply that I refused to share their reading of a text (with what I now see as its significant themes of catastrophe and resurrection); I did not even fully recognize that there was a text to be read. In addition, at that time I did not tend to view my own work reflex-ively and only later came to see the possible significance of the fact that the story was being told to *me,* an outsider, a foreigner.

Obviously in the the sixteen years that passed between the end of my first fieldwork and my return to Tinos in 1986 to conduct research on the shrine and pilgrimage, my views had changed. I now saw the church as offering possibilities for the exploration of significant theoretical and eth-nographic interests. For me, then, the shrine was not a text to reveal the islanders' lineage with the Greeks of antiquity (as it was for James The-odore Bent) but a means of exploring some current anthropological is-sues. At the same time, readings such as Bent's, which did see ancient roots in contemporary lives, came to constitute part of the text I sought to elucidate, a text that I had to read not only in a local and national context but in an international context as well.

THE SHRINE AS TEXT

In chapter 8 I discussed written texts and the ambiguities inherent in reading, translating, and utilizing them. In this chapter I have begun to speak of "reading" the shrine itself, and to discuss what the shrine is "saying," terms that are themselves part of a more inclusive metaphor—a metaphor that suggests the similarities between the Church of the Annun-ciation and pilgrimage on the one hand, and a written text on the other. It is this metaphor that I now wish to make more explicit, and to justify its use to structure the material of this chapter. In what way, however, can the shrine be seen as a text, and what does it mean to "read" it?

Edward M. Bruner, in his discussion of "the anthropology of experi-ence," examines text in relation to performance, viewing culture itself as the "performance of text." Performance "does the structuring of the structure of the text" (1986:22). But from another perspective, performance *is* the text. A postmodern anthropology views culture not as existing beyond and independent of—and hence "expressed" in—such things as spatial arrangements, ritual, and other phenomena to which we and the actors assign meaning. Rather, it is these things by which culture itself is constituted. They are not "expressions"; they *are* culture. An important corollary to this is that "culture" itself is never static or determinate but necessarily always in process.

Such a view of culture is one outcome of anthropologists' attempts to strike a balance between two approaches to culture: functionalist and structuralist approaches on the one hand, and action- and actor-oriented approaches on the other. Functionalist and structuralist approaches subordinate actors to the workings of a social system and/or to a set of rules that constitute "culture." Action-oriented approaches stress practice and take account of meaning and motivation; however, they often do not take account of constraints operating on actors (Moore 1986:6; see also Ortner 1984, and Mouzelis 1978 on Greece). Henrietta Moore points out that the idea of culture as a "pregiven" set of meanings makes it difficult to formulate a theory of change and that "The analysis of symbolic forms must acknowledge the interpretation of social actors as other than simply contingent explanations" (1986:6). At the same time, the stress on the importance of ideas and meanings can lead to neglect of the social, economic, and historical conditions governing the production and transformation of such ideas and meanings. The anthropological tendency to see culture in holistic terms, Moore further suggests, tends to obscure the existence of alternative interpretations and values. Coherence and "systemness" are emphasized "at the expense of concepts like conflict, contradiction, and power" (Moore 1986:74).

The metaphor of performance and text can point to one possible way out of these dilemmas. It can also open up possibilities for a critical reflexivity that seeks to break down the observer-observed distinction. Such a breakdown poses a challenge to the very idea of "objectivity," a challenge central to interpretive and postmodern critiques of anthropology. The use of the metaphor of a text (at least for the purposes of this chapter) says something not only about my view of pilgrimage and its significance in a particular context but also about an approach to anthropology, an approach in which my own positioning in the field plays a significant role.

The adoption of the metaphor of culture as text within anthropology has been stimulated, in part at least, by trends in literary criticism. As Jonathan Culler has suggested, "Since literature takes as its subject all human experience, and particularly the ordering, interpreting and articulating of experience, it is no accident that the most varied theoretical projects find instruction in literature" (1982:10; see also Suleiman and Crosman 1980).[2] The idea of culture as text is appealing to a contemporary anthropology because it provides "an analytical framework which retains . . . [the] emphasis on meaning, while at the same time introducing ideas of social strategy and strategic interpretation" (Moore 1986:75). Texts, then, metaphorically considered, are "read"—not only by the anthropologist (who then writes her own text), but also by those who are at the same time producing them.

The idea of "text" implies that the study of culture is necessarily an interpretive one. Moreover, there is no final authority inhering in any single interpretation; there is always the possibility of multiple "readings." Even the authors (in this case the "natives") cannot give a single authoritative reading (cf. R. Rosaldo 1989:49–50). Meaning emerges from the reading of the text by different readers and is therefore neither identical with the author's aims nor somehow inherent in the text itself. Moreover, interpretation is inherently self-critical. As Taussig puts it, "What truth is being displayed by one's interpretation? Is it nothing more than a mediation between the unfamiliar and the familiar? . . . in confronting the implications of the practice we discern that the interpretation of the unfamiliar in terms of the familiar impugns the familiar itself" (1980:3). Moreover, since fieldwork requires that "anthropologists . . . adapt to events in which they themselves are significant actors" (Herzfeld 1983:151), we must see anthropologists as involved in creating the very texts they purport to "read."[3]

Implicit or explicit in the metaphor of text is the seeking to deprivilege the anthropological act of writing by suggesting that all cultures in some sense "write" (Tyler 1987). Writing itself thus becomes metaphoric. Such metaphorical "writing" may be in the form of behavior (ritual or otherwise) or even objects (see Babcock 1986), or it may take a variety of other forms. This supports and extends the notion that we can regard the behavior of others as a kind of text (see Ricoeur 1979), for like a text, cultures have both "authors" (those members of the culture whose behavior and other forms of "writing" the anthropologist "reads") and "readers" (both members of the society writing the text and outside observers, including the anthropologist). This metaphorical idea that all cultures "write" attempts to erase the distance/distinction between "us" and "them" in which a modernist anthropology is grounded. It is part of the attempt to create a "polyphonic" ethnography in which the "natives" "speak for themselves" and the anthropologist's voice is only one of many in the text that is produced (Tyler 1986).

The distinction cannot be erased so easily, however. The idea that we can accomplish such erasure by stating that other cultures "write" is an illusion. Not only does writing (in the literal sense) have a unique power, but it is through the ethnographer's writing that we know about this metaphoric "writing" of others. The shrine at Tinos can in no way "speak for itself." Nor do the pilgrims "speak for themselves," even when I present what they say "in their own words." For not only are "their own words" translated by me, but I must also transcribe and select what I hear. In addition, their "speaking" may not be in words—the possessed woman of chapter 4 was dramatically eloquent, though she spoke very little. Yet it is in words, my own words, that this "speaking" must be represented here. In this sense, for all writings and all readings presented in this book, the author-ity is ultimately mine. In this sense, also, despite my own use of the metaphor, there is no text but that which I produce, for I create the shrine as text rather than simply "reading" it.

These metaphors of writing, reading, and text are some of the most recent metaphors, in a long history of metaphors, by which anthropologists seek to understand people of other societies.[4] I find that the metaphor of culture as a text provides a useful way for examining the multiple meanings of the shrine and pilgrimage, particularly insofar as pilgrimage is coming more and more to be seen as a context in which meanings and interest are contested. Such multiple meanings—that is, the fact that the shrine is "read" in different ways—and the struggle over the hegemony of certain meanings I see as part of the nature and significance of the shrine.

Bruner points out that not all cultural expressions are designed for consumption "inside" but may be directed at outsiders. To put this in terms of the text metaphor, the "reader" or "intended audience" (see Culler 1982) may be someone outside the creator's own culture or group. This is readily seen, for example, in cultural constructions aimed at tourists, whether these constructions are objects for sale, ritual events, certain kinds of behavior, or other types of performance (see Dubisch 1991b). Even when they have their origins in "authentic" cultural experiences, these constructions may be altered (or sometime reconstructed) in response to outside reaction (whether actual, imagined, or anticipated). Thus one of the reasons offered for the ban placed by the Greek military dictatorship on the exuberant breaking of plates (*spásimo*) at festive events was that it presented an image to outsiders of "primitiveness."[5] Constructions aimed at outside audiences may also take the form of lies. At one tourist shop on Tinos, for example, souvenir items constructed of shells were represented to outsiders (Greeks and foreign tourists alike) as a local product when they were actually made in the Philippines. Thus the shopowner responded to visitors' desire for an "authentic" souvenir in order to sell his goods. As an "insider," however (at least in this instance), I was told the truth when I questioned him about the origin of his tourist goods.

Outsiders, that is, nonbelievers, may also be an unintended audience to cultural performances. As unintended readers of culturally produced texts, they play little or no role in the construction of the performance but nonetheless "read" it in significant ways. The anthropologist as outsider is usually both an intended and unintended audience (sometimes shifting, sometimes simultaneous), and it becomes crucial to the understanding of what is presented to know which position one occupies at any particular moment. The anthropological "reading" is, of course, a peculiar one, for it is purportedly an insider's view, telling us what meaning the events have for the "natives," and yet at the same time claiming a superior understanding, a "true" reading, of what is gong on. But just as "culture" is a process, so is ethnography. Indeed the practice of anthropology itself is "comparable as a symbolic activity to what it observes" (Herzfeld 1987a:185). Anthropology does not simply "reflect" a particular way of looking at the world, it helps to create that view as well. The idea of text thus has a political dimension. The ethnography itself, as a written text, is part of political relationships. "Because ethnography is embedded in the political process, dominant narratives are units of power as well as meaning. The ability to tell one's story has a political component; indeed, one means of the dominance of a narrative is the space allotted to it in the discourse" (Bruner 1986:19).

To return, then, to the questions posed at the beginning of this section: In what ways does the shrine constitute a text,[6] and what will the use of the text metaphor accomplish for me, the anthropologist? The above discussion has already suggested some answers to both questions.

First, there are written texts associated with the shrine in the form of records, accounts of origins, recitations of miracles, and so on. Some of these are connected directly to the church by being housed there or distributed by the church. Others are themselves commentaries on the church, as in locally written histories that interpret the meaning of the church and the events associated with it such as the ones I discussed in chapter 8.

Second, the shrine is a set of material objects and a way of organizing space that are both the product and producers of meaning and can be considered part of the text. The icon itself is the meaningful center of the church, the reason for its existence, the motive cause of pilgrimage. While the icon can be seen as part of a religious system in which icons play an important part—a manner of reading that reveals the icon's "sense" (using Ricoeur's [1979] term)—it can also be seen in terms of its "references" (which include the nation of Greece and its history), part of which this chapter seeks to explore. While the icon "embodies" meaning for pilgrims, and it is this meaning that draws them, at the same time they create the meaning by being so drawn. Their devotions at the icon, as well as the other aspects of their pilgrimage (including their vows), create the icon not simply as a representation of the Panayía, but in fact *as* the Panayía. In addition to the icon, the church is hung with hundreds of *támata,* which both represent past faith and create and reinforce present belief.

The church as a structure, as organized space, is another part of the text.[7] Again, its internal reading relates it to the structure of Orthodoxy, and to the systematic nature of its various components *qua* Orthodox church. But it has outside referents as well. As Moore suggests, "to understand space as a text is to conceive of the spatial order as something more than merely the physical manifestation, or product, of activities conducted in space." She goes on to point out that "what is inscribed in the organisation of space is not the actuality of past actions, but their meaning" (1986:81). As I will suggest, such parts of the church as the mausoleum of the battleship *Elli* and the fountain of the Turkish official, while commemorating past events through physical space and objects, are given meaning by contemporary actors, particularly church officials.

But the pilgrims themselves and the events that occur at the church also make up the text. (In this sense, there is no separation of text from performance, practice, experience; I am considering all as text.) Pilgrims thus both read and are the text, not just for the anthropologist or other outsiders, but for themselves and others as well (townspeople, church officials, foreigners, anthropologists, and other pilgrims). Particularly around major holidays, part of the pilgrim's experience of the shrine are the other pilgrims who are there; part of the meaning for the pilgrim is the presence of these other pilgrims in large numbers, the acts they perform, the conversations they engage in, the offerings they leave. The pilgrims are constantly writing and rewriting the text.

The church and pilgrimage appear as a text also to local people and in a national context. But it is a text read in different ways. Here again the idea of a text is useful in avoiding claims of the determination of *the* meaning of what is observed. Meaning is constantly created, negotiated, contested (cf. Eade and Sallnow 1991b; Bowman 1991). It is variable and emergent. Meaning, as we shall see, is also connected to power. Power adheres not only in the ability to produce texts but in the ability to interpret them. In the case of the Church of the Annunciation, the church as an official organization and as the creator of ideology enjoys a hegemony of interpretation and a greater power to disseminate its interpretations. It also plays a role in local politics. But its power does not go unchallenged. Not only may church officials' readings be opposed by those of the political state (and by those of local politicians as well), they may also be opposed by the pilgrims. In the latter case, interpretation may not take the verbal and written form of official discourse, but may be a reading presented, quite literally, with the bodies of the pilgrims as they seek to accomplish their own ends, sometimes in resistance to official attempts at control (see Dubisch 1990a). That is, meaning resides for the pilgrims in practice, is produced by practice, and is both cause and consequence of their pilgrimage to the shrine. In part, then, one reading of the church is as the source of conflict of, or at least of a multiplicity of, different readings. One means of eliciting this multiplicity of meanings is the examination of "the conditions of meaning," that is, "the relationship between a text and its social and historical conditions" (Moore 1986:85; see also Culler 1982).

It is in all of these ways that I seek to elucidate the shrine as "text."

THE RESURRECTION OF GREECE

Pelayia's vision came at a significant point in Greek history, for only a little over a year before her vision occurred the struggle for the existence of a politically independent state of Greece had begun. According to some accounts, the banner of Greek resistance was first raised on March 25, 1821, the day of the Annunciation (*Evangelismós*). Other sources give the date as March 17, though one Greek author sees the beginning on this day as impatience on the part of Greeks zealous for their freedom who could not wait for what should have been the "real" day of the uprising, that is, March 25 (Theoklitos n.d.:71). Whatever the accuracy of the date in the standard historical sense, the pattern of associating significant events with the nearest holy day makes the Day of the Annunciation the appropriate marker for the beginning of the struggle for an independent Greece. March 25 is now celebrated throughout Greece as a day of double import, for it is both Greek Independence Day and the day of the angel Gabriel's announcement to Mary that she would bear the son of God. In other words, two rebirths—of humankind and of the Greeks—are combined. This double rebirth, implicit in much of the shrine's iconography, ritual, and *istoría*, is also stated explicitly in several written texts. In a contemporary book on the Panayía, for example, among the various of her manifestations to whom the author dedicates his work is the one "who on 25 March 1821 trumpeted the national Annunciation" (*ton ethnikó Evangelismó*) (Theoklitos n.d.:6). Elsewhere the same author speaks of March 25 as the "National Easter" (*Ethnikó Páskha*) and of a "double annunciation" (*dhiplós evangelismós*) (n.d.:71). (The parallel between the words *epanástasis*, the term applied to the struggle for independence, and the word for resurrection, *anástasis*, gives weight to such assertions as well; see Herzfeld 1982.)

The theme of resurrection is also carried out in the *istoría* of the finding of the icon. This *istoría* begins, like the story of the Annunciation, with a divine being, the Panayía, speaking to a virgin, the aged and virtuous nun Pelayia. The virgin Pelayia becomes the vehicle for the (re)birth of the Greek nation as symbolized in the finding of the icon, just as the Virgin

Mary had become the means of humankind's rebirth. Moreover, the icon, once housed in a Byzantine church (itself resting on the foundations of an ancient Greek temple—the Greek word *naós* is used for both church and temple in accounts of this history), was buried by the ravages of barbarians. So also the Greek people suffered, their culture and religion buried by the oppression of the Ottomans and other foreigners. The announcement of Christ's birth thus becomes the emblem of the birth of a nation as well.

But as such texts emphasize, this birth is really a rebirth. The finding of the icon—because of its association with the struggle for an independent Greek state—comes to represent the resurrection of Greekness itself, and the recovery of, and building upon, its earliest foundations (both literally and metaphorically), going back to ancient Greek civilization. This resurrection is also a resurrection of a less distant past, a Christian past. Both of these pasts played a role, to varying degrees, in the attempts to answer the thorny question of who is a Greek, a question with significant political implications.

The Greek struggle for an independent nation required not only convincing Greeks that such a nation should exist (and not all Greeks were united in the belief that it should, nor in how to define Greekness itself; see Herzfeld 1982:17), but also enlisting the support of Western powers by convincing them of the legitimacy of a Greek nation, for it was only with the support of key Western nations that a territory labeled Greece could be wrested from the Ottoman lands. This in turn required convincing these Western European nations, in essence, that such a Greece, rather than being created, was instead to be *reclaimed* by people who were, and always had been, Greeks. This argument hinged in large part on the idea of cultural continuity of present-day Greeks with those of the classical past and on the idea that the rest of European culture was descended from this past. Educated Greeks and foreigners devoted considerable effort to proving this thesis, both before the revolution and afterward.

This effort to legitimize the struggle for Greek nationhood in terms convincing to Western European powers, and to acquire the political and military support of these powers, resulted in what Herzfeld has termed "disemia," a double set of identities, one inward and one outward facing. One identity presented the contemporary Greeks as direct cultural descendants of the ancient Hellenes. This created identity (which Herzfeld calls "Hellenism") ignored the heritage of the Byzantine Empire and the traditions of Greek Orthodox Christianity. At the time of independence (and afterward), however, the majority of Greeks had little acquaintance with a classical past and had difficulty conceiving of themselves as its heirs (Herzfeld 1982:17). Rather, Herzfeld argues, they saw themselves in terms of the second, inward-facing identity, which he calls the "Romeic" image of Greece, an identity that "echoes the Byzantine (East Roman) Empire and hence the Orthodox Christian tradition to which the over-whelming majority of Greeks still adhered" (1982:19). The Hellenic model was and is outward looking, playing an important role in interna-tional relations, and concealing "an internally Romeic social reality in which the Greek Orthodox Church continues to play a directing role" (1987a:181). To put this in the terms in which this chapter is framed, there are two kinds of "texts," aimed at two sets of "audiences" in the representation of Greekness. It would be a mistake, however, to see these two models only in terms of outward and inward looking. Certain repre-sentations of the Church of the Annunciation seek not only to present to outsiders (as well as to Greeks) an image of Orthodoxy as part of the continuity of Greekness but also to merge this "Romeic" past with classi-cal "Hellenic" Greece.

The issue of Greekness was by no means resolved with the establish-ment of the first Greek state, for there remained many who were defined, and who defined themselves, as Greeks but lived outside that first state's boundaries, a situation that determined much of Greece's destiny for the hundred years following the Greek War of Independence. Internally, too, the new nation had its problems of national identity. Among these was the problem of fragmenting regionalism and local identities, coupled with a resentment that independence meant simply that a new state, equally prone to such practices as taxation and conscription, had replaced Otto-man rule.

It is in this context that the Church of the Annunciation of Tinos and its miraculous icon take on significant national and international dimen-sions. As representations of a divinely sanctioned Greekness, as symbols of national unity, and as a focal point of pilgrimage for the Orthodox both within and outside Greece, the Church and its icon could serve to give both a focus and a legitimacy to the notion of Greekness, a Greekness founded on a common faith, legitimated by miracles, and experienced directly through pilgrimage. By combining the Orthodox faith with na-tionalism, officials of the church could forge a powerful political symbol for an emerging nation.

Convincing as such a reading may seem, however, it is unclear to what extent the association of the finding of the icon with the promise of a Greek victory and the establishment of a nation of Greece was actually made at the time of the icon's discovery and how much is instead a later reading by Greek writers, church officials, and politicians (and by the anthropologist). Two present-day authors state that the bishop Gavriíl, immediately after the finding of the icon, prayed to the Panayía for Greek victory (S. Lagouros 1979:27), and that the news of the finding of the icon spread quickly throughout Greece, giving hope to those who were struggling (A. Lagouros 1965:54). Several older histories of the finding of the icon, however, written shortly after this event, do not even mention the struggle for independence that was occurring at the time (e.g., Pirgos 1865), and the finding of the icon does not seem to be conventionally included in histories of the struggle.

However, after the establishment of the first state of Greece in 1832 (of which the Cyclades were a part), the church at Tinos was visited by several of the heroes of the Greek Revolution, including Kolokotronis, Miaoulis, and Makriyiannis. Makriyiannis, although he does not mention Tinos in his account of the war years, sent his memoirs to Tinos for safekeeping some years after the war. Then, in September 1844, he reports that "I went to Tinos to do reverence. I spent twenty-three days there in the service of my vows to the Virgin, recovered these papers and brought them back" (1966:168). Kolokotronis is also mentioned in histories of the church as one of the war heroes who visited Tinos (though he himself does not mention this in his memoirs), and a church pamphlet states that Miaoulis and Kanaris came many times to Tinos to pay their devotions (Anonymous 1986:16).

More recent writings make a clear association with national issues in their interpretation of the events of the time, as the following quotation from a twentieth-century history of Tinos (in Greek) demonstrates:

> The finding of the icon as well as the building of the church as we have told it coincided with the early years of nationalism, with the beginning of the Greek Revolution. In the minds of nearly all those fighting, the finding of the miracle-working icon was a sign of the success of the struggle and the idea was deeply rooted in the consciousness of the people who were fighting. Thus the history of the [shrine] is interwoven with that day of the declaration of independence. (A. Lagouros 1965:54)

The account goes on to point out that not only did the major heroes of the Greek War of Independence come to pay their respects at the shrine but the new king Otto did so as well upon his arrival in Greece in 1833. Such pilgrimage to the shrine "was a pattern not only of religious devoutness but also of national gratitude toward the Panayia" (A. Lagouros 1965:54).

The common bond of Orthodox Christianity played an important role in the struggle for nationhood, and the heroic contributions of local church officials, as well as the role of local priests in keeping alive Greek religion and culture during the years of Ottoman rule, are commemorated today (see Campbell and Sherrard 1968:193–94). This does not mean, however, that official church support for independence was enthusiastic at all levels. Grigorios V, the patriarch of Constantinople, disavowed the Revolution and excommunicated its supporters. This act did not save him from Turkish reprisals once the Revolution had begun, and he was later hanged (Frazee 1977; see also Campbell and Sherrard 1968). (He is now portrayed as an early martyr of the revolution and his remains are housed in the Mitropolis Cathedral in Athens.) What this suggests is that in addition to convincing outside supporters that their cause was just, those engaged in the Revolution might have been concerned to demonstrate divine support to both their own followers and those skeptical of or antagonistic to the Revolution's aims (including officials of the church).

Among those who were antagonistic were the Catholic islanders. Fearful of what their standing might be under a new—and Orthodox—Greek state, the Catholics were not enthusiastic about the war (Frazee 1979) and continued to assert their allegiance to the Porte during the struggle. Even though the first constitution of Greece (adopted in 1822, the year after the beginning of the war) stated tolerance for all religions, it made the established religion of the new Greek state the Eastern Orthodox church (Frazee 1979:321). The announcement less than two years after the beginning of the Greek uprising of the finding of a miraculous icon in the heart of the heavily Catholic islands thus may have had important local political overtones.

These possible political implications of the icon's discovery, and the continuing political role the Church of the Annunciation plays today, have led to somewhat cynical readings of the shrine, by both Greeks and outsiders. Some educated Greeks have suggested to me that the establishment of the shrine with its miracle-working icon was a deliberate political maneuver on the part of the local Orthodox clergy. Certainly there does not appear in the accounts any hint of official reluctance to recognize an apparition or a miracle such as one finds in the stories of such famous Catholic shrines as Lourdes or the Virgin of Guadalupe in Mexico.[8] This political view of the establishment of the church was also clearly expressed by James Theodore Bent, whose impressions of Tinos were quoted earlier in the chapter. While giving credit to the Orthodox religion for its role in Greek independence, he nonetheless describes the shrine as "a cleverly conceived plan, the establishment of a miracle-working Madonna in the center of Hellas; and insinuating rumors were spread at the same time, stating that the picture was found on the same day that the banner of the cross was unfurled for Greek independence" (1965:233). Bent's cynicism about the shrine's manipulations by the clergy is further revealed in his statement that sheets with descriptions of miracles were printed up in advance and distributed to pilgrims when they arrived.

Catholics today on Tinos retain their own churches and celebrate their own holidays.[9] The nearby island of Syros (head of the nomós of the Cyclades) is the seat of a Catholic as well as an Orthodox archbishop. A Catholic monastery with a school for girls, staffed by French nuns, is located in the village of Loutra. But it is interesting to note that although the Catholics residing in the main town have their own church (St. Nikolaos),[10] they may also attend the Church of the Annunciation, at least on the important festival days, and Catholic priests participate in the processions of the icon. When I asked a Catholic shopkeeper about this, she replied with a shrug, "The Panayía is one" (*i Panayía ine mía*). Similarly, when I asked another Catholic friend why he had gone to the Church of the Annunciation for *proskínima* on August 15, he replied that God is one, and that he attends other churches as well as his own. Nineteenth-century accounts of miracles include stories of Catholics appealing to the icon (one was pursuaded by an Orthodox friend). And in the account of the finding of the icon discussed in chapter 8, it is stated that *all* islanders participated willingly in the building of the church (though Catholics are not mentioned specifically; indeed the fact that there were Catholics on the island is not mentioned at all). Thus even though the Panayía is in other contexts divisible (see Herzfeld 1987a), in this context at least she is presented as symbol of Greek unity, indivisible even by the barriers of rival faiths.[11]

The Greek church became independent of the Patriarchate of Constantinople in 1837 (Frazee 1977:131). Under the new constitution of 1833, the Church of Greece became a department of state. Many of the Westernized elite who formed the first government of Greece approved efforts to limit clerical autonomy, seeing Hellenism, not Orthodoxy, as the foundation of a modern state. "They expected the attachment of the population to religion to be replaced rather quickly with nationalism as had happened in the west. What they misjudged was the ability of their Greek countrymen to absorb both Hellenism and Orthodoxy, in fact, to identify them" (Frazee 1977:134).

In this context, then, one possible reading of the shrine (particularly for me and for other outsiders) is as an effort to reconcile the different facets of Greekness. The *istoría* of the shrine asserts both a continuity with, and an evolution from, the ancient past. Continuity lies in the repetition of the pattern of pilgrimage to holy places, from its ancient roots at Delos and Delphi to the present-day Church of the Annunciation at Tinos. This continuity is emphasized in histories of the island and church and in church pamphlets distributed to pilgrims. The church is described as built on the site of an ancient temple, itself a site of pilgrimage and healing in ancient times, and marble from the sacred island of Delos was used in the church.[12] The church and its history also assert an evolution from pagan traditions to Christianity. The church stands on and is built from the past. It does not reject that past; at the same time, however, it transcends it. The Greeks are neither Hellenes nor Byzantines—the contrast is false for, as the history of the church asserts, they are in fact both.

The shrine not only asserts continuity—rather than disjuncture—between past and present, between the classical and the Christian periods; its *istoría* also demonstrates the survival of Greekness through times of darkness and upheaval, through centuries of foreign rule or outside domination. Like the icon, kept so miraculously fresh in its hiding place in the ground when the church that housed it was burned, Greekness merely lay concealed, awaiting its resurrection. In such an *istoría* Greek identity is not problematic (as I have read it earlier), and was not fabricated for the requirements of a modern nation-state; rather, it was simply uncovered, miraculously revealed. That this symbolic resurrection of Greekness was announced by the Panayía is also significant because she in many ways represents Greece (see Dubisch 1990b). Moreover, since the icon's history states that it was painted by St. Luke, from life, and actually blessed by the Panayía herself, there is a continuity from the very beginnings of Christianity.[13]

The Church of the Annunciation has played its own role in the sometimes antagonistic relationship between the Orthodox church and the Greek state. As mentioned earlier, the new king Otto came to pay his devotions at Tinos when he arrived in Greece. Explicit support for the head of state, and the state's acknowledgment of divine power, are also demonstrated on the two reported occasions when the icon actually left Tinos, both times to succor an ailing monarch. In 1915, when King Constantine was very ill, the icon was taken to Athens and, accompanied by large crowds, was carried to the royal palace. As a church pamphlet in English states, "It was for the first time that the Icon left Her House."[14] As soon as the king had kissed the icon, his illness began to recede and within a few days he was healthy again. Out of gratitude he dedicated to the church a gold plate depicting him riding on his horse. The second occasion when the icon was carried to a king was when it was brought to the dying King Paul, who had asked for its consolation in his last moments, and the icon was placed on his pillow by his son and heir, Constantine. The church pamphlet describing these events places the church-state relationship in the following perspective: "It is a fact that our Kings, continuers of the great Byzantine tradition and faithful Christians, have always expressed their reverence and adoration to the Megalohari and Protectress of the Nation" (p. 12, English version). Here again we see the emphasis on continuity of Greekness both in the assimilation of the then current monarchy with the Byzantine tradition and in the continuity of the Panayía's protection.[15]

The fact that the day of the Annunciation (March 25) is both a major religious holiday and Greek Independence Day makes that day, and also the other major holidays celebrated at the church, appropriate occasions for articulating the relationship between nationalism and religion and

10. The icon carried in procession on the Day of the Annunciation (August 15)

11. A poster depicting a jet flying over Tinos and proclaiming August 15 as the Day of Military Strength

12. Mausoleum below the main sanctuary of the church, commemorating the sinking of the *Elli*

between church and state. On March 25 and August 15, representatives of the national government always attend the ceremonies, accompanied by a military escort and lesser officials, and give speeches to the assembled crowd. On August 15, 1988, for example, Akis Tsohatzopoulos, the minister of the interior, was the government representative and he began his speech by emphasizing the double nature of the occasion (*dhiplí yiortí*) as both a patriotic and a religious holiday. On another occasion the government representative spoke of Greece as peace-loving yet determined to be strong to protect her borders, an obvious reference to Greece's ongoing disputes with Turkey. (This was at the time of a series of incidents centering around the two nations' claims of territorial waters in the Dodecanese.) These ritual occasions can also be manipulated in conflicts between church and state. At the March 25, 1987, Feast of the Annunciation, the sermon, in obvious reference to the current struggles between the church and the Socialist government, reminded the gathered crowd that "Greece cannot exist without Orthodoxy" (*horís tin Ortho-doksía*).[16] Socialist Prime Minister Papandreou, on the other hand, had visited another shrine of the Panayía in northern Greece on August 15, the shrine of Soumela, in a political move designed both to elevate another shrine to equal or greater prominence as that of Tinos and to court the Pontic Greeks, for whom this shrine is particularly important (see Hirschon 1989).

What is interesting here is that whatever the current relationship between the government and the church, whatever the particular political parties involved, political discourse makes use of religion and religious symbolism and finds opportunity for its expression in religious occasions such as those celebrated at Tinos on August 15.

Military symbolism also figures prominently in religious celebrations at the church, particularly as it is related to naval power. This seems to be connected both to nationalist concerns and to the Panayía's traditional protection of sailors. According to church literature, during the Greek War of Independence the newly formed church foundation (*ídhrima*) raised money to aid the Greek ships in the struggle.[17] It is sailors who form the procession to carry the icon, and the battleships that bring them are anchored offshore during the ceremonials. The sinking of the battleship *Elli* at Tinos by an Italian submarine in 1940 provided a further means of commemorating this relationship of the island, the church, nationalism, and the sea. A local schoolteacher (now living in Athens) who wrote a poem celebrating the history of the icon has described the sinking of the *Elli* in a manner that evokes the colorful nature of the occasion and the drama and national significance of the incident.

Ta plía íne	The boats are
limenisména	tied up at the dock
ke me simaíes	and with flags
yiortodiména.	dressed for the holiday.

Then, as the liturgy is being conducted in the church and the sailors are leaving the boat to go up the hill to carry the icon down, the *Elli* is attacked and sunk by three torpedoes.

To Élli svíni	The *Elli* is extinguished
i písti anávi	faith is lighted
i Elládha óli	all of Greece
klái to karávi.	weeps for the ship.

(Dhesipris 1980:32–33)

The sinking of the *Elli* reinforced the patriotic and military associations of the shrine, and is permanently commemorated in the mausoleum erected below the main church. In addition, since August 15 has been designated as a national Day of Military Strength, the association between the shrine, militarism, and patriotism is made at a national level in posters displayed for the event. Since the festival commands television, newspaper, and even magazine coverage, knowledge about the shrine is disseminated nationally as well. For example, the newspaper *To Víma* (The Step) ran a three-page feature on Tinos and the Day of the Dormition on August 14, 1988. The feature consisted of three articles accompanied by photographs. The lead article was titled "The Panayía of Miracles" (*I Panayía ton Thavmáton*) and included an account of the history of the church, a discussion of the church's importance for local businesses, and a description of offerings. Another article was titled "Faithful and Faith" (*Pistí ke Písti*—a play on words that loses its force in English translation). The third article had as its subject "The Panayía in Modern Greek Painting" (*I Panayía stin Neoellinikí Zoographikí*) and included a picture of an icon from the Byzantine Museum that depicts Luke painting an icon of the Panayía. It is clear that the Church of the Annunciation and the events that take place there on August 15 are national news.[18]

The major events at the Church of the Annunciation—and particularly the events surrounding the finding of the icon and the building of the church—along with writings about the church, make up a set of texts that can be "read" in a literal and/or metaphorical sense. Yet the Church of the Annunciation "speaks" in other ways as well. As a text it is made up not simply of written documents about the church, nor solely of the public rituals and speeches accompanying major holy days. It is also composed of elements of pilgrimage, both the acts and experiences of pilgrims and the material accompaniments of such acts. It is to these that I turn next.

MIRACLES AS LANGUAGE, OFFERINGS AS TEXT

Part of the text of the church is the vast array of votive offerings that have been left there, usually in thanksgiving for a miracle or other act of grace performed by the Panayía. Some are left only briefly, such as bouquets of fresh flowers, or the *lambádhes,* which on busy days are removed almost as soon as they are lighted. In general, only the richest offerings are left on permanent display. These can include not only *támata* of silver and gold, but also icons, icon stands, and other items that contribute to the furnishing (or even the structure) of the church.

Much of what is given to the church, however, is not retained. Most of the jewelry left as offerings is auctioned in Athens every year, and the livestock, olive oil, and other such items brought as offerings are sold as well. And of course pilgrims' offerings of themselves—the going on the hands and knees up to the church, walking barefoot, wearing black, and even simply making the trip—are all ephemeral. They leave no permanent trace at the church except insofar as they may be written about (or photographed) if the acts are associated with an obvious miracle or other noteworthy event, or if they catch the eye of a camera-carrying journalist or an anthropologist.

Of the thousands of offerings, miracles, and other events associated with the icon and the church since their original finding and founding, a few stand out. They usually stand our materially, since they are prominently displayed. But they also stand out in the written and oral history of the church as some of the most frequently cited manifestations of the icon's power.

The most famous of these votive offerings, however, might easily escape the notice of the casual visitor. Though it hangs near the center of the church, not far from the entrance, it can be overlooked as simply one of a number of representations of ships among the hundreds that hang beneath votive lamps suspended from the ceiling of the church. Knowledgeable pilgrims, however, will point the item out to their fellows, and closer inspection reveals that this lamp has an unusual feature: from the silver hull of the ship protrudes the golden body of a fish. This offering represents a miracle that occurred in the middle of the last century, early in the history of the church. It was given by the captain of a ship that had a large hole opened in its hull during a great storm at sea. The captain prayed to the Panayía of Tinos for rescue. The ship stopped taking on water and the crew thus was able to bring it to shore. There they found that a large fish was stuck in the breach of the vessel, stopping the influx of water. The *táma* hanging in the church is a graphic representation of this event.

The other famous offering is a silver orange tree with branches that hold votive lights. It sits on a counter just to the right of the entranceway to the church. The tree was given by a Greek living in America who had become blind from an illness. He prayed to the Panayía of Tinos, promising to offer to her whatever he first saw should she restore his sight. Eventually his sight returned and the first thing he saw upon recovering was an orange tree—hence the offering.[19]

The frequent recitation (written and oral) of these two miracles and the display of the offerings resulting from them are themselves part of the story. Like boldface type or capital lettering in a book, these offerings and their associated miracles command the attention of the reader. But what is it that they (and those who recite them) are trying to say? Or to put it another way, how do I, as anthropologist and outsider, read them?

Let us consider first the offering of the ship.

The connection between divine power and the sea is represented in the

13. Some of the many votive offerings in the shape of ships

hundreds of votive offerings in the form of ships filling the Church of the Annunciation and other churches in the seafaring areas of Greece. In addition, many of the small churches that dot the landscape of islands such as Tinos are themselves the result of sailors' vows, or built in thanksgiving after a successful sailing career. A captain from the village of Pyrgos, for example, in thanksgiving for a miracle performed, turned his house into a church, incorporating into it the ship's mast and shrouds (Dhorizas n.d.: 19). While a variety of holy beings can be appealed to for a safe voyage or rescue at sea (including St. Nikolaos, who is a patron saint of sailors), at Tinos the chief recipient of such supplications is the Panayía. Alekos Florakis, in his book on marine votive offerings, considers her to be the main patron of sailors in the Aegean (1982:59–60).

The history of such marine votive offerings predates Christianity, stretching back to ancient times (Florakis 1982). In the Church of the Annunciation, the displayed offerings encapsulate the history of sailing since the church's founding: the representations depict everything from sailing ships through fishing boats to steamers to modern passenger ships and yachts. Newly launched ships are brought to Tinos to be blessed, and sailors may be brought as well. One woman told me of having sent her son to Tinos before he set off sailing, as she put it, "for the good of it" (*yia to kaló*), that is, to help ensure his safety on his voyages. On major holidays, the fishing boats and passenger boats tied up in the harbor at Tinos are decorated with brightly colored flags, and a cacophony of boat horns greets the arrival of the icon at the waterfront when it is carried down in procession from the church. The fact that pilgrims must of necessity arrive by boat (no easy journey in the days before the advent of large, modern passenger ships) adds further to the significance of the sea and sailing for the shrine and pilgrimage.

Here is another story of a miraculous rescue at sea, taken from a pamphlet describing some of the Panayía's miracles:

> "Panayia Megalohari, give me your hand," one of the men from the ship-wrecked schooner cried out with all the strength of his soul. They persevered together inside a small boat and under the most dramatic of circumstances. Shortly before, the schooner "Dheliyioryis" had been swept away by merciless waves onto a reef and pounded to pieces. A miracle that they had all succeeded in getting into the lifeboat! A miracle that the lifeboat stayed under control on top of the enormous and foaming waves! A miracle that finally in the midst of this great storm they were saved! The Megalohari Panayía once more gave "Her Hand" and in eternal remembrance of her Grace [*hári*] the shipwrecked sailors, on the 25th of March, 1888, hung [in the church] the image opposite. [The accompanying photo shows the lifeboat filled with men crossing the waves.] (S. Lagouros n.d.: 60)

Votive offerings such as the ones described there, and the stories that accompany them and that they represent, validate the power of the saint to whom they are addressed, bear witness to human faith, and provide a visible testimony to the existence and efficacy of miracles. They are part of a dynamic process by which religion is created and recreated.

This, then, is one "reading" of the votive offerings on display at the church and of the stories, written and oral, that lie behind them. Certainly this is how they "speak" to many of the pilgrims who come to Tinos, as well as to the islanders themselves. And yet this reading—for me at least—is only a partial one, for there are important dimensions of the church, its history, and its politics that such a reading leaves out.

The church as an institution has an obvious interest in promoting accounts and representations of miracles, for these enhance the church's fame, and hence its income and power, and promote belief. For this reason, despite the official current requirement of a medical examination to substantiate miracles of healing, church officials seem to treat a broad variety of requests granted and rescues effected as "miracles." But miracles speak not only to the "inside"—that is, to believers—but to the "outside" as well. To understand this, we must once more consider the founding of the church in historical perspective.

Here is another account of a miracle, one that occurred early in the history of the church, several years after the finding of the icon, while the church was still under construction. In this account, an English ship was anchored in the harbor, the English vice-consul on board. (He was, interestingly enough, a Catholic.) During the night a storm came up, and to their horror, the men on board noticed that their anchor cable had become frayed and they were in danger of parting from their anchor and being blown on the rocks. The vice-consul saw the half-built church on the hillside above the harbor and spontaneously prayed to the Panayía for help. Shortly after, although the seas continued to rage, observers saw that an island of calm now encircled the ship and the anchor was thus able to hold. In gratitude for this miracle, the consul donated money to the church, money that was particularly welcome at this point since building on the church had come to a halt due to lack of funds. The donation allowed the work to continue. (Another version of the account has both the ship's captain and the vice-consul praying and making the donation together afterward).

Moore has stated "what is inscribed in the organization of space is not the actuality of past actions but their meaning" (Moore 1986:81). Although Moore is explicitly referring to space as text here, we can expand her observation to include other textual aspects of the shrine as well, in this case accounts and other representations of miracles. It is the recitation (whether in written or verbal form) of this miracle by present-day actors that interests me (and not some presumed "actuality" of past events). In order to understand such recitation we have to look outside the text itself, and refer back to earlier passages about the conditions of the establishment of the first Greek state, and to the historical circumstances that influenced the text's production. In light of these circumstances, and in particular the need for support from the powerful nations of Western Europe, I suggest reading the miracle of the vice-consul's rescue as a statement about the recognition of the legitimacy of Greece, a legitimacy expressed in divine terms, as the power of the Panayía to rescue in even the most desperate and seemingly hopeless cases. (Note that it is the English vice-consul's gift that allows the continuation of the building of the church.)

In addition, while the common occurrence of miracles connected with sailing and the prominence of the votive offerings that represent them have an obvious connection with Greeks' dependence on the sea and their exposure to its hazards, the sea and sailing have a metaphorical dimension as well. What in fact could more accurately image a struggling nation than a ship tossed upon a stormy sea? What could more dramatically reveal the action of divine power and its ability to effect a rescue *in extremis* than the saving of a sinking ship under seemingly hopeless conditions? In the first miracle I recounted—the story of the ship and the fish—this image is presented at its most dramatic.

Another frequently cited and prominently represented account is the story of the Turkish official from Crete who came to Tinos to be cured of syphilis. He stayed a long time at the church, ignoring orders from his superiors in Crete to return to his duties, and eventually was miraculously cured of his disease. In gratitude he donated a marble fountain, which still stands in the courtyard of the church. Since the main figure of this story was Turkish, and it was from Turkey that most of the present Greek state was wrested (Turkey is both Greece's traditional and its contemporary enemy), this story assumes a special significance as acknowledgment of the power of the icon of the Panayía (and by extension of Orthodoxy and of Greece itself).[20]

What, however, of the story of the orange tree, presented earlier in the chapter as one of the most-cited miracles? This particular miracle might be read as expressing the power and the promise that the icon holds for all Greeks, regardless of whether they actually live within the boundaries of the Greek state. It thus contains a message of panhellenism and of the unity of Greeks.[21] This takes on particular significance when we consider that the first state of Greece consisted of only a portion of what is present-day Greece and many who considered themselves Greek lived outside its borders. The idea of Greek irredentism (*Megáli Idhéa*, the "Great Idea") dominated much of Greece's foreign policy until the Asia Minor disaster of 1922. As Bent (1965) pointed out, Greeks from areas outside Greece came to Tinos to visit the church, and accounts of miracles from this period also show that supplicants came from a diversity of areas, most of which now lie within the state of Greece. Moreover, it is hard to overlook the nature of the miracle in this particular case (just as it is hard to overlook the fact that the disease of which the Turkish official was cured was a venereal one). In this account someone who was blind was allowed miraculously to see, and what he saw was sweet and golden and drew him back to Greece to make his offering.[22]

The association of shrines with nationalism (as well as pan-nationalism) certainly is not unique to Greece. And the association of the Madonna with national struggles is found in much of the Catholic world as well as in Greece (see, e.g., Christian 1984). The shrine of the Virgin of Guadalupe of Mexico, for example, which originated in an apparition of the Virgin that appeared at the sacred site of a pre-Columbian mother goddess, "combines the Indian past with the Spanish present" (Taylor 1987:9), and Eric Wolf has concluded that the shrine is "ultimately a way of talking about Mexico" (1958:39). Likewise, we might see the Church of the Annunciation at Tinos as uniting past and present and providing "a way of talking about Greece." To whom is it speaking, however, and why has its message taken this particular form? As I will show, the shrine is only one way of "talking about Greece," and by no means one with which all Greeks would agree.

INSIDE/OUTSIDE AND THE POSITION OF THE ANTHROPOLOGIST

First let me return to an issue I raised earlier—what does the story of the finding of the icon and the recitation of it mean when directed at *me*? In asking this question, I seek to respond to Herzfeld's criticism that anthropologists "often write as though they were describing a virtually immutable society or culture, rather than a rhetoric of cultural differences in which they are themselves actively engaged" (1987a:181). I ask, to quote Herzfeld again, in "the realization that one is in some sense the representative of an intrusive power and that one's scholarly activity is enabled by that discomfiting fact" (1987a:182).

In order to begin to answer this question, it is necessary to examine the various positions from which I have experienced the shrine and pilgrimage. One position is as part of the general audience of pilgrims. While the shrine does not have the same meaning for me that it has for other pilgrims (or, indeed, the same meaning it has for other foreigners), there is no alteration of the "text" in this context that takes me *qua* foreigner into account (aside from signs in English advising me to dress appropriately, an admonition addressed to Greeks in Greek as well). In the case of pamphlets written in English, on the other hand, as well as stories told directly to me in Greek (stories elicited by my presence and interest and told with the knowledge of the teller that I understand what is being said), it is clear that I am the intended audience.

I am thus part of both unintended and intended audiences, for the shrine as "text" is intended for "reading" not only by Greeks but also by "outsiders." But what exactly does it mean to be "outside"? In seeking to answer this question we begin also to answer the question I raised above about what it means for stories of miracles to be recounted to *me*.

The distinction between insider and outsider, between *dhikí mas* (our own) and *kséni* (strangers or foreigners) is strongly marked in Greek social life and ideology (see Herzfeld 1986, 1987b; Dubisch 1993). The terms *dhikí mas* and *kséni* are contextual; an "insider" in one context may be an "outsider" in another. Athenian visitors to Tinos, for example, may be *kséni* to local inhabitants when considered in their visiting status, but *dhikí mas* when contrasted to *kséni* who are tourists, that is, non-Greeks. Similarly, villagers may consider other villagers *kséni* in their social position as nonrelatives, but *dhikí mas* when contrasted with people from other villages. These contrasts are thus part of a complex shifting of the focus of one's social "field."

This sort of shifting is a constant part of anthropological fieldwork, and understanding of one's own position in regard to the inside-outside dimension in a particular social situation is of great importance in one's analysis of that situation. To move from outside to inside is to change the nature of one's social relationships and the images with which one is presented (Herzfeld 1983, 1986). This is especially important in Greece, where this contrast is so strongly marked and where it determines significant differences in meaning. To put this in slightly different terms, the anthropologist must realize that she or he is an "active" sign (Herzfeld 1983:158). That is, anthropologists themselves carry meanings for those they study, meanings that have an impact on the ethnographic process.

An example of my own shifting classification comes from my recent fieldwork at the church. Once again I return to the occasion of the baptism of the Greek-Australian girl (an event of multiple readings). As the reader may recall, my friends from the village, Marcos and Eleni, had been invited to both the baptism and the baptismal dinner (being related to the girl on both sides of the family) and they had in turn invited me.

Baptisms at the Church of the Annunciation are held in a large baptistry underneath the main church and adjacent to the chapel of the Life-giving Well. (There are two baptismal fonts for infants, and one adult font in its own chamber with doors that can be closed during the actual immersion.) Unlike baptisms performed in a village church, baptisms held at the cathedral may be witnessed by strangers, pilgrims who wander into the baptistry from the chapel out of curiosity while the baptism is in progress and who mingle with the family members gathered around the font, and sometimes even pick up one of the favors handed out afterward.

Thus my own attendance was problematic in that I might not have been a member of the baptismal party, as I would assuredly have been had the baptism taken place in a village church. While several of the villagers recognized me, other guests did not know me and asked each other who I was. "She is one of ours" (*ine dhikí mas*), my friend Eleni replied firmly. I had a right to be there, her statement implied. This is an assertion that would not have been necessary at an ordinary baptism, but in this case my friend wanted to make it clear I was not a gate-crasher. On the other hand, when I was seated at the baptismal table in the village later that evening, in a situation in which I was obviously invited and obviously knew people, the question "Who is she?" was answered by "She's a foreigner" (*ine kséni*), followed by an explanation of who I was (I had once lived in the village). Thus within the same situation, and in relation to the same people, I held simultaneously an "inside" and "outside" position, the relevance of each depending on the context in which my position was being explained.

There is a bias in anthropology toward the "inside." This bias comes from the sense that it is here that the juiciest, the most "authentic" information is to be obtained (see Dubisch 1993). To be regarded as an "outsider," we often assume, is to be denied access to the rich veins of information that we are so concerned to mine. To be outside, we further assume, is also to be like anyone else who is not a member of the culture we seek to understand, and this violates our own sense of identity as anthropologists in a "special" relationship to the people we "study." To be "inside," on the other hand, is to be privileged and different, a status we seek not only because of the information we feel it will yield, but also because it is personally gratifying and makes us feel that our work has been successful and worthwhile.[23]

And yet in Greece at least, where the inside/outside distinction is so crucial to an understanding of social life and ideology, one's position as an outsider can be equally revealing in its own way. It is important to understand, however, exactly what one's position is in a given situation in order to make sense of what is revealed (see Herzfeld 1983; Dubisch 1993). Physical context does not necessarily give us the required clues to such social positioning. For example, the division between "inside" and "outside" is not equivalent to the (much criticized) dichotomy of public and private space. Use of the symbolism of "insideness" can occur in a public context. Conversely, one can be an outsider in a private or domestic situation (as, for example, when one is a guest on a formal occasion in someone's house). Rather, the *dhikí-kséni* contrast is part of what Herzfeld terms "disemia," a two-way-facing system of meanings that can be part of public discourse. Thus, as I will suggest later, the church itself, though highly public, represents certain characteristics of the ("Romeic") inside.

In my own case I realized that many of the islanders I encountered wished to present to an outsider a certain image of themselves. In their accounts of the shrine and its miracles they were demonstrating to me a basis of local pride, saying something to me about the unique character of their island.[24] At the same time, or so I later came to feel, they were also saying something to me, an outsider, a non-Greek (and also a scholar whose stated purpose was to write about the island), about Greekness, and—to extend my reading—perhaps also about the divinely sanctioned legitimacy of the Greek state.

To what extent does this recitation "work," that is, to what extent does it have the effect on its audience (outsiders) that apparently is intended? This is not an easy question to answer. In fact, it has several possible answers. In my own case, obviously, the recitation did not "work" in quite the sense that was probably intended. While it convinced me (eventually) of the importance of the church and its icon, I read this importance in a manner not necessarily intended by those reciting the icon's history and miracles, for my reading is that of an anthropologist, an outsider, who always reinterprets what the "natives" say, even in the act of presenting *their* interpretation (cf. R. Rosaldo 1989:50–51). This is a different reading than, say, that which might be made by a foreigner who believed in miracles and who saw the shrine as a true manifestation of divine power, taking literally the accounts of its origins and miracles and thus "reading" the shrine more or less as those presenting it intend it should be read. This, presumably, would have been the state of mind of the English consul who made the offering after his frigate was saved.

But what of other foreigners who are not believers themselves?

James Theodore Bent was such a skeptic, his own cynical interpretation of the icon's finding already mentioned above. Another nineteenth-century visitor, Fredericka Bremer, a German woman who visited Tinos in the mid-1800s, though a religious person, took a mostly negative view of what she saw because her ideas of what a religion should be were different from those of the Greeks she observed. She noted that the church exhibited "no splendour of ecclesiastical architecture but a hasty erection which has been run up to meet the religious necessity of the moment—a necessity in which, however, old superstition had more to do than genuine religion" (1863:227–28). Nor was she impressed with her visit to the church on the eve of the Annunciation: "It was one human mass packed together in a perfectly stifling manner; the priests were performing service—horribly" (1863.235). Her feelings were not uniformly negative, however. She comments that "the poorer class of people seemed to me earnest, and full of devotion; the higher class somewhat vain and frivolous" (1863:234). And in a statement that sums up well her mixed impressions on the eve of the Annunciation: "The whole night through there was a peaceful and cheerful sound of thronging people in the open air. The report of the Panaghia miracles began to circulate. Filth and bad smells increased every hour" (1863:235). Later she asked the bishop if miracles had really taken place:

> "Yes, certainly; of course," was his reply.
> "But how? What has indeed taken place?" I inquired again.
> "I cannot exactly say," returned he. "Panaghia always performs miracles! Of course she does; no one can doubt it." (1863:24)

Bremer's own religious faith, and her particular view of Greece and Greeks, are revealed in her observation that the islands (which at that time had no steamers except during festivals) would be a healthy residence "for cultivated Hellenes and Philhellenes."

> Patience! It will be different in a while. People will one day have more regard to the intention of a Fatherly providence in His gifts. . . . Then will the glorious fountain of Poseidon—now inherited by Panaghia, be visited not merely at the festival of the Evangelistria; and the weak, and the sick, who then, by a prolonged residence at Tinos, recover health and strength, will be legion. The beautiful life of light of these islands must become that of humanity. (1863:237)

Thus she gathers from her visit a message similar in some ways to that which the island conveyed for Greek pilgrims, but she gathers it from reading a somewhat different text, one colored by a Western European's lens of the classical past.[25] In the end, however, Bremer's final observation of Tinos is a negative one, for the next day she observes that the now-deserted area where the pilgrims were is "in a state which cannot be described." She is unable to even go close: "The filth and the abominable stench drove me away" (1863:242).[26]

For Bremer, as for other Western visitors to Greece, the experience of a contemporary Greece drew an ambivalent response. Since their image of Greece was based on a particular construction of a past society presumed to be culturally ancestral to Western Europe, contemporary Greeks can and did appear unpleasantly "oriental"—primitive, dirty, superstitious, and untrustworthy. Certain elements of this view persist into the present day among foreigners who are drawn to Greece by its ancient past. It is this past that constitutes their notion of Greece, and present-day Greeks and their ways may be viewed as a curiosity of sorts, sometimes even standing in the way of what should be an experience of the real and pure Greece.

Although foreign tourism to Tinos has increased since I first did field-work there in 1969–70, it is still overwhelmed by the pilgrimage of the Orthodox.[27] In this respect, Tinos differs greatly from other islands of the Cyclades such as Mykonos, Paros, and Thira (Santorini), which are popular with foreigners. It is safe to say that many more non-Greek tourists visit the ruins of Delos than ever set foot inside the sanctuary of the Church of the Annunciation at Tinos (itself probably more visited, in terms of numbers, than ancient Delos was).

While the behavior of foreign tourists who visit the church varies somewhat by nationality (French visitors, for example, seem more at ease with Orthodox religious practices, and may cross themselves as they enter), in general their actions are those of sightseers and not devotees. Some never even reach the church, for they approach it in the costume many foreigners seem to consider appropriate for touring Greece—shorts, skimpy tops, even bathing suits—and are turned away by the guardian at the door.[28] Of those foreigners who do visit the church, some are shocked by the activity they witness there, which at the height of the pilgrimage season can be highly emotional in nature. Such emotionalism is contrary to middle-class Western European and American ideas of appropriate religious behavior and, to some extent, to foreign images of Greece. Not only is the view that many foreigners have of Greece framed by particular ideas about ancient Greece, but these ideas are themselves shaped by the ways the West seeks its own roots in this ancient Greece. The stark cleanliness of the ancient ruins that the tourist encounters, and the beautiful simplicity of classical art, contrast with the "clutter" and ornamentation of the Church of the Annunciation and the "flatness" of icons.[29] Fredericka Bremer, for example, was unimpressed by the ceremonies she observed, comparing them negatively to Catholic ones. There were no "plastic images," she observes—only "painted canvas, and the paintings all have a family resemblance to the one ancient original type from Mount Athos" (1863:238). In addition, the rhythm of Greek Orthodox services, in which people come and go and even talk freely instead of sitting in pews for a specified duration is also unfamiliar and seems even chaotic to foreigners used to more orderly church services. To quote Bremer once more, this time from her description of the services of the feast day of the Ascension in the village of Amarousi: it was an assembly "into which people came, and from which they went, according to their own good pleasure, looking about them, and talking and being anything but attentive to the psalm-singing, and other occupations of the priest; at which, however, I did not greatly wonder" (1863:47).

To Western observers such as Bent and Bremer, contemporary Greek religion had little appeal and was often most interesting not for its present forms but for what it might reveal about continuities with a classical past. Greek Orthodoxy, especially as experienced by the European visitor at festivals or at the Church of the Annunciation, is "tainted" (see Herzfeld 1987a:176–77) by too many elements antithetical to Western notions of religion. It is emotional, cluttered, aesthetically unappealing. Its rituals are chaotic, its harmonies alien. Moreover, it violates Western notions of individual dignity and proper relations with the sacred. Joseph Brown, for example, writing in 1877, observed that an Englishman cannot read the Orthodox liturgy

> without being offended and shocked by the style of slavish prostration and trembling fear before the Deity, by an oriental adulation only fit for a Byzantine despot to bear with, and by countless cries for mercy, "Kyrie eleyson," Lord have mercy upon us, repeated in many places *forty times running!!!* The holy monks who composed them renounced their manhood when they approached their maker, and cried out like whipped hounds! (1877:18)

I have moved back and forth between a discussion of contemporary views of the church and pilgrimage and nineteenth-century accounts in attempting to elucidate at least one type of foreign reaction to the church and pilgrimage. This is not to imply that Greece, and foreigners' impressions of Greece, have not changed in the last one hundred years, or that the views of a German woman writing a travel account are the same as those of an English tourist visiting Tinos today. Rather, what I wish to suggest is something more general about Western images of Greece and the way in which these images may shape the "reading" of the church.

Greece, poised between East and West, lies at what Herzfeld (1987a) has termed "the critical margins of Europe." It is part of "our" (that is, western European) roots, yet, as I suggested above, sometimes embarrassingly Oriental. Part of the Orientalness of Greece lies in its Byzantine inheritance, an aspect of Greece's past usually overlooked by the outsider seeking to connect contemporary Greece to an earlier past. Or the outsider may seek (as Bent did in part) the classical roots lying beneath the Oriental surface. "Oriental" may also carry connotations of the "feminine," which is another aspect of the church (and perhaps of Greece as well) that makes it problematic for Westerners (as the above quote from Joseph Brown about the priests who "renounced their manhood" indicates).

I do not mean to imply, however, that foreign visitors to Greece completely ignore Greece and the Greeks of today, or that they necessarily find contemporary Greeks objectionable. Greece is a major "tourist destination," and since tourism has a joint mission—seeing "sights" (usually ancient ones) and having a "good time"—the elements associated with the latter are permitted to expand the image of Greekness, at least to some extent. But while sandy beaches, a bottle of retsina, and perhaps some bouzouki and a little exuberant dancing à la Zorba the Greek may be acceptable additions to the outsider's conceptions of Greece,[30] a miracle-working icon and the behavior associated with it are more difficult to assimilate. These things are too alien, too much "them" and not "us," a situation that is confusing in what is supposed to be the land of "our" ancestors. Additionally, for the tourist bent on "fun" (and many tourists seem to see Greece as basically sun, wine, and beaches) such images may be too "serious" as well.[31]

This does not mean, however, that attitudes toward the church and the miraculous icon can be divided neatly into those of Greeks (approving) and those of outsiders (ignoring or disapproving). Not only do some foreigners find the Church of the Annunciation interesting (and some even believe), but also there are many Greeks who view the shrine negatively, others who see it at best ambivalently. The Greek captain of the ship on which James Theodore Bent was traveling, for example, took a dim view of the events at Tinos. "A fanatical people!" (*fanatikós laós*), he is reported to have sneered, gazing down at the pilgrims on deck (Bent 1965:235). The shrine as text can carry a negative message for Greeks, and for reasons similar to those for which it carries such a message for foreigners. This is in part, I suggest, because such negative attitudes are related to the varied images of Greekness in the contemporary national Greek discourse. As Frazee points out, the participants of the first government of Greece had a Western orientation, seeing Hellenism (in Herzfeld's terms) as the model on which a modern Greek state would be built.

They felt that religion would gradually be replaced by nationalism in the popular mind (Frazee 1977:134). (Compare this to the church pamphlet's view of the modern Greek kings as heirs to the tradition of Byzantium.) Among some of the educated Athenian Greeks to whom I spoke about my research, attitudes toward the shrine ranged from embarrassment to disdain. These attitudes reflect both a negative view of pilgrimage as representing more superstition than religion, anachronistic and inappropriate to a modern nation-state, and a negative view of the Orthodox church as an institution. For others, the shrine seemed to be interesting but exotic, almost as "foreign" to them as it might be to an outsider like myself.[32]

A variation of this perspective is the claiming of certain practices as part of Greek "tradition," and hence part of a national culture. An example of this is a piece by the photographer John Demos, which appeared in *Ena* magazine (August 1988). The striking black-and-white photographs, evoking an older, "traditional" Greece, dramatize the events of August 15 as an expression of faith, and particularly of women's faith and their identification with the Panayía. Such an evocation was in this case addressed to a Greek readership.[33]

As an anthropologist, I must be aware of my own position as audience in the "reading" given to me by those who express their view on Tinos and the church. The interaction between the respondents' views, their view of the outsider doing the questioning, and the sense of how their views should be presented to an educated non-Greek (who was going to be writing about these things for a foreign audience) all need to be taken into account. These factors in no way "invalidate" statements made to me; on the contrary, even if they were statements that would be made only to an outsider, they would be revealing for that very reason. But they do remind us that, as with all such statements, they must be seen in the context in which they were made, a context that includes the ethnographer herself.

This is illustrated by situations during my fieldwork when I was treated as part of, or at least allowed a glimpse of, the "inside." An example is a conversation that occurred with my landlady, Marina, and her husband, Dhimitris, the day after the feast of the Dormition in the summer of 1986. I had wandered up to the church in the early afternoon and found a stark contrast to the crowds and emotional scenes that I had witnessed both before and during the holy day. Now the grounds of the church and the streets of the town were deserted, sleepy in the afternoon heat. Only a handful of people were still camped in the park. A group of Gypsies and a man in a wheelchair resting in the shade of a tree were the only occupants of the outer courtyard of the church, which had the day before been crowded with the belongings of pilgrims. Crushed cans, discarded bottles, pieces of melon rind, and trampled grass marked the areas where throngs of pilgrims had camped. Black plastic bags of garbage were stacked by the curb of the street alongside the church, waiting to be picked up. A lone woman was crawling on her knees up the stairs to the church. Here and there a few scattered groups of people were saying good-bye to friends, their luggage waiting at their feet. At the bottom of the street of shops, a handful of people were buying food and last-minute souvenirs. Several tourists in shorts wandered about, looking aimless and somewhat confused.

As I walked back down the hill I stopped to talk to a shopkeeper, remarking that it was certainly quiet, now that the crowds had left. He replied that more people would be coming, but it would be a different sort of people, a better sort of crowd. This view was echoed by Marina and Dhimitris when I stopped by their shop. Soon, they said, there would be more people coming, a good class of people (*kalós kósmos*), not the Gypsies who came in such numbers for the fifteenth. Since it was rare to have any leisure to talk to my landlady at this time of year, I lingered a while to chat. She and Dhimitris wanted to know what I was writing and would I be telling people in America about everything that I had seen? Yes, I would, I said. Dhimitris, disturbed, commented that people in America would think people here were crazy (*trelí*) because of all the pilgrims going up to the church on their knees. I asked if people here thought it was a crazy thing to do, and Marina replied that personally she didn't think it meant anything to do it (*dhe tha pi típota*). Going up on your knees, getting your hands black—could the Panayía really want someone to do that? But someone, some believer, had done it once, and now it had become a custom (*siníthia*). Dhimitris added that he thought when people made the vow to go up on their knees, they did not have any idea of how far they were from the church (his actual words were "from the Panayía") and how difficult it was to go all the way from the harbor up to the church on one's knees.

This conversation is revealing on several accounts, in particular because in this situation I held the position of both insider and outsider simultaneously. On the one hand, I was allowed to hear negative opinions about some of the activities associated with the church and pilgrimage. On the other hand, it was precisely my position as an outsider who was going to write about "their" church and the impression that this would make on non-Greek readers that led to the expression of these opinions. Marina and her husband recognized that I, as an outsider, would be representing what happened on *their* island (and perhaps even more extensively, in Greece) to other outsiders, specifically to people in America. Hence they were expressing their concern with what my representation would lead Americans to think of Greeks. In this sense I was an outsider who had seen the "inside," a part of Greece about which they themselves had somewhat negative, or at least ambivalent, feelings, and which they would have preferred to hide from outsiders if they could. Moreover, both they and I were aware of my own situation of power—as an American, as a scholar—through my writing. While some things can be concealed from such an outsider, much of what went on at the pilgrimage site could not be since it was of a public nature. It was concealed from outside view only by the average tourist's indifference to what went on at the church. I had thus penetrated to the "inside" and the townspeople could not prevent me from writing about (and showing photographs of) what I had seen (cf. Friedl 1970).

Such quiet moments of conversation with local people as the one I have just described were not a common experience for me. Most of my work was done during the summer, when pilgrimage was at its height and when several major festivals—including the feast of the Dormition—occurred. This was a time of year when most of the townspeople were very busy, with little time to spare for getting acquainted or for leisurely conversation. Moreover, unlike villagers, townspeople had developed ways of dealing with a constant stream of kséni (both Greeks and foreigners) that kept them at a distance. Many of my interactions with townspeople were commercial, that is, they took place in the context of buying, or at least in a context in which I might buy. I often used these interactions for information gathering (for example, asking a vendor of icons, támata, and other religious items questions about these items).

When these interactions became regular, however, they sometimes created confusions as to whether I was "inside" or "outside." Though my relationship with my landlady, Marina, began as a commercial one, she also did various things to make a friend out of me. Often I would go to her apartment in the morning for coffee, and she sometimes treated me to lunch (which she made in the back of her shop), always apologizing that she was not able to do more because she was so busy. When the time came to do the bill for my lodging, she tended to be caught between the cultural expectation that she should give me a discount because of our relationship and her desire to make a profit. Was she hostess or landlady? Was I a customer or a guest? We played both roles, not always comfortably.

Another example of such confusion occurred one day at the vegetable stand where I often shopped. If there were no other customers waiting at the stand, I sometimes struck up a conversation with the young woman, Katina, who worked there and she would even occasionally introduce me to others in the shop, explaining who I was and what I was doing in Tinos. One day after I had made my purchases, Katina came running after me as I left, two large tomatoes in her hand. As she came up, she stuffed them into my bag with the comment, "Let me treat you to two tomatoes" (*na sas keráso dhío domátes*). Her use of the verb *kernó* here is significant for it is often employed in offering hospitality. *Ti na sas keráso* (What can I offer you?) is the polite prelude to the presenting of the food or drink necessary to fulfill the obligations of the host.[34]

In addition to indicating my dual insider/outsider status, the conversation with Marina and her husband also revealed the ambivalence with which many of the townspeople seemed to regard both the church and pilgrimage. For many townspeople, the church is the source of their livelihood; without pilgrimage many of the businesses would not be able to survive, indeed would not even exist. In addition, the church shares its wealth with the island's inhabitants in the form of money for roads, repair of village churches, and public buildings. Moreover, the church and its miraculous icon, as I have already suggested, are also a source of local pride. At the same time, in part because pilgrims are viewed as a source of business, certain classes of pilgrims are regarded as less welcome than others. Gypsies in particular, whose numbers at the feast of the Dormition have been increasing over the years, are seen as undesirables, for not only do they camp in the streets and in their trucks and cook their own food (thus spending little or no money in the town), but they are reputed to steal and are a trial to shopkeepers. "A better class of people" (*kalós kósmos*) means, in part, more affluent pilgrims and summer visitors who are more likely to spend money and less likely to cause trouble.

Spending habits are not the only characteristic by which pilgrims are judged. Certain kinds of pilgrims may be negatively viewed for their religious behavior. Here is where a real ambivalence emerges. On the one hand, those pilgrims who perform such strenuous vows as going up on their knees are impressive in their piety and suffering. On the other hand, their behavior may be viewed as excessive, at least by some townspeople. The ambivalence may be the reason I often found it difficult to get townspeople to express an opinion to me (positive or negative) about pilgrims who went on their knees or performed other arduous vows. It was only from those with whom I could assume more of an "insider's" position (such as Marina and her husband) that I heard negative comments. It was interesting too that my landlady's comments centered around what the Panayía herself might want, and that she was concerned about the *appearance* of the pilgrims (dirty and disheveled) when they arrive at the church.

Another source of ambivalence is the Church of the Annunciation as an organization. It is a powerful force in local politics, but more important, judging from the negative opinions I have heard expressed, it is an organization with considerable money, and it is an organization of priests. Thus it provokes both general sentiments of anticlericalism of the sort found elsewhere in Greece, and particular negative comments because in this case the priests have such wealth at their disposal. The church in this sense is seen as priests with too much money, and this view reflects the ambivalence that attaches to wealth and power, which command both respect and distrust.

The Church of the Annunciation is thus both a source of local pride (and an asset to the local economy) and a source of ambivalence. The ambivalence, however, does not extend to the icon itself or to the Panayía. While there may be varying degrees of belief or skepticism about what goes on at the church, I never heard anyone express doubt about the power of the icon and the Panayía. This complex combination of faith and anticlericalism is well illustrated by my friend Marcos, who was working at the church during my recent trips. Like many village men, he did not particularly like working for someone else, preferring to be his own boss (*afendikó*),[35] but had taken the job out of economic necessity since his family had little land. He particularly disliked being under the command of priests and found small ways to defy their authority (such as drinking the Cypriot wine donated to the church during his breaks in the employees' room). In addition, he was often amazed at the things he witnessed pilgrims doing at the icon, and sometimes commented negatively on them. At the same time, despite a generally skeptical attitude, he did not doubt that the icon had power and that miracles really did occur, and his behavior while he was working in the church and around the icon was always respectful and reserved.

To return then, to my own position—insider, outsider, reader: we can see that the presentations of the church and its history to me by Greeks reflect two kinds of Greek readings. One is of the shrine as a sacred text, proclaiming not only faith but also local pride and Greekness. Another reading is of the shrine as a negative text, as something one does not want an outsider to see because it is an inappropriate revelation of self. In both cases, however, the shrine is viewed as saying something about Greekness, and both positive and negative readings can be viewed, in part at least, as taking place within the context of a discourse about Greek identity.

In my own position as a reader, my initial problems with the islanders' accounts of the church and its miracles was not so much that I misread what they were saying but that I did not at first see the church as an important text, or even as a text at all. Or perhaps I might say that it was a text written in a language too foreign for me to grasp at the time. The language of miracles was not one with which I was either familiar or comfortable. Once, however, I began to see miracles *as* a language (itself a particular way of reading), it became possible to sort out different kinds of human action and statements associated with the shrine and to see (to put it in my terms) what they were "saying," both individually and collectively.

In this framework miracles can be read as a kind of validation. By bridg-
ing the gap between the divine and the human worlds, they not only
validate individual faith but also, in this case, the existence of the nation-
state. What this means is that they (and the activities, objects, and writings associated with the church) cannot be read only in the context of
individual vows and collective pilgrimage, but must be seen in a national
and highly politicized context as well.

In this context I must also place myself, not simply as an individual but
as a representative of a European cultural tradition and heir of European
history. I cannot overlook the fact that the Greece I observe, and (re)create
here in my own text, was itself a European creation, "our" creation.[36]
This is true not only in a political-historical sense (through the support of
European powers for a Greek state and the continued interference of these
powers—and more recently, of the United States—in the affairs of that
state (see, e.g., Couloumbis et al. 1976). It is also true in the sense that the
ways that the multiple ideas of "Greekness" have been constructed have
been influenced by Western notions of what Greekness is and shouldn't
be. These notions have largely been based on Western images of a classical
Greek past and on Western standards of "civilization" (a standard that
contemporary Greeks often do not attain in Western eyes). By this I do not
mean, however, that Greece is or ever was totally a Western creation and
that Greeks have been completely passive in the process. (Certainly the
internal dynamics of Greek politics and class have played a significant
role.) But an important part of the historical and political and ideological
circumstance in which the meaning of Greekness has been forged (by
Greeks and non-Greeks) lies in Greece's relationship with the Western
(and by implication, if only negative, Eastern) world. Indeed, as the use of
the analytic metaphor of text and the discussion of the notions of performance and practice have attempted to show, the meaning of the shrine
and its ways of representing Greekness are diverse and emergent, forged
in a dialectic between inside and outside, politically contingent, historically constructed, and strategically manipulated.

CHAPTER TEN

Women, Performance, and Pilgrimage: Beyond Honor and Shame

> One does not give birth in pain, one gives birth to pain.
>
> A mother is always branded by pain, she yields to it.
>
> —Julia Kristeva, *Stabat Mater*

ON A WARM morning in July 1986, I left my apartment on Tinos and headed into town to pick up fresh bread for breakfast at a nearby bakery. My walk took me down the road along a low cliff above the sea and then along the waterfront, past a large concrete wharf, restaurants, shops, bars, and stores to the bakery, tucked into a narrow whitewashed alley. As always in the summer, the town was bustling at that hour. Local housewives haggled at the produce and fish market in the square near the waterfront, shopkeepers and restaurant owners swept out their establishments in preparation for the influx of pilgrims later in the day, and trucks laden with soft drinks, produce, and building materials rumbled by. In short, it was a typical summer morning.

As I was returning from the bakery, clutching the round, still-warm loaf that would be my breakfast, I noticed that a small crowd had gathered at the edge of the road just beyond my apartment house. Curious, I dropped the bread off at the apartment and then went up the road to investigate. As I drew close to the crowd, I saw several people leaving the scene, shaking their heads solemnly. Those who remained at the edge of the cliff were staring down into the water below. I joined them and peered cautiously over the rim, but I could not see what was attracting such interest. I turned to ask one of the bystanders next to me what was going on. A motorcycle accident, he told me. A young man on a motorcycle had been coming down the road late the night before and had failed to negotiate the curve, plunging off the road into the sea below. The motorcycle was still there, in the water, he added. I turned to look again. Now I could see the motorcycle, clearly visible under the water, several yards from shore. And what of the young man, I asked. He died, was the reply, and the young woman who had been riding with him was badly injured and in the hospital. Neither the driver nor his companion was from the island I learned upon further questioning.

As I was returning to my apartment, I saw my landlady, Marina, working in the little storeroom next to the entryway of the apartment building. I stopped in the doorway to ask if she had heard about the accident. She had not. Busy with her many morning tasks, she hadn't even noticed the small crowd clustered at the top of the cliff. When I told her what had happened, she immediately became very agitated. Dropping what she was doing, she clasped her hand to her heart. Too late I remembered that she had almost lost her son in an accident just the year before. I immediately felt guilty, realizing that what was for me simply an unfortunate and somewhat interesting event had a much more emotional and personal impact for her. Was the young man someone from the island, she wanted to know. I told her no. It was obvious, however, that her concern did not center on the young man who had died, or even on his seriously injured female companion. It was to the boy's unknown mother that her thoughts had flown. "What mother cries?" (*Pya mána klaéi?*), she exclaimed dramatically, summing up what was for her the essence of the tragedy.[1]

Preceding chapters have examined my own position as a woman in the field and as a woman writing within the traditions and dictates of a Eurocentered and androcentric anthropology. I have also noted that despite the fact that the Church of the Annunciation is centered around and owes its existence to two female holy figures—the nun Pelayía and the Madonna, or Panayía—women are nonetheless muted in the history and "reading" of the shrine. They are "the written about" rather than the writers, functioning as "native" and "other" in the writings of men. This chapter approaches such "otherness" from a different perspective, using some of women's activities in pilgrimage as a vehicle for critiquing some anthropological constructs, specifically those of "honor and shame" and the idea of an "anthropology of the Mediterranean," and drawing on the idea of "performance" in order to construct what I term a "poetics of womanhood." The story of the motorcycle accident has already pointed the way to some of the themes of such a poetics. I shall return to this story later, as these themes begin to emerge.

HONOR AND SHAME AND "MEDITERRANEAN ANTHROPOLOGY"

One of the sights that constantly attracted my attention at the Church of the Annunciation (as well as the attention of other visitors to the shrine, both Greeks and foreigners) was the many women who chose to ascend to the church on their knees. This sight was especially common at the busiest times of year (such as the summer season or major holy days). At such times one might see a steady line of women on their knees crawling up the wide avenue to the church. Although the women who performed such acts were a small minority of the pilgrims who visited the church, the dramatic nature of their vows made them highly visible. Moreover they vividly represented (not only for me but apparently for many Greek observers as well) the hope and suffering that characterize the making and the fulfillment of a vow. It was not uncommon to see other pilgrims, especially women, stop and sigh and cross themselves and even wipe away tears when they passed a woman on her knees.

While I tried during the course of my fieldwork to keep this dramatic form of vow in perspective, and to give attention to more "ordinary" religious behavior as well, I felt it necessary, as with other aspects of religion that caught my attention, to ask *why* I found myself so intrigued by the phenomenon of women on their knees, and why it also attracted the attention of other Greeks. Certainly for me the fascination was due in part to the "exoticism" and the dramatic nature of the act. But there was another reason for my own interest, and this was the challenge these pilgrims presented to certain anthropological representations of Mediterranean women, representations that had played a significant role in my own anthropological biography. These representations stressed Greek (and Mediterranean) women's restriction to the private realm and exclusion from the public arena, the social rules that placed women under male control, and the necessity of female modesty for the maintenance of male honor. And yet during their devotions at the Church of the Annunciation, large numbers of women in effect make public spectacles of themselves in front of strangers, as well as family and friends. In order to understand such seemingly anomalous behavior—or rather to consider why it *seemed* anomalous to *me*—it is necessary to consider the ethnographic and theoretical literature that has shaped and constrained work on gender in this particular cultural region. This literature has continued to cast its shadow over our anthropological perceptions, despite the criticisms to which it has been subject in recent years.[2]

Whether or not a category such as "the Mediterranean" or "Mediterranean society" is an accurate or useful one has been a subject of anthropological debate, as have the criteria by which such an area might be defined (see Davis 1977; Boissevain 1976; Gilmore 1987; Herzfeld 1980, 1987b). The most enduring—and most contested—elements of this debate have centered around those cultural conceptions of gender and sexuality labeled "honor and shame." These conceptions have been presented as a significant (if not *the*) distinguishing feature of the region. Despite its regional variations, the moral code of honor and shame has been asserted to have common core features throughout Mediterranean society, from

North Africa through southern Europe.[3] Indeed it is the unity of this code, some have argued, that allows us to speak of "Mediterranean society" at all, and that "defines a Mediterranean World" (Gilmore 1987:17). The honor-shame syndrome, Gilmore states, can be regarded as "a total social fact . . . fundamental and pervasive" (1987:5), an example of what Turner has termed a "master symbol" (Gilmore 1987:17). While this moral code has supposedly derived from certain shared features of geography, history, and social structure (see, e.g., J. Schneider 1971), it is the code itself, whatever the material factors that may have given rise to it, that is presented as the defining feature of the region.

The code of honor and shame unites ideas about power, sexuality, and gender relationships with a rigid spatial and behavioral division between women and men. According to this code, a family's standing within the community depends on the sex-linked maintenance of its reputation. The burden of such maintenance rests on both men and women, although in different ways. The code of honor and shame "delegates the virtue expressed in sexual purity to the females and the duty of defending female virtue to the males" (Pitt-Rivers 1966:45). The male defense of honor is carried out in the public realm. Not only must a man be ready to stand up for his family's material interests and to retaliate for insult, but he must also be prepared to protect the sexual chastity of daughters, sisters, and wives. Women, on the other hand, preserve honor by cultivating their sense of "shame" (*dropí* in Greek). A woman's shame is "an instinctive revulsion from sexual activity, an attempt in dress, movement, and attitude, to disguise the fact that she possesses the physical attributes of her sex" (Campbell 1966:146).

Women must also refrain from behavior that might give rise to gossip or suspicion. This means dressing modestly so as not to attract sexual interest and confining their activities as much as possible to the domestic realm. Women also must not neglect family or household duties or engage in such disreputable activities as gossip, for derelictions of this sort suggest a weak moral character, and therefore at least the possibility of behavior that can lead to familial disgrace (the very possibility is a shadow on a family's reputation). Whatever a woman's efforts, however, she cannot succeed in avoiding dishonor if these efforts are "unsupported by male authority" (Pitt-Rivers 1966:46). "For an unmarried woman shame reflects directly on parents and brothers . . . who did not protect or avenge her honour. The moment a woman is married these responsibilities pass to her husband" (Peristiany 1966:182).

While in general shame is the "sensitivity to the opinions of others" (Pitt-Rivers 1966:52), it differs in its meaning for men and women. "Clearly manliness and shame are complementary qualities in relation to honour. The manliness of the men in any family protects the sexual honour of its women from external insult or outrage. The women must have shame if the manliness of their men is not to be dishonoured" (Campbell 1966:146). A man who has been shamed is emasculated; he has become like a woman (Pitt-Rivers 1966; Delaney 1987:40).[4] Similarly, a woman stripped of her honor, no longer ruled by shame, Pitt-Rivers suggests, becomes like a man (1966:70).[5] Hence behaving in ways that are inappropriate to their own gender places men and women in the category of the opposite one.

Disgrace is thus familial, for honor, while it can be lost through the behavior of individuals, is collective in its attribution and maintenance. A man's honor depends both on his own actions and on the actions of other family members; in particular, honor can be destroyed by women's uncontrolled sexuality. A woman's reputation depends not only on her own sense of "shame" but also on the communal knowledge that the men in her family are able and willing to guard and defend her. Sexual attacks on women are seen as attacks on the men of the group (whether that group is the family or a larger social unit, such as community or nation; see Peristiany 1960:183; Herzfeld 1987a). Women are in this sense the "weak link" in the system of honor, and their protection and seclusion are essential for honor's maintenance.

There are several important implications of this formulation of the code of honor and shame. First, it sets up a series of cultural dichotomies that structure the social and moral world. In particular, it postulates a clear and gendered distinction between the public and the private realm. The boundaries between these realms, according to the moral code, must be diligently guarded. In the public realm, men's honor is claimed, evaluated, defended. Women, on the other hand, contribute to familial reputation by staying inside, confining their activities as much as possible to the domestic sphere. Thus men are public and visible, while women are private and concealed, the social roles of each defined accordingly. In addition, implicit if not explicit in these formulations is a higher evaluation of the "public" realm as the source of both power and prestige.

A second implication of the code concerns the nature of men and women. Women are weaker, more prone to sin, bearing the burden for the destructive power of sexuality, which must be channeled within male-controlled boundaries to serve the socially desirable ends of reproduction. These ideas are reinforced by the major religious traditions of the region: Catholicism, Eastern Orthodoxy, and Islam. In addition, women are associated with the negative side of such symbolic oppositions as left/right, Satan/God, goats/sheep, witchcraft-magic/religion (see Campbell 1964; du Boulay 1974, 1986; Hoffman 1976). These symbolic oppositions both justify and necessitate the control of women by men. "Honour ordains man and woman to behave in a certain way—mostly positive in the case of man, mostly negative and passive in the case of woman" (Peristiany 1966:184; see also Di Bella 1992:152–53). Women maintain family reputation by being "hidden," by restraint, by not doing. Their flaws are inherent and gender based, part of their nature as women, redeemable only by control by self and by others. Men, on the other hand, must actively maintain honor in the public arena, looking after family interests and defending family reputation from insult or threat.

There is, however, another side to women, for they can represent the good as well as the bad. Particularly in the highly valued social role of mother, women can redeem their sinful natures, becoming identified with the Mother of God, and overcoming the fallen Eve within them (du Boulay 1986; see also Rushton 1983). As mothers, women epitomize unqualified moral good (Pitt-Rivers 1977:80). Moreover, women "in their place" that is, in their interior domestic space—may represent inviolable honor, hence the frequent associations of women with sanctuary in the Mediterranean area (Pitt-Rivers 1977).

CHALLENGING THE ETHNOGRAPHIC AUTHORITY OF HONOR AND SHAME

I have deliberately written the preceding summary in a "traditional" anthropological style. It is not only presented as an "objective" and authoritative account, generalized and generalizing, but is also couched in that deceptive tense known as the "ethnographic present." Thus I have engaged in "writing culture" in the sense indicated by Abu-Lughod when she speaks of "writing against culture" (Abu-Lughod 1991). I have adopted this style here for a particular reason: to present this summary of the code of honor and shame in the same style in which those who have described this code have generally written, and also—and more subversively—by so presenting it, to say something about my own view of the account.

The mode of presentation I have employed here—authoritative, "objective," generalizing—represents both the period of anthropological writing and the view of the anthropological endeavor that were characteristic of the time when I was beginning my own academic career. Not only were ethnographies of the period written from the perspective of an invisible but omniscient anthropologist, but also the people described by the anthropologist were presented as members of bounded and unchanging social groups whose ways of life could be encapsulated in such static frameworks as "honor and shame." Since this was the period of my own induction into the field, this anthropological construction of "honor and shame" played an important role in my struggle to understand women and gender relations in Greece. The heavy (male) authority embodied in the sort of anthropological writing represented by the above summary illustrates some of the heavy authority of the idea of a "Mediterranean moral code."

Female anthropologists working in Greece and elsewhere in the Mediterranean area, however, have sometimes found themselves experiencing a dissonance between what they encountered in the field among the women with whom they worked and what was reported and theorized in these earlier, mostly male writings about such topics as honor and shame (see, e.g., Cowan 1991). The Mediterranean women that these anthropologists came to know were not the suppressed, downtrodden, and reclusive creatures that such accounts had led us to expect, but rather active participants in social life and strong personalities, often stronger and more assured than women we knew in our own societies (Dubisch 1986a), seeking in various ways to resist the dominant ideologies of their society. In my own case, such discrepancies between what was written and what I experienced led me (initially at least) to doubt my own competence. Somehow I had failed to "find" honor and shame in the village where I worked. Such failure suggested some fault in my own perceptions and methods—or so it seemed to me at first.

As I look back on the ways in which early writings about "the Mediterranean" and about "honor and shame" shaped both my conceptions of the region and my expectations of what I would—and *should*—find, as well as my experience of myself as a fieldworker, I am struck by an interesting parallel. The dissonance that I experienced between the anthropological ideology of "honor and shame" and my experiences "in the field" was analogous to the dissonance experienced by many women in my own society between ideologies of gender and their own experience as women (cf. Seremetakis 1991:236). And just as I found it difficult to mount a direct challenge to the anthropologically formulated ideology, so women at the time were finding it difficult to express an experience and a perspective that did not fit in with dominant social ideology.[6] "Finding a voice" became an important element of the women's movement as women sought to put into words what had hitherto been "muted." Thus dissonance in the field resonated with dissonance in my own society.

This was early in my academic career. By now many "voices" have been raised to challenge old constructs, including the constructs of honor and shame.[7] For example, Alison Lever (1986) has contested the idea that honor as a moral attribute is in any way unique to Mediterranean society. Drawing on her own fieldwork in Spain, she argues that discussions of honor and shame have been misleading, acting as a "red herring" to draw anthropological attention away from the values of nondominant groups (including men *and* women), as well as from concern with the ways in which values change. Cole has suggested that anthropological concepts of honor and shame mirror the ideology of the Catholic church and of the fascist governments in power in several Mediterranean countries when anthropologists began doing work in the region (Cole 1991). In a different vein, Michael Herzfeld has criticized the glossing of a wide variety of local terms and usages by the single English term *honor* and has challenged the idea of a "Mediterranean unity" (1980, 1987a, 1987b). It has been suggested that the values and behavior associated with honor and shame represent class differences rather than a distinct "Mediterranean pattern" (see, e.g., Fernandez 1983; Lever 1986; Pina-Cabral 1989). Other writers have simply ignored "honor and shame" and approached gender in other ways (e.g., Friedl 1967).

But the debate over "honor and shame" and its relationship to an anthropology of the "Mediterranean" is by no means dead, as a recent volume illustrates (see Gilmore 1987), though it is a debate that for the most part has grown increasingly sterile. Even acknowledgment that "honor" is a "polysemic concept" requiring "comparative emic analysis" (Gilmore 1982:191) does little to revitalize the arguments. But I am not simply beating a dead concept here. Rather I raise the issue of "honor and shame" in order to examine some of the reasons why this construction has exerted such a powerful hold on us (that is, anthropologists) and to explore the implications of this for my own fieldwork.

GENDER CODES AND MARGINALITY

It is significant that anthropological attempts to define a "Mediterranean" have focused so extensively on a moral code based on a deep gender division. The interest in the idea of a "Mediterranean region" and its definition in terms of a moral code that has been viewed as in some sense "archaic" (see, e.g. Hoffman 1974) may reflect the attempts of a Eurocentric anthropology to come to grips with societies "on the margins" of European experience (or to distance itself from such societies; see Pina-Cabral 1989:399). Those who inhabit these margins (Greeks and other "Mediterraneans") have a highly ambiguous status. They are like "us"—that is, they are members of European or Eurocentered societies—and yet in the eyes of western Europe, and often in their own eyes as well, they sometimes wear that membership uneasily. The highly marked gendered division of society and space and the masculine code of honor that defends it are particularly striking indicators of this marginality. These indicators resonate within "us" (the anthropologists and others of the western European tradition; see, e.g., Delaney 1987), and yet they are at the same time alien, marking off a distinctive otherness (cf. Brandes 1987). Are Greeks and other "Mediterranean" people really "us," after all, or are they really "them," the exotic other that "we" study?

In a sense they are both, for they have often been taken to represent our own "primitive" past. As Pina-Cabral has put it, "synchronic difference is explained away as diachronic difference" (1989:403). Pitt-Rivers, for example, writing of the small town of Sierra de Cadiz, states that "a certain bashfulness disguises the expression of attitudes concerning honour in our own society (perhaps because the word has acquired archaic overtones), but this is not so in the small town of Sierra de Cadiz" (1966:39). In another passage from the same essay, speaking of adultery, Pitt-Rivers describes the cuckold as "the object of ridicule and opprobrium according to the customs of Southern Europe (and formerly England and the whole of Europe)" (1966:46). Gilmore refers to "the primordial values of honor and shame" (1987:16).

The interest in a Mediterranean area, then, and the attempts to define it in terms of the moral code of honor and shame, may reflect the particular (and androcentric) interests of a Eurocentric anthropology confronting a distorted and cloudy mirror of itself (cf. Brandes 1987; Herzfeld 1987a; Sant Cassia 1992). In this mirror we seek our own roots. We hope to discover the clear boundaries, which in modern society have become blurred, and to locate the past certainties, which for us have become ambiguities (cf. Rabinow and Sullivan 1979:15).[8] As Fernandez suggests, "There is now a long tradition of giving our deepest psychological impulses Mediterranean roots" (1983:170).

Insofar as it is true that we have searched for the origins of "our" social institutions in "their" contemporary Mediterranean life (see, e.g., Hoffman 1974), it raises the question of whether or not gender, particularly gender as the basis for a dichotomized system of values and social relationships, has been overemphasized in the analysis of Greece and other Mediterranean societies. Is there a Western "nostalgia" embedded in the descriptions of honor and shame? And is it a *male* nostalgia for a presumed past certainty in the notions of maleness and femaleness and the boundaries that divide and sustain them? And if so, does this help to account for the fact that female anthropologists in general seem to have found these notions both less useful and less compelling?

Much of what I had read about Mediterranean women in general, and Greek women in particular, was challenged by my own experience almost immediately upon my arrival in the village where I did my first fieldwork (see Dubisch 1986a). Despite the restrictions placed upon them, village women were hardly the downtrodden, submissive, and self-effacing creatures works such as Campbell's had led me to think they would be. Indeed it was women who introduced my husband and myself to much of village social life, inviting us into their houses, chatting to us about their families, and asking numerous questions about our own (see Dubisch 1986a,

1991a, 1993; see also Clark 1983). While there were individual women who were dominated and restricted by their husbands, there were also women who bullied their spouses, ran their households with a firm hand, and exhibited a self-confidence I sometimes envied.

Not long after my arrival in the village, I became embroiled in an on-going feud between two women—my landlady, Vasiliki, and a woman who lived across the street who had also befriended us. In recounting to me her grievances against my landlady, the neighbor, Frosoula, remarked that Vasiliki had no *filótimo*. I was very excited by this remark, for all that I had previously read on Greece presented *filótimo* (love of honor) as a male possession only. Never had I heard of the term being applied to women. Curious as to whether this was simply an idiosyncratic use on the part of my neighbor (who certainly had many idiosyncrasies—I had to learn to use her information carefully), I made inquiries of other villagers. Yes, I was told, women could have *filótimo*. It was the general quality of being an *ánthropos*, a "person" or "human being" (the term, though masculine in ending, can be applied to both women and men). To be an *ánthropos* involves, among other things, being hospitable and doing the "right thing" as occasion demands, in other words, meeting social expec-tations (cf. Herzfeld 1987b). Not doing the right thing, on the other hand, was a "shame" (*dropí*). There was no mention of gender in the villagers' explanations; the terms applied to both women and men. Thus while terms such as *filótimo* and *dropí* were more likely to be applied to one gender than another—men having more occasions to uphold individ-ual and familial reputation, women being more concerned with *dropí*—in the community I studied (and in other parts of Greece as well), these con-cepts, like ideas of pollution and sin (Dubisch 1986b; cf. Cole 1991:82–84), were potentially and actually applicable to both women and men.[9]

Years later, when I had returned to Tinos to do fieldwork at the Church of the Annunciation, my thinking on these issues was once more stimu-lated by the behavior of a neighbor. I was living in an apartment near the edge of town, in a concrete building, one of many erected in the building boom that occurred during the junta years. Across the street was another concrete apartment building, a narrow street in between. With all of this concrete, and with no trees or other vegetation to soften the noise, a cacophony of traffic, television sets, and voices reverberated between the buildings, often making me long for the pastoral quiet of my first field-work site. One of the especially predictable—and obnoxious—noises was the voice of the woman across the street calling her children in the late afternoon. "Ar-YEER-ee! Ar-YEER-ee!" Her shouts would echo down the narrow concrete canyon every day around dusk as she called her son home. (I don't remember her daughter's name; it was the son who seemed to be most frequently called.) As I sat at my desk trying to concentrate on my notes, I longed for the quiet, retiring (if mythical) Mediterranean women I used to read about. At the same time it also struck me that in the act of calling her child this woman was loudly and publicly proclaiming what may be a Greek woman's most significant status—that of a mother.

Another incident: in the evenings, when not writing up fieldnotes, I would spend time at the shop of my landlady, Marina, or of other acquaintances in the town. One evening I observed the following incident at the ticket office opposite Marina's store: a woman was giving a little girl a scolding because the child wanted yet another snack after she had already gorged on *souvláki*. Taking off her shoe in an exaggerated gesture, the woman shook it at the child, threatening her with a beating (a very common threat in Greek child rearing, and one seldom carried out). The little girl was not at all intimidated by the scolding, or by the woman's threats. Grinning, she drew herself up and, dramatically imitating the older woman's stance, shook her own hand in mockery and boldly answered back. In the child's impudent mimicking of adult gestures, the adult gestures themselves suddenly took on greater vividness, and I saw the way in which, through the use of body language, both adult and child prepared themselves for and delivered a public performance. It was a moment of insight in which the deliberately dramatic nature of Greek social interaction took on particular clarity for me.[10]

In the context of some of the issues with which I was currently concerned, the importance of this incident was twofold: first, it made me aware of the *body* language by which such drama is signaled and by which it is enacted, and second, it also made me aware that despite differences in body language and in the content of performance between men and women, performance itself, and in a public context, is not (as ethnographic accounts of Greece have sometimes led us to believe) the exclusive property of men, but rather a general characteristic of social interaction.

Incidents such as these are small scraps of the sort that anthropologists must constantly sort through in the course of fieldwork. In and of themselves they tell us little. They take on meaning only against a background of other observations, in this case, against a background of observations made by myself (and others) over a period of years. And yet they are more than simply additional bits of information, for the materials of fieldwork are never even or neutral. These incidents stood out for me as epiphanies, as what Fernandez has called "revelatory moments," points in the fieldwork process when other, routinely collected data come together and suddenly take on a meaning and shape they have hitherto lacked.[11]

What, then, is this shape and meaning, and how is it related to my understanding of both gender and pilgrimage?

Toward a "Poetics of Womanhood"

I see two ways in which the anthropological construct of "honor and shame" led to my feeling of dissonance between expectations and experience during my earlier fieldwork. First, discussions of honor and shame (which frequently are more about honor than about shame) place women in an essentially passive role. This did not fit with my experience of women in the village. Second, and related to this, the static nature of the construct inhibited understanding of the ways in which the actual practices of social actors are informed by notions of gender. Increasingly, anthropologists have come to view cultural conceptions of gender not as a rigid set of rules about male and female nature or about how men and women should behave, but as a framework for discourse and negotiation, worked out in the dynamic context of social life (see, e.g., Cole 1991). Thus a critical view of honor and shame would argue that both the construction of gender categories and the dynamics of gender roles are considerably more complex than formulations of honor and shame, or the distinction between public and private, suggest. What is necessary, then, is a more dynamic, integrated, and integrative approach to gender than the fixed, static categories of honor and shame, an approach that not only allows me to propose a possible "solution" (or at least one possible interpretation) to the "puzzle" (*my* puzzle, not theirs) of the women I observed on pilgrimage, but also contributes to a more general understanding of cultural constructions of gender and of certain facets of Greek cultural and social life.

For such an approach I return to the metaphor of "performance," which I developed in chapter 9. In *Persuasions and Performances*, James Fernandez speaks of

> our tendency as social animals to try and maintain ourselves at the center of, or in the right position in, the social world to which we belong and whose roles we have learned to perform with satisfaction. . . . This maintenance of satisfying role performance by argumentative means seems to be a fundamental mission in human life. . . . to preserve our place and our gratifying performances . . . and to persuade others to recognize that place, that performance, that world. (1986:viii)

To perform, then, is to present the socially constructed self before others, to in a sense "argue" for that self (not necessarily verbally but in other persuasive ways as well), and thus to convince and draw recognition from others of one's place and one's satisfactory performance of that role. I would add to this Seremetakis's observation (which she makes in reference to Maniat women's mourning ceremonies) that these performances are transformative and not simply expressive (1991:2). In other words, they are creative endeavors. Such an approach to the analysis of social life has particular implications for the study of women and provides at least a guidepost to the path by which we might bypass honor and shame. To illustrate this, here is another tale from my fieldwork.

I returned to the island of Tinos in the blustery March of 1987 for the Feast of the Annunciation (March 25), accompanied by another anthropologist who had been working in Greece. To my great disappointment, a boat strike began shortly after I arrived, so instead of the thousands of pilgrims who normally arrived for the event, there were only a handful, greatly reducing the scope of the festivities. Because of the lack of business, my landlady, Marina, and her husband decided to close their shop in the afternoon and return to their apartment for a holiday meal. My friend and I were invited to join them (a rare event for me, since during the summer the family spent the entire day, from early morning until late at night, seven days a week, in their shop). In the general conversation after the meal, Marina began to complain about a chronic ailment and revealed that her mother had died of a similar complaint. Her husband, my friend, and I all urged her to see a doctor. How could she possibly see a doctor? she replied indignantly. To do that she would have to go to Athens, and such a trip would require an absence of several days at least. With all the things there were to be done for the upcoming Easter holidays, and all the baking these holidays required, and with getting the shop ready and cleaning the apartments and rooms she rents for the tourist season, there was no way she could take time off to take care of herself. My landlady's husband, Dhimitris, and her son, Takis (a young man in his early twenties), had no response to this monologue and listened in silence, as did my friend and I.

"LIFE IS A THEATER"

The idea of performance (in the dramatic sense) as a part of social life is something that accords with many Greeks' own conceptions of the world. "Life is a theater" (*I zoí íne théatro*), I sometimes heard people in the village remark. Or of a difficult or complicated situation one might say, "It's a drama" (*Íne dhráma*). In addition, as both the incident with the little girl and my landlady's litany of suffering suggest, a dramatic structure underlies much of everyday social interaction. Through gestures, tone of voice, phrasing, and appeal to bystanders as an "audience," an individual "frames" certain statements and acts. Less routine occasions are also marked by performances, as in women's mourning laments (see Caraveli 1986; Danforth and Tsiaras 1982; Seremetakis 1991). All such dramas are, of necessity, "public," a point to which I shall return shortly.

The often implicit assumptions about the "naturalness" of such gender-specific roles as motherhood (assumptions often shared by both anthropologists and their informants) may lead us to overlook the important ways in which gender status is culturally constituted and "performed" (in Fernandez's terms) and the ways in which it may be used to make statements and claims—and even to provide an idiom of resistance—in the everyday context of social life. Discussions of honor and shame have tended to perpetuate this oversight in their emphasis on the dramatic nature of the conferral and maintenance of masculinity, masculinity that must be continually affirmed in a public setting. Less attention is paid to the practice of "being a woman," for womanhood, such discussions suggest, comes passively to women, while manhood must be "earned" by men. The implication (whether intended or not) is that men's roles and identity are more culturally constituted than women's. Gilmore, for example, suggests that the heavy emphasis on the assertion of masculinity in Mediterranean society is a result of the necessity to break away from a female-dominated domestic world in order to become a man. Because there are no formalized rituals to accomplish this, "and without biological markers like menarche to signal manhood, each individual man must prove himself in his own way" (Gilmore 1987:15).[12] Women's transitions do not require such an active effort, it is argued, because they do not need to differentiate themselves from this domestic world. Because "femininity depends more often upon natural functions," Gilmore argues, it is "therefore often less problematical" (1987:9). Less problematical for whom, one must ask here—for the women in question, or for the anthropologist?

An example of anthropological analysis of Greek male performance (though not in Gilmore's psychosocial terms) is Michael Herzfeld's (1985) discussion of what he calls "the poetics of manhood' in a Cretan village.[13] Herzfeld argues that Cretan men present themselves in a type of public performance in which "being a good man" is less important than "being *good at* being a man" (1985:16). "The successful presentation of selfhood depends upon an ability to identify the self with larger categories of identity" (1985:10). Individual performances are part of an ongoing struggle with other men in which individuals act as persons, as members of their patriline, as villagers, as Cretans. In such performances, the individual presents himself in a dramatic way, which concentrates attention on the performance itself.

Could we then speak of a "poetics of womanhood" in Greece? In the context of "honor and shame" the answer would seem to be no. If Mediterranean women's roles generally, and Greek women's roles in particular, are domestic and hence "private," and if women's identity is supposedly less "problematic" and therefore does not need to be "earned" or actively demonstrated, and if, furthermore, women are not engaged in the sort of public struggle of which Herzfeld speaks, there seems little scope (or need) for a public presentation of self. Moreover, the very idea of a public "performance" for women seems antithetical to the cultural rules for appropriate female behavior, especially in a society such as Greece. And if we follow Gilmore's argument, women do not even need such performance to place and maintain themselves socially as women. After all, they "automatically" achieve womanhood by "natural" means.

Indeed general discussions of the idea of performance often *assume* a male performer. And yet if, as Fernandez claims, "the maintenance of satisfying role performance by argumentative means seems to be a fundamental mission in human life" (1966:viii), then women should be as much involved in such endeavors as men, even if the content and form of this performance differs from that of men. (Moreover, to return to Gilmore, the very notion of "need" is a cultural one—in this case the anthropologist's.)

Indeed we can argue that *all* roles are "public" in the sense that they are defined and evaluated by a larger community (see Dubisch 1993; see also Constantinides 1977). Collier and Yanagisako, for example, suggest that gender needs to be seen in the context of "the public discourses through which people describe, interpret, evaluate, make claims about, and attempt to influence relationships and events" (1987:41). The key word here is *public,* for ideas about femaleness are no less publicly expressed and negotiated than those about maleness. Once we begin to think this way, assumptions about "naturalness" and the "unproblematic" nature of women's roles no longer serve as bases for our understanding of womanhood, and we are forced to look at women as no less actors than men, and at womanhood as being no less culturally constructed than manhood.

In what ways, then, might a Greek woman present a performance about "being good at being a woman"?

Performance draws upon culturally "available" material for its construction and is carried out in culturally relevant or appropriate contexts. In a recent article exploring the possibility of a "poetics of womanhood," Herzfeld points out that as Western anthropologists we may share with Cretan shepherds the tendency to recognize performances by men because they *do* something, whereas women *seem* to do very little. He suggests that the *lack* of "doing something" can also be a performance, and that the outward presentation of Greek women (at least in certain situations) is "inarticulacy," an inarticulacy paralleled by the absence of a feminine equivalent in Greek for the terms for masculinity or manhood (1991a:82). Herzfeld goes on to point out that for this reason a verbocentric and androcentric anthropology can easily overlook the extent to which such inarticulacy is itself expressive. "Gender stereotypes," Herzfeld maintains, are "rhetorical strategies that only make sense in terms of social practice" (1991a:80). As an example, Herzfeld suggests that women may exaggerate certain aspects of their supposedly inferior roles as ironic comment on the dominant male ideology and as an expression of their own dissent from that ideology. In his words, women "creatively deform" the tenets upon which their submission is based (1991a:81).

As Herzfeld points out, his analysis in some respects parallels Edwin Ardener's idea of the "muted model," a view of the world held by a subordinate social group (such as women), which differs from, but is muted in the face of, the dominant ideology and which may be only vaguely articulated by the members of the group (Ardener 1975). Herzfeld's idea of a poetics of womanhood suggests one way that muted model might be expressed. Yet his analysis is incomplete, for he seems to present a poetics of womanhood as simply a "subversion" of a male ideology, and the female expression of selfhood and its place within a system of values and social relationships as only a reaction against male dominance, a reaction based on silence. More "articulate" and dramatic performances by women, however, are not difficult to find—or at least they were not in the area of Greece where I worked (nor, it seems, in other areas as well; see, e.g., Cowan 1990; Danforth 1989; Seremetakis 1990, 1991). And Herzfeld admits his limitations as a male ethnographer who was not privy to women's conversations among themselves, suggesting that the defining criterion for "public" in his analysis is the presence of men. Thus if Greek women seem to the observer "to do very little," it may be only because we (the anthropologists) discount women's activities as "not really doing anything," or do not pay close attention to what women's "doing" actually "does."[14] As Seremetakis points out in her discussion of the women of Inner Mani, these women present a "multi-media performance," drawing on a range of cultural materials within their own temporally and spatially bounded locale (1991:7). In what media, then, do women perform?

Being a Woman

We might begin by examining what much of the ethnographic literature on Greece has presented as a Greek woman's most significant role—that of mother. In the framework of honor and shame, motherhood has been described as the means by which women redeem their inherently sinful nature. By bearing children, they overcome the "Eve" within them and become instead like the Mother of God (du Boulay 1986). There are few instances that I or other ethnographers of Greece have encountered of women who have deliberately chosen not to have any children at all. Unintended childlessness is a tragedy, the cause of many prayers, vows, and pilgrimages. Motherhood is a state that is highly respected, one might even say revered, in Greece. A woman without children is generally pitied, and may not be regarded as quite fully adult. A pregnant woman, far from trying to hide her pregnancy in concealing "maternity clothes," will instead exaggerate her condition through her posture and gait.[15] Sexuality, on the other hand, has until recently been something women were required to conceal, by dressing and behaving in such a manner as not to provoke the sexual interest of men. Thus explicit sexual attractiveness plays a lesser, or sometimes even negative, role in the construction of womanhood.[16]

This does not necessarily mean that motherhood is regarded without ambivalence, or that the more children one has, the better a mother one is. A single child often will suffice to satisfy the social and personal demands for maternity, and I have known several Greek mothers of only children to say that the one child they had was work and trouble enough; they did not want another.

Maternity must not be seen only in relationship to children, however, but also in connection with the general duties regarding the maintenance of the house, which is not only the seat of family life but also a metaphor for family (see du Boulay 1974). Therefore, the demonstration of the fulfillment of maternal and housewifely duties, and the carrying out of activities that prefigure this fulfillment (for example, housewifely skills in a young, unmarried woman; see Stanton and Salamone 1986), can be seen as part of "being good at being a woman."

Women's bodies play an important role in a poetics of womanhood, for bodies have social meanings that may be used in public performances, and in Greece, as in many societies, the female body provides an important source of social symbolism.[17] Much of the ethnographic writing on Greece has emphasized the negative aspects of the female body—its inherently polluting nature, its propensity for sin, and its danger as a potential avenue for the loss of family honor (e.g., Campbell 1964; Hoffman 1976)—and the manner in which women's bodies are "redeemed" from their inherent shamefulness in motherhood (du Boulay 1986; Rushton 1983). And yet a view of the female body as completely shameful tends to obscure the public aspects of body symbolism. The female body both creates and represents the family in a variety of contexts. (Even its concealment is a public statement of individual and familial virtue.) For example, by wearing black mourning clothes when a family member dies, women become highly visible symbols of mourning, hence of the kinship relationships between the deceased and the living. Village women told me that adherence to this custom of mourning (*pénthos*) was necessary because of what others (*o kósmos*) might say, that is, because of public opinion (see Dubisch 1989).[18] More generally, Seremetakis has linked ornamentation to the iconic construction of status. In the past, in Inner Mani, a woman who "enjoyed all her kin alive" wore a red strip of cloth on the hem of her skirt. In mourning, a woman stripped this red trim away. Thus her ornamentation indicated her relationship to both the living and the dead (Seremetakis 1991:213–14). In such publicly visible acts women, like men, identify themselves "with larger categories of identity" (Herzfeld 1985:10). As Seremetakis puts it, "The presence and absence of ornaments on the body is a public statement concerning self and collectivities" (1991:214).

Women are responsible for the general well-being of their families. Cooking is one of the most important duties of a Greek wife and mother, and one of the most worrisome of mothers' complaints is a child who won't eat. Although cooking and feeding are usually acts performed in the privacy of the house, they can have a public dimension as well. Once I observed a mother at the beach following her child into the water in order to continue feeding the boy his lunch. On another occasion, I saw a grandmother in a playground periodically stop a merry-go-round on which her grandchild was riding so that she could stuff bits of food in the child's mouth. I had at one time regarded such acts as simply extremes of maternal feeding behavior (see Dubisch 1986b), but I have now come to see them as a kind of performance, an extreme but by no means atypical demonstration of maternalness in a public context.[19]

A woman's cooking, while usually consumed within a family context, may also be displayed publicly at name-day celebrations and other ceremonial occasions, as well as in the course of the hospitality associated with more routine visiting. All of these are public acts, or at least acts with a public dimension. Indeed, in the offering of hospitality, so important to *filótimo* on ritual or other occasions, women play an important role in maintaining a family's communal reputation.

Other aspects of a woman's housewifely abilities may also be publicly displayed. In the village of Falatados, women were responsible for keeping the street in front of their houses clean, no small task with the constant passage of farm animals. They frequently complained to me about the fact that passing animals dirtied the streets, making it difficult to keep them properly swept. They thus called attention to their work by this act of both apology and complaint. In the refugee community of Ammouliani in northern Greece, the display of the household goods accumulated by the women of the family is an important element of weddings, and such display makes public the skill and diligence of the female members of the household (Stanton and Salamone 1986; see also Pavlides and Hesser 1986).

Women also have important ritual roles in village and family life. In the villages of Greece, women not only attend church more frequently than men but they are also the guardians of their family's spiritual health (which cannot really be separated from physical health, given the role of prayers and vows in healing and protection). It is most often women who represent and connect their families to the spiritual world. Women light the oil lamp or candle in front of the family icons on the eve of every holy day and on other occasions when they need divine help, make vows and pilgrimages on behalf of family members who are ill, and guard the house against pollution and the evil eye (see Dubisch 1983, 1986b). Among the most important of women's rituals are those pertaining to the dead, including the singing of mourning laments, the tending of graves, and the preparing of *kóliva,* the ritual food of sweetened boiled wheat offered at memorial services and on all souls' days.[20] Women are also more likely to observe religious fasts than men. Men have to work too hard, several village women told me; they can't be expected to fast. In such a manner these women laid claim to this particular spiritual work as their own. Laywomen are thus much more intimately involved in religion than laymen, and many village men seldom attend church except on the most important holidays, such as Easter.

This greater involvement of women in religious activities, both within and outside the church, has been noted throughout the Mediterranean Catholic and Orthodox world. Pina-Cabral (1986), writing about Portugal, suggests that women's greater sinfulness in the eyes of the church may lead to their greater need for religion.[21] This fails, however, to account for the fact that women perform very "positive" and necessary spiritual activities, often on behalf of others. Another explanation, which is particularly germane to my arguments here, is that while Mary offers an appropriate model for women, the figure of Christ does not provide such a model for men. Juliet du Boulay argues that a Greek woman overcomes her negative association with Eve by striving to emulate the example of the Panayía, the pure mother. Men are likewise associated with Adam and sin, but Christ, with his virtues of meekness and forgiveness, does not provide an appropriate model for Greek men to emulate since these virtues are not appropriate to male behavior: "Modesty, meekness, humility are values only admirable for women" (Campbell 1966:167; but see Herzfeld 1985.) In addition, the restraint that the church attempts to exercise on sexuality, the institution of confession, and the necessity to submit to the authority of other men (men who are often not held in high regard) seem to be sticking points for men both in Greece and elsewhere in the Mediterranean.[22]

Such interpretations, however, limit women's religious roles to Marian devotion and to religious activities that are connected with the church and church controlled. (And they do not account for women's anticlericalism; see, e.g., Seremetakis 1991.) An alternative explanation is that religious activities provide a "space" for women's performances. Visiting the cemetery, attending a liturgy at a country church, going on a pilgrimage—these are all legitimate ways for women to move through public space and to socialize with other women. They provide, in some respects at least, the counterpart of the male *kafenío,* the village coffee-house, which is such an important stage for male performance. Nor can women be criticized for these religious excursions. They are not neglecting their appropriate duties as wives and mothers; on the contrary, they are often engaging in ritual activities on the family's behalf.

Our category of "public" must thus be broadened to include not only the world of men but also the world of women, even when they do not gather in what is conventionally designated as "public" space (see Constantinides 1977). That is, *women* may provide the "public" audience for other women's performances (as well as the critical commentary that determines how such performances will be evaluated; see Caraveli 1986), whether at religious events, while tending the graves of loved ones in the cemetery, or in informal socializing. It is obvious from Herzfeld's analysis that for many of the male performances he describes the audience is other *men,* and that when women do observe, they are not always sympathetic or impressed. (Likewise men may not always approve of women's performances; several village men, for example, made negative comments to me about women's wearing of black mourning clothes.) We must be careful, then, not to fall into the type of tautological thinking that simply equates "public" with "male," thus assuming what it is that needs to be demonstrated.

A final point on women's "multimedia" performance: women's own stories about themselves can be seen as another type of female performance. Seremetakis, for example, sees biography as one of the elements encapsulated within the ritual process of lament performance (1991:7). Similarly, in another cultural context, Valentine (1992) has analyzed a Galician woman's accounts about herself as an example of women's narrative performance. Such accounts are not simply "personal"—they position the teller in relation to her cultural and social world. They are "about" "being a woman."

Suffering as an Aspect of Womanhood

So far I have suggested several kinds of cultural materials upon which women may draw for the presentation of self in the performances that we might term "the poetics of womanhood": the importance of motherhood; proper keeping of the house, including handicrafts and food preparation;[23] the female body, especially as it represents family and social relationships; personal narratives; and women's activities in the religious sphere, which give them legitimate reasons to move through the kind of space that is often designated "public" and male. There is one further cultural element that needs to be discussed, however, before I relate the preceding discussion to the activities of female pilgrims, and that is the idea of suffering.

Relatively little attention has been paid to the cultural role of suffering in the ethnographic literature on Greece, especially outside the context of the study of mourning laments.[24] This may be because expressions of suffering (such as my landlady's)—and indeed most expressions of emotion—tend to be treated as statements of individual feelings, as "natural" phenomena, rather than as cultural idioms (M. Rosaldo 1987). In addition, emotions are generally distrusted or overlooked by social scientists, who seek structure and "rationality" in social life and for whom emotions seem incompatible with both (Lutz and White 1986). This has particular implications for the study of women, not because women are "naturally" more emotional, but because cultural factors often lead women to construct and express their identity through emotional statements and acts. In addition, women may be culturally identified with the emotional side of life. In the West, for example, emotions are generally seen as appropriate only in the private realm (associated with women), and should be suppressed in the public realm (which is associated with men).[25] The naturalistic view of emotion as associated with the body and hence the view of emotional communication as nonverbal (Lutz and White 1986:423) further enforces a Western view of emotion as womanly, childish, weak, nonverbal (and hence inchoate and chaotic) and even lower-class and primitive, a view that has implications for the study of emotion cross-culturally. It also has implications for the study of religion. In American society (or perhaps Western society generally), emotional religions may be viewed as "lower-class" or marginal. Influenced by such views, anthropological studies of religion have often sought to "rationalize" the emotional aspects of religion, presenting emotions as something that religion seeks to "handle," or as a means to, or expression of, something else (for example, social solidarity). And in such an intellectual context, the anthropologist's own emotions also become problematic and something to be suppressed, as I have argued in earlier chapters.

More recently, interpretive approaches to emotion have sought to move from a view of emotions as belonging to an unproblematic "natural" realm and toward the analysis of expressions of emotion as cultural constructions (Lutz 1988; Lutz and White 1986:408; see also Lutz and Abu-Lughod 1990). Like gender, then, emotions must be studied not only in cultural context but as part of the construction of culture itself and of the relationship of the individual to culture. As Seremetakis argues, one must take account of emotions as "embodied, conceptual, moral, and ideational constructs that place the self in dynamic relation to social structure" (1991:4). In other words, we need an anthropology of the practice and performance of emotions.

While it was the activities of female pilgrims at Tinos that first drew my attention to the role of suffering, once I had noticed it, I began to perceive the importance of suffering in other areas of Greek life as well. In fact I came to see suffering as a pervasive cultural expression, not only in the more dramatic representations of religion and of modern Greek history,[26] but also in the context of everyday life, and in the presentation of self, especially the female self. Many Greeks I know—both women and men—engage in what I came to term "competitive suffering," which often manifests itself in constant complaints about the difficulty of daily life and problems with work, illness, or (particularly for women) personal relationships. Even though motherhood is the most highly valued role for a woman, it is not uncommon for women's complaints (and sometimes men's as well) to center on children and how much trouble they are. Children inevitably bring trouble and suffering; hence Marina's exclamation when told of the motorcycle accident: "What mother cries?" Her own cry both identified her with the unknown woman and expressed her own suffering motherhood.[27]

The idiom of suffering is particularly important in the context of women's roles. We see this in the part that women play in mourning. By dressing in black, women make their bodies into representations of their personal and familial loss and publicly proclaim their connection to specific social groups. And by refraining from certain acts (for example, dancing or other expressions of social enjoyment), as well as through public grieving, women's mourning behavior highlights their own suffering.[28] Suffering may also serve as a basis for women's identification with other women. This can be seen in the concept of *ponos* (pain), especially as it is applied to the experience of death and mourning. Anna Caraveli, who has done extensive studies of Greek women's performance of mourning laments, speaks of a "community of pain" that unites women. She feels that her own entry into this community was facilitated by the fact that she, too, had suffered, both from illness and from problems with her children (Caraveli 1980, 1986). The laments themselves are a major form of female performance, created by women from traditional forms and the painful materials of their own lived experience, and they serve as vehicles to express their sufferings and those of others and to protest against injustice on behalf of all the weak and downtrodden of the world (Caraveli 1986; Seremetakis 1991). Thus being a woman in this case means identifying not only with other women but also with others who share women's experience of marginality.

Within Greek Orthodox religion, suffering is a central theme. It was through Christ's suffering, death, and resurrection that humankind was redeemed. The crucifixion is a "lived" drama within the Orthodox ritual cycle, made real every Easter in the services of Holy Week. And although all are affected by this drama, the village women I observed were especially expressive in their empathy. I watched these women weep as Christ's sentence was read, and their fasting during this time was a reminder of the suffering Christ himself endured. And yet it might be argued that the suffering of Mary is, in some contexts at least, as important as the suffering of Christ. Christ died and was resurrected, but Mary remained to bury her son and to mourn. Her experience is directly applicable to other mothers' lives. Indeed, some Greeks writing about women's pilgrimage to the Church of the Annunciation see a clear identification between the suffering female pilgrim and the Panayía,[29] and the painting at the church titled *The Vow* depicts a mother in black holding a child, implying that the basic nature of the vow is built on maternal suffering and hope.

More broadly, most, if not all, vows might be seen as having their origin in *pónos,* so that behind every offering lies a story of pain. In the context of pilgrimage, suffering might be seen as a form of sanctification. Dahlberg, in her discussion of pilgrimage at Lourdes, suggests that healthy pilgrims tend to treat the sick and suffering "in a way analogous to the way the saints are treated," touching them, giving them small gifts, and asking for their prayers (1991:46). While I did not encounter such behavior at Tinos, those who dramatically exhibited their suffering did often become objects of attention and pity and even awe, especially if they had chosen to undertake a particularly difficult and painful form of pilgrimage.

Suffering and struggle are not limited to such occasions as death and pilgrimage but are also seen as an ongoing part of everyday life. A common response of villagers to the question "How are you?" is "We are struggling" (*Palévoume*) (Friedl 1962), or "We are fighting" (*Polemáme*). I found women especially prone to complain about the difficulties of their lives, the amount of work they have to do, their problems with children and relatives, and their various ailments. And both men and women complain about economic difficulties. In her article on the appearance and reality of women's power in Greek village life, Ernestine Friedl suggests that women's complaints to the men of their household are culturally sanctioned and serve as "a constant reminder of the lengths to which the women go in the toil and trouble which they take in the performance of those household tasks which enable the men of the family to preserve their public honor" (1967:108). *Hristé mou* (my Christ) and *Panayía mou* (my Madonna) are both commonly heard expressions, often uttered with a sigh, eloquent with the difficulty and suffering of everyday life. Women's "complaints" and suffering, then, call attention to what they must endure in order to carry out their roles. This does not mean that all women complain, of course (nor that all complaining is done by women).

Rather, such complaints are a part of the available "cultural material" out of which the "poetics" of womanhood can be constructed. Such "complaining," however, is not confined to the "domestic" context, but can take place "publicly" (and nonverbally) as well.

This is an appropriate place to note that performance requires an "audience." I have already suggested that one audience for women is other women, who may be the most interested and critical commentators on each others' performances (just as men most often provide the critical audience for other men). The family also provides an audience, as Friedl's observations and Marina's litany of martyrdom illustrate. In the case of female pilgrims, the audience varies—it may be accompanying family members, friends, fellow villagers. Or it may simply be the Panayía herself, and the anonymous crowds of fellow pilgrims.

But there is another audience involved here too. It was not only in front of her son and husband that Marina voiced her complaints but in front of two foreigners as well. What do such complaints mean when I consider them reflexively? What does it mean that they are voicing such complaints to *me,* that I am the "intended audience"? I must begin to answer this question by saying that sometimes it may mean nothing—that is, the complaints are not different in substance or tone from those I have heard Greeks voice to a fellow Greek. I am simply a general audience, the person who happens to be there to listen.[30]

But I cannot always see myself as entirely neutral. I am not only a foreigner. I am also a representative of a more affluent and more powerful society, one whose actions affect Greece's economic, political, and cultural destiny. Moreover, islanders saw me not only as more affluent but also as more leisured. To the townspeople I knew I did not seem to work. They knew that I wrote and read, that I went to the church a lot, and asked questions and took many photographs, but this did not seem particularly like work to them. A question people frequently asked about my daily activities was whether or not I had gone swimming. If I had, it confirmed my status as a leisured summer visitor; if not, they wanted to know why. (After all, I had the time to enjoy myself even if they didn't, they would remind me.) And townspeoples' recitations to me of all the work they had to do in the course of a day certainly did serve to make me feel guilty. I had nothing to offer in return. Even if I were to tell them about my normal working year—the problems of teaching, the committees, the writing of articles and papers—it would have made little impression upon them, so alien was my world to them.[31] "If we worked this hard in the United States or Canada," one shopkeeper told me, complaining about the lack of tourist business one summer, "we would be rich." To borrow a common Greek expression, what could I say (*ti na po*)?

And yet I feel that my own pain was significant in my fieldwork, not simply in calling my attention to the issue of suffering in pilgrimage, but also in making me aware of the public and performative dimension of suffering. I came to realize that one reason I seldom succeeded in having anyone take my own complaints seriously was that, coming from a very different cultural background, I tended to mute, rather than to dramatize, difficulty and pain. As the example of "the anthropologist's vow" illustrates, when I did make an emotional show of my pain, I was taken seriously and treated very sympathetically. At the same time, I cannot claim that at any point in my work with pilgrims I felt part of "a community of pain" such as that described by Caraveli.[32]

EMOTION, SUFFERING, AND THE SELF

Lutz and White speak of "the culturally constituted self, positioned at the nexus of personal and social worlds. . . . Concepts of emotion emerge as a kind of language of the self" (1986:417). Emotions help form "the actor's sense of his or her relation to a social world" and serve as "a primary idiom for defining and negotiating social relations of the self in a moral order" (1986:417). Emotion, then, is not simply the expression of an internal state but is rather "a statement about a person's relationship with the world, and particularly problems in that relationship." If one views emotion in this way, "the most commonly occurring emotions in a society can be seen as markers of the points of tension (or fulfillment) generated by its structure" (Lutz and White 1986:421).

In the Greek contexts that I have described, suffering—that is, suffering as culturally constructed and expressed through verbal complaint, the body, ritual actions, or other means—can be seen as an expression of social identity and connection, as well as a validation of the performance of social roles. It is a means by which women—and men—can demonstrate to and remind others of the difficulties inherent in the performance of their roles. For many women, the points of both tension and fulfillment center around motherhood and familial responsibilities. For women, especially, the body plays an important role in these expressions of suffering, whether it is through the wearing of black mourning clothes, crawling to the church with a child on one's back, or the numerous expressions of the ways women suffer in the process of bodily reproduction.[33] For women also, the identification with the Panayía as a suffering mother lends a particular moral force to their own performance of suffering as enacted at the pilgrimage site, for it draws on powerful religious imagery and aligns women with the major figure of Orthodox devotional practice. Emotion provides a means of communication and contact with this figure, as women cry out and call upon "my Panayía" (*Panayía mou*). When enacted by such difficult (and painful) activities as crawling on one's knees, a particularly powerful public performance of self is presented, but it is a self that characteristically takes validity through the sacrifice and suffering of the self on behalf of others.

Emotion is not limited to the pilgrim. Her performance of pain can provide a point of connection to others. The pilgrim, after all, has an audience—townspeople, other pilgrims, tourists, anthropologists. These are affected to differing degrees by the pilgrim's performance. When a woman works her way painfully up the church steps on her stomach, supporting her paralyzed child on her back, other pilgrims step back to make way for her. Some weep or sigh and even the anthropologist is moved to tears. Yet at the same time, emotion also separates the performer from others, just as the actor is separated from the audience. This may be part of what Herzfeld means when he states that "the self is not presented within everyday life so much as in front of it" (1985:11). In such a setting, the suffering pilgrim is somewhat "larger than life."

Although I have emphasized that pilgrims do not leave their everyday social worlds and its structures entirely behind but rather carry relationships and familial concerns with them on pilgrimage, this does not mean that I see pilgrimage as devoid of liminal experience. It may be women's at least partially liminal state during pilgrimage that allows for their more dramatic religious performances in this context. Religious activities generally may provide important "space" for women, space in which they can express emotion, socialize with others, and find legitimate time away from family and home.[34] Through religious ritual women can detach themselves from their normal social contexts and create performative space for themselves. This is particularly true of the activities associated with death and mourning, where pain provides an instrument for both separation and community. Women may spend long hours in cemeteries, for example, tending the graves of deceased family members, singing laments, and even speaking with the dead. Though such activities might seem depressing, even morbid, to the foreign (particularly Western) observer, Greek women speak of the peace they experience in such a setting and the satisfaction that their activities by the gravesite afford (Danforth and Tsiaras 1982; see also Hirschon 1983). Similarly, pilgrimage also provides performative and emotional space, and it is not uncommon to see a woman who has put on an emotional performance in front of the icon of the Annunciation later strolling through the streets of Tinos with family or friends, calmly buying snacks and souvenirs.

Such examples do not simply suggest a view of emotional performance as catharsis (though it may certainly be that). Nor do I mean the use of the term "performance" to imply that such expressions of emotion are "insincere." Rather, I see these emotion-laden dramas as a creative act. From this perspective, Greek women on pilgrimage are not simply using the materials of Orthodox religion in order to create expressions of their own identity; they are creating images central to that religion as well.[35] Their ritual and prayer focus not on Christ, but on the Panayía. Instead of the martyred son, they produce and reproduce images of the suffering mother. These are powerful images, reinforced in everyday life as Greek mothers struggle to bear and raise their children, and experienced by those children as their mothers remind them of the difficulties of the maternal role. The mother's own body is constantly offered as a sacrifice in this struggle, and this sacrifice may be dramatized in women's pilgrimage to the shrine.[36]

Stories are even told of women who have died for, or because of, their children. I have heard of several cases of women who are supposed to have been killed by *stenohoría*, a state of anxiety or depression particularly afflicting women. Two cases I heard about involved women who died because of troubles with their children. In another (which occurred in the village of Falatados during my fieldwork), a woman's difficulties with her troublesome daughter-in-law were said to have sent her to her grave.[37]

A mother's death of *stenohoría* is, of course, an extreme, and perhaps stories of such deaths should be taken metaphorically. (My landlady, Marina, who told me she had the same liver ailment that had killed her mother, had earlier told me that her mother died of grief over another daughter's death.) Crawling on one's knees to the shrine of the Panayía is also an extreme. Yet just as in the case of the possessed woman, it is in such extremes that we can discern important cultural themes, themes present in everyday events as well, even if they are not so dramatically portrayed. Marina's litany of her ailments, followed by the statement that her family duties are too pressing for her to take time to see a doctor, expressed very clearly her "martyrdom" in fulfillment of her role as wife and mother. Through both large and small performances women may lay claim to recognition of the difficulties involved in their role (and emphasize the essentialness of that role as well).

On pilgrimage, women's performances take place on a wider stage. Moreover, though conducted individually, they take on a kind of collective power, especially on major ritual occasions when dozens of these individual dramas may be occurring at any one time. Since pilgrimage at Tinos, though focused on the church and icon, is a highly individualistic ritual activity, the scene on such occasions appears to verge on chaos. This chaos is intensified by the heightened emotionalism that these occasions both allow and induce. A naturalistic view of emotion sees it as womanly and weak, but it is also inchoate, chaotic, and therefore even threatening. More specifically we see an emergent opposition between pilgrims and the formal institution of the church.

In *The Last Word: Women, Death, and Divination in Inner Mani*, Seremetakis describes scenes that resonate with my own experience of pilgrimage at Tinos. She speaks of the bifurcation of the ritualization of death by "oppositional performative practices" (1991:163). This opposition is manifested in the split between two terms connected with mourning, *kidhía* (funeral), which is associated with institutional ritual and theology of the church, and *kláma*, the lamenting and noninstitutional rituals carried out by women in connection with death. Older women will either not use the term *kidhía* or will make a distinction between the *kidhía*, which "begins with the moment of the priest's entry into the church and includes the Orthodox service," and the *kláma*, which "indicates the period of 'screaming the dead' and lamentation that takes place at least several hours prior to the funeral and recurs at the completion of the Orthodox burial" (Seremetakis 1991:162). During the *kláma* the church is packed with women. "When *kláma* . . . takes place in the church, the latter is packed with women. The entry of the priest into this feminized space is initially registered in a variety of noises, gestures, talk, and rearrangement of body postures. . . . The mourning continues as he enters, and it is not until he positions himself directly over the corpse that the mourning singers stop." Seremetakis goes on to note: "The entry of the priest . . . creates a disciplinary space. The previous polyphony, in turn, becomes imbued with an aura of chaos. The first overt sign of a disciplined space is silence" (1991:163).

Seremetakis's description not only bears some striking resemblances to what I observed at Tinos but also makes several important points about women, religion, performance, and emotion. Note her point that the women's lamenting, which has its own highly creative structure, suddenly seems "chaotic" at the entry of the (male) priest, who represents the order, authority, and discipline of the church. Similarly, the loud (womanly) expression of emotion falls silent at the (manly) stance of authority as the priest "claims" the corpse, creating "the space of discipline by first imposing a boundary between his body and the bodies of the women through processual movements" (1991:164). Emotion, then, is womanly and chaotic, to be controlled by the ordered authority of men (in this case the Orthodox church, represented by the priest). In addition, it should be noted that much of women's mourning ritual takes place *outside* the church, both literally and metaphorically.

I observed a similar phenomenon in pilgrimage at Tinos. Here, however, the boundaries were not so clearly drawn, the final exertion of church authority not so decisive, even within the physical confines of the church. Such activities as the individual rituals of devotion, which take place both outside and within the church, though they may sometimes involve a priest, are not overseen or directed by any church authority. On a busy day of pilgrimage, the church is full of pilgrims carrying out their own individual devotions, making their own requests, fulfilling their own vows. Inside the church, when the priest emerges from behind the icon-ostasis for the prayer service, there occurs a shifting and rearranging similar to that which Seremetakis describes for Maniat funerals. But the priest never succeeds in establishing a "disciplined space of silence." While some pilgrims cease their activities to attend to the service, others continue to go about their individual devotions, to come and go, and even to converse.

When pilgrimage is especially heavy (as on and around August 15), the church becomes contested space, as pilgrims seek access to the icon that is the object of their journey, and church officials try to control the crowds. Church policemen (*ikonofílakes*) block the main entrance to the church with their bodies as they attempt to regulate the flow of pilgrims into the church. When the icon is carried in procession through the streets, police lines hold the watching crowds at bay as the icon, flanked by a military escort, priests, and lay church officials, is carried over the heads of kneel-ing pilgrims. Even here the attempt to exert control over the "chaos" of pilgrimage is sometimes thwarted as kneeling pilgrims stand to touch the icon as it passes, their outstretched hands beaten down by church offi-cials. The precision and rigidity of the procession, with the martial drum-beat of the military band, contrasts with the individualized and unorganized crowd. At times the procession must even halt in order to allow all the waiting pilgrims to stream underneath. Once the icon has passed, all orderly procession dissolves, and the pilgrims stream en masse behind the icon down to the waterfront.[38]

Pilgrims do not necessarily perform their rituals in defiance of church controls. Nonetheless it is clear that they and their activities are only partially "organized" by the church as official institution. The church seeks to minimize this "disorganization" and to maximize its own claims to control pilgrimage through a variety of mechanisms (in addition to the physical controls I have just discussed). For example, through a variety of pamphlets issued by the church, pamphlets that describe the church's history and miracles, the church establishes its own authority by claiming and encapsulating pilgrims' activities and presenting their vows, rituals, and offerings as manifestations of the faith that the church itself promul-gates. In addition, the ways in which the church portrays pilgrimage is in certain respects at odds with the popular religious activity that takes place there. For example, although pilgrimage is heavily feminized, this is ob-scured by official displays. Women's offerings to the church are frequently ephemeral in nature—acts of devotion such as crawling on their knees or perishable gifts such as flowers or candles—but offerings selected for permanent display tend to be the more durable and expensive ones, most

14. Official ritual: Gypsy children watch the procession of the icon with its military accompaniment

often presented by men (see Dubisch 1988, 1990a). In this process, I suggest, the emotional content of pilgrimage is appropriated and rationalized, the "chaos" created by pilgrims is controlled and ordered, and the feminization of pilgrimage is obscured.

Nonetheless, the tensions inherent in pilgrimage at Tinos are not resolved and clearly reveal themselves on the major ritual occasions of pilgrimage. And while such tensions are not confined to pilgrimage rituals (as Seremetakis's descriptions demonstrate), pilgrimage by its nature creates a situation that can be difficult to control.[39] Officially conducted rituals such as those surrounding the Dormition on August 15 may be one way in which the church seeks to manage the enormous crowds of pilgrims who arrive for such events and to lay some claim to pilgrimage as its own.

We seem to have moved away from considerations of gender—but not so far really. As the parallels between female pilgrims and female mourners suggest, there is a close association here between women and emotion, women and "disorder," women and "anti-structure." Or perhaps a better way of putting it would be that women may use ritual to demarcate their own performative setting, a setting in which they create alternative orders, alternative structures. Pain, as Seremetakis points out, is one means of detachment that serves both to create a performative space and to provide a language for construction of a self (1991:5). For the women on pilgrimage their suffering may be combined with the rich symbolic materials of the Orthodox religion in order to construct distinctive and powerful images of womanhood.

It is for these reasons that I would suggest that it is too narrow an interpretation to see women's involvement in religious activities, including their participation in pilgrimage, as indicating either greater feminine piety or greater identification by women with the church's constructed image of the Panayía. As my own observations demonstrate, women's activities and women's religious constructions of themselves may be at odds with those of the official male-dominated church. Indeed anticlericalism may be quite strong among women as well as men, despite their greater participation in religious activities and their apparent greater submission to churchly authority (see Seremetakis 1991).

This brings me back to a point made by Herzfeld, a point I earlier critiqued: the notion of a poetics of womanhood as constructed through ironic subversion. Does the woman on her knees, by exaggerated submission, provide an ironic commentary on male churchly authority?[40] Or does the mother complaining about her ailments, by calling dramatic attention to her pain and the burden of her duties, protest the inequity of her position? Perhaps. But can this be sufficient for understanding a "poetics of womanhood"? And if not, what are we to make of suffering itself? It is to this issue that I turn next.

POETICS, SUFFERING, AND FEMINISM

When I presented a version of this chapter at a feminist discussion group during the year I spent as a Rockefeller Humanities Fellow in Women's Studies at the University of Arizona, I received a variety of interesting and helpful responses from the women there.[41] The group was interdisciplinary and included several anthropologists. Some of the nonanthropologists were concerned about my model of a "poetics of womanhood" and what it suggested about Greek women. That women adopted suffering as an idiom for the expression of womanhood seemed to them to imply the exploitation of women in Greek society.

Since I had seen myself as taking the "neutral" stance of an anthropologist (I was describing and interpreting, not passing judgment on the "rightness" of what I described), these responses were valuable to me in viewing my own material. In particular, they helped to frame for me a contrast between a feminist agenda and an anthropological one, and to point out ways in which the two approaches did—and did not—intersect in my own work. Up to that point I had not found it advisable or necessary to "take a stand" on what I had described. Whether it was "good" or "bad" that Greek women used suffering as a cultural idiom was not something for me to decide. Moreover, as an anthropologist, I might have argued that a feminist judgment on the rightness of what I had observed was ethnocentric both in failing to understand the cultural role and meaning of emotion and in regarding public displays of emotion generally as bad. I might have gone on to argue that Greek women do not necessarily suffer more than American women—I am speaking of culturally constituted expressions—and that, moreover, if we are going to engage in cultural critique, it could be said that in much of American society (and perhaps contemporary Western culture generally) we do not allow enough expression of suffering, especially public expression, and this makes us unreceptive to the emotional forms of other cultures. Emotion, for many Americans at least, should be private, contained, and not brought into the public realm. Emotional displays such as the ones seen at the Church of the Annunciation are shocking to Western observers and therefore are judged negatively.

I would not, however, dismiss the feminist reaction to my analysis, especially since feminists are part of the audience I wish to address. For that reason I raise the question here: is a "poetics of womanhood" such as I have described always a "negative" one? Does it always involve martyrdom, suffering, and pain? Are Greek women as unhappy and oppressed in their roles as this analysis of public expressions of suffering seems to indicate?

There are two responses to this question. One response is to return to an issue raised earlier: the issue of outer act versus inner state. As I observed with reference to religious ritual, Greeks generally feel that it is difficult if not impossible to know another's inner "real" state of mind. One can only know what is publicly expressed. And from the anthropologist's point of view, what is publicly expressed is culturally constituted. There are, in this sense, no "natural" emotions. A mother might cry and wail and throw herself on the grave of a dead child in one society, stoically and tearlessly endure in another, and allow her grief to be expressed only in the family circle in yet another. It is not what is "felt" in some inner sense (and the idea of the existence of this "inner" state may be a peculiarity of Western and particularly American culture) but what is expressed in culturally conditioned ways and for culturally determined goals that has been the focus of my analysis (see Lutz and White 1986; see also Lutz and Abu-Lughod 1990). It is all that I—whether the intended or unintended audience—can know. The fact that such expressions as I have been discussing use the cultural idiom of suffering is part of a larger system of cultural values from which their meaning is derived. That I became sensitive to this idiom in my later fieldwork is due both to the nature of the fieldwork and to my own experience of pain.

I would also argue that suffering can be a strategy of empowerment, granting those who use it a "moral high ground" in their interactions with others. And it is a strategy that is particularly useful (though not necessarily limited to) those whose social position may otherwise place them at a disadvantage. Hence it may frequently be used by women, as Friedl (1967) has pointed out, or by Greeks speaking to me or other foreigners. It is both an affirmation of one's position and role and a means of protest and even resistance. Suffering thus becomes part of the "politics of emotion" (Lutz and Abu-Lughod 1990). Insofar as it is the strategy of the marginal and disempowered, however, one would have to say that the feminist critique is right—a poetics based on suffering can be seen as a consequence of exploitation, or at least of a weak or marginal social position (though it may also be used to belittle or critique the moral authority of the dominant).

The second response to the question I posed above regarding the "negative" nature of a poetics of womanhood is that suffering is not the only cultural idiom with which women construct their performances of womanhood (though it is a particularly powerful and dramatic one). Earlier in the chapter I suggested other cultural expressions available to women—including preparation and serving of food, the production and care of children, household skills, and religious activities. Nor should the particular focus I have taken for my analysis obscure the other emotional dimensions that pilgrimage offers for both women and men. There are indeed suffering and pain, since it is precisely their troubles and sorrows that have brought many pilgrims to the church. But there is also hope, the fulfillment of requests, the release from pain and anxiety, and the enjoyment of the religious activities and sights. At the same time we must keep in mind that any insistence on pointing out these more "positive" aspects of pilgrimage reflects the value judgments of my own culture. Public expressions of suffering may play the major role for many of the pilgrims, providing both a focus for the pilgrimage and a final sense of release. In some cases, the suffering is essential to the release, as it was for the possessed woman who had to struggle up the hill to the church before the devil relinquished his grasp and she found safety and redemption within the Panayía's sacred space.

In addition, the idiom of suffering is available to men as well as women, as the following story illustrates.

In March 1987, when I returned to Tinos for the Day of the Annunciation (March 25), I found that a local friend of mine, Nikos, a divorced man in his forties, was much preoccupied. He had a good deal on his mind, many troubles (polá vásana), he told me, sighing. Not only was he having some problems with the workmen on one of the houses he was constructing on contract,[42] but he also had his teenage son living with him. This meant he had to hurry home from work in the middle of the day, when the boy returned from school, in order to prepare a midday meal. This in turn meant that he had to be certain he had shopped so that he had food on hand. Moreover, he was not free to come and go as he pleased anymore, for he did not want to leave the boy alone too much.[43] As far as I could tell, my friend was not in any way suggesting that it was inappropriate for him to have responsibility for his son and that his ex-wife should be taking care of the boy instead. (On the contrary, he said that he felt that it was right at this time in the boy's life for him to stay with his father.) Rather, he was expressing to me all of the burdens this parental role entailed, and what he had to give up in order to meet his responsibilities. Although the role of divorced father is a relatively new one in Greece,[44] my friend's recital had a very familiar ring. It was the litany of the suffering mother, recited now by the suffering father instead.

Toward "Creative" Womanhood

I have told the story of female pilgrims, or at least of some of them, in a particular way, as "stories" of a sort (whether verbalized or not) that they tell about themselves. And I have in turned tied these to "stories" told in other contexts of Greek life. These stories, I have suggested, are presented in a variety of ways, through expression of emotions, through complaint, through housework and children and food, through religious ritual. I have labeled these stories "the poetics of womanhood," for they are acts and material representations that have both a public and a creative dimension.

My own telling of these stories was motivated by a "problem"—a problem created for me by women going on their knees and performing other public acts of suffering while on pilgrimage. But the "problem," as I have pointed out, is mine, not the women's. Its nature as a problem was generated by a certain kind of anthropology, an anthropology that has included the notion of the "Mediterranean," a notion in turn heavily informed by certain constructs of gender. It was such an anthropology that shaped the context in which I was socialized as an anthropologist and thus helped shape the context for my own fieldwork as well. Moreover, I was taught to proceed in my intellectual inquiries through the examination of such "problems." Indeed the structure of progress in academia (dissertation proposals, grant proposals, articles) requires that one advance through a series of "problems" (which themselves then generate further problems, providing further opportunities for grants and research).

This does not mean that no Greeks perceive women on their knees as a "problem." but it is an entirely different sort of problem for them. Certainly not everyone I encountered regarded such behavior during pilgrimage as a commendable, pious act (nor indeed pilgrimage itself as a commendable act). The emotional aspects of pilgrimage in particular seem embarrassing to many of the Westernizing, modernizing segment of the population, in much the same way that Seremetakis found the ritual lamenting, the *kláma,* to be embarrassing to urbanized kin (1991:221). Thus for some Greeks I encountered, the acts associated with pilgrimage to Tinos were examples of superstition or religious excess. These individuals have bought into the "modern" notion that emotion is private and not to be publicly displayed. The publicly displayed emotion characterizing such rituals adds to their delegitimation.[45]

Whatever their own opinions about the activities of pilgrimage, some people I knew worried about how such behavior would appear to outsiders like myself. Such was the concern of Marina's husband, Dhimitris. And my landlady herself, as may be recalled, did not feel that crawling on one's knees (and thereby becoming dirty and disheveled) could be acceptable to the Panayía. Theirs was the insider's problem; mine was the outsider's. I could, if I wish, abandon my problem and formulate another. They cannot. And yet the two problems are not entirely separate. As an outsider, I help to create at least part of their problem—the problem of appearance and national sensitivity to outside opinion. In addition, I represent the source of concepts associated with being "modern." How much of a problem would these women on their knees be if it weren't for me and others like me who are there to observe, and possibly to judge?

A problem such as I have created requires an answer, which I have also created. My answer is to suggest that the concept of "a poetics of womanhood" provides a more dynamic view of gender and gender roles than that embodied in "honor and shame." This answer allows me not only to create my own understanding of some of the activities I witnessed at the Church of the Annunciation in a manner that overcomes the apparent anomaly that was my original puzzle, but it also helps to integrate my interpretation of that activity with other interpretations resulting from my fieldwork. Hence it is more consonant with my own experience in that it offers a dynamic framework that satisfies me because it grants a creative role to actors. It suggests ways in which women may present public performances of "being good at being a woman" (of which pilgrimage activities are only one instance). And as the above example of the "suffering father" illustrates, a "poetics of womanhood" is flexible, providing possibilities for expression of newly emerging male selves as well and hence is both sensitive to, and able to serve as a vehicle for, change.[46]

I have told the story of female pilgrims, or at least some of them, in a particular way, as stories they "tell" about themselves and about being women. And I have in turn tied these to "stories" told in other contexts of Greek life. But narrative is power (Bruner 1986:19). In exercising the power of writing, am I not usurping these women's stories? Have I not exerted the very sort of heavy authority of which I accused those writing about honor and shame? In making articulate the nonarticulate, verbalizing the nonverbal, have I simply reduced a "poetics of womanhood" to words, my own words, and written ones at that?[47]

Or perhaps my writing has in some sense empowered. My aim has been to proceed from my own experiences at the shrine in order to find ways to put women's experience at the center of analysis, to see women as "authors of themselves" (Bruner 1986:12). In doing so, I recognize that women's modes of expression have often been given less attention, either by those dominant in the society or those outside studying them (such as anthropologists), or both. Concepts of honor and shame, for example, have often been framed with an androcentric focus that has kept some analysts from seeing women's expression of their own experience and their own modes of constructing selfhood. I have thus exercised my own power as a writer to draw these performances from the wings and into the spotlight. In doing so, I have suggested that Greek women, whether villagers or pilgrims, are not so inarticulate as some have proposed. Both verbally and nonverbally women present the stories with which they construct themselves—thus they actively create womanhood. And just as with men's construction of selfhood, often the context of women's stories is "public"—whether that public is other women, both men and women, only men, or the anthropologist.

But these stories do not speak for themselves. They require a context. For the women's audiences, the context is already there. But for the purposes of my own presentations, I must create the context for my readers. If I were to show a videotape of a woman on her knees or play a tape of my landlady's complaints or her story of her mother's death of *stenohoría* or show a picture of a woman in black or a table of food prepared for a *paniyíri*, these would be meaningful only to those who already shared the context in which these performances were produced. But the context I have presented is complex, for I have created it from the meshing of my own experience of my two intertwined fields, the "field" of fieldwork and the "field" of anthropology.

There is one woman, however, whose performance has been left out of my analysis, and whose words have been touched on only briefly until now. This woman is the Madonna or Panayía. Like the women on their knees, she also poses a "problem." It is to this "problem" and to her story that I turn next.

The Virgin Mary and the Body Politic

IN MAY 1990 a woman made a pilgrimage to Tinos in order to fulfill a vow.[1] In and of itself, this was an event so common as hardly to be worthy of notice. This particular woman, however, was more famous than most of the pilgrims who come to Tinos. She was a former Olympic airline stewardess and former mistress (and now wife) of the recently defeated Socialist prime minister Andreas Papandreou. Their affair prior to Papandreou's divorce from his American-born wife had received considerable attention in the press, and may have helped contribute to the downfall of the Socialist government.[2] But despite her visibility in the public spotlight of politics, the new Mrs. Papandreou's visit to Tinos was purely a personal one. It was to fulfill a vow she had made to the Panayía when Papandreou had been in the hospital with serious heart problems. The vow, she claimed, was not related to her husband's political difficulties, only to his health. It was the sort of vow that any woman might make on behalf of those closest to her, the sort that leads thousands of pilgrims every year to the shrine in search of health, protection, and the Panayía's unfailing grace.

Unfortunately I was not at Tinos for this event. Had I known it was to take place, I would certainly have scheduled my visit that summer accordingly. In fact, Mrs. Papandreou had planned to come on her pilgrimage at an earlier point when I was there, but stormy weather had prevented the sailing of the yacht upon which she was to arrive. Eventually, however, it appears she was able to make the trip and to fulfill her vow. She wore black and went on her knees, a friend of mine in Athens told me. Not so, my landlady, Marina, replied when I questioned her. Dhimitra Papandreou walked up to the church and she wore a suit.

My regret at not being present for this event was all the keener when I learned that both the Papandreous had been feted later that day in the very village where I had done fieldwork, at the taverna where I had attended the baptismal dinner (described in chapter 5), as well as numerous other village events. I have no doubt that had I been on the island at the time, I could have arranged to be in the village for the occasion and at least had the opportunity to observe, if not meet, the famous pair. When I asked villagers about the visit, it was obvious that Papandreou's wife had excited more interest than the former prime minister. She wasn't as good looking as he had expected, my friend Marcos commented to another villager when I raised the topic, and he mentioned the wife of a mutual friend as someone who was certainly prettier than Mrs. Papandreou.

Even if it was his wife who had excited the most interest, Andreas Papandreou had not simply provided her with companionship on her pilgrimage to Tinos. He had reportedly used the occasion for his own purposes as well, seeking to effect a reconciliation of sorts with the church after a rather stormy relationship during the period in which the Socialist government (PASOK) was in power.[3] This was not the first time Papandreou had made a pilgrimage to a Marian shrine, however. While he was prime minister, he had visited the shrine of Panayía Soumela in northern Greece, a site that holds particular significance for the Pontic Greeks who were an important element of support for PASOK.

Papandreou was not the only former head of state to visit Tinos at this time. Not long before, another political figure of note had also made a pilgrimage: Konstantinos Karamanlis, the conservative politician who had headed the Greek government after the fall of the junta in 1974. Karamanlis had attended the celebrations of August 15, 1989, and his presence on this occasion—as Greece hovered between inconclusive national elections—was interpreted by observers as a sign of his interest in reentering the political scene.[4]

A woman visiting a shrine to fulfill a vow made to ensure her husband's health, two politicians visiting the same shrine at significant points in their political careers—what do these pilgrims have in common? Or are their purposes entirely separate, one centered on a purely private matter, the other on a public political statement, their only commonality their presence at the same sacred site?

I will return to this question later in the chapter, but right now I wish to focus upon a somewhat different one—why have all of these different individuals turned to this particular female saint, in one of her most famous manifestations, as the means of carrying out their various purposes, whether private or political? While the answer to the first part of this question, the private part, may be found (to some extent, at least) in conventional analyses of Marian devotion, the answer to the second part, the political, is not as readily apparent. In chapter 9 I discussed some of the patriotic dimensions of the shrine at Tinos and the ways in which it enters into discourses on "Greekness." In this chapter I explore the wider meaning of the particular holy figure around which devotion is centered—the Virgin Mary or Panayía—and her nature as revealed in the acts of devotion directed toward her (including pilgrimage), in the stories that center around her, and in the various contexts in which she is invoked.

Feminism, Anthropology, and the Virgin Mary

The prominence of Mary in European Mediterranean religious devotion has been noted by a number of authors. Her cult is the most widespread, and shrines to her such as Lourdes in France and Medjugorje in former Yugoslavia are some of the most noted of contemporary European pilgrimage sites (see, e.g., Carroll 1986; Marnham 1981; Perry and Echeverria 1988). Not only does devotion to Mary overshadow homage to the other saints in both the Catholic and Orthodox traditions, but she often provides a more central—and certainly a more immediate and accessible—devotional figure than Christ himself.

Mary thus presents a dilemma for feminists. Given the widespread devotion that she has inspired, historically and contemporarily in both the Catholic and Orthodox worlds, she would seem a logical model for feminists seeking female manifestations of divinity as a counter to a patriarchal theology. But the control and manipulation of Mary's image by a male-dominated church, and the glorification through her of all the virtues traditionally considered "feminine" (maternity, chastity, and obedience), offer a difficult—and increasingly questionable—model for women to emulate. As Marina Warner puts it, "By setting up an impossible ideal the cult of the Virgin does drive the adherent into a position of acknowledged and hopeless yearning and inferiority," and hence deepens a woman's need for the church (Warner 1976:337; see also Pope 1985:193–94). Moreover, the use of Mary by the church to combat forces of modernism and rationalism and in support of a conservative political agenda (Pope 1985; see also Perry and Echeverria 1988) has made her unattractive to those who seek models for female empowerment at both the secular and spiritual level. Hence Mary has generally been ignored in feminist literature on religion and spirituality and in works addressing the issue of early female-centered religions. Insofar as the Virgin Mary is acknowledged in such works, it is as a tamed female divinity, brought under male control and bent to patriarchal purposes.

Within anthropology, the Virgin Mary and her cult have been studied in several ways. The largest number of studies have focused on local manifestations of devotion, particularly as these are connected with visions and shrines (see, e.g., Crain 1992; Marnham 1981; Murphy 1993). But there has been little of a more general nature, focusing specifically on Mary.[5] In addition, most anthropological studies of Mary have been carried out in the Catholic context. The literature on her in Orthodoxy—anthropological or otherwise—is exceedingly sparse.

In both the Catholic and Orthodox context, anthropological analyses of Mary have generally focused on her relationship to family and family roles, emphasizing the importance of Mary as mother and as a model and resource for women. For example, Richard and Eva Blum ascribe the continuing importance of Marian devotion in Greece to the need on the part of rural Greek women "for a powerful friend of the same sex" (1970:327), someone to whom they can appeal for help with the problems resulting from motherhood, poverty, and their own subordinate status. Juliet du Boulay, drawing on her study of a village in Euboea, emphasizes the image of the Mother of God as the counterpart to the sinful figure of Eve and as the ideal model for the married village woman, who, in carrying out her duties as wife and mother, fulfills her destiny, which is to become like the mother of God (du Boulay 1986:165–6; see also Campbell 1964; Machin 1983). Eve and Mary are thus perceived as the two poles of feminine nature, and a woman in the course of her life moves from the first (part of her nature and her inherent original sin) to the second (which redeems her through motherhood). Studies that see the cult of Mary in terms of "mother worship" also suggest a direct correlation between family gender roles and Marian devotion (see, e.g., Preston 1982).

The psychoanalytic approach to Marian devotion also proceeds from a family-centered interpretation, in this case using a Freudian framework. In such an approach, the role of the mother in the family, a role that emphasizes nurturance, protection, and self-sacrifice, is seen as a causal factor in the prominence of Mary in the religious devotion. Ann Parsons, for example, in her discussion of the Oedipus complex in southern Italy, states that "the Madonna is quite obviously the ideal mother figure" (1967:365). Her most important feature "is that her love and tenderness are always available; no matter how unhappy or sinful the supplicant, she will always respond if she is addressed in time of need (1967:265). God the Father, on the other hand, is perceived as a remote figure, while Christ takes on the characteristics of the good son.

In a similar vein, Michael Carroll adds a historical dimension, seeking the roots of the Madonna complex in the social structure of the family in late Roman–early Christian Mediterranean society (Carroll 1986). Emphasizing the virginity of the Catholic Mary, that is, her ability to combine motherhood with asexuality,[6] both Parsons and Carroll locate Marian devotion in the Oedipus complex, seeing it as the outcome of the sublimation of the sexual desire for the mother within the particular context of Mediterranean family structure. To quote Carroll: "The distinctive features of the Mary cult over the centuries have been shaped primarily by the son's strong but strongly repressed desire for his mother" (1986:56). Women, on the other hand, identify with Mary "to experience vicariously the fulfillment of their desire for sexual contact with, and a baby from, their fathers" (Carroll 1986:59). In addition, the sometimes punitive nature of Mary is also rooted in this complex. According to Carroll, "we would expect to find an association between excessive Marian devotion and masochism" (1986:62).[7] For Parsons, the Madonna becomes a feminine superego: "She could not be forgiving if she did not have a concept of sins which have to be forgiven" (1967:382).

On the level of popular devotional practice, the prominence of Mary has been used to explain the frequently noted greater participation of lay women in everyday religious life throughout the Christian Mediterranean. Mary, it is argued, provides a model for women in their daily lives, the model of the self-sacrificing and virtuous mother. This model is congruent with expected social roles for women, whereas the virtues exemplified by Christ do not provide such a satisfactory role model for Mediterranean men (see chapter 10). In some ways, however, such arguments presume an *a priori* elaboration of the roles of both Christ and Mary, independent of the context of the social roles in which they are now interpreted. Moreover, they fail to take account of the historical fluctuations in the cult of Mary and of the other roles she plays, particularly those in which she has served as a focus for male-dominated devotion (as in the religious brotherhoods of Spain and in medieval monastic life; on the latter, see Bynum 1987), and the ways in which she stands as a national and local political representation beyond the domestic realm.

THE CULT OF MARY: ROOTS AND HISTORY

The culture of Mary has not been a constant in either the Catholic or Orthodox traditions. Rather, it has varied according to historical and political forces, as well as with popular needs and attitudes. Within church doctrine, however, Mary has been presented as eternal and unchanging. Indeed such a presentation is part of the politics surrounding her cult and has served to obscure the historical context of Marian devotion. As Warner puts it, "In the case of the Virgin Mary, faith has simply wiped out the silt of history in her myth. It comes as a surprise to believers and non-believers alike that she is rarely mentioned in the Gospels" (1976:335). Warner compares this to Jungian psychology, which reinterprets Mary as the archetype of the Great Mother, and hence colludes with the church's presentation of Mary as eternal (1976:335). Such an eternal/natural nature is also suggested in the concept of "mother worship" as applied to Mary.

Mary was not prominent in early Christianity, and was not called the Virgin until the middle of the second century (Davis 1984:27). Perry and Echeverria suggest that certain ideas and practices began to emerge in the early Christian communities that were concomitant with the cult of Mary: "veneration of images, belief in intercessors and in the malignant nature of the flesh" (1988:7). They also state that the veneration of relics played a role in the devotion to Mary because "it inculcated a trust in mediators and the idea of sacredness in material things and places" (1988:9). The first great impetus to Marian devotion may have come with the end of official persecution of the church in 313 under the emperor

Constantine: "Asceticism replaced martyrdom as the chief witness to saintliness; and virginity, chastity, obedience, submission were modelled on the qualities of Mary" (Davis 1984:27). Not long after that, in 431— at the Council of Ephesus—Mary was called *Theotókos* (Bearer of God), a term still commonly used to refer to her in the Orthodox church. In the fifth century the first relics and miraculous icons of Mary begin to appear in the East (Perry and Echeverria 1988:10).

Davis suggests that the history of Mariology is one of attempts by ecclesiastical authorities to prevent Mary from being exalted to a higher place in the Christian economy of salvation than official theology warranted (1984:27). But the church also played a role in the development of Mary's cult. In 470 the Basilica at Salonika was dedicated to the Blessed Virgin Mary, and later the Parthenon, followed by other churches throughout the Christian world. In the fifth century the Feast of the Commemoration of the Virgin was introduced throughout western Europe (while the Feast of the Annunciation was kept in Byzantium). The celebration of August 15 as a key Marian holiday appears to have begun in the seventh century. It was first celebrated as the Feast of the Dormition (a name it still retains in Greek Orthodoxy), and the name was changed to the Feast of the Assumption in some ninth-century liturgical calendars. "Pope Nicholas I (857–67) placed the Assumption on a par with Christmas and Easter—tantmount to declaring Mary's translation to heaven as important as the Incarnation and Resurrection" (Warner 1976:88). Warner suggests that the Iconoclast period in the Eastern church (753–843) was a catalyst for the cult of the Virgin in the West. At this time, many ecclesiastical and lay refugees fled to the West, leading to an infusion of "the fervent, excitable strain of piety that has until iconoclasm been the unrestrained character of Greek worship of the Virgin and the saints" (Warner 1976:108), and to a "current of energy" electrifying Rome, resulting in frescoes, icons, and mosaics.[8]

Iconoclasm marked the beginning of the schism between the Greek and Latin worlds and the emergence of the papacy as a Western power. "The image of the Virgin in triumph therefore served a twofold purpose: it asserted the orthodoxy of images themselves, and its content indicated the powers of the pope as the ruler of Christian hearts and minds at a secular as well as a spiritual level" (Warner 1976:109; see also Perry and Echeverria 1988).

In medieval Catholicism, the body of Mary was often used to represent the body of the church. By giving birth to Christ, Mary gave birth to Christianity. This is most dramatically illustrated by the *vierge ouverte,* the opening Virgin—a statue of Mary that opens to reveal Christ and/or a church within. Mary's body thus contains the church itself, of which she is the mother and protectress. Similarly, the church was sometimes portrayed as a lactating mother (Bynum 1987, plate 17), representing another important dimension of Mary and, as Caroline Bynum argues, an important part of the image of women generally in medieval times (Bynum 1987). After the Council of Trent (1545–63), the cult of Mary became particularly prominent as part of the Catholic church's attempt to exert church control over the household (Wolf 1984:8). Thus the Virgin Mary assumed a new and important role in the Catholic world during the Counter-Reformation. The church, in its efforts against the Reformation (which was anti-Marian), sought to penetrate into households and to exalt the wife/mother as the center of the home by reaffirming the importance of the Virgin Mary, which "not only attracted women, but also served to re-orient husbands and sons away from the external arena of dubious politics and marketing toward the morally subliminated household" (Wolf 1984:8). A similar effort on the part of the Catholic church was stimulated by the French Revolution: "Congregations were founded, miraculous apparitions approved, the Rosary promoted, and dogma altered, partly in response to the anti-clerical movements which recur throughout the century and a half after 1789" (Davis 1984:27).

The Dogma of the Immaculate Conception was proclaimed by the Catholic church in 1854, and the following century saw a number of Marian apparitions, leading to shrines and pilgrimage, among them La Salette (1846), Lourdes (1871), Knock (1879), and Fatima (1917) (see Carroll 1986). In the post–World War II period there was a renewed outbreak of Marian apparitions, most of them anti-Communist in their message (Christian 1984; Carroll 1986), and there seems to have been an upsurge in appearances of Mary in recent years as well, including those at Medjugorje, Bayside, New Jersey, and the weeping icon at an Albanian Orthodox Church in Chicago. In 1980 Mary was seen by an anti-Sandinista cardinal in Nicaragua and was given a new title: "The Virgin of the Contras."[9] She was also supposed to have supported the Pinochet regime in Chile (see Perry and Echeverria 1988:309). In 1987 Pope John Paul II declared a Marian year, beginning June 7 and ending on August 15, 1988, the Day of the Assumption (only the second Marian year in the church's history). This declaration of a Marian year might be seen by the pope as a way of reaching out to a recently opening eastern Europe, and "as a means of rekindling the flame among his Orthodox Brethren."[10]

MARY IN THE ORTHODOX CONTEXT

So far I have been discussing Mary's role mostly in the Catholic context. Her role in the Orthodox world has been much less analyzed. The very term "Virgin Mary"—the common appellation in the Latin church—is inappropriate in the Orthodox context. Although Mary may be referred to as "Virgin" (*Parthéna*) in Greek, this term is not in everyday use. Most commonly she is called *Panayía*, a term that can be translated as "all holy one" and that signifies dominion over all the other saints. Translations from Greek to English, such as those found in museums, sometimes refer to the Panayía as "St. Virgin." She is also sometimes called *Megalóhari* (the one of great grace, or giver of grace), *Theotókos* (the Bearer of God), and *Mesítria* (the Mediator). In addition, she may be known by particular manifestations, such as the *Evangelístria* or the Madonna of the Annunciation.[11] As in the Catholic world, Mary also has various local manifestations, drawing their names from localities, from the manner in which Mary appeared at that particular locality, or from some miracle she has performed. Thus the terms used to refer to Mary within the Orthodox tradition do not generally emphasize her virginity but rather her maternal role as the Mother of God (Sant Cassia 1992:211) and her power within both the heavenly and secular world.

There are also theological differences in the way in which Mary is viewed in the Orthodox and Catholic churches. In the Orthodox church, Mary is not seen as immaculately conceived and bodily assumed into heaven. Thus rather than the Assumption of Mary, the Orthodox church celebrates the *Kímisis* (Dormition). "In Orthodoxy the virgin remains a human intercessor . . . an *ánthropos* and a Mother, and does not become a semi-deified human as in Catholicism" (Sant Cassia 1992:212). The fact that the doctrine of the Immaculate Conception is not present in Orthodoxy is another manifestation of Mary's humanity.

It is in part on the basis of these differences that Carroll justifies his own exclusion of the Orthodox world from his analysis of Marian devotion. He argues that Mary does not occupy the central place in Orthodoxy that she does in Catholicism and suggests that popular religious practice is more Christ-centered in Orthodoxy than in Catholicism. For him, the main difference centers on the fact that it is Mary's role as *Theotókos* that is emphasized in Orthodoxy and not her virginity. For Carroll this reinforces the idea of a Christ-centered religion: "Mary is venerated primarily because of her close association with Christ" (1986:20–21), and she does not stand as a divine personage in her own right. Carroll's focus on the social-psychological dimensions of Marian devotion may, however, lead him to misunderstand the importance of Mary's role within the Orthodox world, an importance that derives not simply from her being the mother of Christ, but from her identity as a holy figure in her own right. Therefore some attention to the manifestations of Mary's central role in Orthodoxy, and to its development over time, are in order at this point.

The history of Marian devotion within the Eastern church has parallels with its history in the West, but also exhibits significant differences resulting from differences in theological doctrine and in the politics and history of Byzantium and of the church under the Ottomans.

The cult of Mary developed a particular importance in Constantinople in the period preceding Iconoclasm. A major reason for this may have been the fact that the city supposedly possessed a number of relics of Mary, acquired in the fifth century. Among these were Mary's robe, her girdle, her shroud, and the swaddling clothes in which Christ rested against her breast and upon which could be seen the marks of her milk (Cormack 1985:158–59). Imperial interest in these relics was reflected in the increasing ceremonial attention they were given during the sixth century, and public interest intensified in the seventh century as belief in the powers of icons and relics grew (Cormack 1985:159). Prayers directed at Mary asked her protection of the city from barbarians, famine, and natural disasters. In 626, when Constantinople was besieged by Avar tribes, the siege was successfully beaten back only after an icon of Mary was carried in procession on the city walls and a vision of her carrying a sword appeared to encourage the besieged (Cormack 1985:159).

Devotion to Mary received a serious setback during the Iconoclast period, when not only was access to her icons denied but prayers to her were discouraged. During this time, a number of icons, including some of the Madonna, were spirited to safer locations in the West, sometimes miraculously assisting in their own escape (see Dhimitrakopoulos 1971). After the defeat of the Iconoclasts, a monumental image of the Mother and Child was created to decorate the Church of St. Sophia in Constantinople. Such a conspicuous display of devotion to the Madonna reflects a general post-Iconoclasm trend. Patriarchal and imperial seals of the period, for example, use images of Mary. Devotion to Mary became an essential element of belief; Iconclasts could be attacked for their refusal to venerate her (Cormack 1985:160). Constantinople itself was seen to be under the special protection of the Mother of God. In addition, "there are increasing examples of visual expression of special devotion to the Virgin among all levels of society, both in Constantinople and throughout the empire" (Cormack 1985:165–66).

Since the sixth century, when the emperor Justin II enlarged and redecorated the churches in Constantinople in which the major relics of Mary were kept, the rituals surrounding her cult had grown. The two festivals that were especially enhanced were the Annunciation on March 25 and the Dormition, which, following the example of the church of Jerusalem, became fixed on August 15. Since the death of Mary is not mentioned in the canonical Gospels, the church relied on an apocryphal narrative attributed to St. John the Evangelist, the earliest version of which seems to have appeared at the end of the fifth century (Cormack 1985:169). In addition to the elaboration of these holy days, illustrations of other events of Mary's life became a standard part of church decoration, with particular events often being associated with particular features of the architecture.

Insofar as icons served as both means of instruction and visual connections to the holy (see chapter 4), these decorations would have served to create Mary as a reality for devotees and to make manifest both her humanity and her role as intercessor for humankind. The scene of the *Kímisis* makes this role especially visible: "The scene illuminates the end of the life of a human being to whom immediate entrance to a heavenly paradise was granted. As the Virgin was in a mystical sense also described as the 'church' and therefore in a position of motherly grace toward all Christians, the picture offers the hope of life after death for all believers, and the perpetual presence in Heaven of someone to whom appeal could be made through prayer for personal intercession with God" (Cormack 1985:176).

The period of Ottoman rule resulted in a markedly different course for the cult of Mary in the Greek Orthodox church than in the Catholic West. As Sant Cassia puts it, "Under the restraining hand of the Turkocratia the emphasis was much more on retaining the continuity and identifiability of icons as the most readily available and accessible aids to the divine" (1992:213). He argues further that "there was an internal dialogue in both text and image in the evolution of Catholicism across time which was largely absent in Greek Orthodoxy" (1992:212). In particular, icons retained their importance during this period, not only as a mode of instruction and religious continuity, but also as a focus of resistance to oppression and persecution (as revealed in the stories told about them). During the Ottoman period, Greek Orthodox theology remained relatively static and there were neither the theological redefinitions of Mary nor the revitalization of her cult (such as occurred during the Catholic Counter-Reformation) that were seen in the West.

The cult of Mary seems to have grown in late nineteenth-century Greece, as well as in other areas of southern Europe. Sant Cassia attributes at least some of her increasing importance (and the changes in her iconography) to Western influences (1992:216–17),[12] but one should not forget her early manifestation at Tinos in 1822, through which the Panayía became, in effect, the first saint of the new nation of Greece.

This brief sketch of the cult of the Panayía in the Greek Orthodox tradition only begins to touch on the history of her devotion. Indeed a thorough history of the phenomenon has yet to be written. Brief and incomplete as it may be, however, we can discern in it at least a sketchy outline of the challenge it offers to conventional interpretations of the relationship between Marian devotion and gender and family roles, particularly within the Greek Orthodox world.

Thus while Carroll, in his analysis of the Catholic Virgin Mary, traces its historical origins to family structure and psychodynamics, Cormack warns against seeing the intensification of Marian devotion in the post-Iconoclast period as a reflection of increasing importance of the family in Byzantine society. For one thing, he argues, it would be an oversimplification to see Byzantine society as divided into Iconophiles who venerated Mary and encouraged family life, and Iconclasts who abhorred her cult and were not concerned with the family. Moreover, "the church and Byzantine society in general encompassed a wide range of sexual statuses, which do not seem to match closely with attitudes to the Virgin" (Cormack 1985:167). In addition, Cormack argues, it is not clear that it was Mary's image as Mother that was the predominant one (1985:168).

With respect to present-day Greek beliefs and practices, Sant Cassia challenges du Boulay's interpretation of women's life-cycle transformation from Eve to Mother of God as based in religious ideology. Such a transition, he suggests, may have to do more with social factors than with spiritual belief: "This ambivalent, developmental cycle perspective which attributes to women a set of diametrically opposed characteristics . . . is not directly and exclusively attributable to religion, but is heavily influenced by domestic arrangements" (1992:204).[13] Church-formulated ideologies may reflect or justify particular popular conceptions of womanhood, but the relationship between these ideologies may be quite flexible. And as Loizos (1988) warns, it is risky to equate church-formulated ideology and popular conceptions of womanhood and to simplistically derive the latter from the former. It is for this reason, in part, that he critiques Warner's analysis of the effect of Catholic doctrine on women's roles.

What such critiques suggest is that in order to understand the significance of Mary, in both the Catholic and the Orthodox world, we need to shift our focus from the domestic context to a wider social and political arena. The tendency to see Mary only in the context of her representation of idealized gender and familial roles (or in psychological terms as derived from family psychodynamics) may represent a cultural bias that sees women generally only in these roles and thus denies a wider role to a female divinity. We may need to give Mary more autonomy in our analysis of her devotion. Indeed we may even need to move beyond her gender to understand her divinity fully. She is a *person*, an *ánthropos*, and a powerful person, once a human, now the most powerful of the saints (hence her Greek name *Panayía*).

In discussing the development of the cult of Mary in the post-Iconoclast period, Cormack suggests that the mosaic of her in St. Sophia reveals her "not only as a tender mother, but also as an awe-inspiring woman in whom the divinity is somehow reflected" (1985:170). In the *Kímisis* her role as an intercessor is emphasized, as she passes immediately into heaven. Her intercession for other Christians at this rite of passage is implicit. In addition, "it may be that the Virgin Mary herself was seen as a mainstay at other rites of passage and that this stimulated her cult and the conspicuous visual representation in icons of other events of her life . . . which showed to Christians that holy persons went through the same experiences as themselves, and could be relied on for help and sympathy by humans passing through the same circumstances" (Cormack 1985:177).

But Mary is more than an intercessor and source of help in the life passage. She is also an active defender of the church, of the Orthodox religion, and of Orthodox nations and communities, as well as the deliverer of punishment to unbelievers and enemies. In addition, as the story of the icon at Tinos shows, she is capable of making her own will known to ordinary humans. Considered in these roles, Mary becomes a strong, active figure in her own right, and not simply an intercessor with a higher power.

In earlier chapters I discussed the ways in which icons are seen to "contain" (rather than simply represent) the saints and are the means through which they express their will and enter into relationships with human actors. Stories surrounding icons, then, are one source of information about beliefs regarding the Panayía and her nature and powers. There are, however, other means of representation as well, and it is to these that I turn next.

ICONS AND OTHER REPRESENTATIONS OF THE PANAYÍA

Within the Orthodox tradition, independent Marian apparitions (such as those of Lourdes and Medjugorje) are less common than in Catholicism. Instead the Panayía more often manifests herself through or in connection with icons. These icons characteristically represent her in certain poses or manifestations. Some show her in various configurations with the Christ child. Others show her by herself, often with scenes from her life, such as the presentation in the temple (*Ta Isódhia*), the Annunciation, and the Dormition. In addition to what is visually depicted, many icons have their own individual *istoríes,* which are transmitted orally as well as in written form and which give such icons a unique character and power. At the same time, every icon is a manifestation of a single divine personage. As we shall see, it is this dual quality of the Panayía and her icons that makes her (and them) an especially powerful and manipulable political symbol.

Dhimitrakopoulos (1971) lists eighty miraculous icons of the Panayía found throughout Greece, each with its own history of miracles or story of miraculous origins. Some of the most famous of these icons are attributed to the Evangelist Luke, who is believed to have painted them during

Mary's lifetime, with her as a living model. Such holy origins give a special sanctity to the icon, tying it to the very origins of Christianity and the image directly to Mary herself. In addition, such icons have often survived the tumultuous times through which they have lived by a series of miracles, which in turn have added to their power and fame. I have already recounted the story of the icon of the Annunciation of Tinos (remember that Tinos's famous icon is also attributed to St. Luke). Several other famous icons of the Panayía and their histories will give some additional sense not only of their role in Orthodox devotion but also of the nature of the Panayía herself.

The Panayía Megalospileotisa (the Panayía of the Cave) is located in the monastery of Spileo near Kalavrita in the Peloponnesus. The icon is one of the first attributed to the Evangelist Luke and shows the Panayía holding the holy infant. It was discovered in a cave by two monastic brothers from Thessaloniki who were visiting Jerusalem following separate visions of the Panayía and eventually arrived at its present location in the Peloponnesus, its fame spreading over the entire region. During its long history the icon has performed many miracles. It was saved from destruction during the Iconoclast period, it survived unharmed when a fire burned the cloth covering it, and it saved the monastery where it was housed from the ravages of the Pasha Ibrahim in 1827 during the Greek War of Independence. The monastery was less fortunate during the German occupation; it was burned by the Germans. It has now been rebuilt and is the site of patriotic pilgrimage, including a yearly gathering of the *andártes,* fighters of the Greek resistance.

Another famous icon is that of the Panayía Soumela, also attributed to Luke and now located in the monastery of Soumela in northern Greece. This particular icon was active in determining its earlier location in the Pontus, commanding two monks who were on their knees before the icon to take it outside the church where it has housed. When they obeyed, the icon disappeared over the horizon. The monks followed and after many adventures arrived in Trebezond and found the icon in a cave filled with swallows. Here they founded a monastery. In 1922–23, after the defeat of the Greeks in Asia Minor, the last monks were thrown out of the monastery. They were not allowed to take anything with them, but they had hidden the icon. In 1932, with the intervention of the archbishop of Athens, the Pontic metropolitan, and requests from Greek prime minister Venezelos to the Turkish prime minister, several monks were able to return to the monastery and brought the icon back to Greece. It remained in the Byzantine museum in Athens until 1951. The refugees did not want to be separated from "the refugee Panayía" (Dhimitrakopoulos 1971:18), and after it was brought out to be displayed in a newly built church, they refused to return it. Eventually they were allowed to keep the icon and it was brought to the newly built monastery of Soumela. It is now the object of pilgrimage for thousands of Greeks every year, particularly those from the Pontus, still called "refugees" (see Hirschon 1989).

The monasteries on Mt. Athos contain a number of icons of the Panayía, many of which also have particular stories attached to them. In the monastery of Vatopedhiou, the largest and richest on Mt. Athos, there is an icon of the Panayía of the Rocket (*Piravolithísa*). The name dates from the War of Independence, when a Turkish soldier "dared to fire off a rocket opposite the holy icon and damaged the Panayía on the outer part of her right hand. The culprit, however, was frightened and committed suicide immediately, hanging himself from an olive tree in the garden. The wound [on the icon] can still be seen today" (Dhimitrakopoulos 1971:46).[14]

Another icon painted on one wall of the church in the same monastery is called the Panayía of the Torment of the Custodian (*I Pedhévousa ton Eklisiárhin*). As the story goes, one evening the church custodian (*eklisiárhis*) was trying to light the lamp of the icon, but it was too drafty, so finally he gave up and was about to leave. He was punished, however, for his neglect and fell unconscious to the ground, where eventually the other monks found him.

In a variety of ways, then, icons of the Panayía, like icons of other saints, exert their wills and resist suppression and destruction. Often they do so in the face of determined opposition. For example, an icon of the Panayía that was thrown into the river when the Turks took Constantinople returned the next day to its place in the church. It was thrown back in the river and once again returned. The next time, the Turks burned the church and threw the icon once more in the river. The icon, now having no place to go, took itself to the place it occupies today (near Nafpakto). In 1455 it was found by a shepherd who had been led to its location by a flame. (Flames and lights are common ways in which icons of the Panayía manifest themselves to believers and are discovered.) A church was built on the spot, and later a monastery, which now houses the icon.[15]

A similar story of an icon's resistance was told to me by a woman on Rhodes. When the island was under Turkish rule, an icon of the Panayía was taken from a local church and transported to Constantinople. But the icon escaped the hands of its enemies and returned to the island. It announced its return as a flame on the hill where the church that had housed it stood.

The Panayía also reacts to the behavior of her devotees. In 533 an old woman had a dream that led to the discovery of an icon of the Panayía. A church was built on the spot and later a monastery. The icon cured many who were sick or possessed. One day in 1480 the custodian opened the doors of the church to find the icon no longer there. It had left because of the sins of the inhabitants. Later it was found in other monasteries, finally ending up in its present location near Metsovo. A similar story of a truant icon is told of an icon on Tinos, the Lady Stranger (*I Kíra Kséni*), recounted in chapter 4. As other examples of the Panayía's power to punish, we might also recall here the behavior of the Panayía when she appeared to the nun Pelayia, threatening to erase her from the book of life if the nun continued to ignore the divine instructions, and then her later infliction of a plague of cholera on the islanders when they prematurely abandoned the search for her icon.

These various stories associated with icons of the Panayía show her/her icons asserting their own will, defending human groups devoted to them, resisting persecution and destruction, punishing enemies of the Orthodox, and punishing sinners as well. It is obvious from such accounts that the Panayía is a powerful personage, capable of both providing succor and inflicting damage on the human world (see Carroll 1992; Perry and Echeverria 1988). She does not "intercede" in these stories but acts directly on her own behalf, on behalf of the Orthodox faith, and on behalf of her followers and supplicants. We might also note that while the Panayía may have specialized, localized manifestations, she is neither specialized in her functions nor limited in her geographic range (unlike many of the saints, who are best appealed to for certain kinds of problems; cf. Carroll 1992:59).

But the nature of the Panayía, and of her relationship to her human devotees, is not only revealed in icons and the stories associated with them. It is also revealed in the manner and situations in which she is invoked. I have given examples of such invocation with respect to individual problems and dangers. But she is also invoked in times of collective crisis, and in such contexts the "militant Madonna" can be seen most clearly (cf. Perry and Echeverria 1988). This happened in Greece during World War II. Here also the political dimension of the Panayía begins to assume clearer outline.

In the National Historical Museum in Athens are several paintings depicting the Greek-Italian war. One of these paintings is of a battleground filled with soldiers, the Panayía and child hovering in the clouds overhead, accompanied by angels, one of which carries a Greek flag. Another painting depicts a naval battle, overseen by the Panayía alone, her hands slightly raised over the scene of the action. Newspapers of the war period also depict the Panayía as the protectress of an embattled Greece. In the December 24, 1940, edition of *Athinaiká Néa* there is a picture titled "Wartime Christmas" (*Polemiká Hristoúyenna*), which shows the Panayía in the foreground, her hands raised in blessing over distant troops going to war. Below it says "May the Panayía be with them" (*I Panayía mazí tous*).[16] In the September 8, 1941, edition of *I Níki* (Victory) there is a similar scene. In this one a soldier is striding forward. Immediately behind him is a larger

244 · Chapter Eleven

figure of the Panayía. The heading reads, "May the Panayía be with him."
In *Kiriakí* on January 1, 1941, a headline read "The Panayía, leader of our
army in battle" (*I Panayía, odhiyítria tou stratóu mas is tas Máhas*).[17] And
Néos Kósmos, on December 19, 1940, ran the headline "We thank the
Panayía who stands by our side!" (*Evharistoúme tin Panayía pou stéketai
plái mas*). And the role of religion in war is even more clearly depicted in a
cartoon in *Ellinikón Méllon* (Greek Future), which shows Hitler carrying a
swastika backing off from a Greek soldier with a bayonet, accompanied by
the Panayía carrying a cross. The cartoon is titled "The Two Crosses" (*I
Dhío Stavrí*).

The Panayía was not alone in the divine defense of Greece. As in the
War of Independence, God and religion, along with the saints, generally
were seen by many as being on the Greek side. "Why Does God Help
Greece—and Punish Italy?" read a headline in *I Níki* on December 14,
1940. The accompanying article goes on to note that "the rock-strong
foundation of the Greek race is RELIGION." Not only is the Panayía part
of Greece's strength, the article points out, but so too are such saints as
St. Constantine and St. George, who defend the nation. But it is the
Panayía who appears to be most frequently invoked as protectress of the
nation.

Tinos played its own special part in the war. Indeed the war might be
said to have begun there as far as Greece is concerned, with the surprise
submarine attack on the *Elli*. It was an attack that did not go unanswered
by the Panayía, according to *I Níki*. When the *Elli* was attacked, "they
begged the Panayía to punish Her dishonorable and crude blasphemer.
And indeed, on the 21st of November, the day of the Presentation of the
Theotókos, at the same morning hour that the Elli had sunk, our torpedo
boat the Aetos sank an Italian submarine, perhaps the same one which
attacked the Elli" (December 14, 1940).[18]

THE PANAYÍA, POLITICS, AND IDENTITY

While any saint can protect and perform miracles, and can inflict punishment as well, the Panayía emerges, true to her name, as the most
powerful of the saints. In addition, as some of the examples above suggest, she has often played a special role as the protectress of the Greek
nation, a role particularly emphasized at Tinos, where she has been associated with Greek nationalism since the War of Independence. Several
years ago the Day of the Assumption, now Tinos's major holy day, was
designated a national Day of Military Strength. Posters commemorating
this day juxtapose military images with ones of the Panayía and/or
Tinos. For example, one poster shows an aerial photograph of Tinos,
taken just above several military jets that are flying over the island. Be-

low the planes can be seen the town and the church. Another poster shows a battleship at sea, with an image of the Panayía floating in the upper-right-hand corner.

The militant role of Mary is not confined to the Orthodox tradition, nor is the Orthodox context the only one in which she is seen as defender of the faith. In the nineteenth century both the Catholic and Orthodox worlds saw a popular and official resurgence of Marian devotion, and many apparitions were sighted in the Catholic countries of southern and western Europe (Pope 1985:173; see also Perry and Echeverria 1988). A number of twentieth-century apparitions of the Virgin appeared in Catholic countries in order to deliver anti-Communist messages. In 1917, for example, the Immaculate Heart of Mary appeared at Fatima and asked for prayers for the conversion of Russia (see Christian 1984). Such apparitions were often co-opted by the church as weapons in their fight against forces of the Left (Perry and Echeverria 1988).[19] Thus while visions of Mary promised hope and comfort to those in need, in her more militant aspect she promised victory over sin and the triumph of the church over its enemies in an increasingly troubled and turbulent age (Pope 1985:176–77). In the post–World War II period in Greece, the Panayía apparently took on a similar role, being portrayed in the conservative media as an anti-Communist crusader.

But the Panayía has served as more than a symbol and protectress of the Greek nation and more than a defender of the faith against the threat of communism. Like the other saints, she may also represent specific communities and groups. Throughout Greece, one finds various manifestations of the Panayía as the patron of particular villages and regions and as a focus of local identity. The exact location of visions in which she appears, and of the churches that she has commanded, become important (and sometimes contested) communal claims. This provides the basis of political struggles centering around images of the Panayía—struggles between communities, and between local communities and the religious establishment.[20] It also provides a basis for the expression of intercommunal hostilities. As Herzfeld has pointed out, in Greece the expression "screw your Madonna" is a counterpart to the often heard exclamation "my Madonna" (Panayía mou), the blasphemy dividing a universal image into refractions associated with particular social segments so that "my" Madonna is different from "yours" (see Herzfeld 1987a). Thus Mary presents two seemingly contradictory and yet interrelated dimensions: a universality that can be, at its widest, national, international, or even pan-Christian,[21] and a localism that serves to separate one community from another. At the same time, her symbolic complexity makes her more than merely a map of social segmentation. I would agree with Carroll, who, speaking of the multiplicity of Madonnas in Italian Catholicism, warns against seeing them as simple reflections of political fragmentation (1992:60).

MARY AS A "PROBLEM" FOR THE ANTHROPOLOGIST

It should be obvious even from this brief discussion that the Madonna or Panayía is a complex figure in both Orthodoxy and Catholicism. Theologically an intercessor, she assumes in popular devotion a great power in her own right. Supposedly a model for obedient and chaste womanhood, she also becomes a militant defender of her people and the church. Celebrated as a mother, she also has the power to punish in sometimes hideous ways those who disobey her will. Venerated in a wide range of local manifestations and appearing throughout the centuries to a variety of humble folk, she also has the power to unify, as does no other saint, both national entities and pan-national bodies of the faithful. She is the premier female within the Catholic and Orthodox faiths, and at the same time she seems to transcend womanhood itself.

The problem that Mary (in both her Catholic and Orthodox forms) poses for the anthropologist is how to understand all her various dimensions and their relationships, and especially how to understand them within particular social contexts. More specifically, we might ask why is Mary, more than any other devotional figure, so often the representation of the body politic, whether that body is community, church, or state? And more generally, why are nations (and to a lesser degree certain other political bodies) so often represented by female bodies, sometimes even warlike ones, when public politics generally, and certainly warfare, are almost universally male activities? As I have already suggested, in order to answer these questions we must move away from the domestic arena in which Mary is usually analyzed (Mary as wife and mother, Mary as a model for women) and into the public arena. We must also move away from such terms as "mother worship," to which Marian devotion is sometimes reduced, and toward a more general exploration of issues both of political ritual and symbol and of the symbolism of the feminine.

Considered in this context, how may we interpret the multiple roles of Mary and, more specifically, of the Panayía as she is known and venerated in Greece today?

Victor and Edith Turner suggest that Mary provides an appropriate metaphor and symbol for human groups for several reasons. First, women in general, and Mary in particular, carry the idea of a container or vessel. In Greek one of the terms for Mary is *Theotókos*, the Bearer of God. Women are the bearers, and in this sense the originators, of human groups. Men in groups, the Turners suggest, are thus "bounded by the feminine" (1978:156), just as Christ, and hence the church, were contained in Mary. Second, though Mary has numerous local manifestations, she is also omnipresent. Mary was assumed *bodily* into heaven, hence there are no relics to provide a cult focus or the basis for claims of preeminence of one site over another for her devotion.[22] She thus has mobility throughout the church and is equally present, and present to all (Turner and Turner 1978:160). At the same time, Mary connects heaven and earth in a "bodily way" through her assumption, and thus readily appears to fleshly mortals in visions that form the grounds for local claims, on the basis of which specific churches honoring her may be built (Turner and Turner 1978:155). Thus, according to Turner and Turner, the relationship between the female body and the body politic follows a certain symbolic logic.

The Greek Panayía and the Catholic Virgin Mary are paralleled, and sometimes countered, by other female symbols of political corporateness. The goddess Liberty, for example, was the personification of a revolutionary France. And during the French Third Republic, the unveiling during the Bastille Day celebrations in 1883 of a statue of Marianne, a militant image of the republic, wearing a red cap (Agulhon 1985:182–83), aroused the derision of the religious Right, which labeled her an "impure Venus" (Pope 1985:186). The Right countered with celebrations of the Feast of the Assumption, designated as the French national holiday in the seventeenth century by Louis XIII. Left and Right contended with each other, mobilizing competing symbolic female figures. Thus not only do we see political bodies symbolized by human bodies, but they are symbolized specifically by *female* bodies that not only signify the more obvious attributes associated with women—motherhood, nurturance, and protection—but militancy and civic virtue as well.

In addition to these attributes, women represent a vulnerability that, like the nation, requires protection. Timothy Ware (1963), writing of the position of Mary in the Greek Orthodox church, states that the Orthodox Mary is less known than the Orthodox Christ because the Orthodox prefer to keep Mary to themselves, to keep her "inside," just as women in "traditional" Greek society are also kept inside, to protect their honor and that of their families (see Dubisch 1986b; Herzfeld 1986). Violation of women, whether of those of one's own group by outsiders or by those of other groups by one's own, is a powerful symbolic act of aggression (see Herzfeld 1987a). Thus the expression "screw your Panayía" is a verbal symbolic counterpart to the rape of the women of another family, community, or nation. In this context, the Turkish abduction of the Rhodian icon of the Panayía, recounted earlier, is a form of rape as well. Thus women generally, and the Virgin Mary in particular, provide powerful representations of political conflict, conquest, and difference. Nations are like women, whose boundaries must be defended from penetration by the enemy.

At the same time, the Panayía transcends womanhood in that she is the protector and not simply the protected. In the case of the Rhodian icon, she is not rescued by others but returns herself to the homeland. She strikes down those who threaten harm to her or her devotees. She leaves her icon at Tinos in order to aid the troops at the front. She retaliates for the *Elli,* treacherously attacked on her own holy feast day. She strides off to war with soldiers and watches over battles. Thus while she may be kept "inside," as Ware suggests, insofar as she is less known "outside" than the Catholic Virgin Mary, this does not mean that she does not play an important symbolic role on the national political stage.

As political symbols, the Panayía, the Virgin Mary, and other feminine political representations usually embody nationhood rather than particular forms of government. That is, they are the eternal spirit of the body politic rather than the transitory corporeal form of a particular government, nationhood rather than particular political states. Female figures symbolize certain abstract and permanent principles on which the Western body politic—whether church, community, or nation—is claimed to be based. The Panayía has thus played an important role both in the defense of Greekness under conquest and in the creation, legitimation, and protection of the body politic. But while the Catholic Virgin Mary has generally been seen as being co-opted by forces of the Right (see, e.g., Perry and Echeverria 1988), in Greece the Panayía does not represent only one shade of the political spectrum but rather may be claimed by competing parties.[23] Although Greek governments have changed over the time I have been visiting Tinos—from military junta to conservative to Socialist—there has always been a representative of the government present to give a speech at the ceremonies of August 15, no matter what the party in power at the time.

This brings us back to Tinos and the pilgrimage of Papandreou's wife.

POLITICS: PUBLIC AND PRIVATE

As much recent anthropological work on pilgrimage has pointed out, pilgrimage sites are often places of contested meaning, visited by pilgrims with a wide range of purposes, and carrying a variety of symbolic messages that are not necessarily the same for all who visit there (see Eade and Sallnow 1991b; Murphy 1994). Moreover, such sites are capable of carrying meaning at a variety of organizational levels, from the individual pilgrim with a request or vow, to the local community where the shrine is housed, to the nation with its own political agenda, to a national or international church that uses the pilgrimage site to demonstrate and bolster the faith. This makes pilgrimage both a significant personal act and a powerful political tool.

Given the nature of the Panayía, then, it is no accident that what is perhaps the major national shrine of Greece—as well as the first pilgrimage shrine of the Greek nation—should center around the figure of the Panayía. Not only does her particular manifestation at this site—that is, the Annunciation—provide a powerful symbol of Greek nationhood as both a birth and a rebirth, but the figure of the Panayía is one that can transcend localism at the same time that it represents it. She is everywhere in her various manifestations, and at the same time she is one. She can serve as a model for women, as a powerful saint who can help with any human problem, and as a defender of the faith and symbol of the nation. And on any occasion of pilgrimage she may be appealed to and praised as any or all of these by the people who come there.

For Papandreou's wife, the Panayía was a source of aid in fulfilling a woman's duty in caring for the health of her family. In addition, for someone whose affair with a married man had caused something of a public scandal, a visit to a shrine of the Panayía, a visit that made clear her wifely concern as well as her piety, was an act that cannot be dismissed as an apolitical one, particularly when the man was (and became again) the prime minister of Greece. And Papandreou's visit, like that of other political figures, was not simply the domestically motivated journey of other men who accompany their wives on pilgrimage. Though no public events attended his visit, his pilgrimage was a public even that took place on the national political stage, one level of the complex structure of pilgrimage to this particular Marian shrine.

CHAPTER TWELVE

Epilogue: In a Different Place

IN JUNE 1993, I returned to Tinos for a short visit. Although I was in Greece for research purposes,[1] my trip to the island was not connected to this research. I had simply come to visit friends and to enjoy the island for a few days. I had, however, timed this visit for a particular event: the arrival of an Elderhostel boat at Tinos. One of the lecturers on the boat was a historian, George Moutafis, the husband of Vasiliki Galani-Moutafi, a Greek anthropologist who teaches at the University of the Aegean on Mitilini. When I had visited the Moutafis on Mitilini the previous week, George had told me about the Elderhostel boat and suggested I time my visit to Tinos to coincide with its arrival.[2] It sounded like an interesting idea, especially since the group would be taking a bus tour that would end up in Falatados, the village where I had originally done fieldwork. So I planned my own visit accordingly.

At that point it had been three years since I had been in Greece, and while the island radiated a welcome familiarity, not surprisingly a number of things had changed as well. My landlady, Marina, and her husband, Dhimitris, had converted their tourist shop into a bar that also sold sandwiches and ice cream. Marina had also opened a second store not far from her apartment building. The apartment she rented to me for the few days of my stay, though smaller than the one I had occupied before, was newly remodeled and very pleasant. And as I strolled through the streets of the town I noticed that a number of the stores that had been familiar to me, some going back to my earliest visits to Tinos, were gone, some empty, others replaced by shops selling gold jewelry and other items aimed at a more affluent clientele. It was clear that Tinos, though still heavily influenced economically by pilgrimage, was also continuing its trend of catering more and more to middle-class summer visitors, more likely to come to the island for vacation than for pilgrimage.

But as it turned out, these small if ubiquitous changes did not prove to be the most striking evidences of the passage of time.

The Elderhostel boat arrived on a Thursday evening at the crowded waterfront. There was much shouting and maneuvering as other yachts were shunted about to make space for the boat to dock. As it was a rather chubby vessel, its docking in the narrow space allotted to it was an exciting affair, watched anxiously by the occupants of the boats on either side of the slip. As often happens during such events, a small crowd had gathered on the quay to watch, myself among them, enjoying the drama as the boat dropped its anchor and then backed slowly, and with much shouting back and forth, into the slip. Then finally it was tied off and the gang-plank was lowered. I saw George in the companionway, waving to me to come aboard, and as soon as the gangway was secured, I clambered onto the ship.

The drama of docking had been missed by most of the passengers, for they were in the dining hall, consuming their evening meal. I was intro-duced to the crew and passengers and invited to sit for a glass of wine and something to eat. Though I turned down the meal, it was arranged that I would join the group for their bus tour of the island the following day.[3]

The tour began with a trip to the church. I was glad to see such a visit included as part of the tour, not only because the church is what gives Tinos its significance for most Greeks, but also because I felt it was good for tourists to be exposed to something other than classical ruins and to gain some understanding of life in contemporary Greece. But even though I was interested in observing the way the guide explained the church and the practices associated with it to an American audience, I felt awkward standing in the church with the Elderhostel group. This was not how I was used to acting while in the church, and although I wanted to listen, at the same time I did not want to be identified with this group of foreigners, a feeling that characterized the rest of my experience on the tour as well.

After the visit to the church, the group boarded the bus and we set off for Pirgos, a village famed for its marble quarries, sculptors, and pictur-esque village square. The trip to Pirgos is spectacular, the road winding up steep mountainsides, with whitewashed villages spilling down the slopes below. The previous winter had been a wet one, and the roadside and fields were bright with flowers. I felt the odd sense of the mingled exotic and familiar that I experience whenever I go back to Tinos, the accumulation of memories that now go back almost twenty-five years.

At Pirgos, George and I left the group at the house (and now museum) of the sculptor Halapas (which I had already seen) and went on to the village square, where we sat under the famous giant plane tree and had a sweet (compliments of the cafe owner) while we waited for the others. The group eventually found their way to the square and were all served the traditional Greek sweet of preserved fruit. We then strolled back to the bus stop and boarded the tour bus for the next leg of our trip, across the central part of the island to the village of Falatados.

It was a strange feeling to enter, as a passenger on an Elderhostel bus tour, the village where I had once done fieldwork. The bus headed up a road around the village, a road that had not existed when I had first lived there. We stopped at a restaurant that had also not existed in those earlier days, though I had eaten there on other occasions since then. The restaurant, which had been a little raw and unfinished when I had last been there, was now completed, freshly whitewashed and enhanced by trees and flowering plants around an outdoor terrace that overlooked an expanse of fields and distant villages. A long table had been set up at the edge of the terrace for the Elderhostel party.

The daughter of the restaurant owner came out to greet us and I asked her if she remembered me. She had been a child when I had last lived in the village, and now she was a lovely young woman. She said she did remember me, though not well, and called to her father, Petros, now aged and gray, who certainly did remember me, as my husband and I had often kept company with him and his wife. We gossiped a little, and then he went off to look for an old photograph he had. We all sat down to eat, the Elderhostel people at the long table, George, the guide, the bus driver, and myself at a separate table where we conversed in a mixture of English and Greek.

The food was delicious. It catered to American eating patterns while at the same time retaining the taste and interest of genuine village food. I do not know if the Elderhostel people appreciated this, but I was impressed. But I was reacting within a framework of comparison that stretched back many years, taking in an earlier village that hardly ever saw tourists, one in which the daughter of a village taverna owner would not have been friends with a Greek-American historian on an Elderhostel boat, one in which a meal like this would not have been served to a group of Americans who were visiting Tinos as part of an Elderhostel cruise of the Cyclades.

As I sat there at my lunch, I was assailed by a complex mix of feelings, for I felt both an insider and an outsider. I had obviously distanced myself from my fellow Americans, the Elderhostel passengers, by sitting at a table with the guides and by speaking in Greek. I was an insider in the village also, from my earlier stay there, and as we ate, Petros came out with the photograph he had been looking for, which showed himself, Marcos, and me sitting at a table at a cafe in town. It was a color photograph that I had sent him, very faded now, and I recognized it as dating from the early 1970s. He offered it to me, but I told him I had a copy and he should keep it himself. How many years had gone by since that photograph, I thought as I looked around. This restaurant, once new, now an established enterprise, obviously run by Petros's daughter, since he was getting on in years. I hardly even recognized the village, for across the street from the restaurant was a row of new summer houses where once before only fields had stood. From where I sat it did not look at all like the place I once knew and I felt like a stranger as I ate my lunch.

I knew that the Elderhostel meals had been arranged in advance and that my own meal had been an extra one, so I offered to pay for it. Petros's daughter refused my offer. "You're one of us," she told me, smiling, "from when you used to live here." Again I was stuck by the mix of familiarity and strangeness, being "one of us" to this lovely, warm woman in whom I now saw only the faint image of the child I remembered from those earlier years. We boarded the bus and headed back down the mountainside toward town.

The Elderhostel tour marked a significant point in my relationship with Tinos and with Greece. In the tour of the island, and particularly in my visit to the village, I found myself in a setting both familiar and strange, in a different place from what I had known before. I felt I had reached the end of something—or perhaps the limits of my own understanding of the place that had for so long played an important role in my life.

"In a different place"—this is the title I have chosen for the book and for this final chapter. It resonates for me in several ways. In my return to the village I was in a different place from the one I remembered, even though the place still had strong memories of the one I used to know, just as Petros's daughter still bore traces of the child she had once been. But I was "in a different place" in another sense as well, in a different place in my own life, in a different place "in my head," to employ a more collo-quial use of the term. Younger than Petros's daughter when I first did fieldwork, I now see myself, or at least my not-too-distant future self, in Petros, with his lined face and gray hair.

But "in a different place" also has another set of meanings, for it joins both the anthropological enterprise and the object of that enterprise. I am in "a different place" in terms of my practice and understanding of an-thropology than I was when I first began research in Greece, and anthro-pology itself is "in a different place" as well.

Anthropologists seek difference. This is hardly a new observation, yet it remains an important one. And in this sense, I have suggested, we are like pilgrims, for they too seek a different place, one where miracles occur and things reveal themselves that are not revealed in ordinary life. This was perhaps best expressed for me by a woman working at the church when I visited in March 1987. It was March 25, the Day of the Annunciation, normally a major holy day for Tinos since it was the feast day of the icon itself. But since a boat strike had kept pilgrims away that March, the only visitor in the church besides myself was an old lady in black slowly making the rounds of the icons. I talked for a while with one of the church caretakers, a woman in her early thirties, asking her about the stories attached to some of the offerings hanging in the church. As we stood by the stand near the entrance where the church's famous silver orange tree is displayed, she gazed around her for a moment and then said quietly, "There is much here that we don't understand."

The statement of the woman at the church might be said to characterize the anthropological enterprise as well. "Much that we don't understand"—this sense increases rather than decreases the more I work in Greece. There is much about what we do, and about how we do it, that we don't understand. This may be why we often seek to describe our work metaphorically (see Karp and Kendall 1982). This may in part also be why anthropologists sometimes identify themselves and their work with the project and people they are studying. This is true in the experiential sense, as with my own vow, made in a moment of danger and stress, or with Danforth's (1989) experience with firewalking, or the dreams experienced by Seremetakis (1991) and interpreted by her informants in the course of her fieldwork. But it is also true in the sense that we often derive metaphors and other organizing principles for our own work from what we are studying. Thus Herzfeld (1985) has drawn on indigenous notions for his concept of "poetics" in Crete, Danforth (1989) has characterized fieldwork as therapy in his study of the therapeutic rituals of the Anastenaria. And I have compared the anthropological enterprise to a pilgrimage.

As anthropologists we journey to a different place to seek understanding, both of that place and of the place from which we have come. And the two places, and the understanding of each, are intimately related, as I have sought to demonstrate in this book.

This brings me to the subtitle of this book: pilgrimage, gender and politics. *Pilgrimage,* as I have pointed out, carries multiple meanings here, for it refers not only to the pilgrimage of Greeks to Tinos but to the anthropologist's journey as well. *Gender* likewise has multiple referents, for it refers to gender in the context of pilgrimage but also in the context of anthropology, both my own gender and my relationship to feminist issues, particularly as they pertain to my discipline and my work within it. And the third term, *politics,* I have used in multiple senses also, referring to the local politics of the founding of the shrine and the politics of the shrine and pilgrimage today, but also to the politics of anthropologists studying another culture, the political relations of Greece and the West, and the politics of anthropology itself.

As "a different place" Greece occupies a particular position in our thought. Seen as both the cradle of Western civilization and at the same time Oriental and hence somewhat mysterious, Greece challenges in specific ways our distinctions between self and other. This challenge may be epitomized in the study of religion, for although Greeks are Christian, hence tied by faith to the West rather than to the East, they are Eastern Christians, whose religious beliefs and practices may confound, and sometimes outrage, Western notions of religion. Pilgrimage, gender, and politics thus take on specific forms in this context, which although familiar, present us with a challenge of difference as well.

During my most recent visit to Tinos, I made the following notes:

June 11, 1993—Tinos
Went up to the church this morning around 11:30—it was very quiet—there seemed to be more tourists than pilgrims, and even when the first boat arrived, there were not many people who headed for the church.

Things seemed a little shabby and very much in need of work—the very worn carpet on the steps had been covered with some black, rubber-like material, and this also was worn away . . . showing the remnants of the carpet.

Otherwise things were much the same . . . I had bought two small *lambádhes* and I trudged up the hill with them—deliberately I had not brought my camera, and I did not stop to look in shop windows—instead I concentrated on my pilgrimage.

This was important to me—even if I go up to the church again while I'm here, it won't be the same as that first time after being away for three years—it's kind of touching base, I suppose.

I sat for a while after lighting my *lambádhes*—feeling my attachment to the church, and perhaps to the Panayía, whoever she is—the age of the church, the accretion of objects and meaning over time, give the church a depth which I found lacking at Ayios Rafaíl [on Mitilini].

As I walked back down from the church, I thought of the woman from Australia I had talked to at Ayios Rafaíl who said that religion had a psychological effect on her, that it lifted the anxiety—I had a feeling of lightness, of well-being just from having gone up to the church—in part one could attribute this to physical factors: after toiling up the hill to the church, I found walking down easy, a sense of freedom—but I think that's only part of it—in some way I gave up a burden while I was in the church and walked away feeling more at peace.

I wouldn't want to confuse this with how a Greek who was a believer might feel, but I wonder about the relief to be found in the act itself, regardless of belief—one only has to believe enough to do the act.

I have shown much of myself in this book—perhaps too much. Even an anthropology that seeks to be reflexive should not be about the anthropologist but about what the anthropologist studies. The anthropologist is a means to an end, and reflexivity a means of better understanding the method and tools used to arrive at that end. Yet insofar as I am an anthropologist, I am what I study. Moreover, it can be argued, what I study, what I write about, is in turn a product of what I am (see Tyler 1987:101). "Ethnographies" do not miraculously emerge from "fieldwork" conducted by a detached observer. And anthropology itself is a construction, shaped by the culture and politics of our own society as well as by what we encounter—and by what we do—in that ambiguous place we call "the field." More and more we are revealing the techniques, the props, even the tricks that shape that construction from behind the scenes, and this includes revealing what we ourselves are, do, and feel.

I have used the terms *field* and *fieldwork,* referring both to the field as the location of anthropological work and to the field of anthropology itself. But we need also to emphasize the term *work*—anthropology is the field in which we toil and we need to understand the nature of work in such a context, especially when it often seems to those among whom we work that we hardly work at all. Even to ourselves the nature of our "work" may be unclear. I spent many days on Tinos watching pilgrimage, talking to pilgrims and shopkeepers, collecting "information" of various kinds and writing everything laboriously in my "fieldnotes," doing the sorts of things that fieldwork is supposedly about and yet feeling as if I were getting nowhere and learning nothing. Yet perhaps the repetitious recording of the same things over and over again does tell me something, just as breaks in the sameness also tell me something (Karp and Kendall 1982). Each is necessary to the other: unusual occurrences can only be identified against the background of the usual, insights regarding the usual often come at unusual or dramatic moments. Therefore an account that truly reflects the "work" I have done is an account that contains both the generalizations that are the summaries of long experience and system-atic investigation and the more dramatic or unusual incidents that both typify and contrast with the more "normal" flow of things.

Would I consider this book to be a postmodern ethnography, or a feminist ethnography, or both (if such a thing is possible)? In the end I cannot put a label on this particular work. Obviously my book has been greatly influenced by the ideas and concerns of both postmodernism and feminism. Postmodernism's emphasis on the verbal, and perhaps also on the masculine ("Postmodern anthropology is the study of man— 'talking'" [Tyler 1987:71]) has limited its appeal for me in dealing with such subjects as emotion and the visual and material dimensions of reli-gion and with a "poetics of womanhood" that may rely on other modes than the verbal for its expression (Herzfeld 1991a). At the same time, postmodernist concerns with writing and language have made me con-scious of the way I, and other anthropologists, use writing to depict others and to exercise our anthropological authority. As for feminism, it is still very much a matter of debate what a "feminist ethnography" could or should look like.[4] Perhaps I could best describe this as a book "in-formed" by feminist concerns, or at least by certain feminist concerns as they are shaped within anthropology.

It is obvious to me as I look back not only on my earlier work in the field but on my earlier experience *of* work in the field that I am indeed "in a different place" today than I was in my earlier years of research. Femi-nism has played a part in leading me to view my experiences and my emotional responses to what I experience as part of my anthropology and not separate or outside of it. In turn, this is related to a postmodern concern with the breaking down or dissolving of boundaries, between self and other, the personal and the professional, theory and experience, the field of fieldwork and the field of anthropology. In addition, I have found that some of the boundaries that I expected to divide the subject matter of my fieldwork into its analyzable categories also became fluid or dissolved: boundaries between the sacred and profane, the material and the spiritual, belief and act, tourist and pilgrim, history and story, pilgrimage and everyday life.

This brings me back to the ostensible object of my study, one that has proved more complex and richer in possibilities than I had originally conceived, and that is the topic of pilgrimage. An old phenomenon, pilgrimage has proved surprisingly fertile as both a subject and a metaphor for a postmodern age. Although involving by definition separation and a journey to a different place, pilgrimage is intimately connected to the context of everyday life. Although it exhibits sometimes strikingly similar features worldwide, it is also highly distinctive within its particular cultural and historical contexts. Although it takes place as a major public event, at the same time it is connected to strongly personal emotions, needs, and inner states. It is in all these senses that pilgrimage has proved a rich metaphor both for and of anthropology, and a fruitful context in which to explore a variety of anthropological interests, from the rituals of politics, to gender and feminist issues, to reflexivity and postmodernism.

Is this, in the final analysis, all that anthropology is—a pilgrimage from which we return with a variety of tales that we shape in conventional ways designed to excite the interest of our audience? Perhaps. But even now, as we challenge some of the conventional ways in which we have told our tales in the past, our goals in the telling have not substantially changed. We still look toward both "fields" in our accounts, the field in which the "other" dwells and the academic field in which we ourselves toil, seeking to bridge the boundaries and barriers between worlds and to understand ourselves better as we do so. And as we proceed with our task, increasingly we come to realize that there is still much here that we don't understand. Perhaps we can only, like the pilgrim, journey to a different place, have faith, and hope for miracles to occur.

Notes

CHAPTER ONE

1. I began my initial research at the shrine in the summer of 1986, spending six months there supported by a research grant from the Fulbright Foundation and by a grant from the Foundation of the University of North Carolina at Charlotte and the UNCC Faculty Grants Committee. Additional research trips were made to Tinos in the spring of 1987, and in the summers of 1988 and 1990 with faculty grants from the University of North Carolina at Charlotte, and in the summer of 1993 with a Faculty Research grant from Northern Arizona University.

2. The first systematic treatment of this issue was Marcus and Cushman 1982, followed by Clifford and Marcus's influential (and much-critiqued) volume *Writing Culture* (1986).

3. Such experimentation leads to, among other things, a sort of "balancing act" between two contrasting (though not necessarily antithetical) modes of ethnographic writing: "evocation" and "referentiality." I would agree here with Birth in his critique of writing and postmodern anthropology that "the implicit assumption that ethnography is either referential or poetic is unsound. Ethnography is better viewed as being both referential *and* poetic" (1990:553).

4. Compare Kondo's discussion of her self-conscious writing strategies in *Crafting Selves* (1990:8).

5. Dwyer's *Moroccan Dialogues* (1982) is an example of a work that seeks to overcome what the author perceives as the deficiencies of both the "scientific" approach and the personal narrative as the means for interpreting the anthropological encounter with another culture. Other anthropologists have taken different approaches to the problem, these differences themselves constituting an important feature of the "experimental turn." (For a criticism of Dwyer, see Hastrup 1992a.)

6. Among other things, such "traditional" structure includes a set of assumed universal categories into which cultural materials can be placed, for example, "economic systems," "family and marriage," "kinship," "religion." The sequencing of topics also reflects an implicit materialist interpretation of culture: one begins with subsistence and economics and works through family, kinship, and politics (cf. Tyler 1987:93). Religion and ideological systems often come last, and a concluding chapter on "change" implies a hitherto static and even "pristine" culture, only recently affected by outside sources. The anthropologist as actor is normally limited to an introduction that describes "conditions of fieldwork." This establishes the authenticity of the account, after which the anthropologist disappears (see Marcus and Cushman 1982). In addition, "theory" is separated from "fact," as reflected in the ethnography/ethnology distinction.

7. On anthropology and autobiography, see Okely 1992.

8. On interpretive anthropology, see also Geertz 1973; Rabinow and Sullivan 1979, 1987.

9. This "presentation" is constructed in the terms of my own culture, particularly my own anthropological culture, though I have made presentations to non-anthropological and nonacademic audiences as well, and to Greeks (including Greek anthropologists and anthropology students).

10. See Dubisch 1988.

11. In addition, "postmodern" has a wide range of referents outside of social science (in architecture, art, and so on). "Postmodern" seems to have subsumed certain earlier terms such as *poststructuralist* and *deconstruction* as a description of a particular intellectual stance. This is not to say that these terms necessarily mean the same thing or that there is universal agreement about what they *do* mean.

12. Some of the critiques of postmodernism by anthropologists include Birth 1990; di Leonardo 1991; Sangren 1988; Ulin 1991. Indeed Pool (1991) argues that much of what is labeled postmodern in anthropology (especially by critics of postmodernism) is really "high modern" or "late modern."

13. For differing views about whether or not postmodernism is inherently politically disengaged, see Pool 1991; Ulin 1991.

14. The deliberate exclusion of feminism from Clifford and Marcus's groundbreaking *Writing Culture* would seem to support this view. Ulin's (1991) article on postmodernism also explicitly excludes feminism.

15. With respect to history, Tilly argues that "all women's history is . . . feminist, and related to the feminist social movement, at least in its roots" (1989:442). The history of the anthropological study of women and gender is a complex one and there is not space to summarize it here. For some recent discussions, see di Leonardo 1991; Moore 1988; Strathern 1988.

16. Like postmodernism, feminism means many things to many people, and it is becoming more common to speak of "feminisms." For an overview of feminist issues and debates, see Tong 1989.

17. This reflects certain cultural assumptions regarding the "naturalness" of womanhood, assumptions that may be reinforced by being shared with those among whom the anthropologist works (see M. Rosaldo 1987; see also Tiffany 1984). An important task of a feminist anthropology, as I see it, is to problematize gender, both male and female (see Dubisch 1991a; see also Flax 1987:629).

18. Whether gender is universally basic enough to form the basis of an entire intellectual approach is part of the anthropology-feminism debate. Strathern, for example, states that "'feminism,' that is, the feminist component of this or that theoretical approach, takes system or structure for granted. It does not pretend to be an independent (holistic) theory of society as such" (1988:25).

19. Renato Rosaldo's *Culture and Truth: The Remaking of Social Analysis* (1989) uses experience and emotion as vehicles for a critique of anthropological theory. While in no way wishing to detract from the value of this insightful and stimulating work, I cannot help wondering if it might have been received differently if written by a woman, especially since many of the things Rosaldo says have previously been written by feminists (and indeed he draws on the writings of several female anthropologists). It might be noted that, like feminists, Rosaldo is writing from "outside," using, in part, his own experience as a Hispanic to critique scientific "objectivism." For Tyler, on the other hand, experience does not

constitute an independent, prior element that precedes the writing of ethnography, but is created in the writing of ethnography itself (1987:215). On the differences in the notion of experience as used by nonanthropological feminists and nonfeminist anthropologists, see Strathern 1987. For two recent works on experience, gender, and anthropology, see Okely 1992; Callaway 1992. Stacey (1988) has also critiqued the idea of feminist ethnography, though from the point of view of branches of social science in which ethnography has not been the usual method of research. The dilemmas of ethnographic fieldwork that she discusses are by no means unique to feminists, as she naively seems to assume, but are ones that have long been discussed in anthropology generally.

20. This emphasis on experience raises the very interesting question of whether or not men can do feminist theory.

21. The earliest work on women and fieldwork (which is now enjoying something of a revival) is Golde's *Women in the Field* (originally published in 1970). For a more recent discussion of gender and fieldwork, see Whitehead and Conaway 1986.

22. See, e.g., di Leonardo 1991; Moore 1988; Strathern 1988.

23. See Dubisch 1991a. Among others who have criticized the neglect of women's writing are Caplan 1988; Cole 1994; Lutz 1990. Gordon (1990) has examined the role of both race and gender in the neglect of the writings of Zora Neale Hurston.

24. Among the earlier female anthropologists whose writings have been thus neglected or downplayed are Ruth Landes, Laura Bohannan (who wrote *Return to Laughter* under a pseudonym), Hortense Powdermaker, Jean Briggs, and Elizabeth Fernea (whose book *Guests of the Sheik* I have used regularly in introductory anthropology classes for over twenty years).

25. This "halfie" position is occupied to some extent even by the anthropologist of non-European descent, since anthropology itself is part of the European intellectual tradition as well as a product of European colonial relationships. Europeans studying other Europeans of different cultural backgrounds are also "halfies." The issue of doing anthropology in the European context was explored in a session I organized for the 1991 American Anthropological Association titled "Self or Other?: Reflexivity in the European Context." For a good discussion of these issues by a Greek "halfie" anthropologist, see Gefou-Madianou 1993.

26. Friedl was one of the first to bring up this issue in the introduction to her groundbreaking work *Vasilika: A Village in Modern Greece* (1962).

27. Danforth reports an encounter with an educated Greek who expressed indignation that an anthropologist should be talking to him rather than to "natives," who were anthropology's proper objects of study (1989:155). At the same time Europeans can themselves create an internal "otherness," defining certain categories of people as appropriate objects of study. There are Greeks who would consider the fire-walkers studied by Danforth an appropriate anthropological object, but might not see urban Greek intellectuals as similarly suitable anthropological subject matter (see Faubion 1993).

28. The issue of the "natives" reading the writing of anthropologists is not confined to Europe. See, e.g., Abu-Lughod 1991:159–60.

29. See Chodorow 1974; Gilligan 1982. The idea of a "feminine" voice is a

general one and does not necessarily apply to individual women and their modes of writing.

30. Some suggest that the term "participant observer" is an oxymoron (see, e.g., Herzfeld 1987a:63). I would suggest rather that it describes a dilemma of anthropological research, a dilemma that may begin to resolve itself as we break down some of the boundaries discussed here (for example, self/other, experience/theory, subjective/objective). This is part, I think, of what Herzfeld means when he states that "we are participant observers only as far as we are also prepared to accept our informants' right to the same title" (1987a:90–91).

31. R. Rosaldo speaks of emotions as "unmanly states" within the Weberian ethic of an objective social science and extols the "analytic possibilities" that these emotions offer (1989:172). This is not to suggest that such states are inherent qualities of male and female but rather are culturally shaped and defined.

32. We can see one manifestation of this in the different attitudes toward male versus female sexual experiences in the field. Such experience on the part of a female anthropologist may be used to cast doubts on her work (see Cole 1994). Rabinow's recounting of a sexual encounter with an apparent prostitute not only had no effect on the evaluation of his work, but seems to have passed virtually without a ripple in the anthropological world (Rabinow 1977), whereas a female anthropologist writing a few years later of her own affairs in the field felt compelled to use a pseudonym (Cesara 1982). The double "otherness" of woman is revealed in her sexual intimacy, which is more boundary threatening than male sexuality. (On the issue of female sexual experience in fieldwork, see Dubisch 1991b; see also Kulick and Willson 1995).

33. Some examples of recent experimental works by women are Kondo 1990, Lavie 1990. For a discussion of these issues, see Abu-Lughod 1990.

34. This may be part of what Tyler means when he states that ethnography "is not a record of experience at all; it is the means of experience. That experience became experience only in the writing of ethnography" (1987:215). In working on this book, I found that in the course of fieldwork I had not recorded certain events and observations I later decided were important (at which point I did write about them; cf. Ottenberg 1990). In part, this was a result of changing ideas about what constituted "data," or perhaps what constituted an anthropologically relevant part of my experience. One could also argue, however, that Tyler's statement tends to privilege writing in the making of anthropology (see Okely 1992 for a critique).

35. As Okely (1992) warns, we must not overly privilege writing and reduce fieldwork itself to "mere" data collection.

36. I find myself in sympathy here with Abu-Lughod's offering of "ethnography of the particular" as a response to the call for textual innovation in anthropology, and with her critique of the postmodern response to this call:

> The proponents of the current experiments and critiques of ethnographic writing . . . reject the rhetoric of social science not for ordinary language but for a rarified discourse . . . packed with jargon. . . . Whatever the merits of their contributions, the message of hyperprofessionalism is hard to miss. Despite a sensitivity to questions of otherness and power and the relevance of textuality

to these issues, they use a discourse even more exclusive and thus more rein-forcing of hierarchical distinctions between themselves and anthropological others, than that of the ordinary anthropology they criticize. (1991:152)

In light of the argument that postmodernism is a last-ditch effort to preserve male academic power, it is interesting to note an emerging bifurcation in current an-thropological writing between the sort of ethnography advocated by Abu-Lughod, which appears more commonly (though not exclusively) to be done by women, and the sort of writing she critiques, which is done mostly by male anthropologists.

37. There have been some interesting attempts to develop what might be termed "ethnographies of muteness." Abu-Lughod's *Veiled Sentiments* (1986) might be seen as one example. Another is Messick's (1987) article on North Afri-can women's weaving.

38. On this issue, see Hastrup 1992a:122; Geertz 1988:140; see also Stacey 1988; M. Wolf 1992.

39. While postmodernism has had an undeniable impact on this book, I do not know that I would call it a postmodern ethnography. Tyler, for example, states that "a postmodern ethnography is fragmentary because it cannot be otherwise" (1986:131). I cannot say that my book fits this description for it unashamedly seeks to "make sense" of things, at least within the framework of the issues I have been discussing. This "making sense" is not complete or perfect—in this I would agree with Tyler—just as the attempt to "make sense" of their own culture by Greeks (or any other people) is not perfect. In some ways, "making sense" calls for constant questioning and for multiple approaches. In addition, some things must remain open-ended, some questions unanswered.So in this respect my narra-tive is postmodern insofar as any attempt at a postmodern ethnography "will always be incomplete, insufficient, lacking in some way" (Tyler 1987:213); see also Brady 1991:12.

CHAPTER TWO

1. The term *Evangelístria*, which I have rendered as the Madonna of the An-nunciation, refers to one of the manifestations of Mary and has no equivalent term in English. *Panayía*—the all holy one, the foremost among the saints—is the most commonly used term for Mary in Greek, and the term one is most likely to hear in ordinary conversation. Another frequently used term is *Megalóhari*—*megálo* meaning large or great, *hári* referring to favor or grace. Pilgrims will often speak of going to the Panayía *yia tin hári tis,* that is, to seek her favor or grace.

2. When I first did fieldwork in Tinos in 1969–70, the only ferryboats were the ones from Rafina. The ships from Piraeus were only passenger ships, and pas-sengers disembarked from the upper deck. This was certainly a more exciting way to approach the island, since a passenger could actually watch the docking pro-cess, which was sometimes tricky, especially in high winds.

3. "Large candles! *Támata!* Little bottles for holy water! Here [are] large candles!"

4. Return visits prior to my research on pilgrimage took place in 1972, 1973, 1975, and 1979.

5. He came for a period of approximately six weeks, from early July to mid-August 1986 (see chapter 4).

6. Like most of the names used in this book, this is a pseudonym.

7. Villages here tend to be visited more often by urban Greeks, who are distinguished from "tourists," the latter term usually referring to non-Greeks. "The village" has come to have an almost mystical quality for these urbanites (many of whom are only a generation away from village life themselves). The village embodies a "traditional" way of life absent in the city, a way of life that includes quaint architecture, clean air, good food and wine, and traditional festivals (*paniyíria*). Some of the villages on Tinos have taken to advertising their village festivals to such visitors, and sometimes even charging admission, a practice unimaginable twenty years ago. Such advertising of festivals is found in other areas of Greece as well. (On "the village" as a cultural construction, see Sutton 1988.)

8. For a discussion and critique of these metaphors, see Karp and Kendall 1982.

9. I am not the first to propose such a metaphor. Turnbull (1992), for example, has used it, but in a somewhat different way than I have here. For a more general discussion of the root metaphor of a journey in discussions of anthropological fieldwork, see Dwyer 1982.

CHAPTER THREE

1. Among the recent anthropological works are monographs by Gold 1988; Morinis 1984; Sallnow 1987; Sax 1991; Slater 1986; as well as edited works by Crumrine and Morinis 1991; Eade and Sallnow 1991a; Morinis 1992; and Naquin and Yu 1992. Eickelman (1976) also has material on pilgrimage. Some recent articles dealing with pilgrimage include Bax 1992; Bilu 1988; Cohen 1992; Crain 1992; Delaney 1990; Eade 1992; Gross 1971; Hudman and Jackson 1992; Jackowski and Smith 1992; McDonnell 1990; Marx 1977; Mernissi 1977; Metcalf 1990; Murphy 1993, 1994; Nissan 1988; Pfaffenberger 1979; Sallnow 1981; Sax 1990; Sered 1986; Vukonić 1992; and Weingrod 1990. Perhaps the heaviest anthropological coverage of pilgrimage has occurred in India (see Gold 1988 for a bibliography; see also Morinis 1984), which has also provided some of the exceptions to my statement on the dearth of earlier anthropological works on pilgrimage. On contemporary Greek Orthodox pilgrimage, the only anthropological work of which I am aware is my own (Dubisch 1988, 1990a), although Bowman (1991) discusses Greek Orthodox as one of several groups of pilgrims who visit the holy city and Chryssanthopoulou (1985) has examined Greek pilgrims from Australia who visit the holy land.

2. Medjugorje was featured in *Life,* July 1991, in an article titled "Do You Believe in Miracles?" For anthropological articles on Medjugorje, see Bax 1992; Vukonić 1992. On the effect of improved means of transportation on Muslim pilgrims from Malaysia, see McDonnell 1990.

3. Some examples of pilgrimage sites not marked by sacred structures such as churches are the Ganges, Irish sacred wells, and Medjugorje (where the appari-

tion site is marked only by a pile of rocks and a cross, though there is a church nearby).

4. In effect, the people of Tinos *live* in a sacred space. One local publication calls Tinos "the sacred heart of the Cyclades."

5. This would apply, of course, only to religious pilgrimage. The topic of secular pilgrimage is considerably less explored, though some have argued that the division between the two should not be sharply drawn (see Delaney 1990). Tourism has also been considered as a kind of pilgrimage by Turner and others; see, e.g., the special issue of the *Annals of Tourism Research* on pilgrimage and tourism (1992:19).

6. See chapter 11 for a discussion of this shrine.

7. This may be one reason why pilgrimage has been less popular in Protestantism, where it has tended to be a metaphorical rather than a physical journey. For a discussion of another kind of Catholic devotion, in which petitions are mailed to a shrine instead of carried there, see Orsi 1991.

8. Other studies of pilgrims within particular communities include Sallnow 1987; Sax 1990, 1991.

9. Other studies of pilgrimage sites include Eickelman 1976; Gross 1971.

10. Other studies of pilgrimage networks include Bhardwaj 1973; Cohn and Marriott 1958; Nolan and Nolan 1989. See Morinis 1984 for a discussion of typologies of pilgrimage sites. For a discussion of the complexity of pilgrimage sites and the problems facing anthropologists studying them, see Preston 1992.

11. Turner distinguishes three kinds of communitas: (1) existential or spontaneous communitas; (2) normative communitas, in which the needs of a social group to mobilize and organize in order to preserve an original feeling of fellowship lead to a more enduring social group; and (3) ideological communitas, which characterizes, for example, utopian societies. Turner suggests that while the pilgrimage situation fosters an existential communitas, normative communitas is the characteristic social bond among pilgrims (1974:169), especially when the pilgrimage journey involves large numbers of people traveling great distances (as in some of the classical medieval pilgrimages).

12. Even the pilgrimage to Mecca, one of the five pillars of Islam, is undertaken at the initiative of the pilgrim, and only if the pilgrim is able to afford the journey.

13. Some perhaps overstate Turner's arguments in the course of critiquing them. Turner does not say that all hierarchies are necessarily abolished, but rather that they have the "sting" taken out of them.

14. For a general critique of anthropological approaches to pilgrimage, see Morinis 1984.

15. Gold's (1988) work on Rajasthani pilgrims is an excellent presentation of the variety of motivations for and interpretations of pilgrimage found even among those from the same village and religious tradition.

16. For a critique of kinship, see D. Schneider 1984; see also Collier and Yanagisako 1987. On the concept of gender, see Bordo 1990.

17. On Muslim travel generally, see Eikelman and Piscatori, 1990.

18. There is a term in Greek for "pilgrim"—*hatzís*—but it refers to a pilgrim to the Holy Land.

19. Or at least Orthodoxy is the marked category when Christianity is viewed from the West. The *Oxford Encyclopedia of Christianity,* for example, includes a separate chapter on Eastern Orthodox churches. Compare also Eade and Sallnow's *Contesting the Sacred: The Anthropology of Christian Pilgrimage,* which, aside from Bowman's article, has no discussion of Orthodox pilgrimage.

20. Two exceptions are the articles by Bowman (1991) and Chryssantho-poulou (1985), mentioned in note 1 of this chapter. In addition, Sandin (1993) has explored Byzantine pilgrimage as expressed in museum objects.

21. An exception here seems to be pilgrimage to Jerusalem; see note 1 of this chapter.

22. Herzfeld (1982, 1987a) conceptualizes this as a split between the "Ro-meic" and "Hellenic" notions of Greekness. This is discussed further in chapter 9. Marginality might be seen as characteristic of the Mediterranean generally, a region often viewed as "a liminal zone between the situational ethics of exotic peoples and the ordered morality of European culture" (Herzfeld 1987a:130; see also Sant Cassia 1992).

CHAPTER FOUR

1. Much of the description of the incident that follows was first published in Dubisch 1990a.

2. I learned later that his name was John Demos, and he eventually produced a pictorial of pilgrimage to Tinos that appeared in *Ena* magazine (August 11, 1988).

3. It has been my observation that Greek audiences seldom are.

4. These are common forms of expression. A busy waiter, for example, when summoned to a diner's table, will reply *Éftasa* (I have arrived) as he hurries off in the other direction.

5. This may seem overly sensitive, but conversations with pilgrims frequently resulted in exchanges of information when they learned I was a foreigner, and in the situation I am describing, I did not wish to have my attention drawn away from the drama before me.

6. For similar accounts of the devil afforded his opportunity, see Hart 1992:107; see also Stewart 1991.

7. This is for safety, I was told by a church employee, even though the church also has an alarm system. It is a practice supposedly instituted some years ago after an attempt to steal the icon.

8. One of the few earlier works to deal with this aspect of Greek life was Blum and Blum 1970. For a more recent work, see Charles Stewart's *Demons and the Devil* (1991). Danforth's book (1989) on the Anastenaria focuses on the dynamics of ritual and its role in healing.

9. I am often asked by people here in the States whether or not I actually witnessed any miracles at Tinos. This is the only one. On "possession catharsis," see Tentori 1982:110–11.

10. It was a much more commonly cited reason for pilgrimage in nineteenth-century accounts I have read (e.g., Pirgos 1865). Although it still occurs, I suspect other diagnoses (for example, epilepsy, retardation) have replaced it to some ex-

tent in the accounts of miracles given in church literature, though belief in possession still exists, as evidenced by the incident described here and by personal communications I have had from other anthropologists working in Greece (see also
Hart 1992; Stewart 1991).

11. It was presented at the 1986 American Anthropological Association meeting in Philadelphia, in a session organized by Ellen Badone.

12. Among such works are Campbell 1964; Caraveli 1986; du Boulay 1974,
1986; Hart 1992; Just 1988; Kenna 1977; Machin 1983; Rushton 1983; Seremetakis 1990, 1991.

13. Not all comparisons are neutral, however. Orthodox islanders told me that
while they have the Holy Trinity, the Catholics have "four"—father, son, holy
spirit, *and* the pope—a comparison meant negatively. Catholics were also looked
down on for presumably having large families.

14. What proved unexpectedly confusing, however, was the fact that the word
for "Jew" in Greek—*Evraíos*—is also the word for "Israeli" in popular usage.
(The official term is *israilitis*.) "You're *Evrai?*" people would say. "But we thought
you were Americans!"

15. I faced a reversal of this attitude in the United States, and especially in the
South, where I discovered that many Protestants did not consider Catholics to be
Christians. Those of the Greek Orthodox faith were so unknown as to hardly be
considered at all, and when I attended a tour of the Greek Orthodox church in
Charlotte, North Carolina, during the annual Greek festival, the guide was at
pains to explain to his audience that not only were members of the Greek Orthodox faith Christians, they were the *first* Christians.

16. There once were more members of non-Orthodox faiths in Greece.
Thessaloniki, for example, had a large Sephardic Jewish population, and there
were Jewish populations in other towns and cities of Greece. Large numbers of
Jews were deported during the Nazi occupation, and very few returned to Greece.

17. For example, I attended a private showing by an Athenian artist in his
home of a recently completed set of paintings, all of which drew their inspiration
from the crucifixion. The friend who had brought me, an outspoken critic of
Orthodox religion and of the church, was nonetheless impressed by the artist's
presentation and his work (cf. Faubion 1994).

18. On the role of liturgy in this practice, see Hart 1992:93–99.

19. On village festivals, see Bennett 1988; Gearing 1968.

20. Nowadays children's birthdays will be celebrated, but I have yet to encounter this practice with adults.

21. A man's name day, at least in the village context, tended to be more of a
public event than a woman's. Whereas a man would preside over the table, dis-
pensing food and drink to those who came to call, a woman celebrating her name
day usually received guests more informally, her female friends visiting her in the
kitchen. Another interesting feature of name days (as opposed to birthdays) is that
one treats one's friends on such days, instead of the other way around.

22. I have encountered other versions of this story. In one, the villagers were
fleeing from pirates (though these were not always different from Turks; see chapter 7).

23. On the layout of the church and its symbolism, see Hart 1992.

24. Icons may be covered with gold and/or silver, the precious metals overlaying the painting itself. Faces and hands, however, are always left uncovered.

25. Children are formally taught the distinction, however, in religious training in school.

26. The empress Theodora reportedly used to sit for hours talking to the icons housed in a special chamber of the palace (Başğmez 1989:12).

27. This story is taken from a series on folklore published in a local newspaper, O Fáros tis Tínou (The Lighthouse of Tinos), nos. 133–34 (August 1971).

28. Because pilgrims draw information from the media and from pamphlets circulated by the church, and because officials who recount these miracles to pilgrims also draw on the same sources, it is difficult, if not impossible, to separate oral from written tradition.

29. Most discussions of the saints in Greek Orthodoxy focus on icons. Not as much attention has been given relics in Orthodox devotion. Though playing a lesser role than in the Catholic church, relics are found in Orthodox tradition as well. Meinardus (1970) records relics of 475 saints located in various Greek Orthodox churches. Remains of saints are found in several major pilgrimage sites in contemporary Greece, including the shrines of St. Rafaíl (Lesvos) and St. Nektarios (Aegina), as well as in the church of St. Pelayia on Tinos (see chapter 8). For a general discussion of relics and the development of the cult of the saints in Christianity, see P. Brown 1981. On the body, saints, and the sacred, see Bynum 1987, especially p. 255.

30. In small communities, for example, morality is generally less defined by what one does than by whether or not others find out about it (see, e.g., du Boulay 1986:406; see also Dubisch 1993).

CHAPTER FIVE

1. Although a villager might say that she or he had gone to the church *na proskiníso* (to make my devotions), I am excluding this sort of religious visit from the category of pilgrimage.

2. I would not necessarily include the Gypsies among those who suffer hardship. Even though they camp out, they are equipped to do so, with tents and trucks and even well-outfitted vans.

3. For a description of how rough the journey used to be, see Hamilton 1910.

4. It is not clear when the focus of pilgrimage began to shift to August 15 (though March 25 continues to an important occasion of pilgrimage).

5. While Tinos is my main point of reference here, much of what I describe would apply generally to pilgrimage at other sites in Greece as well. On Lesvos, for example, people may walk long distances to various churches there, such as St. Rafaíl, as part of a vow or pilgrimage.

6. Several people told me that a *lambádha* should be at least the height of the person on whose behalf they are offered, though I found no agreement on this point.

7. I was told by a woman at the tourist bureau that periodically the church tries to clamp down on topless bathing. Given the island's economic dependence on tourism, however, there is a reluctance to antagonize or discourage tourists

(especially since nude bathing is found on nearby islands, to which tourists could easily go). This split between Tinos as a vacation/tourist site and a holy place of pilgrimage is one that has emerged relatively recently. When I first did research there, tourism was too minimal to have much economic impact.

8. This practice is found elsewhere as well, especially at monasteries, where a variety of appropriate clothing is kept just inside the church precincts to be donned by the unprepared visitor.

9. Turner and Turner (1978) point out that very bad sinners may have special difficulty on their pilgrimage journey.

10. Holy days begin at sundown on the eve before the day itself.

11. On the "domestication" of religious space in Greece, see Dubisch 1994.

12. While in the eyes of pilgrims no distinction may be made—sightseeing is part of the whole religious excursion—some townspeople remarked to me that many people nowadays are not really serious pilgrims but come only for vacation.

13. There are very few local products and most of the objects offered for sale are manufactured elsewhere in Greece, or imported.

14. As described by Turner and Turner (1978:25) and found, for example, in Spain (Crain 1992; Murphy 1993, 1994), Italy (Tentori 1982), Brazil (Gross 1971), and elsewhere.

15. An employee at the church complained to me that Gypsies took up all the free rooms there, even though they could afford to stay elsewhere, and kept out the poorer people who needed the rooms more. His view reflected the common local perception of the Gypsies.

16. Rooms for pilgrims are also found at other shrines. More well-to-do pilgrims as well as the poor may occupy such rooms, especially at shrines (such as Aylos Rafaíl on Lesvos) that have no commercial lodging nearby. Staying at the shrine itself also has a spiritual value. On class and ethnic differences among pilgrims, see Kendall 1991.

17. August 15 is a major holiday in Greece, much like the Fourth of July in the United States. And like the Fourth of July, for many people it marks the beginning of the vacation season, which lasts through September.

18. These are saints who were martyred by the Turks and whose bones were discovered only relatively recently. For an account of these saints and the church, see Cavarnos 1977.

19. This does not mean, however, that the church does not seek to exercise any control over pilgrimage, or to shape the meaning of the church as an Orthodox and patriotic shrine (see chapter 9).

20. Segregation by gender is the norm in village churches: men on the right or in the front, women on the left or in back, an order followed at all services except weddings and baptisms, when men and women mingle around the couple or at the baptismal font. No such segregation is observed during pilgrimage at the Church of the Annunciation, however. Although the high-backed seats along the walls are labeled, respectively, "for men" and "for women," men and women move around and sit indiscriminately, ignoring the signs.

21. The church does play an important local role, however.

22. Her saint's day celebrates the day when she had the vision of the Panayía, which led to the finding of the miraculous icon (see chapter 8). Pelayia was can-

onized in 1973, but even before she became a saint this day was celebrated at Tinos with the much same ceremonies that occur now.

23. The procession up the mountain now seems to be done by car, bus, and taxi, as I discovered when I went to join the procession in 1988.

24. Most of the offerings of any value are sold by the church.

25. The term *afyerómata* may be applied to the plaques as well, though this usage is not common among pilgrims but tends more to be the "official" usage of the church.

26. On patron saints, see P. Brown 1982; Christian 1981. On saints and vows, see Di Bella 1992.

27. On patronage in Greece, see Campbell 1964.

28. My landlady was Catholic, but this view of the world, and the practice of building churches, does not seem to differ much between Catholic and Orthodox, at least on Tinos.

29. The crowns are used in the wedding ceremony and are often framed and placed with the household icons (see Dubisch 1986b). They can serve as a metonym for the wedding itself (e.g., "they were crowned").

30. One might ask here whether in so doing they both represent and reproduce the burden of their own oppression.

31. Black has now become a fashionable color, especially among urbanites, and is not associated with mourning.

32. On the symbolism black/death and white/resurrection in Greek mourning and ritual, see Danforth 1982.

33. While this is an excessively long time to wait for a baptism, it is not uncommon in Greece for baptisms to be delayed until a child is several years old (see Hart 1992:124).

34. Blum and Blum recount a story from the mainland community where they worked about a vow undone by lack of faith. A woman whose children had all died promised the Panayía at Tinos that if she had a child who lived for a year, she would give that child to the Panayía, taking it to Tinos and throwing it from the bell tower. When her request was granted, she went to Tinos to fulfill her vow. But when she threw the child from the bell tower, it landed unharmed. Another woman, hearing of this miracle, made the same vow, and her request was also granted. But when she went to Tinos, she didn't really believe the story and so threw a bottle from the bell tower first. Seeing that the bottle did not break, she then threw the child. The child was killed when it hit the ground (Blum and Blum 1970:45–46).

35. Pilgrims are not, however, getting some of the original dirt from the field. As the attendant explained, since so many pilgrims have taken a sample of this dirt, the original field has been long gone.

36. A young couple visiting the monastery while I was there were upset to learn from one of the nuns that the *philactá* they had purchased in town, which the shopkeeper had assured them were made by the nuns, had been misrepresented. The only place that the genuine item was sold, the nun told them, was at the monastery itself. (However, I knew a woman in the village who made *philactá* for the monastery, so they were not all made by the nuns.)

37. The Australian girl mentioned earlier, whose vowed baptism was post-

poned for so many years, was in a specially liminal state, not having even been baptized.

38. I later realized what was going on here after I heard a paper by Renée Hirschon on the subject of promises in Greek in which she suggested that a promise was a statement of intent or sincere desire rather than a commitment to a specific action, as it would be to an English speaker (see Hirschon 1992).

39. This seems to be a new practice in the island villages; it taps into the growing affluence and the increasing number of urban visitors who come to the island and wish to find "authentic" village entertainment. The greater number of privately owned vehicles (rare even among Athenians when I first did fieldwork) is another sign of such affluence.

40. It should be emphasized, however, that alcohol is not the focus of, or required for, *kéfi* (see Cowan 1990:107).

41. On the concept of *gléndi*, see Caraveli 1985; Kavouras 1992.

42. On the concept of the *kséni*, see Dubisch 1993.

CHAPTER SIX

1. There are also occasions during the winter then pilgrimage is heavy, particularly on January 30, when the discovery of the icon is celebrated, and on March 25, the Day of the Annunciation.

2. There is no airport on Tinos, as there is on some of the other Cycladic islands (including nearby Mykonos), although helicopters sometimes are used in emergencies or to bring important visitors.

3. Pilgrims often head directly for the ticket offices of the various shipping lines when they disembark. They cannot buy a round-trip ticket for the boat trip, hence a return ticket must be purchased on the island. This seems to be a general practice throughout Greece, and certainly keeps island ticket offices in business.

4. I was not simply being naive in trying to use photography as a fieldwork technique. I had based my approach on earlier experiences. When I had first attended the festivities at the church during fieldwork in 1969–70, pilgrims were not so suspicious and taking photographs had proved a good means of initiating conversations.

5. I felt much more comfortable, and was able to have more in-depth interviews, when I visited people in a mainland village who had gone to Tinos. Since I was introduced to village families by an anthropologist who had worked there for many years, I did not have the problem of being a "stranger," and in the familiar setting of their own homes they were willing to talk to me at length.

6. Gold reports a similar problem in her study of pilgrimage in India, and states that she felt more comfortable in private settings among those she knew than in public contexts with strangers (1988, especially pp. 18–22). Since her study was village based, however, rather than conducted at a specific pilgrimage site, the constant approaches to strangers that my own work required were not necessary for her.

7. Pavlos Kavouras, a Greek anthropologist, has told me that on the island of Karpathos where he worked people do not see a contradiction between celebrating a saint's day religiously and getting drunk. Getting drunk is part of the *gléndi*

and continuous with the religious feeling, and if the saint is really a saint (*an ín o áyios áyios*), he will understand (personal communication 1993). For a discussion of the relationship between tourism and pilgrimage, see the special volume of the *Annals of Tourism Research* (1992), vol. 10.

8. I have discussed some of the reasons for this oversight in Dubisch 1988, and it is also addressed in chapter 9.

9. Teaching is an element that seldom enters into anthropologists' discussions about their field, yet it is an experience that most of us share, to some extent at least. It seems almost as if teaching takes place in some separate compartment of our lives and minds, neither influenced by nor influencing the rest of what we do. In fact, this cannot be true, but only rarely does teaching as experience enter into more general writing about anthropology. (For two exceptions, see R. Rosaldo 1989; Turner 1979.)

10. Although it took a different (and more publicly commented upon form), Gold's (1988) dilemma regarding what sort of dress to wear in the Rajasthani village where she worked bears certain similarities to the situation I have described here.

11. On the occasion of an anthropology conference in Mitilini in 1986 in which the participants were taken on a tour of a monastery, I noted that other non-Greek (British and American) anthropologists had arrived at the same solution that I had. An Athenian friend informs me that some Athenians have adopted the same pattern of ritual, and for some of the same reasons as these foreigners (that is, because of discomfort with such rituals as kissing the icon).

12. The significance of performing such an act was reflected for me in the attitudes of church caretakers, especially in areas with heavy tourism. They would sometimes regard me with a hostile or indifferent eye when I entered the church, but this attitude would change once I had performed this minimal ritual.

13. Incense is used outside the church as well. For example, incense may be burned along the route taken by icons in procession.

14. Although writing is taken to be the characteristic activity of the anthropologist in the field, photography is significant for many of us as well, though little has been written about it (aside from works on ethnographic filmmaking, which is not normally part of fieldwork).

15. On death practices in Greece, see Alexiou 1974; Danforth and Tsiaras 1982; Caraveli 1980, 1986; Dubisch 1989; Kenna 1976; Seremetakis 1991. Death practices have also been an important topic of investigation for folklorists and may be seen as a distinctive feature of local identity. The caretaker at the town cemetery in Tinos, for example, explained to me that burial in vaults, with disinterment of the remains after three years, was a special custom of the island (though similar practices are found elsewhere in Greece).

16. The significance of these changes is discussed in Dubisch 1989.

17. Ruth Behar (1987) has described a similar set of experiences and feelings about death connected with the community where she worked in Spain.

18. These sites included the church of Taksiarhis and the recently developed pilgrimage site of St. Rafaíl on Mitilini and St. Nektarios on the island of Aegina.

19. See Kondo 1990 for a discussion of these issues. She also gives an excellent

description of how she began to feel her own identity threatened as she became increasingly competent in Japanese culture.

20. One of the reasons for using initials (in addition to providing a form of shorthand for my notes) was that my earlier research took place during the period of the military junta. Especially when I wrote notes about political opinions or other sensitive issues, I did not want to associate them with individual names.

21. Recently the issue of fieldnotes has received a certain amount of attention; see Sanjek 1990; M. Wolf 1992. As M. Wolf (1992) and Lutkehaus (1990) point out, fieldnotes have a different meaning for someone reading them without their context than they do for someone who has "been there."

22. Although it was maintained at the University of Chicago that "one can't teach fieldwork," somehow I *learned* certain things about it, despite not being taught.

23. Works such as Sanjek 1990 are making the process of writing fieldnotes a more carefully examined activity.

24. The time between event and writing was not as long as this might suggest, since I began work on this book in 1988.

25. I do not mean to imply, however, that fieldnotes play no role at all in the final written product. They are, after all, "the first ordering of 'what we know'" (M. Wolf 1992:91; see also Ottenberg 1990). And certainly fieldnotes are an important check on memory (M. Wolf 1992:87).

CHAPTER SEVEN

1. Most migrants from the Cyclades have gone to Athens rather than abroad (see Kolodny 1974; on Tinos, see Dubisch 1972; on migration elsewhere in the Cyclades, see Kenna 1977).

2. Greek census figures must be used cautiously. Individuals are listed as living where they are registered to vote, and since many migrants continue to stay registered in their community of origin (returning to their home communities on election day), census figures often do not give an accurate idea of the population actually resident at a particular site. In addition, the idea that an individual or family has a single place or permanent residence may be misleading. A number of people from Tinos, for example, lived on the island in the summer and in Athens during the slack winter season, maintaining residences in both places.

3. For discussions of tourism on several Greek islands, see Kenna 1993; Kousis 1989; Loukissas 1982; Galani-Moutafi 1993; Stott 1973, 1979, 1985.

4. Most of the civil servants, including police, are not from Tinos.

5. The Naxos temple of Apollo was formerly thought to be a temple of Dionysios.

6. Recently, AIDS has had a significant impact on the atmosphere at Mykonos. For many Tinians, Mykonos provides a counterpoint to their own island, its "dirtiness" contrasting with the holiness of Tinos and its icon.

7. Some of the ancient ruins can be seen at Kionia today, not far from the resort hotel, the Tinos Beach.

8. Another important Cycladic church, dedicated to the Dormition, is the Church of the Hundred Gates (*Ekatotapilianis*) on the island of Paros. Its found-

ing is attributed to the empress Helena, who stopped at Paros on her way to Jerusalem and had a vision there of the finding of the cross. The building of the church was carried out later by Justianian in accordance with Helena's will (see Frazee 1988:6; Hasluck and Jewell 1920; Mavros 1969). The church is still a major pilgrimage site on August 15, though increasingly it has had to compete with Tinos for this event (even though, as the caretaker at the church on Paros informed me indignantly, the holy day of the church at Tinos is supposed to be March 25, not August 15).

9. Some traces of these fortifications can still be seen in a few of the island villages (see Kharitonidou 1984). Today most houses and walls are whitewashed.

10. By the end of the thirteenth century the fortified islands of the Cyclades included Andros, Tinos, Mykonos, Kea, Syros, Paros, Antiparos, Ios, Sifnos, and Milos (Frazee 1988:34).

11. For a discussion of the social organization of Cycladic island society under Latin rule, see Slot 1982.

12. One of the governors of Tinos and Mykonos during this period, Zanachi Quirini, already owned his own island and tried to put into action a plan to move the inhabitants of his two new islands there, a plan that was quashed by the Venetian senate, which made Quirini return the immigrants to their homeland. Quirini's term ended in 1417.

13. The distinctive cut-stone fanlights over windows and doors on Tinian houses were apparently once a utilitarian as well as a decorative feature, letting in light for silkworms, which were raised in the main living room (*sála;* see Kharitonidou 1984). Such fanlights are now viewed as a significant part of island vernacular architecture, often reproduced in new buildings that seek to recreate a "traditional" island style. Although the growing of silk is no longer practiced, the island still has a number of mulberry trees surviving from the time when their leaves were used to feed the silkworms.

14. Some plausibility is lent to the notion that treachery was involved by the fact that the Venetian commander was put on trial in Venice when he returned.

15. Slot gives the following population estimates for Tinos, derived from various sources: 18,000 in 1637, 7,548 in 1650–60, 12,000 in 1667, and 16,411 in 1828 (1982:264).

16. For example, Dhorizas 1976, 1981; A. Lagouros 1965.

17. For an example of an alternative history constructed by women, see Seremetakis 1991.

CHAPTER EIGHT

1. The Life-giving Well is associated with the Panayía, and chapels and churches with this dedication are common in Greece.

2. Some of these "strangers" or foreigners may have been refugees from places such as Chios, where they had fled the Turks.

3. Greeks may speak of "having letters" (*grámmata*), thus presenting literacy as a kind of possession, something one can "own," just as we might speak of "having power." Such a possession confers (in some Greek contexts at least; see

Herzfeld 1987a:38–39) a superior status on the possessor, who has access to a wider world of power than does the individual who lacks "letters."

4. Thus there is a wonderful irony in the title *The Last Word*, Seremetakis's book on women and lamenting in Inner Mani. Here "the last word" is the spoken one, and spoken by women, the "muted" group.

5. Tyler writes of "the issue of power as symbolized in the subject-object relationship between he who represents and she who is represented" (1986:127). In Greece women may symbolically represent the illiterate other. "We women are illiterate," Greek villagers told Friedl (1962; cf. Herzfeld 1986).

6. It is difficult to say at this point to what extent I have developed such an approach because I am an anthropologist and to what extent I became an anthropologist because of a tendency to see things in this way.

7. On the ways different histories are interpreted, see Gable, Handler, and Lawson 1992:802–3.

8. It should be kept in mind, however, that my own authority (and that of many other English-speaking scholars) would be undermined were we to write in Greek and make similar errors (as I, for one, would undoubtedly do).

9. The Greek version of the church pamphlet does mention that when an old man named Polizois, who had had an earlier vision of the Panayía, went to try to excavate the icon in Dhoksaras's field, he found a stone wall. After the effort at discovery was abandoned by Polizois and his friends, Dhoksaras decided to build an oven with the rocks, but to his amazement and that of the builders, the limestone would not adhere to the rocks and when construction was attempted, something hurled the rocks to the ground.

10. In the English version of the church pamphlet, the past tense is used for the account of the finding of the icon and for subsequent events. An exception is the account of an incident in which the icon was stolen, which, after beginning in the past tense, slips into the present tense as it describes the actual snatching of the sacred object from the church. On the use of the present tense by anthropologists recounting myths, see Davis 1992:19; for a more general discussion of tense in ethnography, see Davis 1992b.

11. It is, of course, very postmodern to play with language; see Tyler 1986. For a discussion of elitism in postmodern writing, see Abu-Lughod 1991.

12. On this issue with respect to the writings of folklorists, see Herzfeld 1982.

13. For a discussion of Greek nuns and their use of metaphors of kinship and family, see Iossifides 1991.

14. Greek parish priests are allowed to marry, a custom several nineteenth-century Protestants remarked upon favorably (e.g., Durban 1897).

15. There seems, however, to have been at least one "secret school" on Tinos, located in a village near the site of my original fieldwork. Such schools were established during the period of Turkish occupation.

16. The same author offers another version of the monastery's origins: the first monastery was not built where it is now but at another site below. One evening when the workers quit for the day, they left their tools at the site. When they returned in the morning, the tools were gone. They started to look for them, and the place they eventually found them is where the monastery is today. Thus they understood that it was necessary to build it there (Amirolis 1972). It should be

noted that the recorder of these stories views them as folklore. They are part of a newspaper series on the traditions (*parádosis*) of Tinos, a series in which such stories are often recounted in the local dialect. Note also the similarity to stories of icons' and saints' assertion of their will in chapter 4.

17. On the monastery, see Kardhamitsis 1987; Protopapas 1984.

18. James Theodore Bent (1965), in his travels to Tinos in the late nineteenth century, noted one hundred nuns.

19. That Pelayia should be buried in such a sacred place suggests her considerable holiness and her removal from the ordinary gendered world, since the altar is normally a male space.

20. The idea of the "sweet odor" of sanctity is found in the Catholic tradition as well, often with respect to saint's bodies, which do not decompose and give off only sweet smells.

21. An account in O *Fáros tis Tínou* (August 1971, no. 133) notes the importance of the first celebration of Pelayia's saint's day in 1971, an event reported in the Athens newspapers and attended by the archbishop of Athens. According to O *Fáros*, the event united the people of the island as well as the thousands of tourists who came. Editions of the paper preceding the event carried stories of the life of Pelayia.

22. There is a female biographer of Pelayia who has presented her story in fictionalized form (Karita n.d.).

23. On ideas of time in connection with the church and pilgrimage, see Dubisch 1991d.

CHAPTER NINE

1. Some of the material presented in this section of the chapter originally appeared in Dubisch 1988.

2. The textual metaphor, however, was suggested even earlier by Clifford Geertz, describing his view of what the anthropologist does: "Doing ethnography is like trying to read . . . a manuscript—foreign, faded, full of ellipses, incoherencies, suspicious emendations, and tendentious commentaries . . . written in transient examples of shaped behavior" (1973:10).

3. As Crapanzano points out, however, anthropologists are not simply translators of culture the way a translator is the translator of a written text, but rather must first produce these texts. Moreover, "ethnography is historically determined by the moment of the ethnographer's encounter with whomever he [*sic*] is studying" (1986:51). Or, shifting the metaphor, if studying a culture is like reading a text over the "native's" shoulder (to use Geertz's image), then Crapanzano reminds us that the ethnographer inevitably casts a shadow over the text (1986:76).

There are a variety of criticisms that can be leveled against the metaphor of culture as text, several of which are discussed in Crapanzano's (1986) article. My own view is that metaphors are to be measured by their utility in expanding our understanding of a subject matter and in stimulating new directions of inquiry. Beyond this, however, I would not want to become mired in ultimately fruitless questions about whether culture "is" text or "is" something else. If my analysis in this chapter is illuminating, to whatever degree, my use of the text metaphor has been worthwhile.

4. Other metaphors that have been used for society or culture include the mechanical, the organic, the linguistic, and the psychological.

5. The ban on breaking plates was continued by the PASOK government, possibly for much the same reasons.

6. The very idea of a "shrine" is one of my own constructions, since no equivalent of this term is used by pilgrims or islanders (see chapters 3 and 4).

7. For a discussion of the architecture of the church, see Dubisch 1994.

8. On Lourdes see Dahlberg 1991; Marnham 1981; on Guadalupe see E. Wolf 1958; Taylor 1987.

9. Some of the villages on Tinos are Catholic and others are Orthodox, while a few are mixed. The main town also is mixed Catholic and Orthodox.

10. The main town of the island is sometimes referred to as St. Nikolaos in travel accounts and guidebooks, but I have never heard the islanders call it by this name. It is simply "the town" (*hóra*).

11. The dual quality of being both divisible and indivisible is an important part of the nature of the Virgin Mary generally (see chapter 11).

12. A Greek anthropologist cautioned me against reading too much into the use of marble from ancient sites in the building of the church, suggesting that such practice is not uncommon and was often a matter of convenience when such places were being built. I would, however, argue that the use of such marble at the Church of the Annunciation, whatever the immediate practical reasons at the time, has taken on symbolic significance. This is reflected both in the presence of a Delian marble lion at the foot of one of the stairways and in the frequent mention in church pamphlets of the use of marble from ancient sites.

13. This is by no means the only Orthodox icon attributed to Luke. Dhimitra-kopoulos (1971), for example, describes a number of icons of the Panayía that are said to have been painted by Luke. A seventeenth-century icon in the Byzantine Museum in Athens shows Luke painting an icon of the Panayía. While some sources attribute only three icons of the Panayía to Luke—Panayía Megaspilotissa in the Peloponnesus, Panayía Soumela in northern Greece, and Panayía Kikkos in Cyprus (see, e.g., Papadopoulos 1962)—the icon of Tinos is sometimes included in such listing as well. Since icons are often copied from other icons, many of them could be said to be descended from originals. (On icons in Greece, see Herzfeld 1990; Kenna 1985; on the "genealogy" of icons, see Danforth 1989.)

14. Note the feminine form here, in the English version, which conveys the identification of "Panayía" and "icon" (both feminine in Greek), as well as the notion of the church as the Panayía's house.

15. Greece is no longer a kingdom; the king was exiled under the junta and the monarchy was later abolished under the Socialist government. The monarchy was not, of course, a direct inheritance from Byzantine times but was established after independence. The Greek royal family was not even Greek by descent but drawn from the royal family of Bavaria (though not all the kings were Bavarian).

16. This conflict centered mainly around the government's plan to place two-thirds of the church's monastic property in the hands of agricultural cooperatives. Among other reactions, this proposal provoked a massive pro-church rally in

Syntagma Square in Athens. For an account of this conflict, and of a local reaction to it, see Herzfeld 1992b.

17. According to Dhaskalaki-Dhoriza (1982), Tinos had about two thousand dead and wounded from the conflict.

18. A stimulus to my rethinking the Church of the Annunciation came from folklorist and anthropologist Anna Caraveli, who told me that when she was in school in Greece, the Church of the Annunciation had been presented in her textbooks as one of the wonders of Greece. This national and nationalistic emphasis on the church contrasted with the lack of attention to such phenomena by foreigners.

19. An oral version of the story I heard places the man in California, certainly a likely place for him to have seen an orange tree.

20. Such stories may also represent a time when those of different faiths worshiped at one another's shrines, unhampered by notions of nationalistic religious purity.

21. It is important to emphasize that I am not suggesting that these accounts were fabricated in order to make such points. Rather, I am interested in why certain accounts of miracles tend to be more emphasized than others, in both written and oral traditions. As Hastrup puts it, "The story of the past is . . . a selective account of the actual sequence of events, but it is no random selection" (1992b:9).

22. One of the *támata* hanging permanently in the church is in the shape of Cyprus, but none of the church attendants could tell me who had left it there or why. The desire for the unity of Greece might also be seen as at least one factor in the large number of Cypriot pilgrims who visit Tinos. Excursion boats from Cyprus stop regularly at Tinos (every week or so, at least during the summer), and passengers disembark and head directly for the church for a few hours' visit before they set sail again. While I do not know all of the ramifications of such visits for these Cypriot pilgrims, I was told by some young Cypriot women that many of the elderly people at home would love to visit Tinos but are too old to make the journey now. It would be interesting to know whether or not Tinos has become a more important symbol for Cypriots since the 1974 invasion by Turkey.

23. It is, however, not always easy for the anthropologist to determine what her or his position is in a particular situation. It is possible to experience a false sense of being inside; see Herzfeld 1983.

24. On the concept of localism or *dopiasmós,* see Bernard 1976.

25. An unexamined aspect of nineteenth-century foreign interest in Greece (echoed faintly here in Bremer's observations) is the notion of Greece as the foundation of the Western Christian tradition (and not just the classical tradition). During the period following the Greek War of Independence there was renewed discussion of the possibility for unification of the Eastern and Western churches (particularly the Church of England), and some searched for evidence of the purity of early Christianity in contemporary Eastern Orthodox (and not just Greek Orthodox) practice. For the most part, those who explored this issue found such evidence to be sadly lacking among the Orthodox peoples of the East (though see Masson 1843). And even those who did manage to see traces of "true

religion" in the beliefs and practices of the Greeks and other Orthodox peoples did not find such traces in ritual activities such as the veneration of icons and saints, which were generally viewed as simply the superstitious practices of the uneducated, hardly better than magic and certainly no better than Catholicism (see, e.g., J. Brown 1877).

26. Being offended by the filth is not confined to foreigners, or to the distant past. A mainland villager to whom I spoke about a trip to Tinos he had made in the early 1970s told me how people were relieving themselves right around the area of the church and what a stink that made. In both cases comments regarding filth might be seen as having a moral dimension, an interpretation strengthened in the latter case by the fact that this informant also told me his wallet had been stolen while he was on pilgrimage at Tinos.

27. Mary Hamilton, during a trip to Tinos in the early 1900s, commented approvingly that "the entire absence of foreigners was remarkable and refreshing. Tenos has not yet undergone the American invasion" (1910:80). Hamilton, like other travelers before her, saw the pilgrimage at Tinos as "one of the most apparent survivals of the ancient Greek religion" (1910:76).

28. Signs in English, French, and Greek posted at both entryways to the inner courtyard of the church notify visitors that proper dress is required, but these signs are sometimes ignored. It should be emphasized that it is not only tourists who are dressed inappropriately. I have also seen a number of Greeks dressed in such a fashion try to enter the church.

29. Western stereotypes may also inhibit the understanding of ancient as well as contemporary Greece. For a different (and controversial) view of ancient Greece, see Bernal 1987.

30. Such tourist images of Greece may also include an affair with a local man (see Dubisch 1991b).

31. It is as difficult to generalize about "foreigners" as it is to generalize about "Greeks." There does however, seem to be a particular category of foreigners (both Europeans and Americans) for whom Greece is simply a place with beaches, sun, and cheap food and wine.

32. Although I have not kept a systematic account of all such responses over the years, it is my impression that the educated Greek women with whom I have spoken have been more likely to consider the study of the church interesting, while the men were more likely to scoff (though there are certainly exceptions to this).

33. John Demos also did some of the photographs for Loring Danforth's (1989) book on the Anastenaria.

34. It is also significant that she used the formal form of "you" (*sas*) in addressing me.

35. This term is usually used in the neuter form (*afendikó*), which is the standard Greek. But I have occasionally heard it used by villagers in the masculine form (*afendikós*). Herzfeld has noticed a similar local use of this form, which he suggests may be "overcompensatory" (personal communication).

36. On the creation of an *anthropologically* significant Greece, see Herzfeld 1987a.

CHAPTER TEN

1. I first described this incident in a paper presented at the 1987 American Ethnological Society meeting in San Antonio,Texas, in a session titled "The Religious Construction of Culture in Europe," organized by Ellen Badone. Many thanks are due to a variety of people for their input during a long series of rewritings, which have resulted in this chapter. Among these helpful individuals were Peter Loizos, Mary Clark, Ray Michalowski, Liz Kennedy, and Susan Philips. The final outcome is, of course, my own responsibility.

2. Among such critiques are Herzfeld 1980, 1987b; Lever 1986; Pina-Cabral 1989.

3. This is clearly illustrated in the title of John Peristiany's early and influential edited volume *Honour and Shame: The Values of Mediterranean Society* (1966).

4. A common term of insult for a man in Greek is to call him a *poústis,* which indicates the passive (that is, womanly) partner in a male homosexual relationship.

5. In certain circumstances a woman can assume the role of a man without losing honor (Mandel 1983).

6. For a further discussion of this, see Dubisch 1986a. It must be kept in mind that at the period I am speaking of here, the "women's movement" was in its infancy and I lacked the language to speak of my experience, a language I am now able to employ.

7. Most of my work on gender did not directly challenge the "honor and shame" construct but instead sidestepped the issue, approaching gender from other avenues (see, e.g., Dubisch 1986a). Similarly, Friedl (1967) wrote about public and private and appearance and reality but did not use the framework of honor and shame for her analysis. And Giovannini (1981, 1987) has written about chastity codes in an Italian community without recourse to the term *honor.*

8. Also, as Pina-Cabral (1989) has pointed out, anthropologists studying "the Mediterranean" generally went to remote villages, where the differences between the Mediterranean and the rest of Europe would seem most pronounced. Compare Pandian's (1985) discussion of anthropology's search for the "other." It is a little disconcerting to realize that we are perhaps not as far from the late nineteenth-century evolutionists in this respect as we would like to think.

9. On this subject, see Dubisch 1986b. Some of the material from this section is also in Dubisch 1993.

10. This was not the first time, however, that I had noticed such dramatic elements. In other instances, the speaker may deliberately create an "audience" by drawing bystanders into the performance. This is sometimes used in disciplining children, when nearby adults may be called on to witness misbehavior or even to administer punishment.

11. See also Valentine 1992.

12. Pina-Cabral (1989) is among those who have criticized Gilmore's ideas, pointing out that the features of boyhood socialization he describes are hardly unique to the Mediterranean.

13. Herzfeld sees "poetics" as related to, but less restricted than, the notion of "performance" (1991a:81).

14. Overlooking what women do is hardly unique to anthropology, of course. A recent newspaper article reported that scientists have underestimated the amount of daily activity in which women typically engage. Questionnaires that focus on exercise and sports do not reveal the extent to which women may actually engage in more steady, moderate aerobic activity than men through housework and other chores (*Arizona Republic,* May 3, 1994).

15. I am indebted to Akis Papataxiarchis (personal communication) for this observation.

16. This is changing as more women, and especially younger women, become interested in style and personal beautification. For an excellent discussion of changing (and sometimes contested) definitions of female personhood, see Cowan 1990, 1991.

17. See, e.g., Dubisch 1986b; Hirschon 1978; Rushton 1983; Seremetakis 1990, 1991.

18. Compare Collier's (1986) discussion of mourning in a Spanish village.

19. A child eating draws approving looks and comments from passers-by, as I experienced myself one time when I knelt down in the street to feed the remains of a pastry to a friend's two-year-old.

20. The importance of women's roles in mourning, however, may be declining in the face of urbanization, "deritualization," and the commodification of death; see Dubisch 1989; Seremetakis 1991.

21. Rushton also emphasizes the idea that Greek village women feel the need for expiation. They are to some extent redeemed in the church as "the Bride of Christ" (1983:67).

22. As explained in chapter 4, however, anticlericalism and lack of church attendance do not necessarily mean that Greek men consider themselves any less Christian than women. In addition, it is unclear whether women's predominance in church attendance is a long-standing or a more recent phenomenon. A late nineteenth-century observer, for example, was struck by "the preponderance of religious *manhood*" in the Eastern Orthodox countries, noting "the magnificent assemblage of men" on Sundays and feast days in Athens and Moscow and commenting that "the women attend in smaller numbers and stay a shorter time" (Durban 1897:101).

23. As with death ritual, women's role in these spheres seems to have declined as handicrafts and homemade products are replaced by manufactured, purchased items (see Pavlides and Hesser 1986).

24. Caraveli (1986) and Seremetakis (1990, 1991) have both examined the role of *pónos* (pain) in connection with mourning and laments. What I have labeled "suffering" here encompasses the notion of *pónos* but also includes other kinds of suffering, such as *stenohoría* (see Danforth 1989). For other writings on the social construction (and social uses) of pain, see Asad 1983; Morinis 1985; Taussig 1987.

25. We can see this distinction clearly in American politics, where the expression of emotions by public figures can ruin political careers.

26. There is not space enough here to discuss suffering in these wider contexts. Greek history—with its emphasis on Turkish oppression and the struggle to

form a Greek nation, the bloody conflicts that resulted, the "Catastrophe" in Asia Minor, the Nazi occupation, and the civil war—is replete with suffering and martyrdom. The National Historical Museum in Athens is a good illustration of these themes, with room after room of paintings and other objects depicting battles, struggle, and death.

27. I have even heard some people say it was better not to have children at all, a comment in apparent contradiction to the supposed high value placed on children and on maternity. Although such comments should be taken seriously, this does not necessarily mean they should be taken literally. Rather I would interpret them as a comment on the difficulties of parenthood as well as a public expression of what one must go through in carrying out the parental role.

28. Again, these expressive elements of mourning have undergone change in many areas. The wearing of black, in particular, and especially of black from head to foot, has been abandoned or modified by many women, especially urbanized ones (cf. Collier 1986).

29. For example John Demos's photographs illustrating an article on pilgrimage to Tinos that appeared in *Ena* magazine (August 1988).

30. The same is generally true in the situations mentioned in note 10 of this chapter, in which I am called upon to witness a child's misbehavior as a shaming mechanism (though in one case my status as a foreigner was exploited when the child was asked if he wanted "auntie" to take him back to America).

31. The one situation in which I have succeeded in impressing people with my own working conditions has been with academics in Greece who are shocked at my teaching load, and further shocked that I sometimes teach classes at eight in the morning.

32. A similar situation occurred one summer on the island of Paros when the boat on which I had booked passage to Athens was canceled and I was told that the next boat was a night one, which would get me into Piraeus early in the morning. Tired from a difficult period of fieldwork and frustrated by the thought of losing a day planned for library research, I burst into tears. The hitherto unsympathetic ticket agent quickly found me an airplane seat (after originally having told me that no tickets were available) and with a smile waved aside my apologies for becoming so emotional. It had taken such an emotional outburst, however, to convince her of my need. (Note also that the outburst was effective in getting me what I wanted!)

33. I have been told that Greek maternity wards are places of bedlam, for Greek women in labor give full voice to their pain. One island woman I knew told me that the doctor assumed she was not in pain during labor because she wasn't screaming. (She told him she was saving her energy for the birth.)

34. Compare Mernissi's (1977) description of Muslim women's pilgrimage.

35. John Demos's photographic essay in the August 1988 issue of *Ena* magazine on pilgrimage to Tinos creates such images.

36. Nicholas Gage (1983), in his controversial book *Eleni*, uses the symbolism of the martyred mother for clear political purposes. The specific political message aside, it is significant that the message was conveyed through a focus on the suffering and eventual death of Gage's mother.

37. On *stenohória*, see Danforth 1989.

38. For a further discussion of "ritual chaos" and "ritual order," see Dubisch 1990a.

39. Turner has suggested that religious leaders may have ambivalent feelings about pilgrimages: "Although operational on a wide scale, pilgrimages have somehow brought features of . . . the 'Little Tradition' into what should have been theologically, liturgically, and indeed, economically controlled by leading representatives of the 'Great Tradition'" (1974:188). For Turner, pilgrimage represents "a kind of institutionalized or symbolic anti-structure" (1974:187).

40. A question by a student after a lecture I delivered to the Department of Social Anthropology at the University of the Aegean on Lesvos in June 1993 seems to represent such an interpretation. The student suggested that the ritual activities performed by pilgrims might be a sort of ironic comment on religion, expressive of lack of faith rather than of strong devotion. I would disagree with such an interpretation, at least as far as most pilgrims are concerned. I think that the student's question itself represented a Westernized view of religion, which sees ritual acts as less real representations of belief than inner faith.

41. I would like to express my gratitude to the Women's Studies Program and the Southwest Institute for the Study of Women at the University of Arizona not only for the Rockefeller Humanities Fellowship (1988–89) that gave me the opportunity to write the original draft of this book, but also for all the stimulation and encouragement provided by many of those associated with the Women's Studies/SIROW program. I would particularly like to thank Susan Philips for her very helpful comments following the feminist study group discussion.

42. It was not uncommon for townspeople to have several businesses. Nikos also worked for a yacht charter company as their island representative, rented rooms, and built houses on contract. The building of houses for Germans represents a relatively recent phenomenon for the island—the building or purchase of houses by foreigners.

43. The boy was a teenager, yet his father was afraid to leave him alone one evening during a thunderstorm. Such protectiveness even of older children is not unusual for Greek mothers. Here the father was being a "mother" in his concern.

44. Divorce is allowed by the Orthodox church, but was not as common in the past as it appears to be now. In this case, my friend was Catholic, so he could only obtain a civil divorce. If he were to remarry, he told me, he would make a civil marriage, an innovation introduced by the Socialist government (PASOK).

45. Seremetakis suggests that, at least in such areas as inner Mani, the binary opposition of women to men (an opposition that informs such constructs as honor and shame) is part of a general series of polarities advanced by modernization theory, polarities that include city/country, past/present, and ritual/science (1991:221).

46. For a good recent analysis of changes in women's roles, especially among young women, see Cowan 1990, 1991.

47. On the various "tellings of tales" and the problems this entails in fieldwork, see Valentine 1992.

CHAPTER ELEVEN

1. Some of the material in this chapter was originally presented in a paper titled "The Virgin Mary and the Body Politic" given at the 1990 joint meeting of the American Ethnological Society and the Southern Anthropological Society in Atlanta, Georgia.

2. I was told by several Greek friends that once the pair had married, their union was viewed positively, especially since Papandreou's American wife, Margaret, was not very popular with the Greek public.

3. For a discussion of the conflict between the church and the Socialist government over the issue of monastic lands, see Herzfeld 1992b.

4. I was told that Mitsotakis's wife also went to Tinos on pilgrimage recently, but I learned this too late to obtain any further information about the visit from people in Tinos.

5. A few exceptions among recent works are Carroll 1986; Christian 1984; Perry and Echeverria 1988; Pope 1985.

6. Perry and Echeverria tie the increasing emphasis on Mary's virginity to concern with establishing clerical celibacy (1988:7–11).

7. For a critique of Carroll's Freudian approach, see Breuner 1992.

8. It is interesting to note the association of the East with a more fervent, emotional strain of religion.

9. From a report by William Scobie in the *Observer Newsletter* 26:VII:1987: 38–39. See also Perry and Echeverria 1988.

10. Ibid.

11. There are other terms for Mary used in the divine liturgy that are not usually found in everyday speech. It is in this context, for example, that the term *Parthéna* is most likely to be heard.

12. The circulation of paper icons, which were inexpensive and issued by the church at Tinos and other sites, may have also been an impetus to devotion at this time; see Papastratos 1990.

13. On the other hand, Machin (1983) warns against seeing the relationship between the Panayía and gender and familial roles in purely materialistic terms.

14. Note the identification of the Panayía and her icon in this account.

15. It is very common for icons to request churches be built in particular places, either through a direct command or by indicating their will through other means. The other events described in such stories are also common, with local variations.

16. All of these examples of newspaper stories are from Florakis 1990.

17. The name *Odhiyítria* is one commonly used for the Panayía.

18. There is an obvious comparison here with Pearl Harbor.

19. Mary herself seems to have recognized the importance of this struggle. As she told a Dutch woman, a seer who had a series of revelations between 1945 and 1959, "This is the era of political Christian warfare" (Christian 1984:245).

20. Such a struggle seems to have taken place over the Panayía Soumela, an icon of special significance to the Pontic Greeks. See Dhimitrakopoulos 1971.

21. Perry and Echeverria (1988) suggest that the Madonna might provide the unifying figure for a future joining of the Eastern and Western churches.

22. However, as mentioned earlier, there were relics of the Madonna (though not bodily ones) in Constantinople, which gave her a special place in that city.

23. The offices of the Communist party, like the offices of the other political parties, were draped with flags and streamers for the fifteenth of August celebrations in Tinos. For a discussion of the politics of interpretation of a local festival, see Cowan 1988.

CHAPTER TWELVE

1. Funding for research during this trip was provided by the a grant from Northern Arizona University.

2. I would like to express my gratitude to both George and Vasiliki for their friendship and hospitality during the two visits I have paid to Mitilini, and to George for including me in the Elderhostel group.

3. I am grateful to the Elderhostel guide, Andromahie Karaniki, for letting me accompany the group on this tour.

4. See, e.g., Abu-Lughod 1990; Cole 1994.

References Cited

Abu-Lughod, Lila
   1986 Veiled Sentiments: Honor and Poetry in Bedouin Society. Berkeley: University of California Press.
   1990 Can There Be a Feminist Ethnography? Women and Performance 5(1):7–27.
   1991 Writing against Culture. *In* Recapturing Anthropology, Richard Fox, ed., pp. 137–62. Santa Fe: School of American Research.
Agar, Michael J.
   1986 Speaking of Ethnography. Beverly Hills, Calif.: Sage Publications.
Agulhon, Maurice
   1985 Politics, Image, and Symbols in Post-Revolutionary France. *In* Rites of Power: Symbolism, Ritual, and Politics Since the Middle-Ages, S. Wilentz, ed. Philadelphia: University of Pennsylvania Press.
Alexiou, Margaret
   1974 The Ritual Lament in Greek Tradition. Cambridge: Cambridge University Press.
Amirolis, G.
   1972 *Paradhósis tis Tínou. O Fáros tis Tínou,* March 1972, no. 139.
Anonymous
   1986 *Perigraphí tis Evreséos tis Thavmatourgóu Ayías Ihónas tis Evangelístrias stin Tíno káta to Étos 1823.* (Pamphlet distributed by the Church of the Annunciation, Tinos.)
Appadurai, Arjun
   1991 Global Ethnoscapes: Notes and Queries from a Transnational Anthropology. *In* Recapturing Anthropology, R. Fox, ed., pp. 191–210. Santa Fe: School of American Research Press.
Ardener, Edwin
   1975 Belief and the Problem of Women. *In* Perceiving Women, S. Ardener, ed., pp. 1–27. London: Malaby Press
Asad, Talal
   1983 Notes on the Body, Pain and Truth in Medieval Christianity. Economy and Society 12(1):287–327.
Babcock, Barbara
   1986 Modeled Selves: Helen Cordero's "Little People." *In* The Anthropology of Experience, V. Turner and E. Bruner, eds., pp. 316–43. Urbana: University of Illinois Press.
Başğmez, Şinasi
   1989 Icons. Virginia Taylor Saçlioğlu, trans. Istanbul: Yapi Kredi Yayinlari.
Bax, Mart
   1992 Female Suffering, Local Power Relations, and Religious Tourism: A Case Study from Yugoslavia. Medical Anthropology Quarterly 6(2):114–27.
Becker, Howard S.
   1986 Writing for Social Scientists. Chicago: University of Chicago Press.

Behar, Ruth
  1987 Death and Memory in Rural Spain. Paper presented at the 86th Annual Meeting of the American Anthropological Association, Chicago.
Benahib, Sylvia, and Drucilla Cornell
  1987 Introduction: Beyond the Politics of Gender. *In* Feminism as Critique, S. Benahib and D. Cornell, eds., pp. 1–15. Minneapolis: University of Minnesota Press.
Bennett, Diane
  1988 Saints and Sweets: Class and Consumption in Rural Greece. *In* The Social Economy of Consumption, H. Rutz and B. Orlove, eds. Lanham, Md.: University Press of America.
Bent, James Theodore
  1965 Aegean Islands: The Cyclades, or Life among the Insular Greeks. Chicago: Argonaut.
Bernal, Martin
  1987 Black Athena: The Afroasiatic Roots of Classical Civilization. Volume 1: The Fabrication of Ancient Greece, 1785–1985. New Brunswick, N.J.: Rutgers University Press.
Bernard, Russell
  1976 Kalymnos: The Island of the Sponge Fishermen. *In* Regional Variation in Modern Greece and Cyprus: Toward a Perspective on the Ethnography of Greece, M. Dimen and E. Friedl, eds., 268:222–31. New York: Annals of the New York Academy of Sciences.
Betteridge, Anne H.
  1985 *Ziarat:* Pilgrimage to the Shrines of Shiraz. Ph.D. dissertation, University of Chicago.
  1992 Specialists in Miraculous Action: Some Shrines in Shiraz. *In* Sacred Journeys: The Anthropology of Pilgrimage, A. Morinis, ed., pp. 189–210. Westport, Conn.: Greenwood Press.
Bhardwaj, Surinder Mohan
  1973 Hindu Places of Pilgrimage in India. Berkeley: University of California Press.
Bilu, Yoram
  1988 The Inner Limits of Communitas: A Covert Dimension of Pilgrimage Experience. Ethos 16(3):302–25.
Birth, Kevin K.
  1990 Reading and the Righting of Ethnographies (review essay). American Ethnologist 17(3):548–57.
Blum, Richard, and Edith Blum
  1970 The Dangerous Hour: The Lore of Crisis and Mystery in Rural Greece. New York: Charles Scribner's Sons.
Boissevain, J.
  1976 Uniformity and Diversity in the Mediterranean: An Essay in Interpretation. *In* Kinship and Modernization, J. G. Peristiany, ed., pp. 1–11. Rome: Center for Mediterranean Studies.
Bordo, Susan
  1990 Feminism, Postmodernism, and Gender Scepticism. *In* Feminism/Postmodernism, L. J. Nicholson, ed., pp. 133–56. New York: Routledge.

Botsis, Peter A.
n.d. What Is Orthodoxy? (A Short Explanation of the Essence of Orthodoxy and of the Differences between the Churches). Athens.

Bourdieu, Pierre
1977 Outline of a Theory of Practice. R. Nice, trans. Cambridge: Cambridge University Press.

Bowman, Glenn
1991 Christian Ideology and the Image of a Holy Land: The Place of Jerusalem Pilgrimage in the Various Christianities. *In* Contesting the Sacred, J. Eade and M. J. Sallnow, eds. pp. 98–112. New York: Routledge.

Brady, Ivan
1991 Harmony and Argument: Bringing Forth the Artful Science. *In* Anthropological Poetics, I. Brady, ed., pp. 3–30. Lanham, Md.: Rowman and Littlefield.

Brandes, Stanley
1987 Reflections on Honor and Shame in the Mediterranean. *In* Honor and Shame and the Unity of the Mediterranean, D. Gilmore, ed., pp. 121–34. American Anthropological Association Special Publication no. 22.

Bremer, Fredericka
1863 Greece and the Greeks: The Narrative of a Winter Residence in Greece and Its Islands. Mary Hewitt, trans. London, 2 vols.

Brettell, Caroline B.
1990 The Priest and His People: The Contractual Basis for Religion in Rural Portugal. *In* Religious Orthodoxy and Popular Faith in Europe, Ellen Badone, ed., pp. 55–75. Princeton: Princeton University Press.

Breuner, Nancy Frey
1992 The Cult of the Virgin Mary in Southern Italy and Spain. Ethos 20:1: 66–95.

Briggs, Jean
1970 Never in Anger. Cambridge, Mass.: Harvard University Press.

Brown, Joseph
1877 Eastern Christianity and the War. The idolatry, superstition, and corruption of the Christians of Turkey, Greece, and Russia, exposed and considered with the present war, and the prospects of a reformation. London: Edward Stanford. (Pamphlet in the Gennadius Library, Athens.)

Brown, Peter
1981 The Cult of the Saints: Its Rise and Function in Latin Christianity. Chicago: University of Chicago Press.

Bruner, Edward
1986 Experience and Its Expressions. *In* The Anthropology of Experience, V. Turner and E. Bruner, eds., pp. 3–32. Urbana: University of Illinois Press.

Buondelmonti, Christoforo
1897 *Description des îles de l'Archipel* . . . Paris: Ernest Leroux. (Publications de l'École des langues orientales. Quartième serie.)

Bynum, Caroline Walker
1987 Holy Feast and Holy Fast: The Religious Significance of Food to Medieval Women. Berkeley: University of California Press.

Callaway, Helen
    1992 Ethnography and Experience: Gender Implications in Fieldwork and
    Text. *In* Anthropology and Autobiography, J. Okely and H. Callaway, eds.,
    pp. 29–49. London: Routledge.
Campbell, J. K.
    1964 Honour, Family and Patronage: A Study of Institutions and Moral Values
    in a Greek Mountain Community. Oxford: Clarendon Press.
    1966 Honour and the Devil. *In* Honour and Shame: The Values of Mediterra-
    nean Society, J. G. Peristiany, ed., pp. 139–70. London: Weidenfield and
    Nicholson.
——— and Phillip Sherrard
    1968 Modern Greece. London: Ernest Benn Ltd.
Caplan, Pat
    1988 Engendering Knowledge: The Politics of Ethnography, parts 1 and 2.
    Anthropology Today 4(5):8–12, 4(6):14–17.
Caraveli, Anna
    1980 Bridge between Worlds: The Women's Ritual Lament as Communicative
    Event. Journal of American Folklore 93:129–57.
    1982 The Song Behind the Song: Aesthetics and Social Interaction in Greek
    Folksong. Journal of American Folklore 93:129–57.
    1985 The Symbolic Village: Community Born in Performance. Journal of
    American Folklore 93:129–57.
    1986 The Bitter Wounding: The Lament as Social Protest in Rural Greece. *In*
    Gender and Power in Rural Greece, J. Dubisch, ed., pp. 169–94. Princeton:
    Princeton University Press.
Carroll, Michael
    1986 The Cult of the Virgin Mary: Psychological Origins. Princeton: Princeton
    University Press.
    1992 Madonnas That Maim: Popular Catholicism in Italy Since the 15th Cen-
    tury. Baltimore: Johns Hopkins University Press.
Cavarnos, Constantine P.
    1977 Orthodox Iconography: Four Essays. Belmont, Mass.: Institute for Byz-
    antine and Modern Greek Studies.
Cesara, Manda
    1982 Memoirs of a Woman Anthropologist: No Hiding Place. London: Aca-
    demic Press.
Charlemont, Lord
    1984 The Travels of Lord Charlemont in Greece and Turkey, 1799. W. B. Stan-
    ford and E. J. Finopoulos, eds. London: Trigraph-London for the A. G. Le-
    ventis Foundation.
Chodorow, Nancy
    1974 Family Structure and Feminine Personality. *In* Woman, Culture, and So-
    ciety, M. Rosaldo and L. Lamphere, eds., pp. 43–66. Stanford: Stanford Uni-
    versity Press.
Christian, William
    1981 Local Religion in Sixteenth Century Spain. Princeton: Princeton Univer-
    sity Press.
    1984 Religious Apparitions and the Cold War in Southern Europe. *In* Religion,

Power and Protest in Local Communities: The Northern Shore of the Mediterranean, Eric Wolf, ed., pp. 239–66. Berlin: Mouton.

Chryssanthopoulou, Vasiliki
1985 *I Hatzidhánes tis Pérthos* (Woman Pilgrims to the Holy Land from Perth). Laographía 3:128–54.

Clark, Mari
1983 Variations on Themes of Male and Female: Reflections on Gender Bias in Fieldwork in Rural Greece. Women's Studies 102:117–33.

Clifford, James
1986 Introduction: Partial Truths. *In* Writing Culture: The Poetics and Politics of Ethnography, J. Clifford and G. E. Marcus, eds., pp. 1–26. Berkeley: University of California Press.
1990 Notes on (Field)notes. *In* Fieldnotes: The Making of Anthropology, R. Sanjek, ed., pp. 47–70. Ithaca: Cornell University Press.

Cohen, Anthony P.
1992 Self-conscious Anthropology. *In* Anthropology and Autobiography, J. Okley and H. Callaway, eds., pp. 221–41. New York: Routledge.

Cohn, B. S., and McKim Marriott
1958 Networks and Centres in the Integration of Indian Civilization. Journal of Social Research 1(1):1–9.

Cohen, Eric
1992 Pilgrimage Centers: Concentric and Excentric. Annals of Tourism Research 18:33–50.

Cole, Sally
1991 Women of the Praia: Work and Lives in a Portuguese Coastal Community. Princeton: Princeton University Press.
1994 Recovering Women's Contributions in Anthropology: Ruth Landes and the Early Ethnography of Race and Gender. *In* Women Writing Culture, R. Behar and D. Gordon, eds. (forthcoming).

Collier, Jane
1986 From Mary to Modern Woman: The Material Basis of Marianismo and Its Transformation in a Spanish Village. American Ethnologist 13:100–107.
—— and Sylvia Junko Yanagisako
1987 Gender and Kinship: Essays toward a Unified Analysis. Stanford: Stanford University Press.

Constantinides, Pamela
1977 "Ill at Ease and Sick at Heart": Symbolic Behavior in a Sudanese Healing Cult. *In* Symbols and Sentiments: Cross-Cultural Studies in Symbolism, I. Lewis, ed. London: Academic Press.

Cormack, Robin
1985 Writing in Gold: Byzantine Society and Its Icons. New York: Oxford University Press.

Couloumbis, T. A., J. A. Petropulos, and H. J. Psomiades
1976 Foreign Interference in Greek Politics. New York: Pella Publishing.

Cowan, Jane
1988 Folk Truth: When the Scholar Comes to Carnival in a "Traditional" Community. Journal of Modern Greek Studies 6:2:245–60.

1990 Dance and the Body Politic in Northern Greece. Princeton: Princeton University Press.

1991 Going Out for Coffee? Contesting the Grounds of Gendered Pleasures in Everyday Sociability. *In* Contested Identities: Gender and Kinship in Modern Greece, E. Papataxiarchis and P. Loizos, eds., pp. 180–202. Princeton: Princeton University Press.

Crain, Mary

1989 From Local Cult to Transnational Icon: The Politics of Re-Presentation in an Andalusian *Romería*. Paper presented at the Annual Meeting of the American Anthropological Association, Washington, D.C.

1992 Pilgrims, "Yuppies," and Media Men: The Transformation of an Andalusian Pilgrimage. *In* Revitalizing European Rituals, J. Boissevain, ed., pp. 95–112. New York: Routledge.

Crapanzano, Vincent

1986 Hermes' Dilemma: The Masking of Subversion in Ethnographic Description. *In* Writing Culture: The Poetics and Politics of Ethnography, J. Clifford and G. E. Marcus, eds., pp. 51–76. Berkeley: University of California Press.

Crumrine, N. Ross, and Alan Morinis, eds.

1991 Pilgrimage in Latin America. Westport, Conn.: Greenwood Press.

Culler, Jonathan

1982 On Deconstruction: Theory and Criticism after Structuralism. Ithaca: Cornell University Press.

Dahlberg, Andrea

1991 The Body as a Principle of Holism: Three Pilgrimages to Lourdes. *In* Contesting the Sacred: The Anthropology of Christian Pilgrimage, J. Eade and M. Sallnow, eds., pp. 30–50. New York: Routledge.

Danforth, Loring

1979 The Role of Dance in the Ritual Therapy of the Anastenaria. Byzantine and Modern Greek Studies 5:141–63.

1989 Firewalking and Religious Healing: The Anastenaria of Greece and the American Firewalking Movement. Princeton: Princeton University Press.

——— and Alexander Tsiaras

1982 The Death Rituals of Rural Greece. Princeton: Princeton University Press.

Davis, John

1977 People of the Mediterranean. London: Routledge and Kegan Paul.

1984 The Sexual Division of Labor in the Mediterranean. *In* Religion, Power and Protest in Local Communities: The Northern Shore of the Mediterranean, E. R. Wolf, ed., pp. 17–50. Berlin: Mouton.

1992a History and the People without Europe. *In* Other Histories, K. Hastrup, ed., pp. 14–28. New York: Routledge.

1992b Tense in Ethnography: Some Practical Considerations. *In* Anthropology and Autobiography, J. Okley and H. Callaway, eds., pp. 205–20. New York: Routledge.

Delaney, Carol

1987 Seeds of Honor, Fields of Shame. *In* Honor and Shame and the Unity of the Mediterranean, D. D. Gilmore, ed., pp. 35–48. American Anthropological Association Special Publication no. 22.

1990 The Hajj: Sacred and Secular. American Ethnologist 17(3):513–30.

Del Valle, Teresa
1993 Introduction. *In* Gendered Anthropology, T. Del Valle, ed., pp. 1–16. New York: Routledge.

Dhaskalaki-Dhoriza, Maria
1982 *I Tínii Agonistés tou 1821*. Athens.

Dhesipris, Stelios
1980 *Ímnos sti Megalóhari tis Tínou*. Athens.

Dhimitrakopoulos, Sofoklis
1971 *Thavmatouryés Ikónes tis Panayía*. Athens.

Dhorizas, Yiorgos
1976 *I Mesoaioniki Tínos* (part 2). Athens.
1981 *I Néa Tínos* (part 4). Athens.
n.d. *I Eklisíes ke ta Proskínima tis Tínou*. Athens: "Tinos."

Di Bella, Maria Pia
1992 Name, Blood, and Miracles: The Claims to Renown in Traditional Sicily. *In* Honor and Grace in Anthropology, J. G. Peristiany and J. Pitt-Rivers, eds., pp. 151–66. Cambridge: Cambridge University Press.

di Leonardo, Micaela
1991 Introduction: Gender, Culture and Political Economy: Feminist Anthropology in Historical Perspective. *In* Gender at the Crossroads of Knowledge: Feminist Anthropology in the Postmodern Era, M. di Leonardo, ed., pp. 1–50. Berkeley: University of California Press.

di Stefano, Christine
1990 Dilemmas of Difference: Feminism, Modernity, and Postmodernism. *In* Feminism/Postmodernism, L. J. Nicholson, ed., pp. 63–82. New York: Routledge.

Dubisch, Jill
1972 The Open Community: Migration from a Greek Island Village. Ph.D. dissertation, University of Chicago.
1974 Honor and Shame in Complex Society. Paper presented at the Annual Meeting of the American Anthropological Association, Mexico City.
1977 The City as Resource: Migration from a Greek Island Village. Urban Anthropology 6(1):65–83.
1983 Greek Women: Sacred or Profane? Journal of Modern Greek Studies 1(1):185–202.
1986a Introduction and Preface. *In* Gender and Power in Rural Greece, J. Dubisch, ed., pp. 3–41. Princeton: Princeton University Press.
1986b Culture Enters through the Kitchen: Women, Food and Social Boundaries in Rural Greece. *In* Gender and Power in Rural Greece, J. Dubisch, ed., pp. 195–214. Princeton: Princeton University Press.
1988 Golden Oranges and Silver Ships: An Interpretive Approach to a Greek Holy Shrine. Journal of Modern Greek Studies 6(1):117–34.
1989 Death and Social Change in Greece. Anthropological Quarterly 62(4):189–200.
1990a Pilgrimage and Popular Religion at a Greek Holy Shrine. *In* Religious Orthodoxy and Popular Faith in European Society, E. Badone, ed., pp. 113–39. Princeton: Princeton University Press.

1990b The Virgin Mary and the Body Politic. Paper presented at the American Ethnological Society/Southern Anthropological Society Meeting, Atlanta, Ga.

1991a Gender, Kinship, and Religion: "Reconstructing" the Anthropology of Greece. *In* Contested Identities: Gender and Kinship in Modern Greece, P. Loizos and E. Papataxiarchis, eds., pp. 29–46. Princeton: Princeton University Press.

1991b Religion, Sex, and "Forty Words for Everything": Expressions of National Identity in Modern Greece. Paper presented at the American Ethnological Society Meeting, Charleston, S.C.

1991c Lovers in the Field: Sex, Dominance, and the Female Anthropologist. Paper presented at the Annual Meeting of the American Anthropological Association, Chicago.

1991d Men's Time and Women's Time: History, Myth and Ritual at a Modern Greek Shrine. Journal of Ritual Studies 5/1:1–26.

1991e The Island of Tinos: Sacred Heart of the Cyclades. Presentation at the Smithsonian Institution, February 6.

1993 "Foreign Chickens" and Other Outsiders: Gender and Community in Greece. American Ethnologist 20(2):272–87.

1994 The Church of the Annunciation of Tinos and the Domestication of Institutional Space. Yearbook of Modern Greek Studies, vol. 10.

du Boulay, Juliet

1974 Portrait of a Greek Mountain Village. Oxford: Clarendon Press.

1986 Women—Images of Their Nature and Destiny in Rural Greece. *In* Gender and Power in Rural Greece, J. Dubisch, ed., pp. 139–68. Princeton: Princeton University Press.

Durban, B. A.

1897 The Spiritual Element in Continental Religions: Vol. 1: The Greek Christianity of Today. The New Orthodoxy: An Evangelical Magazine of Evangelical Verities for Thinkers and Teachers. London: Elliot Stock (Gennadius Library, Athens).

Dwyer, Kevin

1982 Moroccan Dialogues: Anthropology in Question. Baltimore: Johns Hopkins University Press.

Eade, John

1992 Pilgrimage and Tourism at Lourdes, France. Annals of Tourism Research 19:18–32.

——— and Michael J. Sallnow, eds.

1991a Contesting the Sacred: The Anthropology of Christian Pilgrimage. New York: Routledge.

1991b Introduction. *In* Contesting the Sacred: The Anthropology of Christian Pilgrimage. New York: Routledge.

Eickelman, Dale

1976 Moroccan Islam: Tradition and Society in a Pilgrimage Center. Austin: University of Texas Press.

——— and James Piscatori

1990 Muslim Travellers: Pilgrimage, Migration, and the Religious Imagination. Berkeley: University of California Press.

Fabian, Johannes

1983 Time and the Other: How Anthropology Makes Its Object. New York: Columbia University Press.

Faubion, James D.

1993 Modern Greek Lessons: A Primer in Historical Construction. Princeton: Princeton University Press.

Fernandez, James

1983 Consciousness and Class in Southern Spain (review essay). American Ethnologist 10(1):165–73.

1986 Persuasions and Performances: The Play of Tropes in Culture. Bloomington: Indiana University Press.

Fernea, Elizabeth Warnock

1969 Guests of the Sheik: An Ethnography of an Iraqi Village. Garden City, N.Y.: Anchor Books.

Flax, Jane

1987 Postmodernism and Gender Relations in Feminist Theory. Signs 12(4):621–43.

Florakis, Alekos E.

1982 Karavákia Támata ke Thalasiní Afyerómata Praktikí sto Eyéo. Athens: Filopotis.

1990 I Panayía tis Tínou ston Agóna tou '40. Athens.

Foscolos, Evangelos A.

1968 The Panhellenic Shrine of Our Lady of the Annunciation of Tenos: History - Miracles - Activity. Translated by C. Meihanetsidis. (Pamphlet distributed by the Church of the Annunciation of Tinos.)

Frazee, Charles

1969 The Orthodox Church and Independent Greece, 1821–1852. Cambridge: Cambridge University Press.

1977 Church and State in Greece. In Greece in Transition, J. Koumoulides, ed., pp. 128–52. London: Zeno.

1979 The Greek Catholic Islanders and the Revolution of 1821. East European Quarterly 13(3):315–26.

1988 The Island Princes of Greece, the Dukes of the Archipelago. Amsterdam: Hakkert.

1991 Tinos: Venetian Outpost of the Aegean. Modern Greek Studies Yearbook, vol. 7:133–44.

Friedl, Ernestine

1962 Vasilika: A Village in Modern Greece. New York: Holt, Rinehart, and Winston.

1967 The Position of Women: Appearance and Reality. Anthropological Quarterly 40(3):97–108.

1970 Fieldwork in a Greek Village. In Women in the Field, P. Golde, ed., pp. 195–220. Chicago: Aldine.

Gable, Eric, Richard Handler, and Anna Lawson

1992 On the Uses of Relativism: Fact, Conjecture, and Black and White Histories at Colonial Williamsburg. American Ethnologist 19(4):672–87.

Gage, Nicholas

1983 Eleni. New York: Ballantine Books.

Galani-Moutafi, Vasiliki
  1993 From Agriculture to Tourism: Property, Labor, Gender, and Kinship in a
  Greek Island Village (part one). Journal of Modern Greek Studies 11:2:241–70.
Gearing, Fred
  1968 Preliminary Notes on Ritual in Village Greece. In Contributions to Mediterranean Sociology, J. G. Peristiany, ed., pp. 65–72. Paris: Mouton.
Geertz, Clifford
  1968 Islam Observed: Religious Development in Morocco and Indonesia. Chicago: University of Chicago Press.
  1973 The Interpretation of Cultures. New York: Basic Books.
  1988 Works and Lives: The Anthropologist as Author. Stanford: Stanford
  University Press.
Gefou-Madianou, Dimitra
  1993 Mirroring Ourselves through Western Texts: The Limits of an Indigenous
  Anthropology. In The Politics of Ethnographic Reading and Writing: Confrontations of Indigenous and Western Views, H. Driessen, ed., pp. 160–79.
  Ford Lauderdale: Verlag Breitenbach Publishers.
Gilligan, Carol
  1982 In a Different Voice: Psychological Theory and Women's Development.
  Cambridge, Mass.: Harvard University Press.
Gilmore, David D.
  1982 Anthropology of the Mediterranean Area. Annual Review of Anthropology 11:175–205.
  1987 Introduction: The Shame of Dishonor. In Honor and Shame and the
  Unity of the Mediterranean, D. D. Gilmore, ed., pp. 2–21. American Anthropological Association Special Publication no. 22.
Giovannini, Maureen
  1981 Woman: A Dominant Symbol within the Cultural System of a Sicilian
  Town. Man 16(3):408–26.
  1987 Female Chastity Codes in the Circum-Mediterranean: Comparative Perspectives. In Honor and Shame and the Unity of the Mediterranean, D. D.
  Gilmore, ed., pp. 61–74. American Anthropological Association Special Publication no. 22.
Gold, Ann Grodzins
  1988 Fruitful Journeys: The Ways of Rajasthani Pilgrims. Berkeley: University
  of California Press.
Golde, Peggy, ed.
  1970 Women in the Field. Chicago: Aldine.
Gordon, Deborah
  1990 The Politics of Ethnographic Authority: Race and Writing in the Ethnography of Margaret Mead and Zora Neale Hurston. In Modernist Anthropology: From Fieldwork to Text, M. Manganaro, ed., pp. 146–52. Princeton:
  Princeton University Press.
Gross, Daniel
  1971 Ritual Conformity: A Religious Pilgrimage to Northeastern Brazil. Ethnology 10(2):129–48.
Gudeman, Stephen
  1976 Saints, Symbols, and Ceremonies. American Ethnologist 3(4):709–30.

Hamilton, Mary
  1910 Greek Saints and Their Festivals. Edinburgh: William Blackwood and Sons.
Harding, Sandra
  1990 Feminism, Science, and the Anti-Enlightenment Critique. *In* Feminism/Postmodernism, L. Nicholson, ed., pp. 83–106. New York: Routledge.
Hart, Laurie Kain
  1992 Time, Religion, and Social Experience in Rural Greece. Lanham, Md.: Rowman and Littlefield.
Hartsock, Nancy
  1990 Foucault on Power: A Theory for Women? *In* Feminism/Postmodernism, L. Nicholson, ed., pp. 157–75. New York: Routledge.
Hasluck, Frederick William, and H. H. Jewell
  1920 The Church of Our Lady of the Hundred Gates (Panayía Hekatontapiliani) in Paros. London: Macmillan and Co.
Hastrup, Kirsten
  1992a Writing Ethnography: State of the Art. *In* Anthropology and Autobiography, J. Okley and H. Callaway, eds., pp. 116–33. ASA Monograph no. 29. New York: Routledge.
  1992b Introduction. *In* Other Histories, K. Hastrup, ed., pp. 1–13. New York: Routledge.
Herzfeld, Michael
  1980 Honor and Shame: Some Problems in the Comparative Analysis of Moral Systems. Man 15:339–51.
  1981 Performative Categories and Symbols of Passage in Rural Greece. Journal of American Folklore 94:44–57.
  1982 Ours Once More: Folklore, Ideology, and the Making of Modern Greece. Austin: University of Texas Press.
  1983 Looking Both Ways: The Ethnographer in the Text. Semiotica 9: 644–63.
  1985 The Poetics of Manhood: Contest and Identity in a Cretan Mountain Village. Princeton: Princeton University Press.
  1986 Within and Without: The Category of "Female" in the Ethnography of Modern Greece. *In* Gender and Power in Rural Greece, J. Dubisch, ed., pp. 215–33. Princeton: Princeton University Press.
  1987a Anthropology through the Looking Glass: Critical Ethnography in the Margins of Europe. Cambridge: Cambridge University Press.
  1987b "As in Your Own House": Hospitality, Ethnography, and the Stereotype of Mediterranean Society. *In* Honor and Shame and the Unity of the Mediterranean, D. D. Gilmore, ed., pp. 75–89. American Anthropological Association Special Publication no. 22.
  1990 Icons and Identity: Religious Orthodoxy and Social Practice in Rural Crete. Anthropological Quarterly 63:3:109–21.
  1991a Silence, Submission, and Subversion: Toward a Poetics of Womanhood. *In* Contested Identities: Gender and Kinship in Modern Greece, P. Loizos and E. Papataxiarchis, eds., pp. 79–97. Princeton: Princeton University Press.
  1991b A Place in History: Social and Monumental Time in a Cretan Town. Princeton: Princeton University Press.

1992 Segmentation and Politics in the European Nation-State: Making Sense of Political Events. *In* Other Histories, K. Hastrup, ed., pp. 62–81. New York: Routledge.

Hirschon, Renée
1978 Open Body, Closed Space: The Transformation of Female Sexuality. *In* Women and Space, S. Ardener, ed., pp. 66–88. London: Croom Helm.
1983 Women, the Aged, and Religious Activity: Oppositions and Complementarity in an Urban Locality. Journal of Modern Greek Studies 1(1):113–30.
1989 Heirs of the Greek Catastrophe: The Social Life of Asia Minor Refugees in Piraeus. Oxford: Clarendon Press.
1992 Greek Adults' Verbal Play, or, How to Train for Caution. Journal of Modern Greek Studies 10:1:35–56.

Hoffman, Susanna
1974 Kypseli. Men and Women Apart: A Divided Reality. Film made with Richard Cowan and Paul Aratow.
1976 The Ethnogaphy of the Islands: Thera. *In* Regional Variation in Modern Greece and Cyprus, E. Friedl and M. Dimen, eds., pp. 328–40. New York: Annals of the New York Academy of Sciences.

Hondganeu-Sotelo, Pierrette
1988 Gender and Fieldwork (review essay). Women's Studies International Forum 11(6):611–18.

Hudman, Lloyd E., and Richard H. Jackson
1992 Mormon Pilgrimage and Tourism. Annals of Tourism Research 19: 107–21.

Hussey, Joan M.
1986 The Orthodox Church in the Byzantine Empire. Oxford: Clarendon Press.

Iossifides, A. Marina
1991 Sisters in Christ: Metaphors of Kinship among Greek Nuns. *In* Contested Identities: Gender and Kinship in Modern Greece, E. Papataxiarchis and P. Loizos, eds., pp. 135–55. Princeton: Princeton University Press.

Jackowski, Antoni, and Valene Smith
1992 Polish Pilgrim Tourists. Annals of Tourism Research 19:92–106.

Jackson, Michael
1989 Paths toward a Clearing: Radical Empiricism and Ethnographic Enquiry. Bloomington: Indiana University Press.

Just, Roger
1988 Anti-Clericalism and National Identity: Attitudes toward the Orthodox Church in Greece. *In* Vernacular Christianity: Essays in the Social Anthropology of Religion Presented to Godfrey Lienhardt, W. James and D. H. Johnson, eds., pp. 15–30. Oxford: JASO Occasional Paper no. 7.

Kaipofilas, Kostas
1930 *Istorikí Selídhes Tínou: Frangokratía-Venetokratía-Turkokratía 1207–1821.* Athens: Ioann. D. Kollaros.

Kardhamitsis, Ioannis N.
1987 *To Monastíri tis Tínou.* Tinos: Ekdhosis I. Monis Kekhrovouniou Tinou.

Karita, Eleni
n.d. *I Morfí mias Ayías: I Pelayía tis Tínou.* Athens: Ekdhosis "Tinos."

Karp, Ivan, and Martha B. Kendall
   1982 Reflexivity in Fieldwork. *In* Explaining Human Behavior: Consciousness, Human Action, and Social Structure, P. Secord, ed., pp. 249–73. Beverly
   Hills, Calif.: Sage Publications.
Kavouras, Pavlos
   1992 Dance at Olymbos, Karpathos: Cultural Change and Political Confrontations. Ethnografika 8:173–90.
   n.d. Where the Community "Reveals Itself": Reflexivity and Moral Judgment
   in Karpathos Greece. *In* Social Experience and Anthropological Knowledge,
   K. Hastrup and Peter Hervik, eds., London: Routledge (forthcoming).
Kendall, Carl
   1991 The Politics of Pilgrimage: The Black Christ at Esquipulas. *In* Pilgrimage
   in Latin America, N. R. Crumrine and A. Morinis, eds., pp. 139–56. New
   York: Greenwood Press.
Kenna, Margaret
   1976 Houses, Fields and Graves: Property and Ritual Obligation on a Greek
   Island. Ethnology 15:21–34.
   1977 Greek Urban Immigrants and Their Rural Patron Saint. Ethnic Studies
   1:14–23.
   1985 Icons in Theory and Practice: An Orthodox Christian Example. History
   of Religions 24(4):345–68.
   1993 Return Migrants and Tourism Development: An Example from the Cyclades. Journal of Modern Greek Studies 11:1:75–96.
Keohane, Nannerl O., and Barbara C. Gelpi
   1981 Forward. *In* Feminist Theory: A Critique of Ideology. Chicago: University of Chicago Press.
Kharitonidou, Angeliki
   1984 Greek Traditional Architecture: Tinos. "Melissa" Publishing House.
Kolodny, Emile Y.
   1974 *Les Populations des Isles de la Grèce.* Vols. 1–2. Aix-en-Provence: Eisud.
Kondo, Dorinne K.
   1990 Crafting Selves: Power, Gender, and Discourses of Identity in a Japanese
   Workplace. Chicago: University of Chicago Press.
Kornaros, Eleftherios N.
   1969 *I Panayía tis Tínou.* Athens.
Koukas, G.
   1981 Tinos (Brief History of the Island on Tourist Map: Tinos). Athens: M.
   Toubis.
Kousis, Maria
   1989 Tourism and the Family in a Rural Cretan Community. Annals of Tourism Research 16:318–32.
Koutelakis, M. Haralambos
   1981 Tinos: History, Art, Archaeology. Translated by Litsa and Theofanis
   Kakouris. Athens.
Kristeva, Julia
   1981 Women's Time. Signs: Journal of Women in Culture and Society.
   7(1):13–35.

1986 Stabat Mater. *In* The Kristeva Reader, A. Jardin and H. Blake, eds., Toril Moi, trans., pp. 160–86. New York: Columbia University Press.

Kulick, Donald, and Margaret Willson, eds.
1995 Taboo: Sex, Identity and Erotic Subjectivity in Anthropological Fieldwork. New York: Routledge (forthcoming).

Lacroix, M. Louis
1881 *Iles de la Grèce*. Paris: Library de Firmin-Diderot et Cie.

Lagouros, Alexis Stilianos
1965 *I Istoría tis Tínou*. Athens: Ekdhosis "Tinos."

Lagouros, Stilianos Zafiris
1979 *I Ayía Pelayía tis Mónis Kehrovouníou*. Athens: Ekdhosis I. M. Kekhrovouniou Tinou.
n.d. *Thávmata tis Megalóharis*. Athens: Ekdhosis "Tinos."

Lavie, Smadar
1990 The Poetics of Military Occupation. Berkeley: University of California Press.

Lever, Alison
1986 Honour as a Red Herring. Critique of Anthropology 6(3):81–106.

Loizos, Peter
1988 The Virgin Mary and Marina Warner's Feminism. London School of Economics Quarterly 2(2):175–92.

Loukissas, Philippas J.
1982 Tourism's Regional Development Impact: A Comparative Analysis of the Greek Islands. Annals of Tourism Research 9:523–41.

Lutkehaus, Nancy
1990 Refractions of Reality: On the Use of Other Ethnographers' Fieldnotes. *In* Fieldnotes: The Makings of Anthropology, Roger Sanjek, ed., pp. 303–22. Ithaca: Cornell University Press.

Lutz, Catherine
1988 Unnatural Emotions: Everyday Sentiments on a Micronesian Atoll and Their Challenge to Western Theory. Chicago: Chicago University Press.
1990 The Erasure of Women's Writing in Sociocultural Anthropology. American Anthropologist 17(4):611–27.
——— and Lila Abu-Lughod, eds.
1990 Language and the Politics of Emotion. Cambridge: Cambridge University Press.
——— and Geoffrey White
1986 The Anthropology of Emotions. Annual Review of Anthropology 15:405–36.

McDonnell, Mary Byrne
1990 Patterns of Muslim Pilgrimage from Malaysia, 1885–1985. *In* Muslim Travellers: Pilgrimage, Migration, and the Religious Imagination, D. Eickelman and J. Piscatori, eds., pp. 111–30. Berkeley: University of California Press.

Machin, Berrie
1983 St. George and the Dragon: Cultural Codes, Religion, and Attitudes to the Body in a Cretan Mountain Village. Social Analysis 14:107–26.

McNeill, William
1974 The Shape of European History. New York: Oxford University Press.
Makriyiannis, Ioannis
1966 Makriyiannis: The Memoirs of General Makriyiannis, 1797–1864. Edited and translated by H. A. Lidderdale. London: Oxford University Press.
Mandel, Ruth
1983 Sacrifice at the Bridge of Arta: Sex Roles and the Manipulation of Power. Journal of Modern Greek Studies 1:173–83.
Marcus, George, and Dick Cushman
1982 Ethnographies as Texts. Annual Review of Anthropology 11:25–69.
——— and Michael M. J. Fischer
1986 Anthropology as Cultural Critique: An Experimental Moment in the Human Sciences. Chicago: University of Chicago Press.
Marnham, Patrick
1981 Lourdes: A Modern Pilgrimage. New York: Coward, McCann and Geohagen.
Marx, Emmanuel
1977 Communal and Individual Pilgrimage: The Region of Saints' Tombs in South Sinai. In Regional Cults, R. P. Werbner, ed., pp. 29–54. London: Academic Press.
Mascia-Lees, Frances E., Patricia Sharpe, and Colleen Ballerino Cohen
1989 The Postmodernist Turn in Anthropology: Cautions from a Feminist Perspective. Signs 15(11):7–33.
Masson, Edward
1843 An Apology for the Greek Church, or Hints on the Means of Promoting the Religious Movement of the Greek Nation. Part 1. Athens: Royal Printing Office. (Pamphlet in the Gennadius Library, Athens.)
Mavros, Ioannis N.
1969 O Naós tis Panayías Párou (Ekatonapilianis). Athens.
Meinardus, Otto
1970 A Study of the Relics of Saints of the Greek Orthodox Church. Oriens Christianus 54:130–278.
Mernissi, Fatima
1977 Women, Saints, and Sanctuaries. Signs 3(2):101–12.
Messerschmidt, Donald, and Jyoti Sharma
1981 Hindu Pilgrimage in the Nepal Himalayas. Current Anthropology 22(Oct.):571–72.
Messick, Brinkley
1987 Subordinate Discourse: Women, Weaving, and Gender Relations in North Africa. American Ethnologist 14(2):210–25.
Metcalf, Barbara D.
1990 The Pilgrimage Remembered: South Asian Accounts of the Hajj. In Muslim Travellers: Pilgrimage, Migration, and the Religious Imagination, D. Eickelman and J. Piscatori, eds., pp. 85–107. Berkeley: University of California Press.
Moore, Henrietta
1986 Space, Text and Gender: An Anthropological Study of the Marakwet of Kenya. Cambridge: Cambridge University Press.

1988 Feminism and Anthropology. Minneapolis: University of Minnesota Press.

Morinis, Alan

1984 Pilgrimage in the Hindu Tradition: A Case Study of West Bengal. Delhi: Oxford University Press.

1985 The Ritual Experience: Pain and the Transformation of Consciousness in Ordeals of Initiation. Ethos 13(2):150–75.

———, ed.

1992 Sacred Journeys: The Anthropology of Pilgrimage. Westport, Conn.: Greenwood Press.

Mouzelis, Nicos

1978 Modern Greece: Facets of Underdevelopment. London: Macmillan.

Murphy, Michael Dean

1989 Discovering Rocio: Rival Foundation Myths of an Andalusian Pilgrimage. Paper presented at the Annual Meeting of the American Anthropological Association, Washington, D.C.

1993 Politics of Tumult in Andalusian Ritual. Political and Legal Anthropology Review 16:2:75.

1994 Class, Community and Costume in an Andalusian Pilgrimage. Anthropological Quarterly 7:2:49.

Myerhoff, Barbara, and Jay Ruby

1982 Introduction. In A Crack in the Mirror: Reflexive Perspectives in Anthropology, Jay Ruby, ed., pp. 1–35. Philadelphia: University of Pennsylvania Press.

Naquin, Susan, and Chun-Fanf Yu, eds.

1992 Pilgrims and Sacred Sites in China. Berkeley: University of California Press.

Nissan, Elizabeth

1988 Polity and Pilgrimage Centres in Sri Lanka. Man 23:253–74.

Nolan, Mary Lee, and Sidney Nolan

1989 Christian Pilgrimage in Modern Western Europe. Chapel Hill: University of North Carolina Press.

Okely, Judith

1992 Anthropology and Autobiography: Participatory Experience and Embodied Knowledge. In Anthropology and Autobiography, J. Okely and H. Callaway, eds., pp. 1–28. London: Routledge.

Ong, Aihwa

1988 Colonialism and Modernity: Feminist Re-presentation of Women in Non-Western Societies. Inscriptions 79–83.

Orsi, Robert

1991 The Center out There, in Here, and Everywhere Else: The Nature of Pilgrimage to the Shrine of St. Jude. Journal of Social History 25(2): 213–32.

Ortner, Sherry

1984 Theory in Anthropology since the Sixties. Comparative Studies in Society and History 26:126–66.

Ottenberg, Simon

1990 Thirty Years of Fieldnotes: Changing Relationships to the Text. In Fieldnotes: The Making of Anthropology, R. Sanjek, ed., pp. 139–60. Ithaca: Cornell University Press.

Ouspensky, Leonid, and Vladimir Lossky
1982 The Meaning of Icons. Crestwood, N.Y.: St. Vladimir's Seminary Press.

Pandian, Jacob
1985 Anthropology and the Western Tradition: Toward an Authentic Anthropology. Prospect Heights, Ill.: Waveland Press.

Papadopoulos, Kostas S.
1962 *I Ikónes tis Theotókou.* Kathimeriní 23, 25, 26, March 1962.

Papastratos, Dory
1990 Paper Icons: Greek Orthodox Religious Engravings, 1665–1899. Translated by John Leatham. Athens: Papastratos S. A. Publications. 2 vols.

Parsons, Anne
1967 Is the Oedipus Complex Universal? A South Italian "Nuclear Complex." *In* Personalities and Cultures, R. Hunt, ed., pp. 352–99. New York: American Museum of Natural History.

Pavlides, Eleftherios, and Jana Hesser
1986 Women's Roles and House Form and Decoration in Eressos, Greece. *In* Gender and Power in Rural Greece, J. Dubisch, ed., pp. 68–96. Princeton: Princeton University Press.

Peristiany, J. G., ed.
1966 Honour and Shame: The Values of Mediterranean Society. Chicago: University of Chicago Press.

Perry, Nicholas, and Loreta Echeverria
1988 Under the Heel of Mary. New York: Routledge.

Pfaffenberger, Bryan
1979 The Kataragama Pilgrimage: Hindu-Buddhist Interaction and Its Significance in Sri Lanka's Polyethnic Social System. Journal of Asian Studies 38(2):253–70.

Pina-Cabral, Joao de
1986 Sons of Adam, Daughters of Eve: The Peasant World View of the Alto Minho. Oxford: Clarendon Press.
1989 The Mediterranean as a Category of Regional Comparison: A Critical View. Current Anthropology 30(3):399–406.

Pirgos, Dhionisios
1865 *Perigrafí tis Nisóu Tínou* . . . No publisher.

Pitt-Rivers, Julian
1966 Honour and Social Status. *In* Honour and Shame in Mediterranean Society, J. Peristiany, ed., pp. 19–78. Chicago: University of Chicago Press.
1977 The Fate of Sechem, or the Politics of Sex: Essays in the Anthropology of the Mediterranean. Cambridge: Cambridge University Press.

Pool, Robert
1991 Postmodern Ethnography? Critique of Anthropology 11(4):309–11.

Pope, Barbara Corrado
1985 Immaculate and Powerful: The Marian Revival of the Nineteenth Century. *In* Immaculate and Powerful: The Female in Sacred Image and Social

Reality, C. W. Atkinson, C. Buchanan, and M. Miles, eds., pp. 173–200. Boston: Beacon Press.

Pratt, Mary Louise
1986 Fieldwork in Common Places. *In* Writing Culture: The Poetics and Politics of Ethnography, J. Clifford and G. E. Marcus, eds., pp. 27–50. Berkeley: University of California Press.

Preston, James
1992 Spiritual Magnetism: An Organizing Principle for the Study of Pilgrimage. *In* Sacred Journeys: The Anthropology of Pilgrimage, A. Morinis, ed., pp. 31–46. Westport, Conn.: Greenwood Press.
———, ed.
1982 Mother Worship: Themes and Variations. Chapel Hill: University of North Carolina Press.

Protopapas, Nikolaos I.
1984 *Istoriká tis Iéras Monís Kekhrovouníou Tínou*. Athens: Ekdhosis Ieras Monis Kekhrovouniou Tinou.

Rabinow, Paul
1977 Reflections on Fieldwork in Morocco. Berkeley: University of California Press.
1986 Representations Are Social Facts: Modernity and Post-Modernity in Ethnography. *In* Writing Culture: The Poetics and Politics of Ethnography, J. Clifford and G. E. Marcus, eds., pp. 234–61. Berkeley: University of California Press.
——— and William M. Sullivan
1979 The Interpretive Turn: Emergence of an Approach. *In* Interpretive Social Science, P. Rabinow and W. M. Sullivan, eds., pp. 1–24. Berkeley: University of California Press.
1987 Interpretive Social Science: A Second Look. Berkeley: University of California Press.

Ricoeur, Paul
1979 The Model of the Text: Meaningful Action Considered as Text. *In* Interpretive Social Science, P. Rabinow and W. M. Sullivan, eds., pp. 73–102. Berkeley: University of California Press.

Rosaldo, Michelle
1987 Moral/Analytic Dilemmas Posed by the Intersection of Feminism and Social Science. *In* Interpretive Social Science: A Second Look, P. Rabinow and W. M. Sullivan, eds., pp. 280–301. Berkeley: University of California Press.

Rosaldo, Renato
1989 Culture and Truth: The Remaking of Social Analysis. Boston: Beacon Press.

Ross, Ellen
1991 Diversities of Divine Presence: Women's Geography in the Christian Tradition. *In* Sacred Places and Profane Spaces, J. Scott and P. Simpson-Housley, eds., pp. 93–114. New York: Greenwood Press.

Rushton, Lucy
1983 Doves and Magpies: Village Women in the Greek Orthodox Church. *In*

Women's Religious Experience, Pat Holden, ed., pp. 57–70. London: Croom Helm.

Sacks, Karen
1976 State Bias and Women's Status. American Anthropologist 78(3):365–69.

Said, Edward
1978 Orientalism. New York: Vintage Books.

Sallnow, M. J.
1981 Communitas Reconsidered: The Sociology of Andean Pilgrimage. Man 16:163–82.
1987 Pilgrims of the Andes: Regional Cults in Cusco. Washington, D.C.: Smithsonian Institute Press.

Sandin, Karl
1993 Liturgy, Pilgrimage, and Devotion in Byzantine Objects. Bulletin of the Detroit Institute of Arts 67(4):46–56.

Sangren, P. Steven
1988 Rhetoric and the Authority of Ethnography: "Postmodernism" and the Social Reproduction of Texts. Current Anthropology 29(3):405–24.

Sanjek, Roger, ed.
1990 Fieldnotes: The Making of Anthropology. Ithaca: Cornell University Press.

Sant Cassia, Paul, with Constantina Bada
1992 The Making of the Modern Greek Family: Marriage and Exchange in Nineteenth Century Athens. Cambridge: Cambridge University Press.

Sax, William S.
1990 Village Daughter, Village Goddess: Residence, Gender, and Politics in a Himalayan Pilgrimage. American Ethnologist 17(3):491–512.
1991 Mountain Goddess: Gender and Politics in Himalayan Pilgrimage. New York: Oxford University Press.

Schneider, David M.
1984 A Critique of the Study of Kinship. Ann Arbor: University of Michigan Press.

Schneider, Jane
1971 Of Vigilance and Virgins: Honor, Shame and Access to Resources in Mediterranean Societies. Ethnology 10:1–24.

Sered, Susan Starr
1986 Rachel's Tomb and the Milk Grotto of the Virgin Mary: Two Women's Shrines in Bethlehem. Journal of Feminist Studies in Religion 2(2):7–22.
1988 The Domestication of Religion: The Spiritual Guardianship of Jewish Women. Man 23:506–21.
1992 Women as Ritual Experts: The Religious Lives of Elderly Jewish Women in Jerusalem. New York: Oxford University Press.

Seremetakis, C. Nadia
1990 The Ethics of Antiphony: The Social Construction of Pain, Gender and Power in the Southern Peloponnesus. Ethos 18(4):481–511.
1991 The Last Word: Women, Death, and Divination in Inner Mani. Chicago: University of Chicago Press.

Slater, Candace
  1986 Trail of Miracles: Stories from a Pilgrimage in Northeast Brazil. Berkeley: University of California Press.
Slot, B. J.
  1982 *Archipelagus Turbatus: Les Cyclades entre Colonization Latine et Occupation Ottomane, c. 1500–1718.* Leiden, Netherlands: Historisch-Archaeologisch Instituut te Istanbul. 2 vols.
Smith, Valene
  1992 Introduction: The Quest in Guest. Annals of Tourism Research 19:1–17.
Stacey, Judith
  1988 Can There Be a Feminist Ethnography? Women's Studies International Forum 11(1):21–27.
Stanton, J. B., and S. D. Salamone
  1986 Introducing the *Nikokyra:* Ideality and Reality in Social Process. *In* Gender and Power in Rural Greece, J. Dubisch, ed., pp. 97–120. Princeton: Princeton University Press.
Stewart, Charles
  1991 Demons and the Devil: Moral Imagination in Modern Greek Culture. Princeton: Princeton University Press.
Stocking, George, ed.
  1983 Observers Observed: Essays on Ethnographic Fieldwork. Madison: University of Wisconsin Press.
Stott, Margaret
  1973 The Family and Economic Transition in Mykonos. Greek Review of Social Research 17:122–33.
  1979 Tourism in Mykonos: Some Social and Cultural Responses. Mediterranean Studies 1:72–90.
  1985 Property, Labor and Household Economy: The Transition to Tourism in Mykonos, Greece. Journal of Modern Greek Studies 3:187–206.
  1993 Return Migrants and Tourism Development: An Example from the Cyclades. Journal of Modern Greek Studies 11:75–95.
Strathern, Marilyn
  1987 An Awkward Relationship: The Case of Feminism and Anthropology. Signs 12(21):276–92.
  1988 The Gender of the Gift: Problems with Women and Problems with Society in Melanesia. Berkeley: University of California Press.
Suleiman, Susan R., and Inge Crosman, eds.
  1980 The Reader in the Text: Essays on Audience and Interpretation. Princeton: Princeton University Press.
Sutton, Susan
  1988 What Is a "Village" in a Nation of Migrants? Journal of Modern Greek Studies 6(2):187–216.
Tapper, Nancy
  1990 *Ziyaret:* Gender, Movement, and Exchange in a Turkish Community. *In* Muslim Travellers: Pilgrimage, Migration, and the Religious Imagination, D. Eickelman and J. Piscatori, eds., pp. 236–55. Berkeley: University of California Press.

Taussig, Michael
  1980 The Devil and Commodity Fetishism in Latin America. Chapel Hill: University of North Carolina Press.
  1987 Culture of Terror, Space of Death. *In* Interpretive Social Science: A Second Look, P. Rabinow and W. M. Sullivan, eds., pp. 241–79. Berkeley: University of California Press.
Taylor, William B.
  1987 The Virgin of Guadalupe in New Spain: An Inquiry into the Social History of Marian Devotion. American Ethnologist 14(1):9–33.
Tedlock, Barbara
  1991 From Participant Observation to the Observation of Participation: The Emergence of a Narrative Ethnography. Journal of Anthropological Research 47:69–94.
Tentori, Tullio
  1982 An Italian Religious Feast: The *Fujenti* Rites of the Madonna dell'Arco, Naples. *In* Mother Worship: Theme and Variations, J. Preston, ed., pp. 95–122. Chapel Hill: University of North Carolina Press.
Theoklitos, A.
  n.d. *I Panayía: I Mesítria tou Kósmou.* Athens.
Tiffany, Sharon W.
  1984 Introduction: Feminist Perspectives in Anthropology. *In* Rethinking Women's Roles: Perspectives from the Pacific, D. O'Brien and S. W. Tiffany, eds., pp. 1–11. Berkeley: University of California Press.
Tilly, Louise A.
  1989 Gender, Women's History, and Social History. Social Science History 13(4)(Winter):441–80.
Tong, Rosemarie
  1989 Feminist Thought: A Comprehensive Introduction. Boulder, Colo.: Westview Press.
Tress, Daryl McGowan
  1988 Comment on Flax's "Postmodernism and Gender Relations in Feminist Theory." Signs 14(1):196–200.
Turnbull, Colin
  1992 Anthropology as Pilgrimage, Anthropologist as Pilgrim. *In* Sacred Journeys: The Anthropology of Pilgrimage, A. Morinis, ed., pp. 257–74. Westport, Conn.: Greenwood Press.
Turner, Victor
  1974 Dramas, Fields, and Metaphors: Symbolic Action in Human Society. Ithaca: Cornell University Press.
  1979 The Anthropology of Performance. *In* Process, Performance, and Pilgrimage. New Delhi: Concept Publishing Company.
  1988 The Anthropology of Performance. New York: PAJ Publications.
——— and Edith Turner
  1978 Image and Pilgrimage in Christian Culture. New York: Columbia University Press.
Tyler, Stephen A.
  1986 Post-Modern Ethnography: From Document of the Occult to Occult

Document. *In* Writing Culture: The Poetics and Politics of Ethnography, J. Clifford and G. E. Marcus, eds., pp. 122–40. Berkeley: University of California Press.

1987 The Unspeakable: Discourse, Dialogue, and Rhetoric in the Postmodern World. Madison: University of Wisconsin Press.

Ulin, Robert C.
1991 Critical Anthropology Twenty Years Later: Modernism and Postmodernism in Anthropology. Critique of Anthropology 11(1):63–89.

Valentine, Kristin B., and Eugene Valentine
1992 Performing Culture through Narrative: A Galician Woman Storyteller. *In* Performance, Culture and Identity, E. C. Fine and J. H. Sperr, eds., pp. 181–205. Westport, Conn.: Praeger.

Van Maanen, John
1988 Tales of the Field: On Writing Ethnography. Chicago: University of Chicago Press.

Vukonić, Boris
1992 Medjugorje's Religion and Tourism Connection. Annals of Tourism Research 18:79–91.

Ware, Timothy
1963 The Orthodox Church. New York: Penguin Books.

Warner, Marina
1976 Alone of All Her Sex: The Myth and Cult of the Virgin Mary. London: Weidenfield and Nicholson.

Weingrod, Alex
1990 Saints and Shrines, Politics, and Culture: A Morocco-Israel Comparison. *In* Muslim Travellers: Pilgrimage, Migration, and the Religious Imagination, D. Eickelman and J. Piscatori, eds., pp. 217–35. Berkeley: University of California Press.

Wengle, John L.
1988 Ethnographers in the Field: The Psychology of Research. Tuscaloosa: University of Alabama Press.

Whitehead, Tony Larry, and Mary Ellen Conaway, eds.
1986 Self, Sex, and Gender in Cross-Cultural Fieldwork. Chicago: University of Chicago Press.

Wolf, Eric
1958 The Virgin of Guadalupe: A Mexican National Symbol. Journal of American Folklore 71:34–39.

1984 Introduction. *In* Religion, Power and Protest in Local Communities: The Northern Shore of the Mediterranean. E. Wolf, ed., pp. 1–13. Berlin: Mouton.

Wolf, Margery
1992 A Thrice-Told Tale: Feminism, Postmodernism, and Ethnographic Responsibility. Stanford: Stanford University Press.

Zallony, Marco P.
1809 *Voyage à Tine: L'une des îles de Archipel de la Grèce, suivi d'un traité de l'asthme.* Paris: Arthus-Bertrand.

Index

Abu-Lughod, Lila, 10, 14–15, 18, 198, 262–63n.35

Annunciation: and Greek War of Independence, 131–32, 164–65, 170. *See also* Church of the Annunciation

anti-structure: in pilgrimage, 42–43, 45, 222–23

Assumption. *See* Dormition

autobiography: and anthropology, 6, 28–29, 107–9

baptism: at the Church of the Annunciation, 79, 86, 97–98, 181

body: and performance, 203; women's bodies as symbolic, 209–10, 217

Caraveli, Anna, 212, 214, 217, 278n.18

churches: as connecting material and spiritual, 65; nature of in Greece, 61–65; plan of, 65; reputations of, 64; and saints, 61–63

Church of the Annunciation, Tinos: building of, 135–36, 277n.12; foreigners' views of, 109, 156–57, 168–69, 183–85, 279nn. 26 and 27; and Greek nationalism, 164–67, 169–73, 179–80, 182; local attitudes toward, 187–91; and local identity, 158, 182

communitas, 42, 265n.11: in pilgrimage, 42–45, 95–96

Cycladic Islands, 120–22; as "marginal" to history, 130–31, 133; in Ottoman period, 126–27

death ritual, 113–14, 272n.15. *See also* mourning

Dormition, 234, 236, 237–38, 239–40, 244–45

dhikí; *dhikí mas*. See *kséni*

dropí, 196, 202. *See also* "honor and shame"

Elli, 163, 173–74, 244, 248

emotion: as bridge to "the other," 16, 218; as culturally constructed, 213, 224; in fieldwork, 31, 101–2, 105, 111, 114–15, 116, 282n.32; and gender, 213–15, 220; in religion, 119, 213, 218–20, 225; role of in the practice of anthropology, 6, 16; Western views of, 213, 224, 262n.31

Europe: anthropological study of, 15–16, 261n.25; "exoticizing," 15; and Greece, 192

Evangelismós. *See* Annunciation; Church of the Annunciation

experience: and anthropological theory, 12, 14, 56; and anthropological writing, 56–57, 260–61n.19, 262n.34; in feminist theory, 12

experimental ethnographies, 4–6, 16, 259nn. 3 and 5; blurring of boundaries in, 5–6, 19; by women, 13–14, 16; of Greece, 8. *See also* writing

feminism: and anthropology, 9–12, 223–24, 256; and blurring of boundaries, 12. *See also* postmodernism: feminist critique of

Fernandez, James, 204, 207

fieldnotes, 116–18, 273nn. 20, 21, and 25. *See also* writing

fieldwork, 28–29, 31–32, 103–5, 256; and anthropological theory, 6; difficulties of, 32–33, 115, 216–17; and the "exotic," 54–55; and gender, 13; and identity, 114–16; role of emotion in, 31, 101–2; "writing up," 56–57

filótimo, 202. *See also* "honor and shame"

Fourth Crusade, 124

generalization: in anthropology, 6, 46–47. *See also* "writing against culture"

gléndi, 100, 271–72n.7

Greek Catholics, 59, 124–26, 128–30, 168–69

Greek Orthodox religion: attitudes of Greeks toward, 59–60, 186–87, 226–27, 283n.40; as cultural heritage, 60, 75, 187, 267n.17; in daily life, 58–59; as "inward-looking," 74; material dimensions of, 61, 72–73; and

ABOUT THE AUTHOR

Jill Dubisch is Professor of Anthropology at Northern Arizona University. She is the editor of *Gender and Power in Rural Greece* (Princeton).